greek political thought

To George Pepe

greek political thought

Ryan K. Balot

Blackwell
Publishing

BLACKWELL PUBLISHING

350 Main Street, Malden, MA 02148–5020, USA
9600 Garsington Road, Oxford OX4 2DQ, UK
550 Swanston Street, Carlton, Victoria 3053, Australia

First published 2006 by Blackwell Publishing Ltd

1   2006

Library of Congress Cataloging-in-Publication Data

Balot, Ryan K. (Ryan Krieger), 1969–
Greek political thought / Ryan K. Balot.
p.   cm.—(Ancient cultures)
Includes bibliographical references and index.
ISBN-13: 978-1-4051-0029-8 (hardcover : alk. paper)
ISBN-10: 1-4051-0029-X (hardcover : alk. paper)
ISBN-13: 978-1-4051-0030-4 (pbk. : alk. paper)
ISBN-10: 1-4051-0030-3 (pbk. : alk. paper)
1. Political science—Greece—History. I. Title. II. Series: Ancient
cultures (Malden, Mass.)
JC73.B225 2006
320'.0938—dc22
2005013070

A catalogue record for this title is available from the British Library.

Set in 10/12.5pt Stone Serif by SNP Best-set Typesetter Ltd.,
Hong Kong

The publisher's policy is to use permanent paper from mills
that operate a sustainable forestry policy, and which has been
manufactured from pulp processed using acid-free and elementary
chlorine-free practices. Furthermore, the publisher ensures that
the text paper and cover board used have met acceptable
environmental accreditation standards.

For further information on
Blackwell Publishing, visit our website:
www.blackwellpublishing.com

Contents

Preface and Acknowledgments

I have written this book chiefly for advanced undergraduate and graduate students of history, classics, philosophy, and political science. No introductory guide to ancient Greek political thought currently exists; yet there is a particular need for one, I think, because interpreting Greek political thought requires students to utilize a variety of historical, literary, and philosophical skills. Greek political texts are historically situated, and they responded carefully to their contemporary contexts – and yet they do not understand themselves as limited by history. They typically exhibit broader philosophical ambitions that go beyond their local, embedded features. They approach both their contemporary worlds, and the world in general, in a variety of literary genres. Readers must be aware of the conventions of these genres, too, in order to interpret the texts plausibly. Accordingly, my goal is to illustrate and exemplify how such skills are useful in understanding ancient Greek political texts, so as to make students' encounters with ancient texts more enlightening and enjoyable.

I hope, too, that this book will be of interest to scholars. As befits an introductory volume, I have of course made no attempt to locate my arguments within current scholarly discussions. I have stated, boldly and unabashedly, how I interpret the relevant texts and history, and I have explained why, without describing alternative views in any detail. Even so, I hope scholars in the field will recognize my choices and find my historical and normative approach distinctive and plausible. In particular, I have read Greek political texts from the perspective of ancient Greek ethical thought. I have often, therefore, had occasion to discuss the virtues and vices as central elements of Greek political theory and of unsystematic political discourse. Viewing Greek political thought from the perspective of "virtue politics" makes this book distinctive, so far as I know, within existing scholarly discussions.

For both students and scholars, moreover, I have aspired to show that dialogue between ancient and modern political thought is possible, useful, and interesting. The ancient Greek discussions of "virtue politics" furnish valuable resources for modern political thinkers and actors. Ancient Greek political thought is different, often arrestingly so, from what modern theorists are accustomed to, and yet it is equally often familiar and up-to-date. Where possible, therefore, I have explored the comparisons and contrasts so as to invigorate current discussions and to enrich our existing vocabularies. There is much to learn from ancient political thinkers, even if we recognize, in more than one way, that we can never go back.

I have minimized notes and references. Endnotes appear only where I have quoted a published work or directly engaged with another scholar's ideas. Otherwise, I have indicated my scholarly debts in the concluding bibliographic essay. The Bibliographic Essay includes works that I have found useful in writing this book, works that have influenced my thinking, and works that I would recommend to students approaching this field for the first time. Since this is an introductory volume, all ancient sources are cited in translation; occasionally, I include a transliterated Greek term that is especially important. Unless otherwise indicated, all translations are my own. I have consulted and been influenced by published translations, particularly the volumes in the Loeb Classical Library and the translations cited in the Bibliographic Essay. I have made suggestions for translations at the beginning of the Bibliographic Essay; publication information is available there for translators cited in the text and endnotes.

I have incurred many debts in writing this book. Al Bertrand, my editor at Blackwell, has had confidence in me from the beginning; he has provided wonderful advice, encouragement, and inspiration throughout the process. For all of his help and support I am grateful. I would also like to thank Angela Cohen and Ben Thatcher at Blackwell for their excellent support in the production process, and Felicity Marsh for her learned and helpful copy-editing.

Many friends and colleagues have talked with me about this book and have read and commented on particular chapters or sequences of chapters. I received a set of exceptionally helpful comments on the original proposal from Danielle Allen and Arlene Saxonhouse, both of whom have continued to help me, in different ways, throughout the process of writing this book. Paul Cartledge sympathetically and insightfully commented on the archaic chapter and helped me think further about the aims and intentions of the book as a whole. Bob Connor inspired me to see, all over again, why studying ancient democracy and political thought is important to modern citizens and human beings. Brian Warren helped to refine my thoughts on Pericles and Thucydides' representation of fifth-century Athens. Sara Forsdyke insightfully commented on many chapters and was always willing to discuss issues and problems. For help with Thucydides and with Attic oratory, I am grateful to Harvey Yunis. Mark Toher guided me through several thorny issues in the chapter on imperialism; I thank him for this and for his supportive friendship over many years.

For his stimulating comments on the fourth-century and Hellenistic theorists, and for numerous enlightening conversations about ancient ethics and political thought, I thank my colleague Eric Brown. Jill Frank generously discussed Aristotle with me for many hours and helped strengthen my arguments considerably. Through other conversations and written communications, too, I profited from David Depew's deep learning about and insight into Aristotelian political thought. Clerk Shaw kindly shared his illuminating thoughts and work on Protagoras. At a later stage, conversations with Malcolm Schofield helped to sharpen my Platonic and Aristotelian arguments in several key passages.

For his stimulating friendship and his provocative thoughts on a variety of political issues, I thank Josh Ober. Carl Craver provided excellent guidance on biology and metaphysics, while Andrew Rehfeld has engaged me in many fruitful hours of conversation about ethics, politics, and much else. For their friendship and encouragement throughout the writing of this book, I thank my friends and squash partners Hillel Kieval and Joe Loewenstein. Two friends from graduate school, Mark Erwin and Jeremy Goldman, have continued to challenge me intellectually and to inspire me personally. My research assistant, Austin Thompson, provided a great deal of help and saved me from errors and inconsistencies. Through their questions and conversations, students in the Text and Tradition program at Washington University in St. Louis have taught me a great deal about ancient political thought.

Without the encouragement, help, and support of my wife, Carroll, I could never have written this book. Carroll is always there for me. Our daughters, Julia and Corinne, have been a source of joy, happiness, and inspiration.

I dedicate this volume to a "guide, philosopher, and friend" who has been a deep influence on me, both in the writing of this book and otherwise.

Abbreviations

PP	J. Barnes, *The Presocratic Philosophers*, rev. edn. (London, Routledge, 1982)
SVF	H. von Arnim, *Stoicorum Veterum Fragmenta* (Leipzig, 1903–5)
VS	*Vatican Sayings* (*Sententiae Vaticanae*) in C. Bailey, *Epicurus: The Extant Remains* (Oxford, Clarendon Press, 1926)
WD	Hesiod, *Works and Days*

chapter 1
Introduction: How to Do Greek Political Thought

Greek political thought offers us a novel perspective on our own politics and our own lives. The thinkers I consider in this book lived in a far different world from ours. Their world was much smaller; it was pre-Christian; its ethical thought was formulated in terms of virtue and vice; it was primarily agricultural; it was slave-holding; and it was composed of small communities of citizens who played an integral role in politics. Yet ancient Greek political life and political thought overlap with ours to a considerable degree – in the value ancient Greeks placed, for example, on equality, freedom, and justice; and in their public discussions of leadership, self-defense, authority, responsibility, and self-definition. It would be impossible for us to grasp ancient political thought, much less to find it meaningful, if ancient and modern politics did not share a number of similar concepts, underlying beliefs, and collective practices.[1] My goal in this book is to show that Greek political thought is enlightening and educational for us "moderns," both as citizens and as human beings.

Writing an introduction to ancient political thought requires a certain amount of ground-clearing. Traditionally, students of ancient political thought have focused on the systematic theorists of politics in the classical period (roughly 490–323 BC), especially on Plato and Aristotle. They started there for a good reason. Those two authors have defined the terms in which the theory of politics has been understood from their own time until the present day. Their success and longevity are incalculable. From the religious (Augustine) to the secular (Machiavelli), from the revolutionary (Nietzsche) to the conservative (Burke), from pure theoreticians

(Aquinas) to men of action (James Madison), Platonic and Aristotelian political thought has been a touchstone for both theorists of the human condition and rejectionist critics of European traditions. As a result, scholarly work on Plato and Aristotle has been fruitful. But, as I shall argue, this approach is too limited to do justice to the subject we are considering. To say why, I will offer an account of "political thought" that justifies grappling with a much larger ancient tradition – one that includes poets, historians, propagandists, and orators, as well as card-carrying philosophers.

Etymologically, the English term "politics" derives from the Greek *ta politika*, or "the things of the polis." We should not of course be misled into thinking that etymology determines meaning, but, nevertheless, Greek political thought centered on life in the polis. Accordingly, it is important to begin with a working conception of this characteristic political form.[2] The polis, which is usually translated "city-state," was a self-governing political community characteristic of most of ancient Greece. There were roughly 750 Greek poleis in the Eastern Mediterranean by the time of the classical period, often with citizen-bodies of fewer than 1,000 (Athens, with roughly 45,000, was unusual). They were typically controlled by a group of free adult males who shared common religious, civic, legal, and administrative customs and practices. The polis generally included both a population-dense center clustered around a fortified "acropolis," or "citadel," and an agricultural hinterland. Its defining feature was the idea of citizenship, through which a select group of free adult men of native birth secured for itself the power to take binding decisions on behalf of the community. As many classical authors show, it was implicitly accepted that basic standards of equality and mutual respect governed relations among citizens; citizens were, at least ideally and implicitly, free and equal individuals who participated in communal governance. Therefore, the polis is best understood as a "citizen-state."

What do we mean by "the political"? At a highly general and non-culturally-specific level, "the political" refers to a field of activity in which power is exercised and contested and in which collective forms of "association and dissociation" are realized.[3] In order to make this abstract definition meaningful, though, students of politics must give it specific content by focusing on particular cultures or ways of life, or by examining similar, well-defined features (such as political values) across cultures. Understandably, the relevant modern disciplines derive much of their language and conceptual framework from the empirical world of politics. In practice, modern political science has traditionally focused on constitutions, law, and institutions; the trend since at least the late 1970s, though, has been to concentrate on public opinion, socialization, political economy, and so on. Political theory has also undergone important changes. After many years of focusing on constitutions and classification, modern political theory has, since the early 1970s, emphasized "the ideals of justice, freedom, and community which are invoked when evaluating political institutions and policies."[4] Whatever their specific focus, though, modern political scientists and theorists draw sharp distinctions between public and private and take the public as their chief subject; they assume the existence of states with typically large bureaucracies; they exclude consideration of the ethical development of citizens; and they draw a bright line between religion and the state.

The situation was altogether different with ancient Greek politics and political thought. The vagueness and generality of the Greek *ta politika* ("the things of the polis") suggest that to ancient Greeks "the political" was, by contrast, a broad concept. It encompassed both processes of public decision-making and communal self-definition, as well as various aspects of social, religious, ethical, and familial life – particularly those aspects in which the exercise of power was involved. The Greeks' culturally specific conception of the political resulted from the particular social practices, norms, and beliefs characteristic of the polis. Abstractly, "the political" in ancient Greece was of course a field in which power was contested and communities were defined. But, as a distinctive feature of Greek culture, it was the field of activity in which citizens struggled for power by claiming ethical and intellectual virtue for themselves, by showing their concern for the community's welfare, and by discrediting their rivals through charges of vice, selfishness, and injustice. There was an essential link between the political and the ethical. This was not only the experience of political actors but also a widely shared view among political writers.

In their ideologically informed debates and power struggles, therefore, ancient citizens assumed that polis-communities ought to focus on producing virtuous citizens with a view to creating justice and stability for the community. Producing virtuous citizens required paying careful attention to the education and development of the individual as a whole – ethically, emotionally, intellectually, and religiously. Perhaps the most notable difference between ancient Greek and modern politics and political thought is that ancient politics was intensely concerned with the ethical education of citizens. In the background of political debate, accordingly, were communal norms that defined appropriate standards of conduct. Such norms were reproduced over time in the citizens' emotional life, chiefly through public praise and blame, practices of honoring and shaming, and appeal to a traditional vocabulary of virtue and vice. Thus the "emotions of self-assessment," especially honor and shame, were a critical part of Greek political life.[5] These emotions were particularly important in motivating all citizens to undertake the critical task of self-defense: the military and the political were always closely connected in Greek culture. Finally, just as virtuous citizens strove to achieve justice in relation to one another, so too did they aspire to maintain "right relations" with the divine. As a result, the political was always intertwined with religious custom, belief, and practice. The links were illustrated by the patron deities of each polis as well as the public financing of communal rituals and sacrifices.

As in the modern world, so too in the ancient: the everyday experience of politics had a profound effect on political thought. By contrast with modern political thinkers, ancient thinkers believed that the polis should provide for the ethical and emotional education, character development, and appropriate religious participation of its citizens. Such provisions, properly established, would not only make the citizens better off as individuals, but also establish justice, stability, and concord (*homonoia*) for the community as a whole. Whether Greek political thinkers were analyzing politics in the real world, or developing ideas about how politics ought to be, they did so precisely in these terms.

I offer this account of ancient Greek politics and political thought as a working hypothesis. Despite its gestures toward specific content, it is still disconnected from any particular thinker or period or region. Such descriptions can be nothing more than a rough guide, because there was considerable diversity among the Greeks themselves as to what counted as political. We have too little access to most actual citizens in the ancient Greek world to characterize their views precisely. But, as we will see, political thinkers arrived at interestingly different conceptions of the political. One of our goals will, indeed, be to explain how and why this was the case, and what intellectual consequences such differences might have had. Despite the presence of internal diversity, though, this working hypothesis clarifies the content of our subject in a culturally specific way. The differences between ancient Greece and modernity are notable. By the time the Greek polis had begun to develop in the eighth century BC, the invention of private life was some 400 years in the future. The concept of "negative freedom," or freedom from public authority, was as unimaginable as it would have been undesirable. "Pluralism" in any modern sense was impossible. There was no state, no bureaucracy to speak of, no "government" independent of the citizens, no independent judiciary or executive "branches," no professional military.

In light of these considerations, it appears excessively limiting to locate "politics" or "the political" solely within organized state-structures "in which decisions are binding and enforceable" and "in which *binding* decisions are reached by discussion and argument and ultimately by voting [original emphasis]."[6] This account is too narrow in at least two ways. First, such an emphasis on institutional structure is too narrow to do justice to the varied dimensions of activity that were properly considered political in the ancient Greek world. Political thinkers of all sorts took up positions on what we would consider the private, the moral, the familial – and they did so without special pleading or the worry that their views represented any unusual departures. Aristotle started off his discussion of politics with a theory of the household. The "personal," not to mention the religious and the ethical, was unambiguously political in ancient Greece.[7] This meant, for example, that male domination of the traditional Greek household (*oikos*) was political; male power within the *oikos* was integrally related to male power in the public world of the polis. And the ethical behavior of members of the *oikos* was widely, if not universally, considered a chief concern of politics.

Second, politics existed in monarchies and other forms of sole governance, such as tyranny – not only in settings where collective deliberation and negotiation, not to mention voting, were the rules of thumb. Greek political thinkers from Herodotus to Plato described, analyzed, and evaluated the politics of one-man rule. Sole or narrow rule was an exercise of power that controlled affairs in particular communities; and the ordinary people governed by sole rulers negotiated the exercise of power and participated in collective self-definition, not to mention their participation in the religious and legal rituals and quotidian practices of their city. They had a political culture that Greek thinkers took pains to analyze. As a result, for us as for ancient Greek writers, such regimes and their practices fell well within the parameters of "the political." As befits a historical study, we should try to establish a working definition of "the political" that is broad enough to accommodate the phenomena recognized as political by the Greeks themselves.

The term *ta politika*, however, should not restrict our inquiry to the polis itself. Even though the polis became the crucial site of political activity, the polis itself was an artifact of political dynamics such as negotiation, public criticism, communal self-definition, the establishment of means of self-defense, and the development of canons of justice. We must distinguish the institutional structures of the polis from the activity of politics. If, then, we understand politics as an activity that is separable from the specific institutions of the Greek polis, then it is possible to view the polis as a specific political and administrative form resulting from the demands of critical political reflection.[9] The polis took on its well-known historical features – citizenship, shared religion, assemblies, judicial processes, and so forth – as a result of early Greek attempts to define communities through public debate among men who were theoretically equal. Partly because it was an artifact of political thinking, and because it succeeded in working out compromises among different groups, the Greek polis became the normal and characteristic home of politics. The Greeks themselves saw the polis as the typical home of politics. But the question here is one of priority. It makes sense that ideas, often ideas that are critical of the status quo, were the necessary precondition of decisive political change – such as the establishment of the polis. Politics existed before (not because of) the polis, as it also existed in the kingdoms that took center stage in the Hellenistic period (323–30 BC).

This account of "the political" encourages us to examine a broad range of ancient texts, including those of poets, historians, orators, pamphleteers, and others – in addition to systematic philosophers. For it is only through a broad examination of perspectives that we can grasp the pervasiveness of politics in the ancient Greek world. Accordingly, the present book is focused on political "thought", an inclusive term, rather than political "theory", which focuses on understanding systematic philosophical treatments of politics. Political thinking was taking place well beyond the confines of Plato's Academy. Greater inclusion has the additional benefit of showing that Greek political thought constituted a vigorous and self-conscious tradition of adaptation, reinvention, and innovation.

Specifically, the systematic theoreticians did not invent their intellectual worlds from scratch. Rather, their work grew out of a culture of ethical and political analysis that had existed, almost with a vengeance, from the time of our earliest surviving Greek texts, the great epics of Homer and Hesiod. Those poets, whose epics as we now have them grew out of a long oral tradition, dealt in a sophisticated way with many of the themes that recur in the systematic fourth-century theorists – distributive justice, elitism, responsibility, authority, reciprocity, and leadership. Naturally, there are distinctions to be made between these different genres and textual forms. The early poets composed in a highly traditional medium with rigorous rules governing the expression of ideas; their medium was driven by rubrics of genre, meter, vocabulary, and mythological plot. Moreover, they employed narrative and storytelling, rather than straightforward exposition, as their mode of presentation. It is important to remain attuned to these differences in form and expression between the poets and later prose authors. But it is equally important to recognize that later authors, such as Plato and Aristotle, reinvented the substance of early thinking in their own literary mediums, and that they did so for their own local and immediate purposes.

Here is a possible objection. The proposed continuity in thought did not exist, because the poets and historians were offering narratives, analyses, and descriptions of (real or fictional) events, whereas the classical philosophers were providing normative and evaluative pictures of human nature and political relations. To put it more roughly, this objection says that the historians tell us how things were in fact, whereas the philosophers tell us how things ought to be. My response is to deny that such a distinction can be applied to ancient Greek literature. All of Greek political literature is normative in the sense that the authors (or in the case of early Greek poetry, the oral poets and traditional bards) shaped their material in order to provide an ethical analysis and a political evaluation. No doubt a scholar could confront us with this or that bit of text and defy us to explain its normative content. However, it is widely recognized that Greek literature, especially poetry, served a didactic function in its cultural context. It was listened to and read and re-read because its audiences believed firmly that they were deriving moral wisdom from this literature, wisdom that could help them lead better lives and live in healthier political communities. The *History* of Thucydides, moreover, is perhaps the example par excellence of a text that is both descriptive (or analytical) and normative. The standards of (allegedly) objective analysis which are sometimes thought to pertain in modern humanities and social sciences disciplines are not helpful in grasping the self-understandings of ancient authors or their audiences.

By now we have begun to build up a picture of Greek political thought as a set of conversations and reflections on matters of fundamental importance for the identity, self-image, and organization of Greek communities. Therefore, we should not include every particular policy decision or diplomatic mission or declaration of war within the category of "political thought." Such particular events express political thought and they may help us understand underlying political ideas, but they are not our primary interest. Instead, political thought involves more general or abstract reflections about the workings of politics and about human beings in their political capacities. Typically, such reflections can be applied to a wide variety of situations or cases. This general applicability is one reason that a recognizable tradition of Greek political thought could be built up over several centuries. Well-formulated thoughts about hierarchy, equality, justice, and reciprocity could be adapted to make sense of specific situations and to give rhetorical and intellectual support to others who were able to adapt them to other situations persuasively.

On the other hand, even though on the surface it may appear abstract or remote from political reality, political thought was developed at least in part in order to serve immediate local needs or purposes. When, for example, Plato compared the democratic polis to a ship navigated by captains who curried favor with the ignorant crew members (*Rep.* 488a–489a), he clearly had his native Athens in mind (whether fairly or not). In light of this, then, it makes sense to approach political thought historically, to understand both systematic and unsystematic political thinkers as deeply engaged not only with one another, as we have seen, but also with the particular political circumstances in which their texts were produced. This "engagement" is often a sort of dynamic tension, in which authors reflected critically on what they saw, and either rejected contemporary approaches altogether, or proposed avenues of meaningful change for the better. There is reason to think, especially in the case of classical Athens, that more abstract, intellectual engagement with politics had a decisive effect on the actual practice of politics by the citizenry.

Emphasis on the particular, though, need not limit our engagement with these texts or their meaning for us. Suitably translated to the terms of our culture, these texts can help us think through our own political commitments; or, at a minimum, they can show us more clearly why we could never go backwards in time. Cutting across the "historicizing" approach, therefore, is the recognition that the texts themselves do not take a historicizing approach.[10] Their authors believed that they were right, full stop, to put forward their theses about politics and human nature. They had robust normative ambitions of their own. Thus, Greek political texts can be understood outside their immediate ancient contexts, and within the framework of larger philosophical conversations about virtue, justice, the distinction between public and private, political responsibility, authority, freedom, and rights. This second method of interpretation, which de-emphasizes the texts' historical specificity, is also valid in its own right because many Greek texts self-consciously present themselves as models of theoretical speculation. In particular, they are ambitious enough to advance apparently timeless claims about the nature of human beings and the universe.

Both historical and more strictly philosophical methods of interpretation have a place in our reconstruction of the history of Greek political thought. Our goal is both to interpret these texts as responses to particular formations of the economic, political, and social worlds, and to evaluate them normatively, especially through asking what their meaning could be for citizens of modern, pluralistic, democratic nation-states. The trick is to find a balance – to avoid both the Scylla of excessively limiting the texts through historically specific interpretation, and the Charybdis of completely abandoning historical contexts for the sake of modern critical or political agendas.

Asking the question of how these texts can be meaningful for us – citizens of modern pluralistic and democratic nation-states – is crucial, because if these texts were not meaningful and comprehensible to us, then what would be the value of studying them? From the standpoint of the twenty-first century, which has witnessed the widely acknowledged triumph of democracy, and which still has vivid memories of the horrors of oppressive totalitarian regimes, the familiar Greek touchstone might strike us as illiberal, antidemocratic, and even unethical. The ancient Greeks were slaveholders. Many of the political thinkers we shall examine were virulently antidemocratic. Whenever the opportunity arose, Greek city-states were imperialistic, and they made notable arguments to justify their imperialism. Even the most liberal of Greeks excluded women from political power. They maintained rigid, exclusive standards of citizenship that made foreigners into second- or third-class human beings. The Greeks had no conception of universal "human rights" or the dignity of human beings. Clearly, no one would try to re-institute Greek politics as a way of life. Therefore: can we be anything other than tourists in this alien and disturbing, albeit strangely compelling, political and ethical world?

The traditional response to this question is that the Greeks (and Romans) are the cultural ancestors of modernity – of the European world, certainly, but even more globally if we believe that "the modern world was a European creation presided over by the Greek past." Undoubtedly this response and its assumptions are debatable, but such debates are not our concern here. Even if the Greeks are modernity's cultural ancestors, that fact *might* no longer be interesting or important as we devise new ways of thinking about the future.[11] The importance of Greek political thought to us has to be argued for in specific and detailed terms, in the here and now. I would argue that studying Greek political thought provides an important political perspective for us in virtue of its combination of similarity to us and difference from us. At least some ancient Greeks were fundamentally similar to us – in their political convictions about democracy, freedom, and equality – and also fundamentally different from us – in owning slaves, in their polytheistic religion, and in their lack of separation between religion and politics. It is the peculiar combination of similarity and difference that I will emphasize in this book, because it is through appreciating and understanding the unique position of the Greeks in relation to us that looking to the ancient Greek past can become a genuinely educational experience.

To see what this could mean, we must return to, and expand considerably, the point that Greek political thought concerns itself with the ethical implications of individual and collective activity. Greek thinkers assumed that ethics and politics were connected at their foundations. The connection between ethics and politics was not, as one recent scholar has suggested, an invention of the philosophers; it was always an integral part of the Greek experience of the political, whether at the level of theory, ideology, or practice.[12] I am using the term "ethical" advisedly here, in contrast to the term "moral." Roughly stated, "morality" is concerned with the systematic formulation of prohibitions, obligations, and rules of behavior; it specifies what must be done and particularly what must not be done, but without much emphasis on the inner life or dispositions of the moral agent. According to a more strongly Kantian conception of morality, in fact, moral acts are more admirable if they are done through sheer acts of the will, unaided by particular affections for particular others.

By contrast, ethics is concerned with character formation.[13] The term "ethics" derives from the Greek *êthos*, which means "custom, disposition, character." For the ancient Greeks, ethics was primarily a matter of managing one's desires and appetites and keeping them under control, of training oneself to exhibit virtues such as the canonical justice, temperance, courage, and piety – and of acting virtuously because one had the proper motivations, desires, and dispositions. Our term "virtue" was understood by the Greeks as an "excellence" (*aretê*) of the soul or character. The soul – at least according to the Greeks – could be harmoniously managed and set into excellent working order, through proper education of desires, proclivities, passions, and habits. Through such management and education, it was held, the individual could attain an excellent or virtuous condition of soul. In addition to the canonical four, Greeks also constructed political arguments around the virtues of liberality, greatness of spirit, kindness, trustworthiness, loyalty, orderliness, and gratitude. Much of Greek political thought is concerned with defining what the virtues are, how virtue-talk can be applied to particular situations, and why the virtues are important for and necessary to political life. These concerns can be more or less explicit, depending on the contexts and ambitions of the individual writer or political agent. Either way, it is clear and important that the political discourse of ancient Greece was carried on in the terms and categories provided by Greek thinking about the virtues.

Ancient political thought placed a much greater emphasis on character development – on defining what citizens ought to be like – than modern political thought. This connection was present *ab origine* as part of collective efforts to produce individuals who would willingly commit themselves to a just society. There is ample scope to speak of "virtue politics" in the ancient world, by analogy with the "virtue ethics" for which ancient philosophy has become well known.[14] The virtues and vices therefore played a larger and more consistent role in ancient political thought than they could in modern political discourse. That ancient politics was a proper "virtue politics" meant that the ancient polis could never embrace pluralism in any modern form.

Thus, in its normative guise, the ancient "virtue politics" was directed at the flourishing of individuals and communities. The precise nature of such flourishing – that is, what exactly it consisted in, or how we could recognize it if it ever existed – was always in dispute. What was not in dispute was that an objectively flourishing condition was knowable and attainable by human beings. The flip side of this normative virtue politics is the critique of politics that is informed by character defects or vices – cowardice, greed, self-indulgence, mean-spiritedness, selfishness, and envy. These vices stood in the way of achieving happiness, whether individual or political. Even apart from the normative element of Greek political thought, Greek political analysis and exhortation also tended to be conducted in the terminology of virtues and vices. We are working toward an understanding of why Greek political thought is meaningful for us, and traveling through ethics, and therefore the virtues, and "virtue politics," to get there.

Toward the end of our period, Aristotle provided a particularly clear analysis of the link between ethics and politics.[15] In the final chapter of his *Nicomachean Ethics*, he explains that his goal in the study of human affairs is not simply to recognize what is good, but rather also to try to become good, and to make other men good. Although his previous arguments might encourage innately good men to practice virtue, he says, arguments are ineffective at making the majority of men good, since most men follow their passions rather than reason. As a result, most men require the compulsion of laws. In other words, the polis must intervene significantly in the character formation of its citizens, if those citizens are to lead good and flourishing lives. This suggests that the ethical treatise he is finishing should be considered a preliminary study leading up to his account of politics, rather than an end in itself.

He had signaled this point early on in the treatise. Aristotle's entire discussion of "ethics" – his discussion, that is, of the intellectual and character-based virtues that make men flourish – was undertaken with a view to politics (1.2). For Aristotle, politics is the art of making human beings good and successful as human beings. Therefore, Aristotle says, "Presumably the man who wants to make men better through his careful attention, whether they are many or few, must attempt to become skilled in legislating, if we become good men through laws" (10.9.1180b23–5). Thus, he tightly links his ethical thought with a political context by arguing that the science of politics should concern itself with legislation directed toward creating, and creating the conditions for, the living of the best human life possible. As he put it, "Since this science uses the other ones, and also lays down laws about what it is necessary to do and what it is necessary to keep away from, the goal of this science would encompass those of the others, so that this would be the human good" (1.3.1094b4–7).

Talking about the human good in these explicit terms would probably have sounded eccentric, and even farfetched, to most citizens of the Greek polis. However, our sources for the political realities of Greek life strongly suggest that a conception of the good for human beings – really, for citizens of the polis – lay beneath virtually all Greek public conversations about the polis. The evidence for this claim is that a wide spectrum of writers, orators, and politicians in classical Greece, not to mention philosophers, constantly talked about the polis and political life as the contexts for individual and collective flourishing or well-being. They did not conceive of happiness as something individuals experienced in various and sundry ways, on their own terms, and however they wished. The nature of human flourishing was not thought to depend on the individual and his or her subjective choices. This does not imply that everyone subscribed to exactly the same substantive account of what constitutes happiness or flourishing; it means, instead, that most people would have rejected a subjective conception of happiness, even as they fought hard with each other over what happiness actually consists in.

Considered in this way, the ancient Greek "virtue politics" offers
a great deal to the citizens of the modern democratic nation-state,
as they struggle to define their political priorities, commitments,
and aspirations. In particular, Greek political thought, with its
emphasis on "virtue politics," provides a genuine *tertium quid*, a
real alternative to two prevailing modern conceptions of politics
– liberalism and communitarianism. Roughly, citizens of modern
democratic nation-states characteristically use the language of philosophical liberalism to discuss politics – that is, they tend to talk
in the language of individual rights, personal freedoms, protection
from the state, and equality of opportunity.[16] This language is premised on a "thin" or abstract or disembodied conception of the
individual as a bearer of inalienable rights, a person of rational
choice, and a self free to choose a life plan independent of social
attachments and traditional values. Liberal views have been influ-
entially criticized by communitarian thinkers who propose that our
lives have meaning only in view of our partial ties and attachments
and of our "rootedness" in particular social and civic relationships.
Communitarians deny that individuals are free to the extent that
they are detached from such relationships; rather, they argue,
family and community provide the contexts within which genuinely free choices are made possible. Individuals, properly understood, are always already embedded within a fabric of traditional
mores and communal networks.[17]

The ancient Greek "politics of virtue" exhibits many of the
attractive features of both of these conceptions, but avoids the
unhelpful binary and the frustrating debates that have characterized recent writing in this vein.[18] In particular, we find within Greek
political thought approval of individual autonomy, innovation,
private freedom, and equality of opportunity, which are some of
the primary values endorsed by liberal philosophy and culture. For
example, the orator Demosthenes exhorted his fellow citizens to
think autonomously when he said, "When you enter the battlefield, therefore, whoever leads you has authority over you, but at
this moment [in the Assembly] each one of you yourselves acts as
a general" (*Exordia* 50.3). Values such as autonomy, in themselves,
required that citizens exhibit the virtues – to have enough courage,
for example, to air an unpopular view in the political assembly.
Many "liberal" values, in other words, presuppose certain widely
acknowledged virtues. Greek political thought sheds light on the

possible connections between liberal values and political virtues.[19] On the other hand, Greek political thinkers, like modern communitarians, certainly rejected the robust individualism of modern liberals. They believed that individuals were defined by their attachments to their families, religion, and communities and, furthermore, that individuals became happy through participating in the traditions and culture of their poleis. This belief led to the view that individual virtue either naturally was or ought to be directed toward the traditional values of the polis.

Ancient Greek political thought provides a well-articulated conception of good politics and the good life by describing healthy public institutions, by exhibiting respect for the capacities of individuals, by recognizing the human importance of free political association, and by developing non-relative accounts of good character and healthy individual psychology. It achieves all of these important and desirable goals by concentrating on the relationship between politics and ethics – more specifically, by recognizing that politics can play a critical role in making citizens capable of healthy choices about how to live their lives. Such a focus on the ethical, on the individual, and on choice should satisfy the liberal interest in the welfare and autonomy of individuals while also offering a realistic and "thick" conception of the individual as a social and historical agent.[20] Moreover, ancient Greek political thought goes beyond both schools in its admirable grasp of psychology – both of individuals and groups. For this reason and for others that we will explore, Greek political thought offers numerous resources for us as democratic citizens in a very different world. Our goal is now to examine more specifically what their ideals were, how their ideals developed in historically specific ways, and what sorts of translation might be possible to make their ideals a source of renewal and education for us.

chapter 2
Archaic Greece and the Centrality of Justice

"Justice is the first virtue of social institutions." So Rawls begins his famous *A Theory of Justice* (1971). Rawls' development of this premise was a watershed in contemporary political theory. His book helped to move theory from analyzing institutions, administrative power, law, and sovereignty to focusing on ideals of justice, freedom, equality, and community. In studying ancient Greek political thought, likewise, we must examine ideals and ideology as much as the institutional framework that made them possible. It is as important, perhaps more important, to locate the "political" in the interplay of ideology and publicly constructed values as to chart its development in the foundation and growth of institutions. Even if implicitly, institutions reflect normative ideas – that is, ideas about how things ought to work. Moreover, ethical ideals give structure and significance to the behavior of political agents who operate within institutions. Therefore, it makes sense to analyze archaic political thought from the perspective of virtues and values. Justice was the first virtue and ideal of Greece's key political institution, the polis. Not coincidentally, it played an integral role – perhaps *the* integral role – in the most sophisticated political texts of the era spanning roughly 750 to 490 BC. Intellectual conversations about justice evolved in tandem with the historical polis. Because justice illuminates the dialectic between ideas and political history, it is useful to focus on justice in analyzing archaic discussions of political health.

It is especially important to grasp the nature of the sources. Poetry is the chief source for political thought in the archaic period, though it is also possible to make occasional use of art and

archaeology for our purposes. Archaic poetry was highly traditional, composed orally, and fixed in writing only after generations
of development. When we speak of individual poets, such as
"Theognis," or "Homer," or "Hesiod," we are in fact speaking of
poetic personae – that is, figures in whose name many later bards
composed poetry in oral performance. The surviving corpus of
Theognis, for example, contains a mixture of elements that date
anywhere from 625 BC to 490 BC and give voice to sentiments at
many different, and often conflicting, points on the ideological
spectrum. "Theognis" was a prestigious poetic name that conferred
authority on the compositions of many Megarian poets. As we will
see, archaic poetry discussed the ethics of contemporary political
arrangements throughout the Greek world. The poems that have
survived are intertextually related, highly traditional, and general.
Consequently, it makes sense to view them as participating in
broadly applicable conversations about ethical and political
values.[2]

Achilles, Agamemnon, and Fair Distribution

One of our earliest poems, Homer's *Iliad*, presents justice as a
major subject of contention within well-defined communities. The
poem's central term for "justice," *dikê*, means, more precisely,
"the right way," particularly as determined by custom. We will see
that "the right way," in a social and political sense, came quickly
to focus on (contested) issues of justice; doing things "the
right way," moreover, had considerable implications for a community's long-term political health. Through a long process of oral
tradition, this poem assumed its present form, roughly, in the late
eighth century BC. It is contemporaneous with the rise of the polis
and so it reflects upon questions that were important to inhabitants
of the early polis.

In the opening scene, Achilles gets very angry over what he
perceives as the unfairness and arrogance of the supreme
commander, Agamemnon. Pressured by a god to give up his
cherished war prize, Agamemnon proposed to seize Achilles'
prize, a captive woman, in order to restore his honor. Achilles
passionately denounced Agamemnon's greed and insulting behavior (Text 1).

1. Most glorious son of Atreus, greediest of all men, how will the great-hearted Achaeans give you a prize of honor? I do not know of much common property lying around anywhere. . . . Indeed, you threaten to take away my prize yourself, for which I have worked hard, and the sons of the Achaeans gave it to me. My prize never equals yours, whenever the Achaeans sack a well-built citadel of the Trojans. But my hands carry on the greater share of furious battle; but whenever the distribution comes, you get a prize that is much greater, while I return to my ships worn out from fighting, with some small but precious thing. (*Iliad* 1.122–4, 161–8)

Achilles was making an argument about the injustice of Agamemnon's seizure of his legitimate prize of war. This conflict could have turned into a fight – but the goddess Athena commanded Achilles not to kill Agamemnon. Instead of witnessing an open brawl, therefore, we listen to a heated verbal exchange over the appropriate distribution of spoils. The core of Achilles' argument is that he is the best fighter in the army altogether (and kills the most enemies); therefore, he says, he deserves a greater share of the spoils than he typically receives. He is making an early argument about distributive justice. For Achilles, justice prevails only when rewards correspond, in value and magnitude, to actual accomplishments on the battlefield.[3]

Achilles is advancing a distinctive and apparently controversial principle. Even if merit-based claims to fair shares seem natural to us, many other principles of distribution are imaginable. For example, there is the famous Marxist tag "from each according to his ability, to each according to his need" – which might work well in utopias of superabundance, but which is ruled out in archaic Greece, where scarcity of resources, and thus conflict, was an inescapable reality. Certain liberal theorists, such as Ronald Dworkin, have constructed hypothetical systems of (re)distribution that are intended to compensate for class or natural disadvantages (such as physical disability), thereby redefining our very conception of "merit." The *Iliad* represents a tension between claims based on ascribed rank (Agamemnon) and claims based on merit and accomplishment (Achilles).

Agamemnon is the supreme commander, based on the size of his own military contingent and the standing he gains from Zeus.

Therefore, he expects his orders to be obeyed, even though he is outclassed by others in both martial ability and skill in deliberation. Achilles, by contrast, is the best fighter in a group – an army – whose very existence implies the ideal of winning battles. Their conflict makes us think hard about how fairness in distribution ought to be understood, and how political authority is, and ought to be, established. These were the major questions faced by citizens of the early Greek polis.

Whatever answers these questions received in particular contexts, the poet strongly suggests that they are linked. In the Homeric representation, leaders can maintain their authority only if they are genuinely fair-minded. Achilles won a rhetorical victory and undercut Agamemnon's authority because he successfully publicized Agamemnon's lack of fairness. He strengthened his case by explaining Agamemnon's injustice in terms of virtues and vices. He obviously expected his audience to understand and endorse his own application of the terminology of virtue and vice. In particular, Achilles described Agamemnon's injustice in terms of two salient character defects – namely, greed and *hubris*.

The charge of materialistic greed (cf. Text 1) was especially damaging because Homeric heroes valued honor and status above all. Achilles asserted that Agamemnon sacrificed those values in order to satisfy his contemptible materialistic desires. Achilles denigrated such desires as vile and even gluttonous: he said that Agamemnon "devoured" his own people for the sake of his greed (1.231). Agamemnon's greed was especially noteworthy, according to Achilles, because it drove him to dishonor the army's most accomplished warrior. In Achilles' compelling presentation, therefore, Agamemnon's materialistic desire was closely linked to imprudence and *hubris*.

Hubris was a form of arrogant contempt designed to display superiority; leaders who committed *hubris* did so in order to cause their victims shame, by displaying before all their weakness and vulnerability. It was difficult for a tough, status-conscious warrior like Achilles to claim that he had been "victimized." In this case, however, he increased his stature by allying himself with the community and its standards against the unfairness of an oppressive leader. He made his arguments all the more effective by indicating that Agamemnon oppressed not only other leaders, but also the army as a whole.

Later in the poem, the poet deepened his examination of this conflict by exploring its emotional consequences. Achilles felt deep pain over being a victim, as he explains later when Agamemnon's ambassadors ask him to re-join the army: "My heart swells with anger, when I recall how Agamemnon treated me with insolence in front of the Argives, like some wanderer without honor" (9.646–8). Agamemnon's greed and *hubris* made Achilles indignant and angry – very naturally, in context, since anger is an emotion inspired by the painful sensation that one has been treated unjustly and without due respect. Through exploring greed, *hubris*, and anger, the poem shows that both character and emotion play a critical role in the health or breakdown of a political community, especially when its leaders are involved. If justice is to be achieved, then individuals must exhibit the virtues of self-restraint, respect for others, and fairness. If they do not or cannot, then the result will be disorder, feuding, and vengeance. It was, in part, the task of the community to shape the characters and emotions of individuals – even those of its leaders – so as to make them law-abiding, norm-obeying, and trustworthy members.

Justice as "Distinctively Human"

The *Iliad*'s opening scene, then, illustrates both the centrality of justice to communal stability and the complexities surrounding its uses, meaning, and content in concrete circumstances. Justice was a central concern of thinkers of all sorts in the archaic period. Justice was a key term, for example, in the archaic physical theorists' explanation of order and balance in the cosmos; it could either consist in an equilibrium between conflicting "opposites" (Anaximander [*DK* 12 B1]), or, more obscurely, it could be equated with strife (Heraclitus [*DK* 22 B 80]).[4]

But justice was of greater interest still to thinkers whose primary concern was the human and social world. Justice took on special significance for political thought because archaic Greeks saw it as a distinctive marker of humanity. As Hesiod points out using the common imagery of brutish eating, the rule of force is characteristic of the animal kingdom (Text 2).

2. Zeus ordained this law for human beings – for fish, wild animals, and winged birds to eat one another, since there is no justice among them, but to human beings he gave justice, which turns out to be the best by far. Whoever knows and is willing to say what is right wins prosperity from far-seeing Zeus. But whoever swears falsely and intentionally lies in giving evidence, and recklessly and incurably damages justice – that man's family is left in obscurity afterwards. By contrast, the family of a man who abides by his oaths is better off for the future. (*WD* 276–85)

Predatory violence is uncharacteristic and unworthy of human beings, because human well-being is contingent upon individuals' willingness to respect justice and to abide by oaths and impartial legal rules. Hesiod's contrast between human beings and animals depends upon the involvement of the gods. The gods are ultimately responsible for rewarding the upright and punishing wrongdoers. As we saw in the previous section, however, Homer depicted human communities as able and willing to take responsibility for articulating and enforcing their own conceptions of justice. The question of divine involvement in politics, as represented by the archaic poets, will occupy us throughout this chapter.

A similar concern with what is distinctively human underlies the *Odyssey*'s representation of the non-human Cyclopes. These violent creatures, Odysseus says, do not respect the ordinary conventions or standards of civilized human life (Text 3).

3. And then we sailed further on, though we were distressed at heart. We arrived at the land of the arrogant, lawless Cyclopes, who have such faith in the immortal gods that they neither plant with their hands nor plow fields, but all things grow unsown and untilled, wheat and barley and vines, which yield a wine made of fine grapes, and the heavy rain of Zeus makes them increase. They have no public meeting places to take counsel, nor laws, but they dwell on the tops of high mountains in hollow caves, and each one provides the law for his children and wives, and they have no regard for one another. (*Odyssey* 9.105–15)

In the absence of such standards, the most famous Cyclops, Polyphemus, thinks nothing of devouring Odysseus' comrades for three meals a day. In this respect Polyphemus resembles the unjust and predatory animals of Hesiod's poem. Through such memorable characters and stories, Archaic poets established justice as the central mode of talking about properly human relations.

The Cyclopes, moreover, enabled Homer to link justice and humanity to the Greek polis. Homer envisions the early polis as the most suitable context for the development of justice among human beings. Cyclopean society is the polar opposite of a healthy, functioning human community. Odysseus' description of Cyclopean society (Text 3) reveals, by way of contrast, the central features of a normatively defined human society: common laws, a central meeting place, agriculture, and a shared communal identity.[5] His description of a monstrous "community" in which such features are absent helps to define that which is characteristically human. In so doing Odysseus anticipates the standard elements of the Greek polis. It was, many thought, in this self-consciously organized form of political community that justice could be most fully realized.

Institutions and Values of the Early Polis

The polis came into existence in the eighth century BC and was based on an emerging idea of citizenship. Since the polis was a novel political form, citizenship was an inchoate and at best emergent concept at this early period. At a minimum, though, it implied three things. First, that all citizens had a stake in the collective welfare – they participated in common rituals, recognized a common city center, mobilized for warfare and common defense together, and began to take on a self-image as a member of this or that polis. Public life (*to dêmosion*, which means literally "the thing of the demos") took on great significance for members of the *demos*, or the citizenry understood as a collective whole.[6] Citizens were expected to view themselves as "shareholders" in the political community and consequently enjoyed the privileges of participation in community life. Conversely, they also had duties, to perform, such as regular service as soldiers, as voters in the assembly, and as law-abiding participants in the community's economic and social life.

Second, though it was not said outright, citizenship implied a basic equality (albeit in a rough and uneven form) within the privileged group of adult males of proven descent. This meant, not the absence of economic or political hierarchy, but rather minimum standards of behavior and respect owed to men with a stake in the polis. For example, citizens could not be legally sold into slavery, or illegally forced to work for another, or assaulted with impunity. Even citizens of the earliest (eighth-century BC) poleis were beneficiaries of their community's standards of justice. They were also participants in discussions about what those standards should look like. The earliest Greek laws, inscribed on stone, proudly proclaimed that they were sanctioned and passed by the city and the demos.

Third, citizenship implied important exclusions. It went without saying that women and slaves could not hold full and active shares in the political community (women did have public roles to play, for example, in religion). It was rare that free foreign men could become naturalized. Typically, moreover, there were formal exclusions (e.g., from public office) based on property qualifications. In the eighth century BC, these three features of citizenship were not formalized or universal, but the polis was a widespread political form in Greece from this period onward. Citizenship gradually began to manifest these features throughout the world of the Greek polis.

As stakeholders or shareholders in this "joint political venture," citizens owed their loyalties to the community. Conversely, they legitimately expected to be beneficiaries of its legal, religious, social, and economic practices. In the light of citizens' "rights and responsibilities," so to speak, it makes sense that justice was the primary focus of attention when early Greek poets and thinkers turned to politics. For these thinkers, one and all, believed that just dealings were owed to all citizens as citizens. By extension, justice was the critical precondition of political health, either, it was thought, because of the gods' vengeance upon the unjust, or because citizens whose just claims were violated or ignored could become hostile toward their oppressors.

What is Justice? The Voice of the Oppressed and the Origins of Political Thought

If archaic Greeks believed that "Every excellence as a whole is found in justice" (Phocylides 10 = Theognis 147), then can we, or could they, say what justice is? It is perhaps easy to make general, abstract statements about justice. The archaic poet Simonides, for example, is quoted in Plato's *Republic* (331e) as saying that justice is giving to each what is owed. But this is not very informative; it gives us the genus of justice as a virtue but does not specify its content. What is each person, by the standards of justice, owed by the community, or, for that matter, what does each person owe to the community? Even though many poets discussed "fair shares" and the like, no one developed a systematic account of justice as a social virtue of individuals, and no one described in detail what a just political order would look like.

Instead of providing a general theory of justice, archaic Greek poets focused on the particular. Those who were inclined to "speak up" did so out of indignation or anger at the injustice of others.[7] As a rough generalization, in fact, we might say that Greek political thought arose from, and was early on constituted by, the critique of injustice. Often such a critique was aimed at the oppressive rulers of the polis. Hesiod's *Works and Days*, for example, warns the political leaders of archaic Boeotia: "Guard against this, you kings who devour gifts, and give straight judgments; put crooked judgments out of your mind entirely" (263–4). Or, again, Solon of Athens complains, "The mind of the leaders of the people is unjust; their great *hubris* will certainly make them suffer much grief, for they do not know how to restrain their greed" (fr. 4.7–9). These statements echo Achilles' complaint that Agamemnon's excessive desire to get more led to injustice toward his political subordinates. Such behavior was all the more offensive inside a polis. The polis was the site where, institutionally and ideologically, it seemed possible to achieve social justice through encouraging respect for all citizens.

How could poets identify injustice if they had no theory? One traditional approach was religious. Hesiod declared that the gods identify human wrongdoing, take note of it, and then punish it (Text 4).

4. As for those who do arrogant and brutal things, far-seeing Zeus, the son of Cronus, decrees punishment. Often an entire polis suffers because of a bad man's outrageous crimes. . . . Many thousands of Zeus's immortal guardians of mortal men live on the all-nourishing earth; these watch over judgments and shocking behavior. . . . And there is the maiden Justice, Zeus's daughter, whom the Olympian gods honor and respect. Whenever someone harms her by unjustly blaming another, at once she sits beside her father Zeus, the son of Cronus, and describes the unjust thoughts of men, until the ordinary people pay for the arrogant behavior of their leaders (*WD* 238–61)

This was a common belief throughout the archaic period. But, as stated, it was far too simplistic to do citizens much good. For, in this crude form, Hesiod's idea is manifestly untrue: wrongdoers do well for themselves. It is cold comfort to say (as many Greek poets did say) that the gods would harm the wrongdoer's descendants somewhere down the line.

More importantly, religious views of justice and injustice always require human interpretation. Hesiod could not simply leave justice and injustice up to the gods. The poet himself spent a great deal of time *explaining* what was unjust and why, even if he claimed the sanction of divinity. In the Greek polis, unusually for an ancient culture, there were no higher authorities to appeal to in arguing for different religious interpretations. There were no sacred texts; there was no vocationally defined priestly class, or wisdom of the ancestors, or anything of the sort, to appeal to. There was normative argument alone. This meant that human understanding and efforts at persuasion were the key to developing a conception of justice, even from within a religious framework, because the question of how to interpret the gods' relation to humanity was open to public debate.[8]

Therefore, critics of "politics-as-usual" developed interpretations, arguments, and explanations for their opinions. In doing so, they had to appeal, as Achilles did, to the pre-existing and deeply held beliefs, intuitions, and ideals of their audience. Often such beliefs and preconceptions were embodied in law or tradition. Like the appeal to religious norms, however, the appeal to law or custom also required careful interpretation in context. As later ancient theorists saw, the law was a general and blunt instrument; in context, individuals had to reason deductively about legal applications in particular cases. Moreover, and more deeply, it was possible to criticize existing practices as well as legal and cultural norms, provided that poets or political actors hit upon tensions or ambiguities within traditional ideals. This was essentially the form of Achilles' criticisms of Agamemnon; Achilles appealed to his audience's pre-existing beliefs about fair distribution and good character, and his arguments overrode Agamemnon's conflicting appeal to his own stature and authority.

Whatever form their appeals took, the poets and their characters took up positions in a political world that was *contentious*. Citizens differed on questions of distribution and the proper description of the virtues and vices in particular contexts. To help resolve (or at least illuminate) such differences, the poets analyzed justice into its component parts, or its more basic elements. They focused particularly on the belief that justice derives from a commitment to equality.

Equality is a notoriously troubled concept. Nowadays, popularly, equality is usually understood as "equality of opportunity" – all citizens of a modern democratic state are intended to have equal opportunity to appeal to the law, to make a success of their lives, and to exercise their basic liberties. But there is another sense of equality – equal moral respect for other human beings as human beings – that is perhaps more fundamental in the modern world. As slaveholders living in a firmly patriarchal culture, Greeks would hardly have subscribed to this view in general. But, as citizens of a polis, within the community of free adult male citizens, the members of the polis recognized a similar idea, based on their shared "rights and responsibilities" as citizens. The question was how this basic conception was to manifest itself in the distribution of power and resources in the city. This was the crux of the debates. For, obviously to all contemporaries, there was no social or economic equality in the archaic polis. Were the hierarchies in these nonpolitical realms even relevant to political behavior and distribution? How could political hierarchies be justified, if at all? And what special place should be accorded to exceptional individuals, who demonstrated positive capacities for leadership?

To understand what equality could mean, and be based on, early thinkers had to mull over the question of how, if at all, to differentiate between leaders and followers within the community. This is a central issue in the *Iliad* and *Odyssey*. The Homeric epics focus on a group of heroes defined by their beauty, fighting ability, intelligence, rank, and privileges. These heroes were rarely challenged by the mass of ordinary fighters. The low-class Thersites, however, is an exceptional case. He constantly criticized the leaders (2.211–16), and he is shown condemning Agamemnon's insatiable greed (Text 5) and trying ardently to rouse the anger of his fellow soldiers.

5. Son of Atreus, what complaints do you have now, and what more do you want? Your huts are full of bronze, and you have many of the finest women in them, whom the Achaeans give to you first, whenever we capture a city. Or do you want more gold still? . . . It is not right that you, as the commander, lead the sons of the Achaeans into misery. You weak men, you wretched disgraces, Achaean women, no longer men of Achaea, let us go home in our ships, and let us leave this man here in Troy to digest his prizes, so that he can see how men like us help him, or not. (*Iliad* 2.225–9, 233–8)

For his pains he is beaten summarily by Odysseus, to the great delight of the other ordinary soldiers, who laugh disparagingly at Thersites' tears. Homer's representation emphasizes the importance of the leaders and their nearly unassailable authority, as Thersites' criticisms are "contained" by Odysseus' reassertion of Agamemnon's prerogatives. Interestingly, the other ordinary soldiers, who risk their lives for Agamemnon's greater glory, conspire in the system of rank and authority that fails to serve *their own* material interests well.

Through representing Thersites as an inconsequential nuisance, the poet "naturalizes" a distinctive vision of relations between ordinary soldiers and their leaders. Homer's presentation is not a transcript of reality, but rather an ideologically informed vision of how things ought to be in known political groups. He suggests that political health and collective safety are won through deference to the leaders and through the leaders' sensitivity to the claims of one another. It has often been noticed, however, that Thersites' complaints echo those of Achilles. This perhaps hints at the danger to the elite if one of its foremost members breaks ranks. The system would break down if Achilles did the unthinkable and put his weight behind the apparently legitimate claims of men like Thersites. In these episodes, therefore, the poet raises questions about hierarchy and equality that related directly to the concerns of early Greek citizens. As we will see, his elitist vision of political relations was open to attack by poets more sympathetic to Thersites' cause.

In their different ways, Homer and Hesiod alike speak to the contentious relationship between the elite and the ordinary citizens. The early polis was controlled by members of the wealthy landed elite, who usually constructed for themselves elaborate aristocratic genealogies in order to solidify their places in the political hierarchy. At the bottom of the polis were those who, although free men and citizens, owned little or no land – a fact which prevented them from playing a significant role in the defense of the city against attack. The largest group, probably 50 percent of the whole, was in the middle.[9] These were the "middling" farmers who were able to purchase heavy armor and were the city's primary source of military power. This latter group, sometimes referred to as the "hoplite" class after their method of fighting, came to be the backbone of the early Greek polis. These men were the paradigmatic citizens of the polis and served in three main capacities: as farmers, as fighters, and as voters in the public assembly. With this rudimentary sociology in mind, we can better understand class tension in the early Greek polis and its relationship to political thinking about justice.

There were many calls for class differentiation, based, for example, on wealth, birth, superior morality, fighting capacity, and so forth. When Theognis said, "Although he is a stronghold and tower of defense for the empty-headed people, Cyrnus, a good man has only a small share of honor" (233–4), his words were an inflammatory call for political hierarchy, based on the valuable qualities supposedly inherent in nobility. Such calls to hierarchy often translated into the social or moral realm the "logic of merit" utilized by Achilles in the military context. This logic helped to establish the basic principle of political justice: equal shares to equal people, and unequal shares to unequal people. In light of this principle, the important question became, What does the polis – a much more complex group than an army – exist for? It was only through determining the goals of the polis that citizens could specify what counted as "merit." Theognis' "noble man" made a meritorious contribution to – what?

The Egalitarian Response

It is useful to divide the responses to these questions into two main categories, the "egalitarian" and "elitist."[10] The egalitarian response centered on the small farmers who served as hoplite soldiers and voters in the assembly. These men were often represented as being "in the middle." They were in fact in the middle ranges of the economic hierarchy, but their "middling" position was an ideological construct that created an ethical space for them apart from both the very wealthy and the very poor. As Phocylides stated very simply, "Those in the middle have many excellent things; I want to be in the middle in the polis" (fr.12). This laudatory reference to the "middle" implies that Phocylides wants to live the public life of the polis, to be publicly accountable for the distributive choices he advocates, and to be separate from and more politically virtuous than the upper and lower fringes of the hierarchy. The famous ideas of the "golden mean" and "moderation in all things" are based, ultimately, on this politically "middling" position occupied by the small farmers. This middling ideal rejected what it saw as the disruptive aspirations of the elite (Text 6).

> **6.**   I have no interest in the wealth of Gyges, rich in gold, and jealousy has not yet taken hold of me, nor do I envy the deeds of the gods, and I do not long for great tyranny. These things are far from my eyes. (Archilochus, fr. 19)

In order to flesh out their political values, egalitarian poets chose to concentrate on what, in their view, good human beings and good human lives look like. They approached the often abstract issues of justice through a highly concrete language of the virtues and vices. Hesiod's *Works and Days* (ca. 700 BC) conveys the egalitarian vision of what the archaic polis was and what it ought to be. Framed as an agricultural manual and almanac, teaching its audience how to succeed at farming, it is usually categorized as "wisdom literature." Like the Homeric epics, this poem takes a particular stance in controversies over justice and political health. For Hesiod, the elite tended to be "bribe devouring," abusive of their power, and careless of the punishment that, he trusted, the gods would eventually visit on them. As the judges in his own inheritance case, these "kings" of the polis meted out decisions to serve their own interests. To the extent that he criticized elite greed and lack of self-control, at least, Hesiod was refashioning the critique of unjust rule offered by Achilles.[11]

He also criticized those at the very bottom of the socioeconomic hierarchy. Hesiod found fault with the laziness and lack of prudence he attributed to the poor. Developing a common and often harmful ideological construct, Hesiod held people responsible for their poverty – a view he supported through the belief that Zeus makes the diligent farmer, like himself, successful. He also condemned those ordinary citizens who conspired with the elite, thereby casting himself as a more credible and powerful Thersites. He vituperates against his brother Perses, a liar who "stole with his tongue" in court and cheated him out of his inheritance. In addition to taking more than his fair share, Perses lacked truthfulness, a central feature of the respect owed to one's fellow citizens. Thus, through using the language of vice, Hesiod began to articulate the conditions under which fair and unfair distributions in the polis were made. He thereby came to specify, as concretely as the subject would permit, what justice and, relatedly, virtuous behavior meant in the archaic polis.

Hesiod's criticisms of others contrast profoundly with his positive evaluation of his own character. His standing motto was "Work with work upon work" (382). Work, he supposed, would guarantee his possession of a modest but sufficient agricultural holding, provided that he remained self-reliant, industrious, and careful. He abhors unjust profits but respects the gains that can be made through hard work; he finds borrowing and begging to be disgraceful; and he emphasizes measure, good timing, and proportion in all things (cf. 694). Through his articulation of these virtues, and conversely the vices of his fellow citizens, Hesiod gives us a clear picture of the egalitarian ideology. Hesiod claims for himself fair-mindedness, just acquisition, modesty, prudence, and industry. Even without explicitly articulating the ends of the polis, it emerges evidently that Hesiod aspires to realize a simple life of prosperity, with no large ambitions either to achieve fabulous wealth, to win political power, or, much less, to fight wars. He powerfully explains why the vices of others lead to political corruption. Strikingly, however, in view of his celebration of the "middling" virtues, he drew no revolutionary conclusions in relation to the existing political hierarchy. For a robust version of such calls for change, we must wait, as we shall see, for the Athenian democracy. Even so, the prudence and moral wisdom he claims for himself would be central to the self-image, and therefore the political claims, of other egalitarian thinkers who rejected elitist political dominance in favor of a broader based distribution of offices. Like Hesiod, of course, these thinkers would have to frame their arguments in terms of what is good for the polis.

The Elitist Response

The "elitist" tradition, by contrast, was more fragmented and, partly for that reason, had less ethical power than the egalitarian vision. As we have seen, the Homeric epics were narratives that tended to "naturalize" elitist politics. The most specific and credible argument for elitist politics, moreover, can be found in the *Iliad*: as Sarpedon explains to Glaucus, heroes earn their positions of honor through their leadership, particularly military leadership, of their communities (Text 7).

> **7.** Glaucus, why are the two of us honored most of all in Lycia with the seat of honor, cuts of meat, and full cups, and all men look upon us as gods, and we have been granted immense estates beside the banks of Xanthus, rich in orchards and wheat-bearing land? We must now stand in the first rank of the Lycians, and enter the raging battle, so that some one of the well-armed Lycians might say, "Not without fame – our kings who rule Lycia . . . their strength is outstanding, when they fight at the front of the Lycians." (*Iliad* 12.310–21)

Though these characters are non-Greeks, Sarpedon's logic is typical of the arguments made on both sides of the battlefield. The underlying idea was that providing protection for the community was the ultimate form of merit; therefore, reliable heroes deserve the greatest privileges.

The *Odyssey* made a similar, though less explicit, argument for the justice of the monarchic rule of Odysseus. There the argument, drastically distilled, was that Odysseus was like a father to his people, who protected them from foreign enemies, from less self-restrained aristocrats and from each other. When Odysseus left Ithaca, everything went downhill, because of the greed and hubris of wealthy, well-born men without a sense of decency – the suitors of his wife, Penelope. Odysseus' son, Telemachus, did not reach adulthood until roughly 20 years after Odysseus' departure, and so, as a youth, he was hardly in a position to restrain the suitors. Meanwhile, the political community could exert some – though not enough – pressure on these aristocrats to amend their behavior; beyond this, and as long as Odysseus was gone, those who would normally have been in his charge were left with pious hopes that the gods would rescue them. Therefore, practically speaking, the well-being of Ithaca depended on Odysseus' return and his forcible reassertion of his power. In its emphasis on restraining the elite for the collective good, the *Odyssey* provides a nearly Hobbesian justi-fication for preeminent leaders. Either way, the Homeric epics pro-vided the sorts of explanation that the elite of the early polis might have offered for their own claims to political and economic preeminence.

This Homeric form of elitism was powerful because it made no concessions to the egalitarians on the question of equality itself. As a fundamentally egalitarian concept, citizenship tended to give a distinct moral advantage to egalitarians in their arguments over justice in the polis. But the Homeric epics could still claim to sub-scribe, if implicitly, to an "equal things for equal people" concep-tion of justice; it was simply that monarchs were *very* unequal to the ordinary citizens, because of their extraordinary contributions to the welfare of the polis. As Sarpedon points out, therefore, no one should get angry at them for receiving extraordinary privileges, as though that were somehow *unfair.*

Outside Homer, though, it is striking that few arguments on these lines can be found. How might we explain the relative scarcity of elitist arguments based on military leadership? One factor may be that in the course of the seventh century it had become increasingly clear that the middling citizens, in their massed hoplite armies, and not leaders or heroes, were responsible for the defense of the polis.[12] The elite monopoly on military "merit" became less credible as time went on. As a result, the elite had to rely instead on claims to superior intellectual ability, morality, education, and refinement. For example, Heraclitus of Ephesus (550–480 BC), the early philosopher, wrote, "I think that one man is equal to ten thousand if he is the best" (*DK* 22 B 49) – which, probably intentionally, left the grounds of his man's superiority unclear. Theognis, more specifically, connected moral and intellectual superiority to privileged birth and wealth. He enjoins his young friend Cyrnus to learn the noble virtues, especially self-restraint, from those who are noble (Text 8).

> **8.** With good intentions, Cyrnus, I will give you words of advice such as I myself received from good men when I still a boy. Be wise, and do not draw honor, nobility, or wealth to yourself by doing shameful and unjust deeds. Know that these things are so; and do not keep company with bad men, but always hold fast to good men. (Theognis 27–32)

The problem was that such arguments utilized much less tangible claims to merit than the arguments presented in the Homeric epics. Calls for political hierarchy based on refinement or self-restraint must have been a hard sell.

Even so, it is worth focusing on such arguments because Theognis and other poets developed the language of justice and the virtues in interesting ways, and often in the context of strife and competition within their cities. In Text 8, for example, Theognis was articulating a code of virtues appropriate to the nobility of his city, because his position was threatened both by other aristocrats who had taken power and by others of questionable descent but unquestionable wealth. As Alcaeus laments elsewhere, the great regret is that "Money is the man" (fr. 360, attributed to the Spartan Aristodemus). Against the prevailing atmosphere of greed and injustice, Theognis praised virtues such as a noble sense of shame, loyalty to one's friends, self-restraint in money matters, and fair-mindedness. For him these were virtues of the nobles exclusively.

The nobles were destined to remain preeminently virtuous because their virtue was natural, not learned: "You will never turn the base man into a noble man by instructing him" (437–8). It was possible for aristocrats to argue, then, that their positions of power were based on moral and intellectual superiority, which ultimately derived from a superior nature.

Such attitudes of superiority, however, often led to unrealistic hopes and, from there, to anger at the vices of others. The primary poetic energy in Theognis' corpus is anger directed at those he calls "base-born" or "ignoble" (*kakos*). By this term he means lower-class individuals who had recently become wealthy as well as other aristocrats who, in his view, had seized political power unjustly or otherwise "sold out" the values proper to them. For Theognis the engine driving the decline of values is essentially greed: "By now greed has destroyed more men by far than hunger – all those who wanted to take more than their share" (605–6). He laments the world of excessive desires elicited by the bewilderingly complex economic changes of his day. The upshot of moral decline is that the polis is faltering (Text 9).

> **9.** Truly, one is saved with difficulty, such things are they doing; they forced the noble steersman to stop – who used to keep expert watch; and they seize wealth by force, and order is lost, and there is no longer equal distribution in the middle; merchants rule, and base men are above the noble. I fear lest a wave gulp down the ship (Theognis 674–80)

Using the ship-of-state image, Theognis makes it clear that disrespect for fair distribution, motivated by greed and the lust for power, is destroying his native city. This is a highly secular interpretation of the way in which injustice destroys the possibility of politics.

For Theognis, political chaos threatens to promote the rise of tyranny. As he says, "From private profits that harm the community come civic conflict, murder of men who are kin, and tyrants" (50–2). A tyrant was a sole ruler, nearly always an aristocrat, who had beaten out his aristocratic rivals to such an extent that he needed to pay little heed to the competition. Later in the fifth century tyrants were almost universally lambasted as icons of political wickedness. In the archaic period, however, we find little political analysis of the tyrant's role in the polis, beyond the disgruntled commentary from defeated aristocrats.[13]

For example, Alcaeus of Lesbos abuses the tyrant of Mytilene, Pittacus, for being base born, fat, and destructive to the city. Unlike Theognis, however, he does not provide anything approaching a positive account of the aristocratic character – just standard invective because he had lost the political competition and was, apparently, forced into exile. Alcaeus occasionally tries to escape from politics through the pleasures of friendship and drinking wine, but he is haunted throughout his poetry by the success of other aristocrats. Speaking of Pittacus, he says, "Let him marry into the family of the Atridai and devour the polis as he did also with Myrsilus, until Ares wants to turn us to arms; and may we forget this anger; and let us let go of our heart-eating strife and our civil conflicts, which one of the Olympians has stirred up, leading the people to ruin, but giving to Pittacus lovely glory" (fr. 70.6–13).[14] Alcaeus deeply resents the power wielded by Pittacus, an aristocrat who is, he says in the traditional idiom of greed, "devouring" the city. The poet desperately wants to escape from his anger but finds relief to be elusive. There are glimmers of "community service" to be found elsewhere in Alcaeus (e.g., fr. 129), but his poetry tends more toward self-serving invective than critical thinking about justice. His poetry makes him out to be a classic man of *ressentiment.*

Other elitist poets took a radically different approach. Many encouraged aristocrats to seek self-respect and legitimacy by rejecting the polis altogether, in favor of cultivating a style of life unavailable to the less wealthy. A fragmentary poem of Sappho's reads: "for my mother once told me that when she was young it was a great ornament if someone had her hair wrapped around with a purple wreath – this was very great indeed; but the girl with hair more golden than a torch is better off with garlands of flowers in luxuriant bloom. Recently . . . a multicolored headband from Sardis" (fr. 98).[15] This is the poetry of luxury, wealth, and a cultivated lifestyle.[16] It values physical beauty, precious or delicate objects of adornment, and close connections with famously wealthy areas of the East, such as Sardis, the capital of Lydia.

Such values are part of a distinctive class and status phenomenon. They represent a reaction against Hesiod's rugged dedication to the civic virtues of the polis, on the part of a cosmopolitan elite who claimed superiority on the basis of style, manners, and looks. One may compare the similarly luxurious lines from Mimnermus, put into an unselfconsciously erotic register: "What is life, what is pleasant without golden Aphrodite? I would die, when such things no longer interest me, secret love, gentle gifts, and the bed, such blossoms of youth that entice men and women" (fr. 1). Another expression of this ideal can be found in the poetry of Solon: "That man is truly blessed who has dear boys, horses with a single hoof, hunting dogs, and guest-friends abroad" (fr. 23). Solon is praising aristocratic pastimes such as hunting and horse rearing, as well as the formation of foreign friendships and perhaps pederastic relationships.

In turning away from politics, such poetry made a political state-ment: that the politics of the polis was not the context in which genuine aristocrats could achieve their well-being. To the extent that they turned away from the polis, elitists also abandoned the debate over justice. Their move could be nothing other than a retreat into an idealized past, a withdrawal from the public space of the city to the private luxuries of the "compound." "Politics" in this mode, such as it was, had to mean the formation of alliances with similarly positioned elites of other cities (Solon's "foreign friend"), who struggled to create a meaningful public space for themselves outside the polis. The small agriculturalists, like Hesiod, who formed the backbone of the polis in the spheres of politics, economy, and warfare, would have had robust contempt for such delicacy, refinement, and extra-polis attachments. These elitist moves away from the polis were the origin of anti-politics.

By considering a variety of archaic poets, we have identified two major strands of elitism. The Theognidean strand is politically and emotionally engaged with the polis, but ultimately resigned in its acceptance of exclusion. What Theognis has left is his snobbery. Theognis's nobility provides a vantage-point for the ethical criti-cism of those, whether base-born or aristocratic, who have found a way to be politically successful. Theognis and others like him, such as Alcaeus, were attached to the "anti-polis" world only in the sense that they rejected their poleis as currently administered, but not the polis or political engagement as such.

By contrast, the "refined" aristocrats who advocated a luxurious lifestyle were anti-political in a much deeper sense. They feared the diversity of the archaic polis to such an extent that they rejected the rough-and-tumble of political conversation altogether and sought out the more placid world of like-minded aristocrats.[17] This is political thought, to be sure, but its point is to reject politics and to create a closed, unified community. As Aristotle pointed out in his *Politics*, though, "It is clear that if a community goes on becoming more and more unified, then it will not be a polis; for a polis is by nature a certain multitude . . . And not only does the polis consist of a number of human beings, but also of different kinds of human beings. For a polis is not made up of similar people" (II.2.1261a16–24). In Aristotle's view, without diversity, a polis stops being a place for politics – the process where differences can be hammered out through conversations about character and distribution. Readers should interpret the aristocrats' withdrawal from politics against the account of the "political" offered in chapter 1.

Whatever the relation of the elite to the political, we have conducted this analysis in terms of "ideal" categories. Elitists could, in practice, put on different faces depending on the contexts in which they found themselves. Indeed, the tyrants that Theognis and Alcaeus worried about were often aristocrats supported, militarily and financially, by their cosmopolitan "friends abroad." It turns out, therefore, that the anti-political "refined" aristocrats who sought extra-polis connections could easily utilize those connections to attack the government of the polis they had earlier absented themselves from! That does not mean, of course, that they would have done so with genuine political justifications . . .

Case Study: Sparta and the Politics of "Courage"

Many poleis experienced infighting among rival aristocrats, along with attacks on aristocratic claims to superiority. Because of widely shared political experiences throughout the Greek world, and because most early poets took part in a panhellenic conversation about politics, we have, understandably, treated early political thought as a unified conversation. It is also worth delving deeply into regional differences. A better understanding of polis-particularity helps us chart the evolution of political thought in the archaic and later periods. Of two poleis, Sparta and Athens, we hear a significant amount from their famous poets, Tyrtaios and Solon. Because of the survival of their poetic texts, and because these two city-states were to play a key role in politics of the classical period, it is worth singling them out for special treatment. With Sparta, in any event, special treatment is almost a given, since Sparta self-consciously distinguished its social and political arrangements from those of other poleis very early in its history. It is difficult, however, to distinguish the "real" early Sparta from what is now known as the "Spartan mirage" – that is, the mythologized image originating in late fifth-century Greece, which depicted Sparta as a tightly disciplined home of virtue and equality.

Sparta was distinctive chiefly because of its hegemony over the poleis of Laconia and its enslavement of the neighboring people of Messenia. In the late eighth century, Messenians became state-owned slaves, known as helots, who worked the land of the Spartans. This freed Spartans from the need to become small agriculturalists, like most other Greeks, and enabled them to concentrate on military service and political participation. Indeed, their (historically justified) fear of helot revolt virtually necessitated the creation of a standing army of citizens. Sparta gradually became the most militarized of Greek poleis, with rigorous training devoted to the formation of a widely feared fighting corps of citizens. Early in their history, the Spartans also instituted a system of state-owned land, which created an economic minimum standard for all citizens and enhanced the basic idea that all Spartans were *homoioi*, or "similars." It is generally agreed that by the seventh century Sparta had a professionalized army, rough (but certainly not complete) economic equality, a strong conception of citizen identity fostered by contrast with the helots and other dependants, and a formal hierarchy within political institutions.[18]

Sparta's political hierarchy is embodied in what might now be called its "founding document," the so-called Great Rhetra ("utterance") quoted by Tyrtaios: "Having heard the voice of Phoebus, they brought home from Pytho the god's oracles and predictions that would be fulfilled: the kings honored by the gods, whose care is the lovely city of Sparta, will begin counsel, along with the elders; and then the men of the people, responding with straight words, will say honorable things and do everything justly, and counsel nothing crooked for the city; and victory and power follow upon the mass of the people" (fr. 4). This fragment shows that two kings, a council of elders, and the mass of *homoioi* were all formally assigned privileges and responsibilities in Spartan politics. There is some dispute, in other fragments and citations from later authors, as to whether the people or the elders had the ultimate right of decision, but the main point is the quasi-constitutional formalization of hierarchies that were elsewhere observed informally.

These roles created a polis that remained stable, with very little civic strife, for almost 400 years. It was perhaps for this reason that Tyrtaios' poem mentioning the Great Rhetra was later known as "Eunomia" – "Orderliness." Sparta achieved stability through establishing a socially and economically just distribution of benefits among citizens. To some extent, indeed, that picture is accurate within Sparta's citizen ranks. The irony is that the culture that plumed itself on equality, stability, and fighting power was the one that lived off the backs of forced slave labor by the people of another region – slaves who, moreover, posed a constant military threat to their owners. Seen in this light, Sparta nearly provides an example of a so-called "utility monster" – that is, a counterexample to the utilitarian principle that happiness must be maximized, no matter what, even if that involves the subjection of some for the sake of making others happy. The enslaved Messenians produced benefits for Spartans, no doubt, but their existence promoted an atmosphere of fear and severely reduced the Spartans' ability to be free. From our perspective, Sparta looks more like a militaristic camp posing as a polis, than a political culture in which human well being, in any diverse and rich sense, might be achieved.

Sparta's highly militaristic culture gave this polis pride of place in courage and manliness. The virtue of courage was the quintessential excellence of the early Greek polis, so much so that the generic Greek word for "virtue," *aretê*, usually means "courage" or "bravery" in early Greek poetry. The Homeric heroes had well-developed conceptions of this paramount virtue. For example, Idomeneus reassures one of his crew by giving a strikingly reflective account of his courage, including careful attention to physiology, emotions, and the context of display (Text 10).

> **10.** "I know your style, your courage. No need for you to tell it. If we all formed up along the ships right now, our best men picked for an ambush – that's where you really spot a fighter's mettle, where

> the brave and craven always show their stripes. . . . The skin of the brave soldier never blanches. He's all control. Tense but no great fear. The moment he joins his comrades packed in ambush he prays to wade in carnage, cut-and-thrust at once. Who could deny your nerve there, your fighting hands?" (*Iliad* 13.275–87, tr. Fagles)

By contrast with Idomeneus' focus on the individual hero, the Spartan Tyrtaios exalted courage as displayed in the massed ranks of the hoplite phalanx (Text 11).

> **11.** For no man is good in war unless he endures seeing the bloody slaughter and, standing nearby, reaches for the enemy. This is excellence, this is the best prize among men and the noblest for a young man to win. And this is a common good for the city and all the people, whichever man stands firmly among the first ranks, and stays there without pause, and does not think of shameful flight at all, committing his spirit and his stout heart, and, standing by his side, emboldens the man next to him with his words (Tyrtaios fr. 12, tr. Gerber, adapted).

In Tyrtaios' conception military courage is the truest expression of *aretê*, or human excellence, by contrast with other poets who emphasized refinement, loyalty, self-control, or justice. Courage, not the other virtues, is what is supposed to benefit the city. This is a powerful re-use of the Homeric emphasis on military merit, now praising the value of ordinary citizens, who, as hoplite equals, contributed most to the safety and well-being of their polis.

What are the implications of this single-minded dedication to militaristic courage? What does it mean to place "manly courage" at the center of one's politics? Plato and Aristotle harshly criticized Sparta for over-valuing courage at the expense of other virtues such as justice or self-restraint. *Aretê* and its classical equivalent *andreia* can also refer to the less morally admirable pugnacity, as well as the more all-encompassing virtue of courage. I think the later criticisms are correct. Placing "courage," or perhaps "machismo," at the center of politics makes a polis imperialistic, on the one hand, and incapable of enjoying the benefits of peace, on the other (cf. "Aristotle Analyzes Imperialism" in chapter 5). Those who grant primacy to courage tend to provoke fires that only courage can put out; they interpret situations so as to make their militaristic pro- clivities seem necessary and inevitable; and they usually corrupt the possibility of genuine public dialogue by making macho vio- lence the only acceptable response to genuine dilemmas.[19] Thus, Sparta's vaunted stability may have resulted more from a type of macho anti-politics, than from the search for just and justifiable solutions to real political differences. In other words, Sparta's emphasis on courage as the quintessential human virtue created very narrow parameters within which political discussion could take place. Stability and unity became possible for Sparta because the state, threatened by helots within and aggressive neighbors outside, was constantly kept on wartime alert. This made it impos- sible, and indeed seemingly unnecessary, to enjoy a peaceful politi- cal life. Although ancient writers typically extolled Sparta for its discipline, frugality, and traditionalism, such supposed virtues exacted heavy and self-evident costs in human freedom.

A Second Case Study: Archaic Athens and the Search for Justice

Athens, by contrast, later became the home of political freedom – and it was often condemned for that reason by thinkers, such as Plato, who valued Spartan austerity and mistrusted the ability of ordinary Athenians to think for themselves. But, in its early history, Athens suffered from many of the same problems as other Greek poleis, in particular social and economic tensions resulting primar- ily from the competitiveness of its elite. To see how key political principles were formulated in early Athens, it is necessary to explore these tensions in some detail.

Of the Athenian elite Solon says, "They grow rich, trusting in unjust deeds" (fr. 4.11) – by which he meant primarily greed and rapacity. Much of our understanding of the seventh and sixth cen- turies in Athens comes from Solon's poetry and from archaeology. Both showcase the self-aggrandizement of the elite, who were imi- tating the Homeric heroes in their quest for individual prominence. For example, archaeological finds indicate that members of the Athenian elite asserted their status through holding sumptuous banquets with lavish furniture and utensils – luxury items that must have been purchased through their ability to utilize the community's resources for their own benefit.[20] Within the polis their competitiveness turned destructive when they used the community's resources in their own quest for status: "Sparing neither sacred nor private property, they steal rapaciously, one from one source, another from another, and they do not respect the august foundations of Justice" (fr. 4.12–14).[21] The elite used the community as if it were their own possession, often selling poor debtors abroad and otherwise abusing their positions of power.

In Athens elite competitiveness was not limited to symbolic display among the politically powerful. It was a complicated phenomenon. There were also tensions between the politically powerful and other rising men, perhaps *nouveaux riches*, whose political ambitions were left unsatisfied by the traditional arrangements. Beyond these sources of unrest, elite materialism placed harsh economic burdens on small Athenian sharecroppers, who were traditionally expected to give one-sixth of their yield to wealthy landowners. In short, out of these manifold sources of frustration and infighting arose a crisis situation in late seventh and early sixth century Athens. In 594 BC Solon was chosen to be an arbitrator charged with establishing a formal body of laws to heal Athens's political divisions.

In the event both rich and poor benefited from Solon's law code.[22] The poor could no longer be legally enslaved for debt; if they found fault with the legal decisions of elite magistrates, they could launch an appeal in a popular court of ordinary citizens; sharecroppers were freed from any economic obligations to elite landowners; and ordinary citizens could thereafter conduct a formal review of magistrates leaving office. The rich, by contrast, held onto most of their political and economic privileges. They came through Solon's reform without ceding power to a popular tyrant; they retained a stranglehold on the most important political offices; and they did not suffer a wholesale redistribution of land, a populist measure that many elites throughout Greece feared at this time. A measure of Solon's insight is that he re-created the upper classes as an elite of wealth, not birth, thereby reducing the resentment of rich men who were, for one reason or another, excluded from political power. Since all these groups benefited from the reform, it seems likely that Solon was originally appointed by the community as a whole. His appointment expressed the recognition that Athens's political chaos could be put to rest only through the establishment of fair, decent, and widely acceptable political principles.

Even so, ancient scholars such as Plutarch (late first to early second century AD) recognized that laws would not be effective unless they were based on broadly shared beliefs about justice. Enter Solon's poetry, which helped Athenians understand the political value of two key virtues – self-restraint and fairness. Thus, in Solon's law-code and poetry we can see the deep engagement of Greek political thought with the evolving political norms of the polis. Solon's approach to solving Athens's crisis was to focus on justice as the source of political health. He interpreted justice as the fair distribution of power, honor, and resources. In this equation "fair" meant, as usual, "proportional to one's stature or merit." For example, he summed up the spirit of his code of laws as follows: "I gave the people sufficient privileges and neither detracted from nor added to their honor. But those who had power and were admired for their wealth – I took care that they too should not suffer anything shameful" (fr. 5.1–4).[23] Solon's proportional justice meant that there could be no redistribution of land on the basis of simple equality (fr. 34.7–9): already he abided by the principle "equal things to equal people, unequal things to unequal people." Seen in this light, Solon was neither a ruthless populist nor a self-obsessed aristocrat, but rather a reformer who looked impartially to the good of the city as a whole. Solon's appointment as arbitrator was driven neither by aristocratic selfishness nor popular greed, but rather by both groups' recognition that political stability could be achieved only if a non-partisan reformer established pragmatic ways of thinking about and practicing social justice.

A logically prior point, as Solon himself must have seen, was that this vaunted proportional justice could make sense, and could create political health, only if all Athenians viewed themselves as members of a single political community. In retrospect it seems obvious that Athenians would come to view themselves as fellow citizens, but Solon's poetry indicates that contemporaries viewed this polis as a city at war with itself: "This inescapable wound is coming upon the entire city, and the city is swiftly arriving at an abject condition of slavery, which stirs up civic strife and rouses sleeping war . . . a lovely city is quickly being worn down by hostile men in meetings dear to the unjust" (fr. 4.17–22). Solon is hinting in these lines that the competitive, grasping elite has turned Athens into a battleground of self-aggrandizement. The elite were acting like enemies – real enemies, foreign enemies – of Athens.[24] This is why Solon's legal prohibition on debt bondage, as well as his wealth-based redefinition of the elite, was so important: it formally defined citizenship at Athens and therefore, quite literally, defined the Athenian political community. Henceforward all members of that community were owed a basic "citizenly" respect by virtue of their status as citizens. This status, free of formal coercion and constraint, was materially embodied in Solon's liberation of the dark earth, as he put it (fr. 36.1–7) – that is, his abolition of the sharecropping system that had once both put pressure on and stigmatized the non-elite Athenians. Athens could still be a battleground but, in the wake of Solon's reforms and because of his political vision, the combatants would be forced to recognize the bonds of their citizenship and so, hopefully, political tensions would be susceptible of peaceful resolution.

Through Solon's insistence that all members of this community show a basic moral regard for one another, the idea of politics was born, albeit late, in Athens. This baseline respect is an essential precondition of public dialogue about matters of communal importance. But to leave matters at that would be to reconstruct history too idealistically, and in the process to do Solon's own far-reaching political insight a deep injustice. For Solon saw that, if his plans for social and economic justice were to work, he had to develop a new self-image for Athenians. He saw himself as an educator of his fellow citizens: "My heart commands me to teach this to the Athenians, that Disorder brings the most evils to a city, while Good Order arranges everything well and makes it fitting, and it frequently places fetters on the unjust" (fr. 4.30–3). He used a powerful set of images and arguments to explain that justice and political health depended on the virtuous conduct of each individual citizen. In part he conjured up unappealing stereotypes of insatiably greedy characters, whose self-presentation, he hoped, said all that was necessary. In one of his poems, for example, Solon took on the role of ventriloquist, exalting, in the voice of his rivals and enemies, the goods that come from tyranny (Text 12).

12. "Solon is not deep-thinking or wise; for when the god gave him good things, he did not take them; although he had cast a huge net around his prey, he was too astonished to capture it. He lacked courage and good sense. If I had power, unlimited wealth, and the tyranny of Athens for just one day, I'd gladly be skinned alive and have my family destroyed." (fr. 33)

The standard materialistic desires, Solon hinted, reflect a blind, distorted, and absurdly narrow view of self-interest and one's personal well-being. For Solon, true well-being could be found only if citizens showed self-restraint and mutual respect within the Athenian political community.

Solon himself exemplifies the model virtues of the new Athenian citizenry. He says that he considers his self-restraint, his avoidance of tyranny, and his rescue of his homeland a victory (fr. 32). These civic virtues, rather than selfish, militaristic excess, would, in his view, enable him to gain the fame that every ambitious Greek of this period desired. By giving up short-term goods, such as wealth and tyrannical power, and dedicating himself to the good of the city, Solon modeled a conception of enlightened self-interest that would be utilized again and again in Athenian political rhetoric and, later, in systematic philosophy. Athenian orators held fast to the idea – Solon's idea, I think – that the individual's well-being, correctly understood, could best be secured through virtuous dedication to just dealing and, by extension, to the common good. To put it more concretely, even if the would-be tyrant avoided being flayed like a wine skin (Text 12), he would be worse off than a self-restrained and fair-minded citizen, if his ambitions led him to destroy the fabric of the polis.

Solon is explicit – as explicit as one could be in his highly traditional generic language – about the reason for this: "Thus the public evil comes home to each man, and the doors of the courtyard are no longer willing to restrain it, but it leaps over the high wall and finds him by all means, even if someone flees and hides in the inner part of his bedroom" (fr. 4.26–9). It made no sense to Solon to envisage a sharp distinction between public and private interests.[25] For his political program originated in the problematic conflicts between selfish members of the elite and the collective interests of the polis. His major point was that true self-interest, correctly understood, could only be pursued if individuals sought happiness in the polis. The narrow pursuit of self-interest would lead, even without any divine intervention, to political unrest. Notice the differences between this view and the much more religious formulations of Hesiod (Texts 2, 4).

Thus, for Solon, the truly self-concerned individual would both exercise the virtues and attend to the good of the polis, considering that his own private welfare depended on the health of the community. This enlargement of Athenian "self-interest," which is an enlargement of sympathy for one's fellow citizens, is Solon's most radical and important political idea. In early Greek political culture, needless to say, it was extremely ambitious to argue that the virtues, even the virtue of justice, were good not only for others, but also for oneself. Solon arrived at this idea through his astute observations of early Athenian political strife and through his aspirations to achieve justice politically. Later thinkers, including the Anonymus Iamblichi, Socrates, and Aristotle, would develop these ideas significantly, but Solon's redefinition of the relationship between individual and community stands as a profound intellectual, not to mention political, achievement. It originated as a response to very practical, dirty, and (all things considered) somewhat mundane features of early Athenian political life.

One worry might be that Solon appears to envision an invasive state, one that, to modern eyes, might illegitimately and disturbingly invade the individual's choices, life plans, and self-conception. In other words, Solon might define the individual citizen's "self" too completely and too politically, in that he proposes that well-being, correctly understood, can only be achieved through a primarily political self-identification. Certain modern liberal philosophers, particularly democratic individualists writing in the tradition of Emerson and Thoreau, would find this proposal to be oppressive. They would argue that the individual should make up his life as he goes along; that he should live episodically and by his own lights; that he should resist the pressure to conform to another's definition of well-being; and that he should, first and foremost, consider himself to be an individual moral agent, rather than the duty-bound citizen of a possibly intrusive state.[26]

This concern should not be dismissed lightly. True, Solon's exhortation to consider oneself a citizen, and to make political affairs one's own affair, were rooted in a context of ruthless self-promotion. Therefore, his emphasis on the shared values of a community was welcome, and his political definition of the individual is, in this light, understandable. Moreover, it is fair to say that in the political conditions of his day, the invasive state in any later sense was not much of a practical possibility. The question that remains, though, is whether his historically grounded prioritizing of the community over the individual had negative consequences, in that it tended to impose constraints on freedom and to induce conformity to the group. These are problems that later political thinkers would continue to grapple with as they revised and extended the archaic poets' ideas about the virtues, the vices, and justice within the polis.

chapter 3

Democratic Political Thinking at Athens

The political ideas of Solon were more important than his reforms: a little over 30 years after he held office, Athens saw the rise of a tyrant, Peisistratos, whose family ruled the city for half a century. There are no contemporary literary sources for this period, so there is an inevitable gap in our understanding of political thought for roughly a century after Solon (594 BC). However, the late sixth century BC witnessed one event of major importance for classical political thought: the Athenians' establishment of democracy in 508 BC. By turning the ordinary citizens into regular participants in government, this brought about a major change in the way politics was practiced not only in Athens, but also in the Greek world at large. The term *dêmokratia* means, literally, "people-power." Under this system, all Athenian citizens, rich or poor, were full-fledged political equals, whatever socioeconomic hierarchies still existed. That political revolution, in turn, created the possibility for novel, and sometimes astonishing, developments in political thought. For, as many thinkers then and now have realized, democracy was and is not only a constitution or set of laws, but, perhaps more importantly, a political culture with characteristic values, aspirations, and associated ways of living.

Democracy was established through a popular revolution in which Athens's ordinary citizens united in order to drive out the invading troops of the Spartan King Cleomenes.[1] Upon his return from exile, the Athenian leader Cleisthenes established a new constitution in which citizenship was legally defined through a free adult male's membership in a "deme" – that is, a village community in Athens or its vicinity, which, under the terms of the reform, received formal political definition. He thereby made citizens more secure in their status as citizens. Cleisthenes also established a Council of 500 citizens to prepare business for the popular Assembly, which at this same time became the central organ of governance. Through stipulating that only citizens over 30 years of age could be in the Council, and that citizens could serve on the Council only twice, Cleisthenes ensured that a high percentage of the citizenry would become familiar with the everyday business of running the democracy. This encouraged a culture of participation, a meaningful context for freedom and self-determination, and a concrete legal framework within which Athenian citizens could justifiably view themselves as political equals.

At the core of democratic political ideology lay a commitment to equality and freedom. Promoting democratic freedom and equality was the democracy's distinctive way of interpreting the archaic poets' demand for justice in the polis. As a matter of fairness, that is, the citizens of Athens were considered political equals with carefully defined liberties both to participate in public affairs and to live as they chose without state intrusion. As political equals, citizens deserved equal respect from their fellows. We will find that equal respect, in turn, lay behind the democrats' encouragement of each citizen to speak freely in debates about decisions affecting the polis. The democratic commitment to freedom and equality meant that over the course of roughly two centuries, from 508 to 322 BC, the democracy maintained a stable ideology, but not a monolithic one. The Athenians elaborated their values in context-specific ways in order to meet their immediate needs. Their baseline ethical commitments gave rise to political and conceptual opportunities, rather than limitations.

Evidence and Sources

To come to terms with democratic political ideas, we must explore the literary worlds of tragedy and comedy, the speeches of orators, public inscriptions on stone, and the literary and philosophical texts written by members of the elite. This does not imply merely extracting political ideas from these works, like gems, and then rationalizing them into a theory that makes sense to us; it means, rather, understanding these texts on their own terms, with an appreciation for their literary purposes, generic backgrounds, and political contexts. The first step is to keep in mind that these "texts" represent what were, in their day, impassioned political speeches, energetically staged dramas, hilarious comedies, and publicly sanctioned decrees carved on stone.

Democrats did not develop a systematic philosophy to support or defend their emphasis on freedom and equality. This is perhaps why historians have often maintained that antiquity produced no democratic theory. Democracy arose and was maintained as a practice and as an ideology; it was not the result of a well-heeled, systematic theorist's sketch. On the contrary, the democracy was resolutely populist: its foundational value was the political equality of *all* citizens, not just those with education, good breeding, or property. But, despite its lack of systematic theory, Athenian ideology embodied distinctive concepts of how politics *ought* to be done. (By "ideology," I mean an unsystematic and self-justifying set of beliefs concerning politics, human nature, and human values.) Democrats thought through and justified their beliefs and practices. And they often raised their pragmatic reflections to higher levels of abstraction about the nature of democratic government and its governing values. This is why, as we shall see, the antidemocratic philosophers often argued vigorously against democratic principles. The Athenians' ideology and practices of freedom and equality can make an important contribution to the study of political thought.

Because the Athenian orators are a particularly valuable source for democratic ideology, a special word needs to be said about the corpus of Attic oratory. This corpus is made up of roughly 140 speeches, mostly written between 403 and 322 BC by members of the wealthy Athenian elite and by professional speechwriters such as Lysias and Isaeus. Most of these speeches were delivered before a popular audience of ordinary Athenian citizens, either in court, in the Assembly, or at public rituals such as the traditional funeral oration.[2] In court or in the Assembly, the speakers' main goal was to persuade their audiences. To do so, they had to accommodate themselves and their rhetoric to the underlying values of their audiences. Such "accommodation" to popular sentiment was also the standard in funeral orations. Public speakers at Athens were accountable, in short, to popular values maintained by ordinary citizens. And so their speeches are especially useful as sources for democratic ideology.[3]

Dealing with fifth-century speeches is more difficult. The speeches reported by Thucydides are potentially very important to us. Among these are the funeral oration of Pericles and assembly speeches delivered by Pericles, Cleon, Diodotus, Alcibiades, and Nicias. What makes these speeches problematic is that ancient historians as a rule did not adhere to the same stringent canons of accuracy as modern historians, and they often fabricated speeches that they believed were necessary or suitable to the particular situations they were describing.[4] Thucydides, in particular, had ethical, didactic, and critical purposes in presenting his speeches as he did.[5] As I will explain in the next chapter, Thucydides was a critic of Athenian democracy. He rejected many of its central ideological tenets. He judged the ordinary citizens to be fickle, selfish, and imprudent. Great care is needed, therefore, in using his speeches as a source for anything other than the political thought of Thucydides himself.

As a result, I have avoided basing any claims about democratic ideology on the exclusive basis of Thucydides' speeches. However, I refer to these speeches when they represent especially vivid articulations of points that can be paralleled in the less problematic corpus of fourth-century Attic oratory.[6] One reason for doing so is to illustrate that democratic ideology, as embodied in the fourth-century speeches, can sometimes be "read back" into the late fifth century.[7] It would be surprising, in fact, if many elements of democratic ideology were *not* being developed and articulated already in the fifth century. By contrast, Thucydides' evidence on the events and actions of the Peloponnesian War is much less open to doubt, although we must recognize that what we have in his text is his own interpretation of important events. He selected, shaped, and organized the material in order to fit his own ideological and interpretative positions.

Democracy Ancient and Modern

An ocean separates the democracy of the ancient polis from the democracies of the Western nation-states. Frankly, modern democracies have progressed beyond the inequalities and abuses of human dignity that were characteristic of the ancient world. We are not slave-holders; modern democrats are repelled by the idea of excluding women from politics; we are attracted by political and cultural pluralism; we have reduced the role of luck in human life in ways that were unimaginable to the ancients; we have developed unthinkably rich private and social lives because of our distinctive individualism; and we have developed much more complete concepts – and practices – of freedom and equality. There is little, therefore, to recommend nostalgia for ancient democracy. Athens is gone for good, and in many ways that is a good thing. Even Athens's vaunted patriotism and solidarity were based, in critical ways, on the exclusion of women, slaves, and foreigners from political participation. The self-respect and freedom of the Athenian citizens were principally distinctive by contrast with the stunted lives of slaves and other non-citizens. Modernity is not in need of "therapy" from this ancient world.

What contribution, then, can this historical inquiry make to our contemporary political world? First, and honestly less interesting, is that we "moderns" might come to appreciate more fully the nobility and value of modern expressions of freedom, equality, dignity, respect, and tolerance – by contrast with the ancient Athenian example. Examining ancient Athens is specially instructive in this regard because the evaluative vocabulary of this ancient democracy was both broadly similar to and different in detail from our own. Second, and more important, is that ancient democracy might act as a cultural resource as we continue to reflect upon the meaning and ethical possibilities of our democratic commitments. With its example before us, we become increasingly attuned to other successful ways of looking at politics. Athenian democracy provides alternatives that might, if suitably translated, suggest ways of remedying our own deficiencies. We might ask ourselves what ancient *dêmokratia* could be, or would look like, in a modern world that values universal human rights, that rejects slavery, that affirms the value of technological advance, and that cherishes private life.

To take a specific example, a large question in contemporary political thought is that of political motivation: how do liberal nation-states motivate their citizens to respect, participate in, and promote liberal institutions of governance?[8] Are the shared values of freedom, justice, and equality enough to secure the citizenry's willing and fair-minded participation? The empirical evidence suggests not. Apathy and cynicism are on the rise; voter turn-out is dismal; and young people have little if any political knowledge or interest. But then what are we to do about this, believing, as we do, that individual liberties and life choices must always be respected by the state, even if those choices include apathy, cynicism, and political ignorance?

Athenian politics might provide novel ways to explore such questions. Athenians recognized that justice, the laws, democracy, freedom, and equality could become pale abstractions unless citizens understood their value and took responsibility for implementing and, where necessary, enforcing them. For, in themselves, these values do not necessarily inspire citizens to action. As the orator Demosthenes once pointed out, the laws remained inert letters on stone if the citizens did not take self-conscious responsibility for them (Text 1).

> **1.** What is the strength of the laws? If one of you is injured and cries out, will the laws run up and help you? No: for they are simply written letters and would not be able to do this. What then is their power? It lies in your establishing them securely and giving them authority to help whoever needs them. (Dem. 21.224)

Taking responsibility for their values meant that the Athenians had to develop standards of good citizenship and to hold citizens accountable to them. To do so, they developed a powerful rhetoric of good citizenship centered on the virtues. The education of citizens took place through their participation in public affairs, where they observed the virtues and vices in action. The community's practices of praise and blame, reward and punishment, helped to promote a particular self-image among citizens – and their self-image motivated them to live up to normatively defined standards of good citizenship.

What were the collectively sanctioned virtues of Athenian citizenship? The most generic word for "virtue" in Greek was *aretê*, a term with traditional, heroic connotations. Through reinterpreting this term in their political discourse, Athenians made *aretê* a virtue of the demos; or, in other words, they "democratized" this and other entries in the traditional lexicon of the virtues (and vices). Specifically, Athenian democrats could praise citizens in terms of generic virtues such as *aretê* and the synonymous *andragathia*, which referred to the meritorious contributions expected of "manly" citizens; in terms of communally oriented virtues such as loyalty and patriotism (*eunoia*), courage (*andreia*), honesty or fairness (being *dikaios*) and eagerness to serve the city (*prothumia*); and individual virtues of orderliness (*kosmiotês*), piety (*eusebeia*), and self-restraint (*sôphrosunê*). These virtues crop up again and again in political speeches, jury trials, and inscriptions on stone – as do their opposing vices (Text 2).[9]

> **2.** For criminals with no respect for Athenians of the past will try to imitate this man [Leocrates], reckoning that while in previous generations the traditional virtues were held in high regard, in your case shamelessness, betrayal, and cowardice are considered most noble. (Lyc. 1.110)

Athenians saw that inculcating these virtues was critical to their shared project of making their democratic values practicable.

To give one example, the Athenians collectively believed that their democracy was founded by two "tyrannicides" known as Harmodius and Aristogeiton, who in 514 BC had murdered Hipparchus, a brother of the then-tyrant Hippias. (In fact, it was the Spartan military, not the tyrannicides, that had driven out the Peisistratid tyrants, but that is not the point here.) These tyrannicides were immediately established as culture heroes who provided inspiration for Athenians to act courageously in order to defend their democratic values. The freedom and equality won through expelling the tyrants could only be effective to the extent that citizens exemplified the virtues of the tyrannicides in their own lives. That is why Demosthenes could, almost two centuries after Hipparchus' death, hold up the tyrannicides as the quintessential examples of courageous freedom-fighting (20.159–62). The Athenians offer us an empirical example of how ancient democracy could combine an emphasis on virtues of character with respect for the abstract values of freedom and equality.

By contrast with modern democracies, then, Athenian democracy developed a robust language of civic virtue to which citizens held one another accountable. Through communal praise and blame, citizens were trained to exhibit virtues such as courage, honesty, generosity, discipline, respect for others, patriotism, and self-control. They also shared innumerable traditions and founding cultural myths which promoted solidarity among the citizens and strengthened the legitimacy of public institutions. They combined such "thick" social sources of motivation with an emphasis on freedom, equality, and the intellectual autonomy of individuals; for them, the one supported the other. Contrary to a popular belief among scholars and theorists, then, public encouragement of virtuous citizenship is not necessarily elitist or illiberal. Within certain limits, as we will see, Athenian citizens were encouraged to render autonomous judgments in the assembly and the courts and to develop their own meaningful life-plans within the context of the polis.[10] Classical Athenian political thought exemplifies a genuinely democratic and meaningfully populist discourse on the virtues – a discourse that Athenians utilized to promote the free and responsible choices of citizens. Modern democracies would do well to contemplate the success of Athens's example.

It is time to get specific about the ideals characteristic of ancient democracy. Here, again, it is fruitful to compare and contrast democracy ancient and modern.[11] Democracies of both periods share an emphasis on freedom and equality, a belief in the need for self-questioning, and a willingness to take risks. The differences, however, are profound. Some we have already discussed: the existence of slavery in ancient Athens, the exclusion of women from politics, and the lack of any separation between what we would call "church" and "state." Perhaps the most striking difference, along the same lines, is that ancient Greece had no conception of human rights comparable to the modern one(s).

But, even as regards the citizen body, there were major differences. First, classical Athens was a direct democracy in which all citizens could vote in the Assembly on major issues; there was no politics by representation. As a result, the "government" as such didn't exist and certainly was not conceived of as operating thousands of miles away, say, in Washington, D.C., or in London. Athenian citizens were the government; they were the court system; they were responsible for the calendar, public finance, foreign policy, and the laws. There was no highly developed bureaucracy in the ancient world. Second, and related to this, political debates in Athens were settled by majority vote, full stop. There was nothing to stop a strong-willed majority from trampling on the interests of minority groups – by which I mean, not historically unprivileged groups, but rather simply citizen minorities. There was no independent judiciary to protect minority views or interests (see below for the problems of legitimacy such treatment of minority groups might raise). Jury courts were made up of the same demos one would find in the Assembly.

Finally, there is the more complicated and ambiguous issue of individual freedom. On this subject, the Athenian democracy looks different depending on whether we view it historically, within its ancient context, or compare its beliefs and practices to those of modern democracies in the Western nation-states. The Athenian democracy arguably respected individual freedom more than any other ancient Mediterranean city-state, territory, or kingdom. To ancient observers, therefore, Athens's democracy often, and understandably, appeared to be an extremely tolerant, free, and liberal form of constitution. On the face of the matter, this description makes Athens sound very modern. Yet, from the modern vantage-point, the Athenian democracy put significant pressure on citizens to conform to socially and politically constructed ideals. Athens maintained a highly politicized definition of the citizenry by comparison with modern democracies. And so it is necessary to consider carefully the complexity and ambiguity of Athenian democracy on the subject of individual freedom.

Athenian citizens were expected and encouraged to identify strongly with the polis and to give priority to the community's values over their own or their families'. The classical democracy took over Solon's civic conception of the self with enthusiasm, urging its members to put the interests of the polis above their own interests, and to regard political participation as one of the highest of human activities. In the early fourth century, for example, Lysias' speech *Against Philon* emphasized that prospective office-holders must identify strongly with the fortunes of the polis: "To these men it matters a great deal whether the city does well or poorly, because they believe that they must share in the city's sufferings, just as they also share in its advantages" (31.5–6). Speakers commonly claimed in their own favor that they subordinated private, familial interests to the welfare of the city, even to the extent of risking their lives for the safety of Athens (Lys. 21.24). They sometimes indicated that their first allegiance, from birth, was to the city rather than to their families (Dem. 18.205). Such sentiments can be found in many Euripidean tragedies (e.g. *Heracleidae* 503–34), as well as in Plato's *Crito* (51a).[12] A particularly striking justification of this position can be found in an Assembly speech reported by Thucydides and assigned by him to 430 BC (Text 3).[13]

> **3.** I believe that, if a polis is successful collectively, it benefits private citizens more than if it flourishes citizen by citizen but trips up as a whole. For a man who is successful on his own account is nonetheless lost if his city is destroyed, but if man is doing badly, he is much more likely to come through safely in a thriving city. (Thuc. 2.60.2–3)

And, finally, similar sentiments were also reflected in the non-Athenian, but (broadly speaking) democratic, political thought of Democritus of Abdera (*DK* 68 B 252; cf. below, "Democratic Political Thought outside Athens?"). We are undoubtedly familiar with modern calls to patriotism and public service, but such calls had a special intensity in the democracy of ancient Athens.

Through such expressions of patriotism and self-sacrifice, the Athenians publicly constructed a particular image of themselves as oriented toward the welfare of the community above all else. On the one hand, then, Athenian democratic ideology held that individuals best satisfy their own self-interests, narrowly construed, when they reckon the state's interests as an essential – or, rather, *the* essential – part of their own interests. The underlying idea was that individuals achieve their well-being through fulfilling meaningful social roles, within the context of authoritative communal traditions. This self-image underlay the community's imposition of certain duties on citizens, such as military service, as well as its use of shame and honor to enforce those obligations.[14] On the other hand, the democracy promoted individual freedom to an extent never before seen in the ancient Mediterreanean. It is particularly interesting and instructive for modern citizens to examine how such a strongly "communitarian" polis could also emphasize individual freedom as a central value.

Democratic Conceptions of Freedom

In many respects, then, the Athenian democratic experience was consistent with Benjamin Constant's famous view of ancient liberty as the public freedom to participate in politics without the corresponding private freedom to live as one pleases, that is, without intrusion by the community (Text 4).[15]

---

4. Thus among the ancients the individual, almost always sovereign in public affairs, was a slave in all his private relations. As a citizen, he decided on peace and war; as a private individual, he was constrained, watched, and repressed in all his movements; as a member of the collective body, he interrogated, dismissed, condemned, beggared, exiled, or sentenced to death his magistrates and superiors; as a subject of the collective body he could himself be deprived of his status, stripped of his privileges, banished, put to death, by the discretionary will of the whole to which he belonged. (Constant, "The Liberty of the Ancients Compared with that of the Moderns," pp. 311–12, tr. Biancamaria Fontana)

But democratic Athens, as we have seen, presents a more complicated picture than Constant recognized. Constant contrasted ancient freedom with modern freedom, but he did not contrast the freedom promoted by democratic Athens with the lack of freedom that characterized other ancient Mediterreanean polities. As we will now discover, the Athenians' ideas of "good citizenship" also left in place important private freedoms.

Both supporters and opponents of democracy emphasized the value democrats placed on private freedom. Athens's tolerance of individual diversity so annoyed Plato that the philosopher disparaged democracy as a place where criminals could run free, where citizens could choose any constitution they wished, and where individuals had riotous, disordered desires in their souls, rather than clean and stable life-plans (Text 5).

---

5. First, then, aren't they free, and isn't the polis full of freedom and free speech, and isn't it possible, in the democratic city, for a person to do whatever he wishes? . . . It has all types of constitution because of the license it grants to citizens. . . . And what of this – isn't its gentleness toward some of those who have been condemned refined? . . . It seems likely to be a pleasant constitution, with no one in power, and beautifully diverse, distributing some sort of equality to both equals and unequals alike. (Plato, *Republic* 557b–558c, Tr. Grube, rev. Reeve, adapted)

His satirical vision of the overly tolerant democratic city would have resonated with many non-democrats. As Aristotle put it, albeit in a less critical tone, one mark of a democratic constitution was "to live as one likes; for they say that this is the function of freedom, since not living as one likes is characteristic of a slave's condition" (*Politics* 6.2.1317b11–13).

Far from being ashamed of their esteem for private freedom, the Athenians themselves were proud of it and valued it immensely.[16] That is why such freedoms are held to be characteristic of democracy throughout the democratic literature of the classical period. One speaker in Thucydides, the general Nicias, compellingly invoked private freedom in his exhortation to his (obviously democratic) troops just before a life-or-death battle in Sicily (Text 6).

> **6.** He [Nicias] reminded them of their fatherland, the freest anywhere, and of everyone's ability to live his own life in Athens without being subject to anyone's orders. (Thuc. 7.69)

In a speech written for the "scrutiny" of a certain Evandros, who hoped to become an Athenian magistrate, Lysias assumed private freedom as a general characteristic of the system (26.5). Aristotle (*Pol.* 5.9.1310a25–34) referred to a passage from a lost play of Euripides in which individuals in democracy are said to live as they choose and to aim at whatever they happen to desire. The ideal of private freedom was a commonplace of democratic political thinking.

It is in this context that we can place one of the most famous passages of classical literature altogether. In the funeral oration reported by Thucydides, Pericles (Text 7) voiced sentiments characteristic of private freedom and democratic individuality.

> **7.** We enjoy freedom in our politics and tolerance in our private lives. We are not suspicious of one another in the conduct of daily life, and we do not get angry with our neighbors if they live as they please. Nor do we convey through our looks that we are annoyed with others – which causes people pain even if it does not impose a formal penalty. We conduct our private relations without offense. (Thuc. 2.37.2–3)

Pericles' funeral oration represents Thucydides' interpretation of the best possible arguments an articulate spokesman might make on behalf of democracy. It is an idealistic image of the possibilities inherent in democratic culture. In this speech, Pericles celebrates private life, a prized possession for individuals who aspire to live freely – free, that is, from the constraints of convention, the authority of the commonplace, and the pressures of other citizens' expectations. It is in private life that the citizen becomes (again, if necessary) an individual, as opposed to an agent and defender of the state. This is reminiscent of modern liberalism's emphasis on the individual's free choice in creating a life for himself, without governmental or social intrusion.

The sensibility embodied in the Athenian commitment to private freedom was also reflected in laws that protected individuals from physical punishment and from execution without due process, and in laws protecting their households from unjust entry by polis officials and from the arbitrary redistribution of their resources.[17] Yet there were limits to such protections: the classical Athenian democracy practiced ostracism, an institution in which the citizenry could vote to exile an individual for 10 years (though leaving his property intact). The freedoms enjoyed by Athenian citizens were not absolute rights, but rather privileges granted by the community – and they were, therefore, susceptible to being taken away by the community when it found its interests threatened.[18] Thus, though it was not protected as a right, private life was invented in classical Athens, and it was a powerful source of democratic pride.

The tolerance that characterized private life was based on egalitarian respect for all citizens. No one should incur anger or contumely if he lived as he liked, because, as a citizen of Athens, he deserved such freedom and commanded the respect of his fellows. Private freedom is one facet of the democratic interpretation of the archaic poets' insistence on justice within the polis. Private freedom meant that individual citizens had a certain latitude in relation to lifestyle choices and conceptions of the good. How can such latitude be compatible, though, with the social pressures we have charted, which encouraged individuals to develop communally valued virtues of citizenship?

One answer to this type of question, more characteristic of modern liberalism than of ancient democracy, is that the virtues can be viewed instrumentally, as the necessary condition of political health. They should not be dictated to individuals as part of a state recommendation as to how to live a good human life, because for modern liberals the state must remain neutral about conceptions of the good life. Therefore, the liberal response holds that civic virtues should be encouraged as helping us defend liberty and other independently valued public ideals.[19]

The Athenians agreed that the virtues were instrumentally useful to achieving political health. Yet they also believed something different and more robust: that it is impossible for individuals to live a good human life without possessing the virtues as defined by the democracy. By contrast with modern democracies, the Athenians did define normative standards for the character and flourishing of individuals. This goes beyond the limits that modern liberal thinkers could happily tolerate. But the Athenian community left such standards vague enough for individuals to find significant room to develop their own life-choices, within the context of the publicly sanctioned virtues. The Athenian definition of a good life was thus "thick" but also "vague."[20]

The ambiguities in the Athenian stance can be illustrated by examining the Athenians' attitudes toward political participation. As part of the Athenians' thick but vague normative description, individuals were expected, though not legally required, to participate in the political and religious life of the city.[21] There was a strong cultural ethos encouraging participation, the exercise of the virtues, and self-sacrifice for the public good. Yet citizens were also legally allowed to abstain from participating in the Assembly, the law courts, and many other public activities. Citizens were expected to find political and military activity to be highly meaningful, but they were allowed to withdraw from politics and to live privately. Thus, at least in relation to individual freedom, it is necessary for us to view the differences between ancient and modern democracy as a matter of emphasis. But the balance tips in favor of saying that the Athenians granted priority to the community and to its definition of the individual. Athenian speakers and playwrights emphasized the community's way of life as the context within which individual choices made sense. If it was legal to opt out of such lifestyle paradigms, and simply to mind one's own business, then it also took more psychological work than modern liberal individualists would be comfortable with.

Such tensions within Athenian democratic ideology cannot ultimately be resolved. But this is one of the chief reasons for studying classical Athens in the first place: Athens provides us with a fresh look at our own political ideas and categories. Because of its unique blend of liberal and communitarian elements, democratic Athens might provide a genuine *viam tertiam* – a third way – that can serve as a thought-provoking alternative to current forms of political practice and theory. Its "third way" came into existence through its ambiguously defined relationship between publicly required virtues and private choices (Text 8).

> **8.** I ask you, then, men of the jury, to have the same opinion about me now as you have had up to this time, and not only to be mindful of my public liturgies, but also to consider my private practices, supposing that this service is the most difficult, to be orderly and self-restrained for the whole of one's life, and not to be overcome by pleasure or excited by gain, but to exhibit virtues such that no other citizen would find fault with you or dare to bring you to court. (Lys. 21.19)

We have been considering democratic freedom primarily in private terms. But the question of political participation brings up another, much less ambiguous dimension of ancient democratic freedom – namely, the citizen's privilege of participating in the city's political and judicial life. This privilege corresponds to what Isaiah Berlin has called "positive liberty," i.e. the freedom *to* participate (as opposed to "negative freedom," or freedom *from* governmental intrusion).[22] With very few exceptions, all citizens could hold offices and magistracies in Athens, where selection by lot was the normal procedure. No theory underlay the use of lot as opposed to election, only the pragmatic belief that selection by lot probably reduced the level of corruption in elections (however, widespread use of the lot implies a radical belief in the equal capacities of ordinary citizens; see below). The generalship was the only elective office in democratic Athens, perhaps because it was thought that there, if anywhere, real talent had to be promoted, since the defense of the community was at stake. But the most theoretically interesting feature of the Athenians' positive freedom was the freedom of all citizens to speak in the cardinal venues of public decision-making. This was something the Athenians were especially proud of. One fourth-century orator famously said that at Sparta men were forced to praise Spartan laws, and to abstain from praising the laws of other *poleis*, whereas at Athens one could praise whatever laws one wished (Dem. 20.105–6). This privilege was embodied in the standard question asked at the beginning of every discussion of the Assembly: "Who wishes to speak?" (e.g., Dem. 18.170).

Democratic Deliberation

The underlying principle of free and democratic deliberation was the belief that every Athenian had something potentially important to contribute to public discourse. Notice the sea change that had taken place since the time of Thersites, who was violently silenced for publicly dissenting from Agamemnon. By contrast with Thersites, all Athenians, even the poor, the laborers, and so forth, were encouraged to speak their minds about political decisions. Athenians made different types of arguments for the value of free speech. On the one hand were "deontological" arguments which asserted that, regardless of the consequences, Athenian citizens had to be treated with respect because they were all citizen equals; therefore, the "right of free and equal speech" (*isêgoria*) was viewed as especially characteristic of democracy. According to Herodotus, *isêgoria* defined democracy as opposed to the Peisistratid tyranny from which it grew (Text 9).

> **9.** Thus the Athenians grew strong. And it is clear that, not only in one area but altogether, free and equal speech is a fine thing, if the Athenians, when ruled by a tyrant, were not better than any of their neighbors in war, but became first by far once they gained their freedom from the tyrants. These things make it clear that, when they were held down, they shirked their duty since they were working for a master, but once free each and every man was eager to work on his own behalf. (Hdt. 5.78)

So central was this value to democratic self-definition that Herodotus could use it as a synonym for the term *dêmokratia*. As Herodotus also suggested, this all-important value inspired

Athenians to work and fight, as equals, to preserve their freedom (Text 9). As democracy's very existence demanded courage of those who had expelled the tyrants and Spartans, so too did its culture produce courageous citizens, capable of defending democracy from attacks from inside or out. In this sense the freedom to speak derives from a prior belief in citizen equality, while both freedom and equality were preserved and maintained by the virtue of courage.

Perhaps more common were utilitarian or "consequentialist" arguments that found the candid, open speech of all citizens essential to the democracy's capacity to make intelligent decisions. For example, in one of his many speeches attacking Philip of Macedon, Demosthenes urged that the demos profited significantly from listening to all possible angles on questions of foreign policy (Text 10).

> **10.** Men of Athens, I think that instead of a great deal of money you would choose to know clearly what would benefit the polis in relation to what we are now discussing. Since this is so, then, it is your duty to listen eagerly to those who want to give counsel; for not only would you thereby hear and accept the proposal of someone who comes forward with a useful idea, but you are also fortunate, in my view, that several men might think up appropriate suggestions on the spot and say them aloud, so that from all these things the choice of what is advantageous for you is easy. (Dem. 1.1)

This implied, perhaps idealistically, that the city's leadership would be thoughtful and energetic, and that the citizenry would actively participate, if not in articulating proposals, then in deciding which proposal put before them was best. As Demosthenes put it, "Therefore you, the mass of citizens, and especially the oldest among you, do not have to be capable of speaking as well as the most skillful speakers; for this is the work of those who are accustomed to speaking; but you must have good sense like these men, and even more so; for practical experience and having seen many things put good sense into us" (*Ex.* 45.2; cf. Thuc. 6.39.1).[23]

Why would this conception have sounded plausible to Demosthenes or his contemporaries? Many throughout history have regarded ordinary citizens as less intelligent and less capable than their wealthier, better educated fellow citizens. As we shall see in the next chapter, there was a vibrant culture of antidemocratic thought in classical Athens that made arguments on these lines. By contrast, the Athenian demos viewed itself as sensible, wise in judgment, and capable of determining the city's best interests. Perhaps that was simply self-serving propaganda. But genuine arguments for the intelligence of democratically produced decisions can be found in classical Athens. For example, one prodemocratic verdict can be seen in the so-called "summation argument" found in Aristotle's *Politics* (Text 11).

> **11.** As for the many ordinary citizens, even though each individual is not an excellent man, it is possible that when they come together they are better than the excellent types, not as individuals, but all together – just as potluck dinners are better than those furnished by one man's expenditure. For, it is possible that, in cases where there are many citizens, each one has a share of virtue and intelligence, and when they come together, just as the mass of citizens becomes a single individual with many feet, many hands, and many perceptions, so too does it become a single man in relation to habits of character and to intellect. (Aristotle, *Politics* 3.11.1281a42–b7)

Aristotle is applying an additive principle to propose that the many, gathered together, could have a greater portion of virtue and insight than their better bred fellows. A different, and (strikingly) perhaps even deeper, argument can be found in the democratic speeches themselves. Speakers asserted that frank speech makes possible true democratic deliberation – a public conversation in which ideas are floated freely, objections and dissent are confidently and respectfully aired, further revisions and refinement of different opinions can take place, and a collectively supported decision issues in the end.[24] This runs deeper than Aristotle's additive argument because it insightfully assigns a central place to dissent, confrontation, self-conscious revision, and the necessity of making one's revised views adequate to satisfy the judgments of one's fellow citizens.

The key to such a model of democratic deliberation was the latitude with which individuals could respectfully criticize one another, and the demos as a whole, in the interests of constructing the best policy for the polis. In other words, democratic deliberation depended on self-criticism. This could take the form of dissent, as for example when one speaker said, "As I see it, men of Athens, no one with sense would reject the idea that it is best of all for the city to do nothing disadvantageous at the beginning; but, if that does not happen, no one would deny the value of having those who will immediately object present" (Dem. *Ex.* 49.1). It could also take the form of criticism of the audience for being lazy, cowardly, and passive (Dem. 3.31; cf. Thuc. 3.38).[25] In each case the point was to make the assembled demos listen carefully to others, learn from their views, and create rationally viable arguments to guide the city's policy. The effectiveness of such a conception of the public sphere depended on the citizens' ability to approach political questions autonomously, on their trust in the mutual good will of their fellow citizens, and on their intellectual courage to say what they really thought.

Put in these terms, Athenian democratic deliberation sounds strikingly similar to the public conversations advocated by modern theorists of deliberative democracy. Notice the echoes in the account offered by Gutmann and Thompson, two modern theorists of "deliberative democracy": "Compared to other methods of decision making, deliberation increases the chances of arriving at justifiable policies. More than other kinds of political processes, deliberative democracy contains the means of its own correction. Through the give-and-take of argument, citizens and their accountable representatives can learn from one another, come to recognize their individual and collective mistakes, and develop new views and policies that are more widely justifiable."[26]

These theorists have advanced the deliberative model of democracy as the fullest realization of democratic ideals, because deliberation enables all citizens both to come to respect one another's views and to contribute actively to the process of democratic decision making. The Athenians promoted an ideal of democratic deliberation that was comparable to this modern ideal, since they based their own ideal on free speech combined with respect for the opinions of others (for reflections on possible differences between the ancient models of deliberation and those of modern deliberative democrats, see chapter 7, "Classification of Constitutions"). The "discovery of freedom" in ancient Athens, as it has been called, therefore had profound implications for those who wished – rightly, I think – to claim a heightened form of practical rationality for democratic politics.[27]

The democracy's justified claim to heightened rationality poses a serious problem for those conservative exegetes, such as Leo Strauss and his followers, who return to antiquity in order to diagnose and rectify the alleged "crisis" of modernity. Strauss found in classical antiquity a belief in natural inequality, based on the differing intellectual capacities of individuals. In his view this belief was true, full stop; furthermore, it was enlightening and even liberating for philosophers dissatisfied with modern egalitarianism. It is true, as we shall see, that certain philosophers, such as Plato, believed in natural hierarchies. But the Athenian democracy was able, quite dramatically, to stake a claim for the rationality of ordinary citizens – the "wisdom of the masses," understood as a collective group. This argument, along with the undoubted success of the democracy, poses a profound challenge to any politics informed by belief in natural hierarchies.[28]

Yet, at the same time, the ideal of free speech brings to light further complications in the Athenians' way of relating individual to community. Intellectual independence, frank speech, and dissent were encouraged by democratic ideology, but the community could take away the privilege of speaking freely as easily as it granted that privilege. For example, Socrates was brought to trial before a democratic jury-court in 399 BC and executed on the charge of impiety. Admittedly, this was an anomaly in Athenian democracy; other reports of suppressing the free speech of intellectuals are probably exaggerated and derived from the sanctifying narratives about Socrates.[29] But Socrates' case makes clear both the priority of community to individual and the possible limits on free speech when the community felt threatened (for further reflections on Socrates' case, cf. chapter 4, "Socrates and Athens").

On the same subject, another sort of enlightening case is that of the everyday experience of speakers in the courts and the democratic Assembly. Democratic audiences often heckled, interrupted, and shouted down speakers in the courts and Assembly. This tendency, which was not exactly an "institution," was called the *thorubos* – "commotion" or disruption." It was not uncommon for speakers to cry out, "Please do not raise shouts at what I am about to say, but listen to me and then make your judgment," in the midst of advancing serious policy proposals ([Dem.] 13.3). Here Demosthenes was calling on the citizens to exercise self-restraint: to listen before rushing to judgment about complex policy issues.

It is perhaps possible to view the *thorubos* as a form of "free speech" for ordinary citizens who might otherwise not have had the gumption to speak out as individuals,[30] but this traditional practice of Greek audiences poses obvious risks to the model of democratic deliberation formulated by the orators. It stops opposing viewpoints from being articulated and it makes speakers more likely, as the orators themselves saw, to curry favor with the audience, instead of saying forthrightly what they thought best. The *thorubos* posed a practical constraint on freedom of speech and, in turn, on the masses' capacity for political wisdom.

Courage, Trust, and Leadership

No "solution" to this problem was explicitly theorized in democratic Athens. Instead, the orators constructed, in practical contexts, a redefinition of traditional virtues, especially courage, so as to stimulate and reward intellectual autonomy and its public expression in the Assembly. Democrats redefined the paradigmatic military virtue of courage along deliberative lines, in order to provide reasons for individuals to resist the majoritarian pressures of the demos. Thus, as a counterpart to the self-restraint that speakers requested of their audiences, courage became the central virtue of the outspoken, dissenting politician who was unafraid to expound the genuine best interests of the city, against the immediate pleasures of the short-sighted demos. Or so they put it (Text 12).

> **12.** I am not reckless or brutal or shameless – and may I never be – and yet I believe I am braver than many of your foolhardy politicians. For, men of Athens, whoever disregards what is of benefit to the city, and engages in trials, confiscates property, gives bribes, and makes accusations – he does these things without any real bravery. Instead, he ensures his own safety through speaking and making policies so as to win your favor. In this he is "safely bold." But whoever opposes your desires in many cases for the sake of what is best, and says nothing simply to win your favor, but also speaks what is best, and prefers measures in which chance has more power than calculation, and yet makes himself accountable to you in both cases, that man is genuinely courageous. (Dem. 8.68–70)

In the militaristic culture of ancient Greece, it was a noteworthy accomplishment to divest courage, now a moral and political virtue too, of its prototypically military content.

In its concentration on the risks run by speakers, this passage from Demosthenes sounds superficially similar to the "political courage" described, with a particularly modern agenda, but with loose reference to Athens, by Hannah Arendt: "To leave the household . . . demanded courage because only in the household was one primarily concerned with one's own life and survival. Whoever entered the political realm had first to be ready to risk his life, and too great a love for life obstructed freedom, was a sure sign of slavishness."[31] Arendt proceeds to flesh out this idea in a revealingly inaccurate way. For Arendt courage is "present in a willingness to act and speak at all, to insert one's self into the world and begin a story of one's own."[32] It leads to the individual's creation of a memorial to himself, to the possibility that he will be remembered in story or song for generations to come. Arendt devised such a description of Athenian politics in order to re-inscribe a certain quasi-heroic dignity into our own, modern conception of politics.

This heroically laden description, however, does little to advance our understanding of ancient democratic politics, which centered on the thoughts and behavior, perhaps sometimes heroic, of the citizenry as a collective unit. The courage Demosthenes describes in this passage is not part of individual, heroic self-creation, but rather the capacity to participate in a community that was always questioning itself and its traditions, for the purpose of enhancing the flourishing of the polis as a whole. The democracy socialized heroism. If free-speaking courage was the Athenians' method of stimulating independent and thoughtful contributions to public debate, then that courage was always, yet again, entrenched within the collective goals and projects of the polis. That is indeed why Demosthenes specifically explains his own courageous dissent as a contribution to the real, if unnoticed, interests and well-being of the polis. Ancient democracy's contribution to our own (self-) understanding is greater, not less, if we get our historical interpretations straight. The history of democratic politics and political thought can, by itself, be a springboard for our imaginations and a way of summoning up our own democratic aspirations.

These reflections on civic courage point to a further ambiguity in the democratic self-understanding – namely, the problem of leadership. Certain "elitist" theorists, notably Robert Michels, have argued that democracy or "people-power," truly so called, is impossible.[33] The purported reason is that energetic members of the elite will naturally rise to positions of leadership in organizations or states. From these positions they will determine policy in their own interests and even control the proper vocabulary of politics, thereby naturalizing their own positions of power and dominating the inherently apathetic ordinary citizens. Democratic Athens had recognized leaders and "politicians," who held the spotlight for many years and influenced policy over a wide range of important issues and on numerous occasions: one thinks of Pericles, Cleon, and Demosthenes, to name a few. Did their leadership create a conundrum for democratic politics, since their knowledge, expertise, and ability – in short, their civic "merit" – had to be recognized and rewarded, if the democracy was to realize its full potential? Did Athens's leaders introduce an undemocratic element of hierarchy into the system?

The key to Athens's response to this problem was the power of the people – the quotidian control exercised by ordinary citizens over political affairs. As a Herodotean character explains approvingly, Athens's magistrates were chosen by lot, were held strictly accountable by the demos, and had no special authority in the outcome of political debate (Text 13).

13. Rule by the people first has the finest name of all, equality under the law (*isonomiên*), and second the people, when in power, do none of the things which the monarch does; ordinary citizens win offices through casting lots, all offices are accountable to the people, and all decisions are referred to the community. My view, therefore, is that we should rid ourselves of monarchy and grant power to the people. For the entire polis is summed up in the body of its ordinary citizens. (Hdt. 3.80.6)

Thus there was no long-term, formal leadership in the democratic polis. Rather, each speaker had only as much authority as he could convince the demos to grant him on any particular occasion; he was "only as good as his last speech."[34] This solution itself raises certain practical and theoretical problems about the bonds of unity in democratic society and about the nature of democratic equality.

First, this line of thought raises the central question of political trust. Trust might be viewed as a calculated risk in which individuals agree, without compulsion, to rely on others to carry out their promises.[35] Trust is usually spoken of as an unalloyed good. So, indeed, it is, especially when it enables citizens to rely on one another, for good reasons, in carrying out difficult tasks, and particularly in carrying out the difficult task of planning a political future together. In his famous portrayal of civil war in (formerly) democratic Corcyra, Thucydides pinpointed trust as the key to political functioning: for the absence of trust causes the breakdown of law, ritual, mutual respect, and, in short, politics itself (Text 14).

> **14.** Rashly rushing into action was considered characteristic of real men, while contriving plots in order to keep safe was considered a legitimate excuse for failing to act. Anyone violent was always thought trustworthy, and whoever opposed him became the object of suspicion. . . . If people happened to make pacts of reconciliation, they made them only for the moment, because both sides were in difficulties; and they had force only while neither side could call on forces from elsewhere. But when an opportunity presented itself, the first to see his opponent unguarded, and to act boldly, took revenge that was sweeter because of the pact than it would have been if taken openly. (Thuc. 3.82)

In contrast, Thucydides shows that the success of democratic Athens was based on the well-founded mutual trust of citizens, who dedicated themselves to patriotic ideals. To a large extent, it is historically true that Athenian citizens achieved "lateral" trust among themselves in classical Athens. It is, moreover, important for the history of political thought that contemporary observers such as Thucydides could recognize their trust as a key element of their success.

Even so, democracies also benefit from directing a certain level of distrust toward their leaders. Indeed, such distrust appears to be necessitated if the citizenry is not to relinquish power altogether, even for a time, to its leaders. And a certain level of necessary distrust is precisely what we find, over and over, in the Athenians' own thinking about politics. According to Thucydides, for example, the Athenians held Alcibiades in check because they were suspicious of his extravagant lifestyle and anti-egalitarian rhetoric (Text 15).

> **15.** Many people feared him because of his unusual conduct of his private life and because of the drive with which he did everything he was involved in. They became hostile to him because they thought he was aiming at the tyranny. (Thuc. 6.15)

To Thucydides, the demos's distrust of Alcibiades was detrimental to its own interests, but this opinion derives from Thucydides' fundamentally antidemocratic bias (see chapter 4, "Democratic Epistemology and Untrustworthy Rhetoric"). Although Thucydides criticizes the Athenians for their distrust, distrust of leaders such as Alcibiades in fact helped ordinary citizens maintain power over a potentially self-aggrandizing elite. Distrust was therefore a central facet of the democracy's real elevation of ordinary citizens to positions of political and ideological power.

The contemporary debate over trust was revisited in a comic register in Aristophanes' *Knights* of 424 BC. Like other Aristophanic comedies, *Knights* subjects an Athenian leader, Cleon, to a hefty share of comic abuse. Cleon is represented as devoting his political energies to greedily manipulating the democratic system for his own benefit. He flatters the ordinary citizens in order to maintain his power; he diverts the revenues of the Athenian empire into his own pocket; and he trumps up accusations against political rivals. Much of this is standard comic invective: on the comic stage, the Athenian demos did not show special deference to its leaders. It deeply annoyed the democracy's critics, in fact, that the demos was self-confident enough to encourage such abuse. Late in the play, however, things become more serious. The chorus accuses the personified Demos of being, in two words, stupid and fatuous. To this Demos responds with a surprising show of perceptiveness regarding the Athenian leadership (Text 16).

> **16.** There is no sense in your long hair, if you think I don't have my wits about me; I play dumb for a reason. I delight in my drink each day, and I want to nourish one of the thieves we have for leaders; I lift him, and when he is full, I strike him down. . . . Keep your eye on me, to see whether I fool them – the ones who imagine they are intelligent and that they are cheating me. I watch them all the time even though I appear not to see them stealing from me.

And then I force them to spit up whatever they have taken from me, using the voting urns as a probe. (Aristophanes, *Knights*, 1121–50)

Demos says, in short, that he is fully aware of the tricks perpetrated by the "leaders." As he is ultimately responsible for their success, so too he can bring about their downfall, when it suits his own interests. This is a powerful comic presentation both of the demos's understandable and necessary distrust of the democratic leadership and of its fundamental power over politics in the democratic city.[36]

Democratic Political Thought outside Athens?

We have concentrated on democratic Athens in this chapter because Athens was the first, largest, and most fully developed democracy of the classical period. It is the democracy (indeed the polis), moreover, about which we have the most ancient evidence on which to draw. But democracy was not confined to Athens. Other classical poleis, such as Syracuse, were also transformed into democracies in the fifth century.[37] Not surprisingly, non-Athenian thinkers also developed ideas about democracy, although we know far too little about their views, generally, to describe them in any detail. As we will see shortly, Protagoras of Abdera is represented in Plato's *Protagoras* as advancing theoretical considerations in support of democracy.

Democritus of Abdera, a fifth-century atomist and ethical philosopher, also espoused broadly democratic political views. We know more about his ethics than his politics.[38] His ethical and political ideas survive primarily in quotations and second-hand notices. As is often the case, they were adapted to the purposes of later scholars or thinkers who collected and used them. To the extent that we can grasp them in their fragmentary state, they sound conventional: Democritus recommended a calm life of tranquility and moderation, the measured pursuit of pleasure, and the avoidance of excess. In short, he advocated the simple, enlightened enjoyment of life that we normally associate with the later atomist Epicurus (chapter 8). What, then, of Democritean politics?

Democritus says that "Poverty in a democracy is as preferable to so-called prosperity among oligarchs as freedom is to slavery" (*DK*

68 B 252).[39] In the absence of any intellectual context, this statement does not convey its message precisely: for example, we do
not know whether Democritus meant the same thing by democracy
(*dêmokratia*) as his contemporaries at Athens, or to what sort of
arguments he may have intended this statement as a response. We
can supplement our interpretation of this fragment by recognizing
that Democritus elsewhere used democratic key words, such as *par-
rhêsia* ("frank speech") (*DK* 68 B 226), and assumed ordinary democratic features such as popular voting, accountable elected officials,
and deep respect for law. At least in the surviving fragments, though,
Democritus does not outline in detail his reasons for endorsing
democracy.[40] His political thought appears to be directed at a broad-
based participatory system that might or might not have included
all citizens, even poor ones, as equal members.

The surviving fragments are clearer, though, in stressing the
city's development of individual character as the key to maintaining political order. The law, for example, was supposed to benefit
citizens by training their dispositions of character (*DK* 68 B 248).
The result of such training, when applied from youth onward, was
the development of a proper sense of shame and respect (*to aideis-
thai*, *DK* 68 B 179). The sense of shame encourages individuals to
live up to their community's ideas and values, which they have
come, through education, to internalize; Protagoras, as we will see,
made much of shame as a stabilizing political force (cf. *DK* 68 B
181). Democritus provides an interesting set of reflections on politics viewed chiefly from the perspective of the ethical development
of citizens, rather than the broader level of social or political organization. Although there are glimmers, then, of broadly democratic
thinking in the surviving fragments, we must turn elsewhere for a
more detailed account of the political virtues of democracy.

Protagorean Arguments for Democracy

To return to the Athenian thinkers, then, Aristophanes' presentation of Demos, as we saw, helps to explain something of the pragmatic thinking that underlay the Athenian demos's relation to its
leaders. What of the theoretical problem that the leaders, as opposed
to the people, might have expert knowledge of what contributes
to democratic political health? We have seen arguments for a

heightened democratic rationality based on the alleged wisdom of democratic deliberation. These arguments were strengthened by the Athenians' understanding of equality. In short, the Athenians saw themselves as self-respecting equals; every citizen had a role to play in the production of democratic wisdom. This understanding can be appreciated more fully if we examine the political ideas attributed to Protagoras in the Platonic dialogue *Protagoras*. One scholar has called Protagoras "the first democratic political theorist in the history of the world"; we will have to see how, and in what ways, this characterization might be accurate.[41]

Protagoras was a so-called sophist – that is, an itinerant professor of rhetoric, who received pay for his teaching, and who claimed to make his students wise in the art of politics. Plato's sympathetic portrait of Protagoras makes it likely that he interpreted the basic arguments of the historical Protagoras charitably and gave them a genuine run for their money.[42] The dramatic premise of this dialogue is that Protagoras has come to Athens to find students for his expensive education in "political virtue" (*politikê aretê*). Plato's character Socrates challenges Protagoras's claim to teach political wisdom, since leading Athenian statesmen, such as Pericles, have proved unable to pass their wisdom on to their sons, despite giving them the best educations they could find. This might suggest that political wisdom cannot be taught. Socrates also points out that the Athenian Assembly regularly consults experts in fields such as architecture and shipbuilding, but on questions of politics the Athenians are willing to listen to all citizens, including humble tradesmen with no noticeable education. This might suggest that there is no such thing as the political art, or else the Athenians would find (and listen to) experts in politics, too.

In response to Socrates' points, Protagoras offers a myth of humankind according to which human beings, powerless against wild animals, were forced to create early communities. When these communities broke down because of human violence, the gods imparted to men two essential political virtues: the sense of respect for others, or moderation, (*aidôs*) and justice (*dikê*). Each citizen had to possess these virtues on pain of death. Therefore, Protagoras says, it is reasonable for the democracy to listen to all citizens in political forums, since political wisdom necessarily derives from justice and moderation – virtues that all citizens must possess, if the state is to exist at all (*Protagoras* 323a). Protagoras is making a slightly less sophisticated argument for democratic prudence than the democratic orators themselves, since he does not attribute an important deliberative role to dissent, conflict, and self-correction. But Protagoras adds an important ingredient to their discussions: namely, a justification of the democratic view that all citizens have a (roughly) equal capacity to contribute to political discussions. His myth illustrates the egalitarian basis of the Athenian commitment to free speech and it grounds that egalitarianism in the citizens' common sense of respect and justice. This is why, according to Protagoras, everyone at Athens was a teacher of virtue to the extent he was able (322d–323a), and this is why, furthermore, the Athenians are willing to listen to all citizens in the assembly.[43]

To justify these egalitarian ideas, Protagoras expounds a theory of civic education, which explains how all citizens acquire the virtues of justice and respect. After all, he says, no one believes that these virtues are inborn qualities. He first argues that virtue is teachable and that the Athenians believe it, correctly, to be so. His argument is that with inborn faults, such as weakness or ugliness, no one rebukes a person; rather, pity is the normal reaction. By contrast, the citizenry becomes angry and indignant with someone who exhibits political vices such as injustice, on the grounds that the contrary virtues can be acquired through training. Their assumption must be that individuals are responsible for living up to the community's standards of virtuous behavior. This assumption, according to Protagoras, lies behind the Athenians' enlightened theory of punishment as deterrence (this is, incidentally, a historically inaccurate description of Athenian punishment).

Next, Protagoras wants to rebut Socrates' point that men of political virtue do not often pass on their virtues to their sons. Protagoras denies that such men take no pains over their sons' education. They bring them up themselves, and send them to school, in order to learn the virtues through traditional methods of admonishment by elders, reading the inspirational works of poets, and then, at last, through following the laws of the city in order to give shape to their lives. They evidently believe that political education is possible. But, as it happens, this education sometimes works and sometimes does not. When it does not, the explanation is that wealthy statesmen occasionally have sons of inferior virtue through no fault of their own, but rather because of the admittedly unequal distribution of natural talents.

This argument leads Protagoras to draw interesting conclusions about the relationship between political equality and natural differences in ability. Within the rough equality that Protagoras evoked in his myth, there is also room for differential levels of talent. Recognition of such differences makes Protagoras' arguments more realistic: while he argues for the justice and value of democratic political equality, he does not ignore the well-known fact of inequality in natural talent. Rather, he finds a place for such inequalities within his theory, by suggesting that those with greater natural abilities and superior training can become the leaders of the demos. It would be sensible for the city to make its specially talented citizens leaders within the democratic framework we have discussed above.

To make such arguments plausible, Protagoras compares membership in a political community to membership in a linguistic community or a community of craftsmen. In such communities, everyone is roughly, if not exactly, equal; this corresponds to rough equality among members of the Athenian demos. Moreover, to put a finer point on his conception of rough equality, Protagoras points out that every member of such a community is significantly more skillful at the language or craft than those who have no language or craft at all. But, beyond this, there are also specially (though not preternaturally) proficient members, who, for example, are particularly articulate and imaginative users of a language, or are particularly masterful craftsmen. Such exceptionally proficient members of their linguistic or craft communities correspond to the political leaders of the demos, who have special talent in and training for political deliberation. This analogy enables Protagoras to justify his own claim to educate aspiring politicians without damaging his general arguments for democratic equality (Text 17).

17. All men teach virtue as much as they are individually able, and no one appears to you to be such a teacher. Similarly, if you should ask who teaches the Greek language, no single individual would appear, nor again (in my view) if you should ask who teaches the sons of craftsmen the very craft which they have learned from their fathers, to the extent that the father and his friends in the same trade were able to teach it, I don't think, Socrates, that it would be easy to find a teacher of these men, but it would be easy in every way to find

> the teacher of the unskilled; thus it is with virtue and all other things;
> we should be satisfied if someone who is a little superior to us leads
> us on to virtue. (*Protagoras* 327e1–328b1)

Protagoras's theory goes a long way both toward justifying egalitarianism and toward explaining how democratic leaders could be
trained to manage the system without putting the democracy's
underlying equality at risk.

Protagoras's speech would be significant evidence even if it
stood alone, but many of the key points are also paralleled in the
Athenian orators. What is particularly important is Protagoras's
emphasis on virtue as the key to political success and his explanation of how education in virtue takes place. Civic education in such
fundamental qualities as justice, self-restraint, and respect for others
occurs through growing up and living in the community – that is,
through experiencing the largely informal social expressions of
praise and blame in highly concrete circumstances. For ordinary
citizens, such virtues are explicitly said to be cultivated in successive generations through the democracy's laws, public ceremonies,
and judicial decisions. This is a commonplace in the forensic and
deliberative oratory of Athens (Text 18).

18. For know it well, men of Athens, that the young men are educated not only by the wrestling halls and schools and traditional
training in the arts, but much more by public proclamations. It is
announced in the theater that someone is being crowned for virtue,
valor, and loyalty, a man who is shameful in his lifestyle and disgust-
ing. Seeing this, a younger man is corrupted. Some worthless brothel-
keeper gets punished, like Ctesiphon: through this the others are
educated. (Aesch. 3.246).

The belief that all citizens were publicly educated in virtue helps
to explain the Athenian democrats' unwavering commitment to
equality.

Democratic Conceptions of Equality

Theorists and historians normally distinguish between several different types of equality within citizen groups. The first of these is

equality of nature, in the form of equal moral regard. We find this expressed in the American Declaration of Independence: "We hold these truths to be self-evident, that all men are created equal, that they are endowed by their Creator with certain unalienable Rights, that among these are Life, Liberty and the pursuit of Happiness." Obviously the American Founding Fathers did not believe that all human beings were equal in talent or natural ability; they meant that all human beings deserved equal moral regard, because God endowed them with dignity as human beings.

As slave-holders, Athenian democrats did not believe in universal human dignity given by nature. But Protagoras's myth offers a version of democratic thought according to which all citizens were, indeed, roughly equal in the political capacities that were of importance to the city. Because of this roughly equal capacity to contribute, Athenian citizens deserved equal respect and were thus protected by law from acts of outrage or indignity (*hubris*). Again, though, within this rough equality there was room for greater or lesser talent. Invoking the analogies of a linguistic community and of a community of flute players, Protagoras argues that members of the community will, admittedly, have different natural talents and so individuals of greater than average accomplishment will be discoverable. However, compared to those outside the relevant communities, all members (i.e., all Greek speakers, all flute players) will be roughly equal and, as Protagoras puts it, "sufficiently competent when compared to individuals with no understanding of how to play the flute" (327c).

This argument can be found throughout Athenian oratory and was inherent in the Athenians' political practices. Everyone was free to speak in the Assembly in part because people believed that everyone had something potentially important to contribute. Among public offices, only the generalship was elective, all the others being chosen by lot. Moreover, all citizens were deemed capable of making a significant contribution to the defense of the city; it was a serious duty to serve Athens militarily, and military desertion, cowardice, and failure to answer the military summons were often prosecuted as capital offenses. Conversely, Athenian litigants commonly cited their own and their ancestors' participation in the city's wars as evidence of their loyalty: by doing so, they were not claiming special valor, but rather asserting that they had carried out the basic duties expected of all citizen-equals (Text 19).

19. Men of the council, if I demonstrate only this to you, that I am loyal to the established constitution and that I have been forced to share in the same dangers as you, I do not consider myself worthy of special consideration. But if I demonstrate that I have lived an orderly life in all other respects, very much to the contrary of the opinion and speeches of my enemies, I ask you to confirm me at this hearing, and to think the worse of these men. (Lys. 16.3)

Their ability to contribute to Athens's military machine helped to justify their participation in political decision-making, since it was often claimed that those who failed to serve did not belong in the Assembly. On top of all this, the Athenians subscribed to a myth of autochthony, according to which all Athenians were indigenous because they could trace their ancestry back through citizen parents to the first inhabitants of Attica. Thus, they were all brothers and sisters and shared a common nobility based on their lineage. Plato satirizes this myth in the mock funeral oration known as the *Menexenus* (Text 20), but Athenians took this myth seriously as a sign of their collective identity, their rough equality, and their common nobility.

20. But we and our fellow citizens were all born brothers from the same mother, and we do not think it is right to be either slaves or masters of one another. Instead, natural equality of birth forces us to seek equality under the law, and to yield to one another for no reason other than the reputation for virtue and good sense. (*Menexenus* 238e–239a)

Judging, then, by their practices, their ideology, and their collective myths, the Athenians subscribed to what Robert Dahl has called the "strong principle of equality": "All members are sufficiently well qualified, taken all around, to participate in making the collective decisions binding on the association that significantly affect their good or interests. In any case, none are so definitely better qualified than the others that they should be entrusted with making the collective and binding decisions."[44] Although the Athenians did not recognize natural equality as a basic human principle guaranteeing universal rights, nonetheless they believed in a rough equality of political and military ability within the citizen group.

Beyond their belief in natural equality in the specified sense, the Athenians also envisioned equality as a normative value. The most important form this took was equality of opportunity. For example, in Euripides' *Suppliant Women* (423 BC), Theseus urges that Athens is a city ruled by law, in which the poor have an equal share in politics and equal rights to justice (Text 21).

> **21.** To begin with, stranger, you started your speech on a false note by asking for the master here. The city is not ruled by a single man, but is free. The people rule, and offices are held by yearly turns: they do not assign the highest honors to the rich, but the poor also have an equal share. . . . When the laws are written, both the powerless and the rich have equal access to justice, and the little man, if he has right on his side, defeats the big man. (Theseus in Euripides, *Suppliant Women*, 403–8, 433–7, tr. D. Kovacs, ed. and tr., *Euripides III*, Loeb Classical Library, Cambridge, Mass., 2002)

Aristotle viewed democracy as a system of "liberty based on equality" (*Pol.* 6.2.1317b16–17). By this he meant, among other things, that democratic citizens had the privilege of ruling and being ruled in turn, that the system had no or low property qualifications for holding office, and that jury courts were composed of all citizens and were competent to judge on the most important cases (*Pol.* 6.2.1317b17–30). Thus, a subset of equality of opportunity was "equality before the law" (*isonomia*). This boils down, in essence, to the idea that all Athenian citizens, bar none, could bring legal cases against others, all could put their names forward for the lottery drawings for magistracies, all cast an equal vote in the Assembly (*isopsêphia*), all were equally permitted to speak in the Assembly (*isêgoria*), and all deserved to be granted the same legal treatment by juries. Aeschines (1.5) cited equality of law as a distinctive and admirable characteristic of democracy as opposed to other political systems. These ideas were widespread in the literature of the classical period, appearing commonly not only in tragedy and Aristotle, but also in public oratory and in Thucydides.[45]

Equality of opportunity made a striking appearance in Pericles' funeral oration (Text 22).

> **22.** Whereas before the law there is equality for all in private disputes, nevertheless regarding popular esteem the individual receives public preference according to his recognized achievement in some field – not by rotation rather than by excellence – and furthermore, should he be poor but able to perform some service for the city, he is not prevented by insufficient public recognition. (Thuc. 2.37, tr. J. Rusten, *Thucydides: The Peloponnesian War, Book II*, Cambridge, 1989)

Pericles' main point is that all Athenian citizens, of whatever economic or social background, have the opportunity to rise to key positions in the city's government, provided they have genuine ability to offer. Despite the rough equality of all Athenians implied by the "strong principle of equality," Pericles points out that there will undoubtedly be further distinctions to be made in natural talent and in meritorious achievement on behalf of the polis. Pericles' ideal is a pure meritocracy of ability and achievement. The fourth-century expressions of the ideal of equality were continuous with those of the fifth century.

In light of these descriptions, it is worth noting a certain fuzziness about separating natural equality from normative equality. The fuzziness results from two evident facts. First, that normative equality would be difficult to sustain without a belief in some sort of rough natural equality. Since the Athenians, as slaveholders for example, did not believe in equal moral regard for all human beings, they based their normative citizen equality on the belief that all citizens could make a substantial and roughly equal contribution to the life of the city. Second, those who consider themselves naturally equal have always found it difficult to accept any political system other than one valuing normative equality.[46] Thus, whereas many historians would say that Athenians promoted normative but not natural equality, it is more plausible to find both concepts present in their ideology and, what is more, to argue that normative equality derived from a basic belief in natural equality.

Even so, one of the most striking features of democratic Athens is that, despite the ideological emphasis on freedom and equality, in reality Athenians rarely lived up to these ideals. All could speak in the Assembly, and were expected to do so if they had something important to say, but statistical studies show that very few members actually did speak up.[47] Moreover, the most important financial offices of the city, such as the office of the treasurers, were reserved by law for those of the highest two property-classes (though some evidence exists showing that these laws were not observed by the late fourth century). Finally, from a different angle, members of Athens's lowest class, who were called "thetes," were not often officially recognized for their substantial contribution to the city's defense – they rowed the ships that gave Athens its empire (cf. chapter 5, "Debating Athenian Imperialism").[48] The thetes were not entirely forgotten: the comic playwright Aristophanes celebrated the warships that made Athens powerful and said that the rowers save the city (Aristophanes, *Acharnians* 161–3). But public monuments, such as the Parthenon, or the casualty lists, illustrate that the efforts of the cavalry and the hoplites received much higher esteem than those of the lower classes. Thus, even though the democratic ideology of equality resembles modern conceptions of equality, nevertheless the Athenians' practices maintained a more traditional bias toward the upper classes and generally valued the cavalry and the hoplites over the thetes. Perhaps that, or something like it, is equally true of democratic equality as practiced in the modern nation-state.

Yet, despite these continuing inequalities, the Athenians went beyond most modern democracies in socializing both the talents and the resources of their elite. By this I mean that the Athenian elites were legally and socially pressured to use their advantages (such as talent, education, or wealth) to benefit the demos as a whole. The democracy instituted such redistributive schemes both for the sake of justice and for the common good. Through the democratic institution of "liturgies," members of the wealthy elite were required to fund state festivals, choruses, ships for the navy, and so forth. This mechanism of financial redistribution drew heavy criticism from antidemocrats (cf. chapter 4, "Mapping out the Problem"). But, as contemporaries recognized, socializing resources in this way helped to create grounds for rational trust across lower and upper classes, and further to reduce the evident potential for envy, hostility, and class conflict. As countless litigants and politicians said, they and their ancestors provided lavish outlay for the demos in order to show their loyalty to the city and the democracy (Text 23).

> **23.** When I became an adult, I was able to do things that followed upon my upbringing – to furnish a chorus, to fit out a war-ship for the city, to pay the property tax. I did not fail to perform any honorable service, either public or private. Instead, I provided useful services to both the city and to my own associates. (Dem. 18.257)

They articulated their self-image in terms of the virtues that, I have argued, the Athenians tried to inculcate in all citizens. In return for their generosity, they expected the demos to show respect to them as individuals, to grant them public honors, to look with favor on their leadership, and to consider their policy proposals carefully. The demos did this in deliberative forums, for example through voting on such leaders' advice, and in proposing honorific decrees, as in the case of an inscription from the tribe of Pandionis (Text 24).

> **24.** "The tribe of Pandionis decreed: Callicrates made the motion: to praise Nicias of Cydathenaeum on account of his noble service to the tribe, since he well and eagerly (*eu kai prothumôs*) provided for the chorus of boys and won at the Dionysia, and for the chorus of men at the Thargelia; and to crown him." (*IG* ii² 1138.1–7)

Justice and the Demos

The demos used the approbatory language of virtue to encourage wealthy individuals to contribute funds for the good of the city as a whole. The virtues associated with good citizenship encouraged members of the elite to socialize their talents and resources for the common good. Note too that the demos was truly in control, but it accommodated those of special talent and means by granting them places of honor, provided, again, that they voluntarily socialized their advantages for the good of the city. As a result, the Athenian democracy instituted, and enjoyed the benefits of, a redistributive mechanism that bears similarity to the Rawlsian "difference principle": "Assuming the framework of institutions required by equal liberty and fair equality of opportunity, the higher expectations of those better situated are just if and only if they work as part of a scheme which improves the expectations of the least advantaged members of society."[49]

It is worth keeping in mind two points as we compare Rawls' interpretation of justice to that of the ancient Athenians. First, the Athenians' self-conception required more than simply establishing institutions that corresponded to their interpretation of just social arrangements. It required, in addition, that the better situated give generously and voluntarily to the demos, and that the demos, in turn, respond with express gratitude. If just institutions were to be worth having, then they required, in the Athenian conception at least, certain habits of character, even habits of the heart, which would promote solidarity and civic friendship. This does not imply civic invasiveness into the individual's soul so much as a conception in which individuals adhered to a more robust sense of civic responsibility than our more "atomized," if you will, conception of the individual would allow.

Second, justice in Athens was really *justice* in the sense that it could be interpreted as (a type of) fairness in the distribution of power and resources, based on an egalitarian sensibility within the citizen group. However, justice was also valued for its contribution to civic stability. For Athenians saw clearly that inequities in social distribution, of whatever sort, would lead to anger among the disadvantaged and, from there, to civic strife. From the mid fifth century BC onward, as it happens, a critical literature arose in Athens which was designed to show, not that traditional inequities persisted under the democracy, but rather that the demos had so reversed the traditional hierarchies as to become, itself, positively tyrannical and unjust. In other words, certain members of the elite felt taken advantage of by the demos's mechanisms of redistribution. Antidemocratic authors capitalized upon their anger and found a willing audience among those dissatisfied with the interpretation of justice promoted by the Athenian democracy. Their work focused both on criticizing democracy and on offering alternatives to the democracy's egalitarian distribution of power. In both positive and negative registers, they had a long tradition of political thinking to draw on. It is to their work that we now turn.

chapter 4

Criticizing Democracy in Late Fifth-Century Athens

Because of the power of traditional aristocratic ideals in Greece, one might have thought "aristocratic thought" to be a more appropriate title for this chapter – on the grounds that not everyone cared about democracy. Yet political thought flourished in democratic Athens between 490 BC and 330 BC. Partly this flourishing was due to Athens's freedom of speech, partly to its wealth, partly to its status as a cultural center. The Athenians' empire and democracy arguably made these developments possible. Thus it came about that many of those advocating nondemocratic systems were forced to situate their work as a response to democracy. The Athenian democracy, moreover, was strikingly successful. This success placed a certain onus on its opponents; they had not only to explain what was wrong with democracy, but also to show that another conceivable political arrangement could be better. Similar conditions prevail today: democracy *seems* to have prevailed as the best form of constitution. An important difference, though, is that ancient Greeks could find examples, e.g. Sparta, or the Macedon of Philip II, and others, of flourishing non-democratic states. This helped to relieve the considerable burden that modern anti-democrats must confront.

Antidemocratic thought was historically important. Provided that the time was right, democracy's critics could inspire revolutionary political action. Since its foundation in 508 BC, the Athenian democracy met with few interruptions. In the first half of the fifth century, we hear vague reports of two attempts to overthrow the democracy (Plutarch, *Aristides* 13.1; Thuc. 1.107), first in 480 and then in 458. In neither case are the conspirators' motives certain. They may have aimed to attack their political opponents or to oppose a particular foreign policy (such as continuing the war with Persia), rather than to attack democracy in principle.[1] The debate between democracy and oligarchy became polarized only in the second half of the fifth century. And it was only in the last decade of the century that antidemocrats found an opportunity to act. This they did with some success in 411 BC, when they instituted a narrow oligarchy for four months, after which democracy was quickly restored; and then in 404–403 BC, when democracy was restored after eight months of oligarchic rule. In fact the *brief* success of these regimes highlights the entrenchment of democracy within classical Athens.

Examining late fifth-century political thought with a focus on democratic Athens is one reasonable way to approach a vast body of complicated, diverse, and, for us, fragmentary material. Greeks outside Athens thought deeply about politics; many of the thinkers we discuss came from outside Athens; democracies flourished in other Greek poleis; and there were continuities between political thought prior to 430 BC–400 BC and political thought in that three-decade period.[2] Even so, the present chapter's focus on late fifth-century Athens is useful for two reasons. First, thinkers of all sorts were attracted to the financial and cultural opportunities of Athens and expected, rightly, to be hospitably received there by all sectors of the citizenry. Second, the novelty and intensity of the Peloponnesian War, as it was experienced and understood at Athens, provides an illuminating context within which nondemocratic thought might be understood. Analyzing political thought historically helps to clarify the principal interests of thinkers in this period.

The Peloponnesian War (431–404 BC) was the overarching political concern of thinkers and engaged citizens throughout the last three decades of the fifth century. This war pitted democratic Athens and its allies against oligarchic Sparta and its allies. Thus it brought home to careful observers the problems and potentialities of democratic rule, by contrast with those of Athens's chief nondemocratic rival.

In his excursus on Corcyra (3.82–83), Thucydides illustrated the potential for violent reactions over the choice between democracy and oligarchy. At the outbreak of the Peloponnesian War, Athens had contracted an alliance with the island of Corcyra, in northwest Greece, in order to fortify its navy. In doing so, the Athenians knowingly upset relations with Corinth, a leading Spartan ally, which had experienced decades of hostile relations with Corcyra. Thucydides explains that political partisans on the island seized this opportunity to attack their rivals – oligarchs calling in the Corinthians, and democrats relying on Athenian help.

According to Thucydides, the ensuing civil war (*stasis*) liberated the worst human passions, including envy, selfish ambition, greed, and other sociopathic appetites. Social trust, loyalty to fellow citizens, and common civic purposes were all destroyed, since, as Thucydides says, "War is a violent teacher," which brings men's minds down to the level of their (difficult) circumstances. The breakdown of Corcyra's political community was reflected in the growing lack of consensus over significant items in the Corcyraeans' ethical lexicon (Text 1).[3]

> **1.** They reversed the usual way of using words to evaluate activities. Ill-considered boldness was counted as loyal manliness; prudent hesitation was held to be cowardice in disguise; and moderation merely the cloak of an unmanly nature. A mind that could grasp the good of the whole was considered wholly lazy. Sudden fury was accepted as part of manly valor, while plotting for one's security was thought a reasonable excuse for delaying action. (Thuc. 3.82, tr. Woodruff)

This passage makes a crucial point: citizens who are violently at odds with one another no longer share common standards of ethical evaluation. They disagree over what counts as virtuous or vicious behavior. That means, more deeply, that they maintain opposed or, rather, contradictory visions of what constitutes good citizenship and a healthy polis culture, so much so that shared activity becomes impossible. Such was the Thucydidean analysis of civil war and its consequences.

With this we might contrast both the pluralism of modern democratic life and the "virtue politics" of classical Athenian citizenship (chapter 3). For principled reasons, modern democrats allow multiple visions of the good life to coexist peaceably in a single polity. Tensions between competing groups naturally arise, but they are typically limited by the citizens' endorsement of fundamental principles of civic engagement – as embodied, for example, in the American Constitution. Ancient Athenians, by contrast, cultivated particular forms of good citizenship, based on beliefs about what citizens ought to be like – courageous, moderate, just, and so forth, as those terms were understood democratically. These features of virtuous character made it possible for Athenian democrats to enjoy their key values, freedom and equality, without interruption.

In representing Corcyra, Thucydides wrestled with the potential for violence that he viewed as latent in human culture – even in democratic culture. In Thucydides' view, war tends to turn fellow citizens into partisans and competitors. And, as he points out, stasis began to arise all over Greece in the last third of the fifth century. The Peloponnesian War itself – which was an outgrowth of Athenian imperialism – gave rise to bitter polarization between democrats and oligarchs. This polarization was both an expression and a cause of the theoretical and ideological battleground that we explore in the present chapter.

In an increasingly violent atmosphere, democrats developed a powerful self-image and a plausible way of relating their civic virtues to their bedrock freedom and equality. Their ideological developments took place rapidly because democracy was itself an innovation. As the political system promoting novel extensions of freedom and equality, democrats had to justify their system to themselves and to others. But non-democrats took a much longer time, roughly 50 or 60 years after 508 BC, to develop their own ideological and theoretical structure. They made such moves in response to the democrats' self-justifications.[4] In other words, certain members of the elite developed antidemocratic ideas chiefly because, and when, they felt threatened by the power of democratic ideas. Their primary strategies were two: first, to argue that proper civic virtues, and political wisdom, could only be found in those with wealth, leisure, good birth, and education; and second, to argue that democratic freedom and equality were either unfair, or positively harmful, or both. They extended the archaic elite's focus on both virtue and just distribution, now in order to confront a rhetorically powerful democratic competitor.

Given the basic argumentative strategies of anti-democrats, we might distinguish, at least theoretically, between two types of criticism of democracy.[5] The first type is characterized by satirical or philosophical "attacks" on democracy, the demos and its leaders, or Athenian culture, which have as their goal the improvement of the system. Critics of this sort did not encourage their audiences to overthrow the democracy, or to reconsider whether democracy itself was a good system. This category is exemplified by comic satire, which mocked individual politicians for their shortcomings and foibles, and the demos for being litigious, fickle, and greedy. Into this category, too, fits the standard invective that characterized debate between rival (democratic) politicians. Aeschines, for example, called Demosthenes cowardly (3.81, 3.175), sacrilegious (3.130–1), and disloyal (3.64), while maintaining that many politicians in contemporary Athens were deceptive and selfish (3.3–4). These were common charges and had nothing antidemocratic about them. Their point was either to make a joke or to score political points, or both, on the assumption that Athenian citizens should do everything in their power to make democracy better. To put it differently, these criticisms respected democracy's bedrock values and virtues, while questioning the citizens' – or often *a* citizen's – capacity to enact them. This mode of criticism can be called "ameliorative."

The second type of criticism rejected democracy altogether. The primary complaint was that ordinary citizens were not qualified to share political power equally with their betters. Others, that is the elite, it was said, were more intelligent, well educated, and therefore competent, to establish a healthy politics in the city. There was a powerful dose of snobbery in such criticisms, which were inherited from the aristocratic values of early Greece. In ancient Athens, though, aristocrats had their backs against the wall. Aristocrats who were so inclined had to reinvigorate their traditional ideals, so as to explain why the rule of the few, or political exclusivity, was justified despite the success of Athenian democracy. Often their first, perhaps their only, step was to translate their sentiments into a commentary on the faulty character of democratic citizens and the democracy's defective system of governance. Like the democrats, they too saw politics through the lens of ethics, but, as befits their critical purposes, they stressed the need both to deplore the democracy's many vices and to reconfigure the politics of virtue on a more solidly aristocratic footing.

Keep in mind, however, that ameliorative and rejectionist criticism, taken out of context, might sound the same. For example, Andocides, an Athenian politician with possible oligarchic sympathies, once criticized the democratic leader Hyperbolus by calling him a foreigner, and his father a slave, and by ridiculing his livelihood (Text 2).

2. About Hyperbolus, I am ashamed to speak, since his father, who is branded, still, even now, works as a slave at the public mint, while he himself, a real barbarian, makes lamps for a living. (Andocides fr. III.2 = Schol. Aristophanes, *Wasps*, 1007)

His criticism is similar to what Aristophanes, an ameliorative critic, says about other democratic leaders of similar stature (Text 3).

3. Similarly, looking at Cleonymus the shield-tosser yesterday, they saw that he was the worst sort of coward, and therefore turned into deer. SOCRATES: And now that they have seen Cleisthenes (do you see him?), they've turned into women. (Aristophanes, *Clouds* 353–5)

Thucydides, no admirer of democracy, called the politician Cleon the "most violent" of his contemporaries (3.36), a miserably wretched human being and a "disgrace" to Athens (8.73). The lines can be blurry.

Invective denouncing individual politicians could, at times, be raised to the level of an attack on the system as a whole, provided that critics built in certain assumptions. When Aeschines abused Demosthenes as a traitorous coward, for instance, an antidemocratic thinker might argue that, because of the demos's stupidity, democracies tend to promote defective and untrustworthy leaders, thereby depriving themselves of prudent counsel. Or, differently, critics might argue that the demos was incapable of living up to its own ideals – which made democracy a self-defeating system. The greatest sting came from critics who attacked democratic ideals themselves as wrongheaded.

Yet, despite its possible blurriness, we should keep the distinction in mind because it will provide us with a useful spectrum of possibilities, particularly when we deal with ambiguous cases. For example, it will emerge that Socrates' arguments partook, in paradoxical ways, of both types of critique. To get a clearer handle on Socrates' attitudes, it will be helpful to ask whether his arguments reflect a desire to improve the democratic system, or to establish another system altogether. Criticism is a slippery slope and often the surviving record leaves us with nearly inscrutable cases. For the historian of ancient political thought, everything depends on over-lapping contexts: to read critical texts of this period properly, we must draw attention to their "embeddedness" in history, to their intended audiences, and to their self-positioning in relation to democratic ideology.

Mapping out the Problem: The "Old Oligarch"

Unlike democratic ideology, antidemocratic criticism is one area where we can start at the beginning – at least given our incomplete source materials. Probably in the 420s, a political writer known to modern scholars as the "Old Oligarch" translated his anti-demotic sentiments into a wide-ranging analysis of the democrats' character defects and selfishness. His identity is uncertain, though he appears to be a native Athenian explaining, rather defensively, to foreign aristocrats why the Athenian elite has not instituted "good govern-ment" (*eunomia*). "Good government," or "orderliness," the old archaic term of approbation (see chapter 2, "Sparta and the Politics of 'Courage'"), had become an aristocratic watchword by this period; it connoted discipline, hierarchy, and order, such as one found at Sparta, as opposed to the prevailing democratic pande-monium. Therefore, in his "Constitution of the Athenians," as his pamphlet is called, the Old Oligarch wanted both to cast aspersions on democrats and to explain the secrets of their success. The com-bination is revealing. His focus is resolutely critical and ironic, with few positive proposals, and it pours unrelenting scorn on his social inferiors who (yet) happen to be politically ingenious. The great surprise awaiting his readers was his uncontained admiration for the democrats' success both at preserving their constitution and at achieving their other political objectives.

This author's political outlook was shaped by the belief that the rich are favorably disposed to the rich, and the poor to the poor (3.10). Economic class was for him the source of political motiva-tion. This view implies a rejection of the democracy's efforts to establish civic unity across class lines, through speeches, shared values, and civic rituals. For the Old Oligarch, the polis is by nature a battleground, rather than the site of public dialogue and exchange "in the middle" (as Greeks had put it since the time of Homer). The middle ground was lost in the fragmenting world of competing democratic and oligarchic interests. These class-based interests arose, according to the Old Oligarch, from nature and were cultivated and shaped by life in polis culture (Text 4).

4. I think that the Athenian demos knows which of the citizens are good and which are worthless, but despite their knowledge the people cherish those who are useful and beneficial to themselves even if they are worthless, whereas they hate good men. For they reckon that the natural virtue of good men will not benefit them, but harm them. On the other hand, some, although they are truly men of the people, are not by nature demotic. I forgive the demos its democracy; it is understandable that each man wants to fare well on his own account. But whoever is not demotic and still chooses to live in a democratic city rather than an oligarchic one, is preparing to commit a crime and knows that bad men can escape notice more easily in a democracy than in an oligarchy. (Old Oligarch, 2.19–20)

Rather than inculcating shared virtues, as Protagoras had hoped, life in the polis breeds ever-increasing hostility for those of opposing factions. By including nature and natural traits in his analysis, the Old Oligarch suggested that, despite the importance of polis culture in shaping our characters, we are also born with certain class affiliations that we abandon at our (ethical) peril. On his picture, individuals should side with others of their socioeconomic rank, and avoid alliances across class lines, on pain of being (or at least resembling) criminals and traitors. The Old Oligarch's treatise represents a simplistic and polarized, but not quite incoherent, attempt to apply thinking about nature to the observed political world.

In the Old Oligarch's view, then, natural class divisions made politics inherently a stasis-ridden battleground. In this light, Thucydides' Corcyra could appear to be only an extreme extension of the competitive, suspicious world of politics altogether. An inevitable fact of this world was, for the Old Oligarch, the existence of rulers and the ruled, as well as conflict between them. As he declared, "It is necessary that the ruler will be hated by the ruled" (1.14). This is a stark comment on the late fifth-century world, since democrats in Athens abided by the democratic principle of ruling and being ruled in turn; they avoided the political divisions implicit in the Old Oligarch's theorem that rulers are necessarily hated.

Such ideological differences were expressed in charged political arguments and terminology. As a Syracusan speaker in Thucydides once said, democrats held that "the name for the entire people is 'demos', whereas 'oligarchy' is the name for only a part of the citizenry" (Thuc. 6.39; cf. chapter 3, "Evidence and Sources" and "Democratic Deliberation" for discussion of this speech, and Thucydides' speeches as evidence). His argument was that democracy is inclusive and healthy, whereas oligarchy is exclusive and therefore destructive. Or, again, the Herodotean character Otanes approvingly said that the "entire polis is to be found in the mass of citizens" (3.80). Democrats represented themselves as inclusive of both rich and poor; those in the Old Oligarch's camp, by contrast, had a stake in defining *demos* more narrowly as the poor (Text 5).

> **5.** The best element is opposed to democracy all over the world. For among the best men there is the least amount of self-indulgence and wrongdoing, but the most precise dedication to what is noble, while among the demos there is the greatest ignorance, disorder, and vice. Poverty leads them to shameful behavior, and some of the people lack education and are ignorant because of their lack of means. (Old Oligarch, 1.5)

This distinction speaks to the oligarchs' desire to differentiate themselves – and, conversely, to the democrats' desire to establish unity on a firm basis of equality. Thus, by reinterpreting a single item in the sociopolitical lexicon, that is, the word "demos," the rival camps clarified their political allegiances and their respective political aspirations.

What could make such extreme contrasts and emotions possible? Certainly the Old Oligarch's strongly antidemotic sentiments were shared by others. The oligarchic Megabyzus in Herodotus' "Constitutional Debate" (3.80–3) emphasized the violence, arrogance, and self-indulgence of the demos, as though no community of interest could ever be forged between the upper classes and the ill-informed and "unwashed" masses (3.81). This is very traditional snobbery. The Old Oligarch was an anachronistic, and equally horrified, Theognis (cf. chapter 2, "The Elitist Response"). Like the bitter and powerless Theognid *persona*, the Old Oligarch fantasized indignantly about "good government" in which the worthy types "punish bad men," establish selfish policies, and forbid the poor and ordinary citizens to speak up. Through such policies, he says, "The demos would very quickly be enslaved" (1.9).

The formulas through which the Old Oligarch expressed his anger were traditional and ethical. Character, and therefore like-mindedness, develop as a natural outgrowth of material circumstances. This premise gave the Old Oligarch cause to oppose the rich and well born to the poor, the base, and the "worst" types chiefly on ethical, and even aesthetic, grounds (Text 5). Ethics and aesthetics, for him, were ultimately rooted in economics, but they took on a life of their own in this angry treatise. Modern scholars often say that the ancient economy was "embedded" in ethical reasoning, but the Old Oligarch shows how thinking could proceed the other way, from economics to ethics. The author's ethical stance, broadly construed, had an aesthetic component in that he imagined the demotic types as poor, ill-educated, and unworthy citizens. As a group, however, these citizens had united and acquired the material resources to enjoy luxury that they neither deserved nor understood. Thus, in his view, they became powerful but ill-equipped *arrivistes*. Implicit in such ethical and aesthetic judgments was the Old Oligarch's recognition of an irreconcilable conflict of human ends at play in the contemporary political scene.

To oligarchs of his stripe, democratic success was the problem that demanded a solution. For, if the demos had been as unjust, tacky, and stupid as our author asserted, then democracy would truly have been a castle made of sand. It is a tribute to his honesty, however, that the Old Oligarch paradoxically recognizes the democracy's success even as he denigrates the demos. He abhors the resulting picture but is gritty enough to confront the inner workings of democratic success. That success, as he shows, was based on the democrats' prudent and fair-minded politics. They justly distributed political power and material rewards to those who sustained the city's military – namely, the rowers, petty naval officers, and shipbuilders (1.2). They wisely left the serious offices, like the generalships, to men of high status while claiming the paid sinecures for themselves (1.3). They allowed all citizens to speak out in Assembly, since they knew that the poor and unwashed would offer good advice to the democracy, even if Athens could never become "the best city" through allowing just anyone to air his views! Athenians advanced the principle of equality to such an extent that uncertainty reigned as to the free or slave status of passers-by on the street (1.10–12). Strictly speaking, of course, this was untrue, but the author's hyperbole properly hints that the democracy's power depended in part on the democrats' unabashed willingness to promote equality and freedom. These values were the core of the democratic interpretation of justice. Democrats pursued them to the hilt and with extraordinary success.

In his grand finale, on revolution, the Old Oligarch says that Athenians typically disenfranchise only those who behave unjustly in office or "do or say what is wrong" (3.13), that few Athenian citizens have been disenfranchised at all, and that fewer still have been unjustly disenfranchised. At Athens, therefore, there was little hope of finding an embittered "fifth column" inside the polis to mobilize an antidemocratic revolution. In his speech of self-defense, the oligarchic leader Antiphon confirmed this point, by arguing that he was unlikely to have resisted the democracy, since it had not treated him unjustly. The Athenians' promotion of freedom and political equality for all citizens was a sign of the basic justice of the system. Antiphon, of course, was playing to the democratic audience when he made this point, but he couldn't have done so unless such ideas had real plausibility. On the evidence provided by the Old Oligarch, antidemocrats at Athens were in a quandary. They hated the system for its presumed character deficiencies and failure to recognize the aristocrats' natural nobility, but they also comprehended the reasons for democratic success and had little hope of establishing a politics more suitable to their tastes.

The Old Oligarch's psychology comes through in his analysis of the Athenians' empire. Theirs was a novel species of military power, which was independent of hoplite discipline, glamorous generals, traditional manliness, and so forth. The Athenians' ships provided speed, flexibility, safety, and a hitherto unimagined capacity to exert their will on other Greeks. This matched the novelty of their political structures at home. In both cases, the Athenian democrats distributed power and material rewards to all citizens, not to the few. Ruling over the aristocrats within their polis, the Athenian demos had created, at home, a microcosm of their power over other Greeks abroad. (Such, at least, was the Old Oligarch's view; Athenians, to say it again, viewed all citizens as beneficiaries of the empire and of democratic governance. The historical reality, so far as we can discern it, is that Athenian aristocrats who led the city's imperialist ventures profited inordinately compared to the ordinary citizens.)

The Athenian demos' success at home and abroad, ultimately, was the source of the Old Oligarch's indignation. Although he couldn't articulate convincing reasons, he firmly believed that democracy was not a healthy system, that its distribution of social and material goods was unfair, and that aristocrats both at home and abroad deserved better. They deserved, in particular, to be Homeric-style leaders; to win the material rewards and social esteem that Glaucon and Sarpedon enjoyed (cf. "The Elitist Response" in chapter 2); and to feel aesthetically and ethically confident about their way of life, and to be admired for it. The Old Oligarch's unwitting effort to combine elitist prejudice with admiration for Athenian *realpolitik* thereby led to an inconclusive stalemate. The Greeks called this type of stalemate *aporia*, which means literally "lack of passage." There was nowhere for the author to go. The *aporia* of this text is perhaps its most revealing feature. The democracy had created not only a successful political and imperialist culture. More than that, its core belief that justice demands democratic equality and freedom appeared to carry a high level of conviction even among the oligarchic opposition.

Modern and Ancient Quandaries

Modern antidemocratic theory faces similar difficulties. In his *Anatomy of Antiliberalism*, Stephen Holmes has argued that antiliberalism is a multifaceted tradition "whose unity does not consist in uniformity, to be sure, but in a handful of basic assumptions, plus, above all, a common enemy" – namely, the liberal traditions of toleration, free discussion and elections, constitutionality, impartial law, the consent of the governed, and so forth.[6] Holmes shows that antiliberal writers – chiefly de Maistre, Schmitt, Strauss, MacIntyre, Lasch, and Unger – share a tendency to set themselves up as doctors trying to cure the "crisis" of liberal modernity through recovering ancient cultural traditions. They often focus on the "atomism" of modern society – that is, on the (alleged) isolation of individuals who have lost their moral compass. Without a cadre of superior individuals to promote a proper culture, the uneducated masses will live an aimless and worthless life, and intellectuals, particularly, will be sacrificed at the altar of the masses' crude, ignorant, and selfish desires.

Even such a brief characterization enables us to see that ancient antidemocrats shared with modern antiliberals the desire to return to an exalted and presumptively superior past, in the hopes of curing the moral pandemic brought about by democracy or liberalism. Among those antiliberals who have looked back nostalgically to the classical past, such as MacIntyre and Strauss, there is a marked effort to revitalize elitist traditions of ethics and character as they were later filtered through Plato and Aristotle. The irony, though, is that ancient democracy had created its own powerful discourse on justice and the virtues, which not only proved successful pragmatically, but which was never refuted intellectually.

To construct truly compelling alternatives, then, the rivals of ancient democracy had to pose more radical and, frankly, more successful challenges to key democratic ideals, both through criticism and through imagining a positive program of their own. There was no better way to proceed than to probe the question of justice. As we have argued in earlier chapters, justice was widely agreed to be the core value within the Greek polis. But justice also began to assume center stage in the international political discussions of the Athenian Empire (see chapter 5). The most common complaint at the end of the fifth century was that the Athenians treated their allies unjustly by (often metaphorically) enslaving them, demanding tribute, and interfering with their domestic politics. These complaints were at the heart of the Spartans' ideological campaign during the Peloponnesian War. As a result, the historical moment encouraged contemporaries to reconsider the nature of justice. Accordingly, the most successful philosophical challenges to democracy came from those who could reinterpret justice in a convincingly antidemocratic way. That meant, above all, proposing alternative conceptions of equality. This in turn encouraged antidemocratic theorists to knit their alternative ideas of equality into wider theories of nature, sociology, and self-interest, so as to "denaturalize" the overwhelmingly successful democratic positions on equality. The political world didn't have to be this way.

Nomos and Phusis

As the Old Oligarch had turned to nature in order to ground his political sociology, others too explored the relation of nature (*phusis*) to law, custom, or convention, all of which were embodied in the Greek word *nomos*.[7] Hesiod and Heraclitus both notably affirmed that human law was based on divine ordinance or decree. This religious thought also underlay Protagoras's idea that Zeus, upon witnessing human violence and folly, had immutably fixed the cardinal virtues of political life, *aidôs* and *dikê* (cf. chapter 3, "Protagorean Arguments for Democracy"). Such moves soften the apparent conflict between (pre-existing) nature and (humanly constructed) laws or customs. But they were not enough to stave off persistent worries: the relationship between *phusis* and *nomos* is a deep question that has troubled thinkers throughout human history. Such questions became politically important in the last third of the fifth century BC. The reasons were both intellectual and social.

First, a number of teachers now called "sophists" began to look more deeply into questions of ethics and politics – questions that had traditionally been the poets' exclusive province. These teachers included Protagoras of Abdera, Hippias of Elis, Prodicus of Ceos, Thrasymachus of Chalcedon, Gorgias of Leontini, Antiphon of Athens, and possibly (though controversially) Socrates of Athens. These thinkers were not members of a coherent group. They were part of an intellectual trend characterized by probing questions of politics, doing empirical research, thinking deeply about rhetoric and how to teach it, and speculating about the objective basis of morality, or the lack thereof.[8] Most of these thinkers are known chiefly through Plato's negative picture: for Plato, the "sophist," a self-proclaimed teacher of rhetoric, or a professor of political knowledge, was rather "a paid hunter of rich young men" (*Sophist* 231d). At any rate the labels are less important than the impact of their teachings on politics; and we should probably view these men, simply, as philosophers.

Second, the intensity and novelty of the Peloponnesian War encouraged contemporaries, including the sophists, to focus on the relationship between *nomos* and *phusis*. This war overturned all previous customs of war making in the Greek world. Greeks traditionally expected that battles would be fought between two heavily armed corps of infantry, on a flat plain, mostly over a questionable borderland region, within the space of several hours, and according to strictly defined rituals that limited casualties and protected noncombatants. The Peloponnesian War was different in nearly every respect because of the "grand strategy" of the Athenian leader

Pericles.[9] At his suggestion, the Athenians withdrew into the city, rejected land combat, fought by sea, planned on a protracted struggle, and made every effort to erode the enemy's economic infrastructure and system of political alliances. They developed an "island mentality" that even the Old Oligarch had to admire. By defying convention in every way, the Athenians powerfully expressed their democracy's independence of traditional limits. Their independence affected the entire Greek world, not just the polis of Athens.

In particular, the Athenians' strategy made this war a peculiarly long and intensely painful experience for their enemy and, it turned out, for themselves. One effect was the pervasiveness of civic strife; Thucydides' account of Corcyra was meant to be exemplary, not exhaustive. At Athens itself, where we have the clearest picture, citizens experienced economic distress, loss of property (including farms) outside the city walls, and all the uncertainty of how they and their empire would fare. Pericles had to fortify the standard patriotic rhetoric in order to address the Athenians' suffering optimistically (Text 6).

> **6.** Each of you has by now experienced suffering, but a clear vision of how this will benefit us all is still far off. . . . Nevertheless, since you live in a great city and were raised with a way of life which matches the city's greatness, it is necessary to withstand the greatest misfortunes willingly and not to obscure your reputation. . . . Put away your private grief and work to secure our common safety. (Thuc. 2.61.2–4)

Even if these were not Pericles' precise words, the speech as reported is highly credible as a response to such difficult circumstances.

The Athenians' suffering was especially acute because of the destructive plague that hit Athens in 430 BC and lasted for several years, with minor interruptions (Thuc. 2.47–54; 3.87). Four thousand and four hundred hoplites, 300 cavalry, and very many others perished in the plague. In Thucydides' description, people began to renounce traditional customs and laws, whether sacred or civic: for example, he says, it was common for people to steal others' funeral pyres for their own dead, and to forsake obedience to the law for the sake of immediate pleasures (Text 7).

7. The disease was responsible for establishing lawlessness through-out the city in other matters also. People dared more readily to gratify their desires for pleasure, whereas earlier they had kept such desires hidden. For they saw that change came about quickly: the rich died suddenly and those who previously had nothing immediately took over their property. As a result, they deemed it right to pursue imme-diate pleasures for their own enjoyment, supposing that their lives and possessions alike were ephemeral. No one eagerly took pains to do what appeared noble, since no one knew clearly whether he would die before achieving noble aims. But whatever seemed at the moment pleasurable or useful for attaining pleasure – this was set up as the noble and useful. (Thuc. 2.53)

It is hard to believe in the literal truth or historicity of Thucy-dides' account in this case. Rather, we should understand his description of the plague as his own devastating commentary on the fragility of Athens' politics as evoked in Pericles' sanguine funeral oration. But the basic historical point holds that, as in Corcyra, so too at Athens: under the intense pressure of circum-stances, certain darker facets of human nature came to override the healthy operation of *nomos*. If democrats could defy traditional strictures through their popular decisions, then so too were human beings driven to abandon convention, even more awesomely, by their natural passions.

It was in such a bewildering and frightening world that theo-retical reflection on *phusis* and *nomos* took center stage. The most striking fact, perhaps, is the scarcity of reflective thinkers promot-ing *nomos* as a source of security and order in such an unstable world. Thinkers whose works have survived mostly elevated the claims of *phusis* over those of *nomos*. (Of course, most actual citizens must have continued to believe in the value and importance of *nomos* in practice, or else civilized life would not have been poss-ible.) And, in some cases, those who promoted "nature" can also be securely identified as leading figures in the oligarchic revolutions of 411 and 404 at Athens. For the historian of political thought, therefore, the late fifth century offers an opportunity to show how intellectual trends influenced political action, and vice versa. But, as it turns out, the surviving evidence does not point to firm connections, in any individual case, between specifically antidemocratic thought and participation in the oligarchic revolutions at Athens. The surviving evidence is suggestive, but not sufficient to establish the case conclusively.[10]

Even so, I believe that it is substantially correct to see connections between revolutionary action and the political thought of this period. By 411 BC, after 20 years of war, the Athenian elite judged that their contributions and level of suffering were disproportionate to the benefits they derived from the city and its empire. The poorer classes, on the other hand, benefited handsomely from continuing the war and from redistributing the income of the wealthy for public festivals, services, and amenities. Many members of the elite were ready for a political change. Contemporary thinkers explained why the democrats' high-minded ideals of lawfulness and justice had no firm basis in nature, and why it was justifiable for members of the elite to jettison conventions when self-interest was at hand. Nature provided a fixed standard by which existing conventions could be criticized and rejected. Fidelity to the law had once appeared to be a noble idea, but, contemporary thinkers argued, law is simply a human product. Law often conflicts with our self-interests as defined by our nature as human beings. Therefore, when the opportunity presented itself, the elite acted on the basis of contemporary thinking and overthrew the democracy first in 411 and then in 404. Some such picture makes the best sense of all the available evidence. Such a reconstruction, as we shall see, illustrates why political ideas should be assigned a significant role in enabling and inspiring political action.[11]

Antiphon of Athens, who was admired by Thucydides as a key luminary (8.68), capitalized upon the *nomos/phusis* antithesis in order to pose a challenge to conventional morality and law. For Antiphon, justice "is not transgressing the laws (*nomima*) of the city in which one is a citizen" (*DK* 87 B 44 A1). This was a traditional and widely shared view of justice. Antiphon's challenge to law and custom came from the role he assigned to nature. By contrast with law, he argued, nature provides a different and truer standard of advantage for human beings. As a result, Antiphon proposed that law should not be obeyed if it conflicts with nature (Text 8).

8. So a man would employ justice best for his own interests if he were to regard the laws as important when witnesses were present, but, when no witnesses are present, he were to regard the demands of nature as important. For the demands of the laws are artificial, but the demands of nature are necessary. And the demands of the laws are the result not of natural disposition but of agreement, but the demands of nature are exactly the opposite. (Antiphon, *DK* 87 B 44, fr. A, tr. Morrison in Sprague, *Older Sophists*)

And such conflicts between law and nature are very likely. For, in Antiphon's view, many things are advantageous by nature but unjust by law, while "most of what is legally just is inimical to nature." Transgressors of the law would often benefit themselves (truly and according to nature) if they acted secretly and escaped punishment, whereas those contravening nature's demands would be harmed no matter what.[12] Nature provided Antiphon with a foundation from which to criticize law, convention, and traditional morality.

Antiphon's analysis is not specifically antidemocratic. Antiphon was, however, a leading intellectual figure behind the oligarchic junta of 411 BC. After the suppression of the oligarchy in 410 BC, Antiphon was condemned to death for his participation in the junta. He is reported to have said after his trial that "a man of great spirit (*megalopsuchos*) would care more about a single virtuous man's opinion than that of many ordinary people" (Aristotle, *EE* 3.5.1232b6–8). It is understandable that, knowing these biographical details, we would read his extant works with an eye to politics. Imagine how different the case would look if Antiphon were known to have written exactly the same treatise while living an uneventful life as a resident alien in the suburbs of lonely Phocis. Provided that the revolutionary and the theorist were the same man, we are entitled to read Antiphon's discussion of law and nature with one eye, at least, on contemporary politics.[13] The question remains, however, whether Antiphon's hoped-for oligarchic constitution would not also be subject to his own critique of existing law and convention!

Similar issues surround the political thought and activity of Plato's cousin Critias. Critias was a leader of the oligarchic government in 404–403 BC. Not much of his corpus has survived, but what remains reveals his strong antipathy toward democracy. For example, he wrote a "Constitution of the Spartans," apparently in

order to express his admiration for this exemplar of order and
"good government." Over Critias's tomb, we are told, his fellow
conspirators dedicated a personification of Oligarchy setting fire to
Democracy, with the following inscription underneath: "This is a
memorial to good men who restrained the accursed populace of
the Athenians from arrogance for a brief period."[14] Critias was a
staunch antidemocrat; that much is clear. The question is how to
interpret the most famous of his surviving fragments.

In his satyr-play *Sisyphus*, the title character gave a speech pur-
porting to explain that civilization, law, and religion originated as
"mechanisms of social control" (Text 9).

> **9.** There was a time when the life of men was uncivilized and bestial
> and subservient to brute force, a time when neither was there any
> prize for the good nor for the wicked did any chastisement arise. It
> seems to me that men next set up laws as chastisers, that justice
> might become tyrant <equally of all> and might have arrogance as a
> slave. Should anyone commit an error, he was penalized. Next, since
> laws hindered them from committing obvious crimes by force, yet
> they acted secretly; it seems to me that at this point some clever and
> wise man <for the first time> invented fear <of the gods> for mortals,
> that the wicked might experience fear, even if they act or say or think
> <something> in secret. . . . With such fears did he encircle men,
> through whom he settled the deity well via discourse and in a suit-
> able location; and through laws he quelled lawlessness. (Critias, *Sisy-
> phus*, DK 88 B 25, tr. Levin in Sprague, *Older Sophists*)

Like Protagoras in his "Great Speech" (cf. chapter 3, "Protagorean
Arguments for Democracy"), Sisyphus offers a narrative of the
human advance from a "natural condition" to the origins of civilization, law, and religion. But Sisyphus' theology and anthropology were far different from those of Protagoras. Human beings
invented laws, he says, in order to establish just conditions for all.
But they were unsuccessful, to the degree that clever individuals
could keep their crimes secret. The only way to stop crimes from
being committed in secret was to invent the gods, who could
monitor wrongdoing at all times and in all places. (It is hard not
to hear echoes of Antiphon's idea that acting in secret, and according to nature, was often the best course for those able to escape
detection.) Belief in, and fear of, the gods – the clever devices of an

ingenious human inventor – removed lawlessness from human society altogether, even though, the speech continues, there is in reality no strong reason to believe that the gods exist.

The speech presents itself as an example of religious anthropology. On a minimalist reading, Sisyphus aimed to explain human religious beliefs in rational, humanistic, and secular terms. Other thinkers of this period, such as Protagoras, questioned the possibility of knowing anything about the gods (*DK* 80 B 4); Prodicus theorized that religious beliefs were derived from the agricultural experience of fear and uncertainty (*DK* 84 B 5).[15] Such theories do not have obvious political implications. Again we are left to speculate. Critias was imprisoned for his involvement in the sacrilegious mutilation of the Herms in 415 BC. As Thucydides reports (6.27–8), these statues of the god Hermes were defaced one night while preparations for the Sicilian Expedition were underway. Athenians regarded this act of vandalism – along with the roughly contemporary mockery of the holy Eleusinian Mysteries – as a bad omen for the expedition and as part of a plot to overthrow the democracy. Religious beliefs and practices were deeply intertwined with the politics and welfare of the city. Sisyphus' "genealogy" of religious belief *might* have embodied a threat to the religious conventions and political practices of Athens – a threat that *might* have been realized in Critias' sacrilegious behavior and his revolutionary politics. But no conclusive proof is available as to the suggestive link between Sisyphus' speech and Critias' actions.

The Challenge of Thrasymachus and Callicles

I will consider Thrasymachus and Callicles more fully in the discussion of Plato in chapter 6. However, it is also worth integrating them, albeit briefly, into their fifth-century context, because their views help to fill out the contemporary discussions of *nomos* and *phusis* and to show how those discussions could be brought home, quite specifically, to those discontented with democracy.

Thrasymachus of Chalcedon was a fifth-century sophist whose views are discussed in Plato's *Republic* Book 1. Like most other sophists, Thrasymachus is largely unknown to us outside the pages of Plato. I remain agnostic as to whether Plato's representation of him is accurate in philosophical essentials. The views attributed to him, though, are likely to have had currency in late fifth-century Athens. Thrasymachus' basic point was that justice is the good of another. He expressed this point in various ways, centering either on powerful individuals or, more relevantly for us, on governments (Text 10).

10. I say that justice is nothing other than the advantage of the stronger. . . . Each regime makes laws with a view to its own advantage. Democracy makes democratic laws, tyranny makes tyrannical laws, and the others do likewise. They say that this is what is just for their subjects: what benefits themselves. They punish anyone who transgresses their laws as a lawless wrongdoer. This, then, my good man, is what I say justice is, the same thing in all cities: the advantage of the existing regime. This surely is stronger; and so it turns out, for anyone who reasons correctly, that the same thing is just everywhere: the advantage of the stronger. (Plato, *Republic* 338c1–339a4)

For Thrasymachus, justice existed solely by convention and was a kind of "noble foolishness," in which people were taught to act contrary to their own real self-interests. (Strictly speaking, of course, his formulations appear to apply only to the weaker, law-abiding members of society, rather than to the law-making rulers. For the rulers, justice was by his definition *their own* good.) The life recommended by Thrasymachus is that of the strong man, or tyrant, who wins both happiness and others' approval through successfully acquiring as much wealth and power as possible (*Rep.* 343b–344c).

Thrasymachus' "sociology of law" constituted a serious attack on democratic "justice." Note the contrast with the Old Oligarch. In accordance with a long-standing political equation, the Old Oligarch had argued that the democratic system was essentially just in distributing political power to those who defended the city, i.e. the rowers. (It might also be tasteless, rude, uncivilized, etc., but it was basically just.) Thrasymachus, on the other hand, tried to "debunk" justice as it was understood and practiced in existing cities, including democratic Athens.[16] His view was that prevailing conceptions of justice are motivated by selfishness. The laws are rigged so as to benefit the rulers; democratic laws and "justice," as it is called, were designed to benefit the demos. Moreover, he

argued, anyone whose real interests are harmed b
regime, and who yet behaves "justly" and according t
standards, is merely foolish or cowardly or both.

Even though they were expressed in general formu
would have resonated with the resentful Athenian (
of Athens were set against the elite – at least in the perception of
some. Why should wealthy, exceptional Athenians be legally
required to contribute their bodies and money to a cause, such as
the Peloponnesian War, that they did not believe in? Moreover,
why did they not then derive greater benefits from the empire than
their poorer fellow citizens who contributed less? Such angry, even
revolutionary, questions follow from Thrasymachus' sociological
critique of contemporary practices of "justice."

According to other characters in the *Republic*, at any rate,
such attitudes were widespread in late fifth-century Athens. (Imperial Athens itself arguably educated its citizens to adopt Thrasymachean and Calliclean attitudes; see chapter 5, "Debating Athenian
Imperialism"). Plato's brothers Glaucon and Adeimantus report
that they constantly heard such arguments from Thrasymachus
and others (358c). Another form of this argument was put forward
by the brothers in *Republic* Book 2. They argue that, upon recognizing their own infirmity, the weak came to make laws, and to use
the word "justice," in order to prevent others from taking advantage of them. The weak rigged the system out of fear. In such
defensive social compacts the brothers find the origins and nature
of justice (Text 11).

> **11.** Justice is not approved because it is good; rather, it is honored
> because of people's inability to do wrong, since anyone capable of
> doing injustice, and any real man, would never make a compact with
> anyone not to do or suffer injustice. He would be crazy to do so. And
> so the nature of justice is this, and such as this, Socrates, and such
> are its natural origins, as the argument goes. (*Republic* 359a7–b5)

One might think such social compacts necessary or even
good, on the grounds that some natural impulses ought to be
limited by society. But the brothers argue that such a social compact
is contrary to our nature. To illustrate this point, they follow
up their "social contract" story with a narrative of the Lydian

shepherd Gyges, who once found a ring of invisibility. They use this narrative to ask the following question: why should someone with power, like Gyges, not pursue his selfish interests to the hilt, provided that he can be confident of never being caught and punished? After all, they say, we naturally pursue self-aggrandizement and self-indulgence as good, "but nature is forcibly led by law to honor equality" (359c). This contrast between *nomos* and *phusis* was not the subject of idle speculation. The brothers' overlap with Antiphon's theories is significant. The picture we are building shows that such "immoralist" challenges to conventional morality had a great deal of currency in certain elite circles in late fifth-century Athens.

Platonic characters did not have a monopoly on the politically embedded analysis of law and justice. Others too found that such apparently "objective" elements of social organization were based on a calculus of self-interest. Utilizing the *nomos/phusis* opposition, for example, an early fourth-century speaker said that "no human being is oligarchic or democratic by nature; but, rather, whichever constitution happens to benefit each man, that constitution is the one he exerts himself to establish" (Lysias 25.8). Nature was given a much more active role in the social thought of Callicles the Athenian, a star figure in the Platonic *Gorgias*. By proposing new theories of equality, natural justice, and self-interest, Callicles cast radical doubt on the democratic equation that added freedom to equality in order to yield justice.

Callicles is not known outside this Platonic dialogue, but most interpreters have understood him to be, like other Platonic characters, a real person who lived during the Peloponnesian War who possibly espoused the views attributed to him by Plato.[17] Callicles offered an analysis of convention and law similar to that of Plato's brothers. But he made the case against convention more powerful by proposing that nature establishes hierarchies among human beings, and therefore a standard of "natural justice." By the standards of "natural justice," democratic equality is manifestly unjust. Thus, natural hierarchy produces different standards of justice from those normally found in egalitarian society. The powerful, the strong, the intelligent, and the courageous have claims of justice, according to nature, that conventional law does not recognize – to its discredit. It would be an injustice to keep Callicles from speaking for himself (Text 12).

12. Shaping the best and most powerful among us, and taking them from youth, like lions, subduing them by charms and bewitching them, we enslave them, saying that it is necessary to have an equal share, and that this what is noble and just. But if (in my view) there arises a man with a sufficient nature, then shaking off all these constraints and bursting through them and escaping them, and treading upon our documents, our deceptions, our spells, and our laws, all of which are contrary to nature, and rising in rebellion, our slave is shown to be our master, and then the justice of nature shines forth. (Callicles in Plato's *Gorgias*, 483e4–484b1)

Like Antiphon, but unlike Thrasymachus, Callicles used nature as the basis from which to criticize conventional morality. We do not know whether Callicles was involved in the oligarchic activities of the late fifth century, but his ideas certainly speak to a revolutionary antidemocratic mentality. That this mentality was important and shared within the elite would help explain why Plato returned again and again to these themes.

Upholders of tradition, however, had to hand a set of responses to Callicles' arguments. It was possible to view *nomos* as itself the outgrowth of *phusis*. For example, an anonymous late fifth-century political thinker whose short treatise was found among the works of Iamblichus – who is therefore known as the "Anonymus Iamblichi" – argued that cities, justice, and law arose because of nature and natural needs (Text 13).

13. For if human beings are by nature incapable of living alone, but they came together with one another, yielding to necessity, and they discovered our entire way of life and all the crafts that are useful for it, and if it is not possible for them to live together with one another in a state of lawlessness (for this would be a greater punishment for them than living on their own), then law and justice rule over human beings because of such constraints, and in no way would they change; for they are fixed securely in our nature. (Anonymus Iamblichi 6.1 = DK 89, 6.1)

Contrary to Callicles, he argued that greed and self-interest were rooted in fear of death; that true power resulted from large groups' obedience to law and justice; and that, within a polis, lawfulness produces trust among citizens, strong resistance to tyrants, and a pleasant lifestyle. As we shall see, the idea that the polis was the product of nature, rather than *nomos* or a social compact, was developed powerfully by Aristotle in the late fourth century.[18] In context, though, the point is that Protagorean ideas about social unity and polis origins could be developed so as to counteract the prevailing sophistical antithesis between *phusis* and *nomos*.

We have no way of knowing whether the Anonymus Iamblichi was specifically prodemocratic or not, but his ideas solidify the institutions of democratic law and the value of democratic justice. Moreover, he provided a way to confront Callicles on his own terms. For if might naturally makes right, then the masses arguably had right on their side. The power of the masses could overwhelm that of any individual, however strong he may be.[19] Thus, the Anonymus offered resources for a powerful response to Callicles: he renewed the credibility of democratic institutions by accepting Callicles' premises and arriving at antithetical conclusions.

Thucydidean Imperialists Revisit *Nomos* and *Phusis*

Even so, the Anonymus did not pay sufficient attention to possible divisions within the citizen body. True, perhaps a single individual could not overcome the masses' power, but a group with outside help might be able to do so, not to mention a tyrant who could cynically persuade the masses to follow his self-interested lead. That is why a veritable chorus of voices exploited the fertile *nomos/phusis* distinction and attacked the democrats' ethics, laws, and system of distribution on that basis. The Anonymus did not stifle the conversations of the likes of Callicles. But where did such a selfish figure as Callicles come from? As we will explore in "Aristotle Analyzes Imperialism" in chapter 5 and "Plato on Rhetoric and Order in the *Gorgias*" in chapter 6, Plato and Aristotle often linked an individual's character to the character of the city in which he was raised. Through its imperialism, the Athenian democracy itself might have taught individuals to be selfish and self-aggrandizing, and therefore to exploit the *nomos/phusis* distinction for their own benefit. Several essential elements of such an analysis can be found in Thucydides' representation of the Athenians at Melos.

In 416 BC the Athenians attacked the tiny island of Melos, which had tried to remain independent of Athens. When that strategy failed, the Melians had gone over to the Spartan side. The Athenians arguably had to eliminate such signs of independence, and *a fortiori* of defiance, in order symbolically to maintain their stature throughout the empire. In his fifth book, Thucydides reports a conversation between certain Athenian ambassadors and unnamed Melian leaders in which both sides explored the implications of the Athenians' international *realpolitik*. The conversation probably never took place, at least in the form we have it. Real Athenian ambassadors would have avoided any implication that their position was less than just or honorable (cf. chapter 5, "Debating Athenian Imperialism"); consequently, the conversation represents Thucydides' own interpretation of the ethos that governed Athenian foreign policy. Since Thucydides had been an Athenian general, his views might approximate to the reality on the ground, in the sense that he grasped clearly the impulses, passions, and self-justifications that led the Athenians to act as aggressively as they did. His description gives us insight into how the *nomos/phusis* relationship could be exploited to suit particular policies of self-interest. But we should keep in mind that Thucydides drew a particular portrait of Athens in order to criticize the Athenians for their aggressiveness and abandonment of honorable political ideals.[20]

Throughout the so-called Melian Dialogue, the Melians exemplified traditional Greek religious beliefs and diplomatic ideas (Text 14).

14. Nevertheless, we have faith that the fortune which the god sends us will not be less than yours, since we are just men standing against men who are unjust. We also believe that our Lacedaemonian allies will help us in our weakness. They are bound to help us – if for no other reason, then at least because of our kinship and out of a sense of shame. (Thuc. 5.104)

They believed that the gods would help those who are just; they relied on vague hopes of good fortune; and, strikingly, they trusted in the Spartans' dedication to justice, nobility, and honor. Such views come across as wonderfully naive in the context of the ethical and military upheaval that had prevailed in Greece for roughly 15 years. With a coldly rational response, the Athenians sliced through the Melians' fleshy traditionalism in an arresting, and completely revealing, way (Text 15).

15. In our view the gods, as far as we can tell, and men, clearly, always rule over anyone they can through natural compulsion. We did not set up this law nor are we the first to abide by it. But we took it as it is; we will leave it for posterity; and we abide by it. We know that you, or anyone else with our sort of power, would do the same thing. . . . Don't you see that advantage comes with safety, and that doing what is just and noble means running risks? . . . Do not be seduced by a sense of honor, which very often destroys men when they foresee danger in which shame might be involved. Even to many men who see in advance the dangers into which they are led, the thing called "honor", through the alluring force of the word itself, draws them on, overcome by a mere word, to a point where they voluntarily fall into irreversible misfortune and incur a shame that is more shameful because it resulted from stupidity rather than chance. (Thuc. 5.105, 107, 111)

Nature itself contains laws of advantage and realities of power that override the mushy conventionality of value-terms such as honor. Like Callicles, the Athenians appealed to nature in order to justify their break with convention; like Thrasymachus, they evoked political (and military) realities in order to question the unthinking approval given to traditional value-terms, such as justice or honor. As his presentation shows, Thucydides' analysis is that the Athenians were, whether explicitly or (more likely) implicitly, acting on principles of self-interest similar to those articulated by Callicles.

At least until 411 BC, the Athenian democracy was a stable political system. The Athenians had apparently channeled ordinary human competitiveness and selfishness outward against other states, thereby establishing harmony in their domestic politics. As Thucydides Book 8 shows, however, their domestic harmony was fragile. The city had reared citizens who were willing to introduce greed, selfishness, and violence back within Athens. This would not be surprising, in view of the city's commitment to imperialism and (if Thucydides is correct) its use of the *nomos/phusis* antithesis to justify and explain its aggression. Combined with the view of the polis as a battleground, and with the anti-egalitarian theories of

law and justice we have explored, such a political "e
the citizenry was likely to have explosive results.
democracy itself was growing the seeds of antidemocra⌐
tion. Thucydides understood the relationship between the ⌐⌐
foreign policy and its education of its own citizens. He shaped the
Melian Dialogue with this relationship in mind, so as to advance
vivid and memorable criticisms of Athens's long-term imprudence
and injustice.

Socrates and *Nomos*

Even after the revolution of 411 BC, it is evident that the war had
taken its toll on the democrats' adherence to customary procedure.
In 406 BC, the Athenian navy won a critical battle amidst the
islands of Arginusae, but, because of a storm that arose immediately
after the victory, the generals were unable to rescue shipwrecked
Athenian crews. Two generals did not return to Athens; when the
other six returned to the city, they were put on trial as a group in
the Assembly. They were then pronounced guilty and executed for
failing to save their crews. According to Xenophon's account (*Hell.*
1.7.23–25), and according to the Platonic Socrates (*Ap.* 32b–c), this
contravened the Athenian law against giving "corporate" verdicts.
Scholars have disputed the legality or illegality of the Athenians'
procedure, but there is no doubt that the Athenians broke with
their customary rules in order to satisfy their anger.[21] Many contemporaries found their behavior unjust; antidemocrats took their
verdict as a sign of the democracy's intemperate and unjust character; and the Athenians themselves soon afterwards began to regret
this needless execution (Xen. *Hell.* 1.7.35). Thucydides was right:
war is a violent teacher and a teacher of violence (3.82).

The philosopher Socrates is reported to have made his political
debut by standing out against the Athenians at the trial of the
Arginusae generals (Text 16).

16. Men of Athens, I never held any other office in the city, except
when I served on the Council. And it happened that my own tribe
was presiding over the Council when you decided to put on trial, all
together, the ten generals who had not rescued the survivors from

the naval battle – illegally, as all of you later came to see. Then I alone of the presiding group opposed your desire to act contrary to the law, and I voted against you. Although the speakers were ready to hale me before the magistrates and take me off to prison, and you shouted encouragement for them to do so, nevertheless I knew I had to run the risk on behalf of the law and justice, rather than to side with you in your unjust deliberations, out of fear of prison or death. (*Ap.* 32a9–c3)

In this Platonic text, Socrates emphasized his commitment to law and justice. His words confirmed Xenophon's report that, in the midst of fear and suspicion during the trial, Socrates the son of Sophroniscus "said that he would not do anything except according to the law" (Xen. *Hell.* 1.7.15; cf. *Mem.* 4.4.2). At this trial, and at his own trial seven years later, Socrates adamantly affirmed his dedication to upholding the laws of city. In 406 BC, he implicitly stood as a reproach to the demos for not abiding by its own best principles. Only seven years later, in 399 BC, Socrates was sentenced to death on the charge that he "did wrong through corrupting the young men, and through not recognizing the gods which the polis recognizes, but instead other new divinities" (*Ap.* 24b; cf. *Euthyph.* 2b). His trial and execution were symptomatic of the democracy's anger, suspicion, and fear at the end of the fifth century.

Ever since, philosophers and political activists have viewed Socrates' execution as a powerful statement about the philosopher's relationship to politics. More particularly, they have tried to understand why Socrates, who believed in his own innocence, did not wish to escape from jail when offered that opportunity. Even as he waited to drink the notorious hemlock, Socrates insisted that trying to escape from prison would be unlawful and therefore unjust. As Xenophon says, "He preferred dying while abiding by the laws to saving his life through violating the laws" (*Mem.* 4.4.4). What is the significance of this mysterious figure for the history of Greek political thought, and particularly of his adamant affirmation of *nomos* in the late fifth-century world?

In order to answer these questions, it is crucial to locate Socrates in his historical context. To do so, however, is a delicate task of interpretation. Our sources for the historical Socrates are notoriously complex, so much so that the question of which representation is most accurate has long been known as "the Socratic problem." This appellation is striking because there are so many interesting philosophical questions that might have received the same title. The importance of "the Socratic problem" speaks to the widespread agreement that Socrates is a "patron saint" of philosophy even today; to his followers, it has always been critical to understand the relationship between Socrates' (real) life and his thought.

So too in the late fifth and early fourth centuries. Just after Socrates' death, many of his associates began to write "Socratic conversations" in order to commemorate this great figure and, often, in order to provide a defense of his life and thought. Some of these associates were Aeschines of Sphettus, Crito, and Antisthenes, but little of their literary output has survived. The chief extant sources are Aristophanes, Plato, Xenophon, and Aristotle. In the *Clouds* (423 BC), Aristophanes represents Socrates as the head of a "Thinkery" where students are taught sophistical rhetoric for a fee, and where intellectuals investigate natural phenomena such as the movements of the heavenly bodies. Although we learn from this comedy certain details of the public perception of Socrates in Athens, most scholars do not accept that Socrates taught rhetoric, investigated the natural world, or accepted fees for teaching. Such features of the Aristophanic character conflict radically with the representation of Socrates in the works of his sympathetic associates Plato and Xenophon. By contrast, Aristotle (*Metaphysics* 1078b27–32) provides the details that Socrates explored inductive reasoning and general definitions, but did not view universals or definitions as having a separate existence as Forms (on Forms, see "Philosophical Rulers" in chapter 6). These details help us to understand the representation of Socrates in the Platonic dialogues and perhaps, from there, to glean information about the historical Socrates. Even so, they do not directly help us grapple with Socrates' importance as an intellectual figure in late fifth-century Athens.

For insight into the relationship between Socrates' life and thought, and for more detailed study of his ethical and political philosophy, Plato and Xenophon are the principal sources. These are the only two early "Socratics" whose works have survived in entirety. As for the Platonic texts, our suspicion at first glance must be that these are literary works shaped and created by the thought of their author. However, the corpus of Plato, including certain works that are probably spurious, contains 20 works that might be labeled "Socratic." By this I mean that they represent Socrates conversing at Athens on topics and in ways that appear on independent evidence (such as that of Xenophon) to be true of the historical Socrates.[22] This says nothing about the precise chronology of their composition, either among themselves, or in relation to many other Platonic works. Among these works are *Apology, Euthyphro, Crito, Charmides, Laches, Lysis, Ion, Euthydemus, Protagoras,* the two *Hippias* dialogues, and *Gorgias.* In these dialogues Plato is interpreting Socrates' life and thought as he understood them. In them, for example, Plato does not show Socrates speculating about the Forms – a fact that, read alongside the Aristotelian evidence (above), suggests that Plato did not stray far from Socrates' own philosophical conversations, as Plato interpreted them.[23]

Because of Plato's status in the philosophical tradition – and because of the coherence, plausibility, and brilliance of his picture – his has long been regarded as providing a more accurate representation than the works of Xenophon. Many have preferred these dialogues to the works of Xenophon because of the perception that Xenophon used Plato's dialogues as a source for his own work, and because Xenophon's Socrates is (it is often said) not as philosophically interesting as Plato's. Plato's Socrates is at once gripping and maddening, whereas Xenophon's is duller, more traditional, and less moving. The contrast has led scholars to argue that Xenophon's hero, who is chiefly interested in home-spun morality and conventional advice-giving, could never have grabbed the attention of such a genius as Plato or given rise to the Western philosophical tradition.

I would argue that it is impossible at our distance to recover the historical Socrates in any satisfying detail. One of his most important features, indeed, was his ability to give rise to highly divergent interpretations of his life and thought.[24] And that is what we have – multiple interpretations, by two very different individuals, of what was important about Socrates' life and philosophy. Normally, as historians, we assume that authors shape their recollections of the past in such a way as to express and defend *their own* interests and concerns. Writers might preserve facts and plausible data, of course, but they interpret that data according to their own premises, commitments, anxieties, and world-views. As a result, their work often tells more about them and their own circumstances, rather than any prior period. This case is no different. Both Plato and Xenophon arguably preserved independent data about Socrates, and both interpreted that data in accordance with their own literary and philosophical agendas – including chiefly an interest in defending Socrates against attackers. Their facts may well be accurate; their interpretations are more likely their own.

To understand the opportunities – as well as the conflicts and problems – offered by our extant evidence, we can discuss the representations of Socrates in relation to *nomos*. Like the Anonymus Iamblichi, Socrates parted company with those contemporary philosophers, such as Callicles, who attacked commitment to the law in favor of self-interest. Plato explored Socrates' commitments through depicting a jail-house conversation between Socrates and Crito. Since the jury's verdict condemning Socrates was unjust, Crito asks, and since there is much philosophizing left to do, wouldn't it make sense for Socrates now to leave the city, save his own life, and carry on with his philosophical mission?

In the *Crito*, Socrates clarified his thoughts on that question through an imaginary conversation with the city's personified Laws (*Nomoi*). This was Plato's representation of how best to understand Socrates' behavior and thinking at the end of his life. Through the Laws' argument, Socrates affirmed that he (like other adult citizens) had benefited from the city's laws on procreation, marriage, child rearing, and so forth, and was therefore obligated either to persuade the city to change its laws, or to obey the existing laws (*Crito* 50e, 51d, 51e–52a). After his patriotic service to the city, he would cut an absurd figure if he now disobeyed the jury's verdict (Text 17).

17. "You left the city less often than the lame, the blind, and others similarly affected. Clearly the city and we, the laws, appeal to you so much more than to other Athenians. For who would love a city apart from its laws? Now, despite this, will you not abide by your agreement?" (*Crito* 53a)

His arguments emphasized the social compact between the citizen and the laws. Since the Athenian jury had condemned him through legally valid procedures, his disobedience at this point would irrevocably damage the laws.

Among many important issues, let us observe that Socrates presents himself as the child and servant of the laws (50e).[25] This is a powerful image. Read in the context of democratic law, this commits Socrates to a strongly authoritarian conception of the city's power over the individual. To a large extent, his attitude is continuous with the Athenian democratic belief that the individual must fear, respect, and obey the law. But, like Athenian democrats, Socrates could also criticize and try to change laws where he found it necessary. Moreover, Socrates recognized the possibility of legitimate disobedience to human law, if it conflicted with the divine mission to philosophize (*Apology* 29c–d); perhaps in that case the argument would be that the human law was not valid in the first place. (Note of course that it suits Plato's apologetic purposes to portray Socrates – who was convicted for impiety – as interested, above all, in abiding by the commands of the gods.)

Socrates argues however that, in the present case, civil disobedience is impossible for him because he has failed to persuade the jury of his own innocence. And his highest principle, he says, is the "no harm" principle (Text 18).

> **18.** Consider very well, then, whether you agree with me on this point, from which we can begin our discussion: that it is never right to do injustice or return an injustice or to defend oneself from suffering by retaliating – or do you disagree with this starting point? (Socrates, in Plato's *Crito*, 49d5–9)

This doctrine entails, in Socrates' view, that he not damage the laws with whom he has made a compact. Even if the jury's verdict harmed him (a controversial matter), he still could not return harm for harm.

Socrates' reasoning *resembles* what modern philosophers call "deontological" reasoning: he believes that the "no harm" doctrine must be followed for its own sake, as a matter of principle, and regardless of the consequences. But Socrates' case is different in an intriguing way. Socrates follows the no-harm doctrine, not so much because it is a non-negotiable rule, but because of his own self-image: his self-respect depends on not harming others. His principle derives from his character, not from his rigid adherence to rules. At the same time, he believes he must not damage the laws because doing so would have the harmful *consequences* of influencing young people negatively, and of damaging the well-being of the polis (*Crito* 53c, 54c). Thus we also find "consequentialist" moral reasoning – that is, reasoning driven by concern for the positive or negative consequences of behavior. By combining these two explanations, Socrates offered a model of ethical reasoning about his relation to the state that differs from most twentieth-century moral philosophy.

Xenophon's Socrates offers a less elaborate argument for the importance of law. According to Xenophon, Socrates equated the just with the lawful (*Mem.* 4.4.12). On the face of it, this theory holds little water: surely there can be unjust laws? Furthermore, what possible basis could a city have to change its laws if all laws were just? In the course of a notable mini-dialogue (*Mem.* 4.4), Socrates stresses the positive results of abiding consistently by all the laws of the state. He explains to the sophist Hippias that law-abiding cities fare well in war and peace and that, above all, they achieve the harmony that is crucial to, or even constitutive of, political health.[26] Xenophon's Socrates thus emphasizes the positive consequences of obeying the law, rather than adherence to any non-negotiable, or deontological, principle. He does not argue that the *concept* of justice can be specified by saying what is lawful, or vice versa; rather, his position is the less ambitious one that lawful acts are just acts. Thus, disobeying positive law can never be just, because, as he explains in detail, its consequences are destructive. The only ground for criticizing positive laws could be that the laws as written violate higher (i.e. divine) laws, not that they are unjust. This is a simplified form of the "consequentalist" argument designed to show that the legal is always just, because obeying the laws is always beneficial.

On the basis of this fundamental agreement in our sources, we have strong reasons to view the historical Socrates as both interested in theoretical questions of law, and as doggedly committed to upholding the laws of the state. This commitment applies even when an individual law or ruling appears to him wrong – possibly because disobedience, or even picking and choosing which laws to follow, would cause great harm either to the laws or to his fellow citizens or both. The likelihood that Socrates was strongly interested in questions of law is increased by Plato's presentation of Socrates in the *Hippias Major* (284d1–e8), where Socrates maintains that law, truly so called, can never be unjust, even if many existing laws are unjust. Such rules simply do not deserve the name of "law."

Note how much this legal "idealism" conflicts with Xenophon's picture of Socrates as committed to legal "positivism."[27] It also conflicts – albeit less forcefully – with Socrates' affirmation of Athens's positive law in the *Crito*. We will probably never know with certainty which of these stances, if any, was Socrates' own – or whether his views changed over time. Even so, it is fair to say that the historical Socrates worked to counteract the late fifth-century challenges to law. Because of his commitment to his native city of Athens, it is also arguable that he thereby strengthened and deepened the democratic commitment to law.

Logos and *Ergon*

Socrates' case shows that arguments about *nomos* and *phusis* could be framed with reference to integrity. Socrates maintained integrity by renouncing the trial of the generals and by adhering steadfastly to his earlier agreements with the law. By upholding the value of law even at the cost of his life, he matched his deeds with his words and abided by his life-long commitment to the laws of Athens. He exemplifies democratic ideals better than all living democrats. To this extent his life and thought constitute a criticism of democrats, but an ameliorative one. Democracy's ideals are generally worth subscribing to. Real-life democrats, however, often do not recognize what their ideals demand, nor have they cultivated an ethical character capable of living up to their ideals.

In the *Laches*, Plato repeatedly emphasized Socrates' efforts to match words with deeds and deeds with words. Socrates argued that courage (which the discussants are trying to define) cannot exist without a genuine harmony of the two. Of all the speakers involved, including two Athenian generals, Socrates is represented as being the most likely to achieve such a harmony. This aspect of Socratic integrity is also strongly emphasized by Xenophon (*Mem.* 4.4.1, 4.4.10). Since there is no reason to think that Xenophon took the idea from Plato in the passages cited, it is reasonable to suppose that matching words with deeds was an important attribute of Socrates' own self-image and way of life, which his students tried to capture, explain, and glorify. Note that, in these authors' treatments, a recognized Athenian ideal – that of matching deeds with words – was best exemplified by a single Athenian, Socrates. Other

Athenians, by implication, had difficulty living up to their own political ideals. Even if Xenophon and Plato later used this feature of Socratic integrity to criticize and reject democracy, it is likely that Socrates' way of life, and his public arguments, provided guidance to democrats on how to become their "best selves." Socrates had a genuine interest in improving the ethical character of his fellow citizens.

Others, by contrast, exploited the distinction between words and deeds in order to dignify their pursuit of selfish and materialistic goals. When, for example, the Athenians at Melos poured scorn on the word "honor," they contrasted speech (*logos*) with deeds or realities (*ergon*, pl. *erga*) and implicitly set the latter in a privileged position. This rhetoric had a substantial impact on individuals. For individuals within Athens could equally well argue that conventional values (such as those of Athenian democracy) were simply words, or names, with no firm basis in reality. And that sequence of thought could lead to arguments such as those of Callicles.

A dramatic adaptation of such arguments can be found in a moving confrontation in Euripides' *Phoenician Women*. This play was staged in 409 BC, just two years after the violent oligarchic revolution of 411 BC. It might be read as a commentary on the oligarchs' violent uprising. After Oedipus had gone into exile and left Thebes in political disarray, Oedipus's son Polyneices returned to Thebes in order to stake his rightful claim to the throne. His brother Eteocles, now in power, refused to abide by their agreement to rule in turn. Their mother Jocasta urges them to avoid immediate violence, on the grounds that careful deliberation will lead to the best outcome (453).

But their conversation quickly turns into a quarrel. Polyneices declares that the justice of his claim to the throne is obvious, because of their previous agreement; compare Socrates' arguments from previous compacts. Eteocles retorts that mere words do not even reflect, much less produce, shared values among those with competing conceptions of self-interest (Text 19).

19. If everyone defined justice and wisdom the same way, there would be no quarreling or strife among men. As things stand, the only similarity or equality mortals show is in their use of words: the reality to which these refer is not the same. . . . I would go to where

> heaven's constellations rise, go beneath the earth, if it lay in my
> power, in order to possess Tyranny, greatest of the gods. . . . It is
> unmanly to give up the greater thing and take the lesser. . . . I shall
> never surrender my kingship to him. If one must commit injustice,
> it is best to do so for the sake of tyranny, being god-fearing in all
> else. (Eteocles, in Euripides, *Phoenician Women*, 499–525, tr. D. Kovacs,
> ed. and tr., *Euripides V*, Loeb Classical Library, Cambridge, Mass.,
> 2002)

Eteocles transforms his interesting observations on the meanings
and referents of words into the basis for his "immoralist" pursuit
of tyranny. In the absence of shared moral understanding, Eteocles
reverts, like Callicles and the Corcyraeans, to the value of "manliness" or "courage" in pursuing his own narrowly defined self-
interest. Words are merely a "technology" of power for those capable
of utilizing them effectively. Eteocles refuses to "rule and be ruled
in turn" – a democratic catch-phrase – but rather, in the absence
of compelling *nomoi*, falls back confidently on his desire to get
more. Courage and greed – those, at least, were the pragmatic values
that a man like Eteocles could understand. Mere words made little
difference.

Democratic Epistemology and Relativism

Yet in democratic Athens mere words made a great deal of difference. Words uttered in the Assembly could be translated into laws
and decrees, with lasting results, as the Melians found out; and
words uttered in the courts led to judicial decisions (themselves
embodied in words), which also had practical significance, as
Socrates knew. Thus it was only natural for democracy's critics to
lodge complaints against the regime's public "words." They did so
chiefly through their focus on democratic *epistemology* – a transition
made easier by the Greek term *logos*, which means both "word" and
"reason," "account," "argument." How could the intemperate and
uneducated demos correctly harness its public "words" to achieve
positive results in the real world? How could the demos govern the
city, much less an empire, with adequate foresight? What, if anything, could the demos allege as its source of knowledge for using
language to establish a healthy political culture? Such questions

usually informed the elitist tenor of antidemocratic thought we have thus far considered.

To see what the antidemocrats were attacking, let us consider again, but from a different perspective, what might be said on the democrats' behalf. Scholars sometimes point out the connections between democratic deliberation and the relativist epistemology most famously articulated by Protagoras. Protagoras' general relativism was summed up in his well-known "Man-measure" doctrine (Text 20).

> **20.** Man is the measure of all things, of the things that are that they are, and of the things that are not, that they are not. (Protagoras, cited by Socrates at Plato, *Theaetetus* 152a2–4, tr. Guthrie, *Sophists*, 171)

Plato's Socrates interpreted this to mean that if the wind feels cold to me, then it is cold for me; whereas if it feels cold to you, then it is cold for you (*Theaetetus* 152b). To probe the complexities of this provocative claim would take us beyond the scope of this book, but most of the discussion is irrelevant for our specific purposes.[28]

What is relevant, however, is that one might attempt to defend democracy on the basis of Protagorean relativism. Some scholars, indeed, have viewed Protagoras' Great Speech (cf. chapter 3, "Protagorean Arguments for Democracy") as closely connected to his relativism. Relativism might be held to support democratic procedure in two ways. First, one could argue that relativism encourages people to grant respect to the opinions of their fellow citizens, on the grounds that all perceptions must be taken into account.[29] The opinions of ordinary people are worth considering by virtue of their human capacity to "measure." Thus, through its practices of deliberation, etc., democracy would be recognizing this fact of human epistemology. Note that if categories such as the "just" and the "fine" are relative to the individual, then Eteocles' analysis of justice might have an epistemological plausibility that it would not have had otherwise.

Second, one could raise Protagorean relativism to the level of a political culture as a whole: democratic deliberation results in decisions that seem (and therefore *are*) best for democrats, and so forth.

Therefore, Protagoras's epistemology, like his Great Speech support-
ing equality, might help to justify the decision-making procedures
of the democratic Assembly. Even if the democratic citizenry is
largely and necessarily composed of non-experts, the Assembly can
still make good political decisions, by virtue of acting on what *seems*
best to the citizens. Note, however, that Protagoras's relativism
could, given the right conditions, also strengthen and embolden
antidemocrats who viewed politics as simply a game of power. In
other words, Protagorean relativism, if understood at the level of
the entire culture, does not grant any privileges to democracy as
opposed to oligarchy, monarchy, tyranny, and so forth.[30]

Whichever path one chooses, however, the chief problem with
Protagorean relativism in general, but particularly at the level of
political culture, is that it appears to be self-refuting.[31] Take, for
example, the case of Assembly decisions. As Socrates points out in
Plato's *Theaetetus* (177c–179b), the Assembly might make decisions
one day on the basis of what the citizens think best; and that, on
the premises given, will be best for the city. In the future, however,
the citizens might come to believe that their decision has been
harmful to the city, in which case their former decision was wrongheaded, full stop.[32] Even at this point, however, some have tried to
save Protagorean relativism by distinguishing between claims about
advantage and claims about the fine and the just. Whether or not
such moves work, in the end, is unclear; in any event, relativism
turns out to be a hard position (or set of related positions) either
to justify or to dispose of quickly.

It might also be relevant, finally, that the "'live and let live'"
character of Athenian private freedom was based on a kind of relativism.[33] But Athenians themselves were not known for relativist
views. Athenian private freedom, for example, derived from respect
for other citizens rather than from relativism. Athenians respected
their fellow citizens enough to allow them to make their own,
potentially misguided choices, at least when such choices did not
adversely affect the community. Although they legally allowed a
variety of lifestyle choices, Athenians often criticized one another's
choices in terms of the virtues and vices (cf. chapter 3). This would
not make sense if they subscribed to (individual) relativism.

In public forums, moreover, Athenian democratic ideology took
a strongly non-relative stance in relation to the well-being and
wisdom of the city. Democrats thought that their assembly-

meetings and other public practices helped them arrive at the best decisions, full stop. They also believed that others' opinions should be taken into account as a matter of respect and equality, not because of a relativistic epistemology. They criticized one another's views as wrong, full stop, and did not allow that equal weight should be given, in the end, to all views. They believed that the democratic virtues turned people into more flourishing human beings, full stop. They argued, moreover, that their way of life was best; that their lawgivers generally got it right; and so forth, without qualification. This did not mean that mistakes were impossible; rather, it meant that in general and over time the institutions, laws, and citizens of Athens would produce the best results for the community at large. And Athenians believed that their city was an education for others, the best possible place to live, and the most conducive to the happiness of its citizens (cf., e.g., Thuc. 2.37.1, Aesch. 3.4–6). Without expressing the point philosophically, Athenian democrats believed strongly in the existence of clear and nonrelative standards of individual and political health.

By the late fifth century, of course, many democrats were familiar with cultural diversity. For example, Herodotus's *Histories* illustrated the diverse customs and political structures that could be found throughout the known world. But it is not clear that he or many others would have taken this as an argument for cultural relativism. Herodotus's endorsement of the Pindaric line "*nomos* is king," and his statement that "everyone judges that his native *nomoi* are by far the finest" (3.38), might appear, at first glance, to imply cultural relativism. Yet, upon reflection, even Herodotus' statements carry no such implication.[34] In these and other passages, Herodotus observes that customs differ without arguing that all beliefs are equally plausible. Herodotus did argue that human cultures ought to be respected, or at least not ridiculed, for their diverse beliefs (3.38). But he also implied that political systems with values such as *isonomia* (equality under the law) achieved better results than others, e.g. the Persian monarchical system, that lacked such values. His *History* conveyed the message that one could arrive at an understanding of healthy politics through observing who won important wars, whose system was durable, and whose citizens were happier.

The Athenians agreed. Democrats hoped to arrive at correct ethical and political decisions through submitting questions to public scrutiny and debate; they believed in the possibility of a prudent and informed democratic citizenry; and, therefore, their public speeches were thought to lead, and to a large extent did lead, to successful practical decisions and behavior. Their success in the world depended on their correct perceptions of political and military realities, full stop.

Democratic Epistemology and Untrustworthy Rhetoric – or, Where Does the Truth Lie?

It was principally the democratic claim to practical wisdom that democracy's critics seized upon and rejected. Democracy's critics were not relativists, either; they thought the democracy often made ethical and prudential mistakes. Consider the powerful image utilized by Herodotus' Megabyzus to characterize democratic imprudence and stupidity (Text 21).

> **21.** If a king does something, he does it on the basis of his judgment; but the masses lack intelligence. How could they understand anything? They have not been taught and do not understand anything noble and proper. They rush into politics rashly and without sense, just like a river flowing furiously. (Megabyzus, Hdt. 3.81)

Or the heartfelt words of Euripides' Theban Herald in the *Suppliants* (420s BC): "How would the demos be able to rule the city in the right way if it cannot judge speeches correctly?" (417–18). Thucydides and Socrates rank as the chief fifth-century critics of democratic epistemology.

Thucydides' *History* scrutinizes democratic "knowledge" and finds it wanting.[35] For example, he ostentatiously corrects democratic traditions about the deposal of the Peisistratid tyrants at the end of the sixth century (6.53–9; Text 22).

> **22.** The mass of Athenians, at any rate, imagine that Hipparchus was tyrant when he was killed by Harmodius and Aristogeiton. They do not know that Hippias, the oldest of Peisistratos' sons, had power then, and Hipparchus and Thessalos were his brothers. (Thuc. 1.20.2)

In his Assembly scenes these criticisms proved even more devastating. In 415 BC, for example, the Athenians debated the feasibility and prudence of attacking Sicily while carrying on the war against Sparta at full tilt on the mainland. At the beginning of his sixth book, Thucydides had provided a detailed history of Sicily's complex habitation patterns, inter-ethnic contacts, and political development. This alerted his careful readers to take note of the unfounded assumptions that guided the ensuing debate over Sicily. The eventual "winner" of the "Sicilian Debate," Alcibiades, established a coalition of citizens willing to fight for all the wrong reasons: personal gain, excitement, feelings about their own masculinity, destructive ambition, and fear. Their emotional decision was guided by the superficially plausible, but ultimately untested and perhaps self-interested, assertions of the leaders (Text 23).

> **23.** The cities are full of mobs of people, all mixed together, and their citizen bodies often experience changes and additions. Therefore, no one arms himself for battle or defends the countryside in the usual sorts of fortifications, as though he were doing it for his own fatherland. . . . It is unlikely that a crowd like this would be united in its purpose or embark on action in common. More likely is that they will come over to us if we say things to gratify them, especially if they are in a state of civil war, as we have learned is the case. (Alcibiades, at Thuc. 6.17)

Only the eventual *ergon* of defeat could convince the Athenians that their *logoi* had gone badly astray. Thucydides exploited the *logos/ergon* distinction to explain why the Athenians were defeated in Sicily. By the time they lost, Alcibiades had gone into exile and was fighting for the other side.

Thucydides' concerns about democratic rhetoric were widespread. Both democrats and their rivals worried that public rhetoric was a slippery and uncertain tool with which to make life-or-death decisions. Practically speaking, this worry was understandable: what if unscrupulous speakers using the latest techniques persuaded citizens to behave unethically or imprudently or both? Correctly perceiving what is just and advantageous is more difficult that it might appear.

Aristophanes rendered the humorous possibilities of unscrupulous rhetoric in his *Clouds* of 423 BC. As the head of a comic

"Thinkery," Socrates taught students to master verbal tricks so as to gain release from paying debts, criminal prosecution, and the wearisome responsibilities of quotidian life. To draw attention to the untrustworthy cleverness of contemporary politicians, Aristophanes staged a mock debate between two personified arguments, "Better Argument" and "Worse Argument." Worse Argument declares that he will outshine his rival through inventing novel rhetorical devices – to which Better Argument replies, "Such things flourish here, through the ignorance of these men (the spectators)" (897–8). The exchange suggests that, even in their crucial civic capacity, the Athenian citizens had become mere hedonistic spectators of speeches (cf. Thuc. 3.38). This criticism gained force from Aristophanes' indication that sophistical rhetoric was impressively clever, but ultimately selfish and empty (Text 24).

> **24.** In fact, for a long time I've been choking in my bowels and I've been wanting to confound all this with contrary arguments. For I am known as the "worse argument" among those with any sense, for this very reason, that I first invented ways to argue against the laws and against what is right. This ability is worth more than many millions – to choose the weaker position and then to win the argument. (Worse Argument, Aristophanes, *Clouds*, 1036–1042)

The emptiness became all the more complete when Worse Argument asked why Zeus hadn't been punished for chaining up his own father, if justice truly resides with the gods!

Rhetoric had potentially subversive qualities.[36] Rhetoric became particularly problematic in Athens because certain sophists had worked to strengthen its philosophical and pedagogical basis, and came to Athens to disseminate their discoveries. Gorgias of Leontini, for example, sent to Athens as an envoy in 427 BC, argued that speech had an enchanting effect on the soul, even to the extent of being capable of exonerating Helen of Troy of any wrongdoing (Text 25).

> **25.** For speech, persuading the soul which it persuaded, forced it both to obey what was said and praise what was done. . . . The power of speech has the same relation to the state of the soul as the power

of drugs has to the nature of bodies. For just as some drugs draw out certain fluids from the body, and others other fluids, and some put an end to disease, and others put an end to life, so too with speeches: some cause grief, some bring delight, some cause fear, and others make their audience bold, while still others drug and charm the soul with an evil persuasion. (Gorgias, *Helen*, 12, 14 [= *DK* 82 B 11])

Moreover, apparently building on his own relativist theories, Protagoras wrote a work in two books called *Contradictory Arguments* (*Antilogiai*). This is a mere title to us, but Aristotle ascribed to Protagoras the promise that he could "make the weaker argument stronger" (*Rhet.* 2.1402a23) – precisely the rhetorical strategy satirized by Aristophanes.

Such works appear to have influenced the anonymous writer of a short treatise written around 400 BC, called the *Dissoi Logoi* (*Double Arguments*). This treatise puts forward arguments about the nature of good and bad, the fine and the disgraceful, justice and injustice, and so forth, in a way that illustrates the potential problem: "Twofold arguments are also put forward concerning the just and the unjust. And some say that the just is one thing and the unjust another, and others that the just and the unjust are the same. And I shall try to support the latter view" (*Dissoi Logoi* 3.1).[37] Relativism and rhetoric constituted a powerful and dangerous combination. In such an intellectual climate, contemporaries might well question the value of sophistically informed public speaking as a proper guide to democratic decision-making.

Interestingly, the relativist views embodied in these works were viewed by democrats as potential problems, not as the basis of their democratic politics. However, since careful observers tended to view "sophistical" rhetoric as characteristic of democracy, the Athenians seemed to be always teetering on a slippery slope. For one thing, Plato represented Gorgias as teaching rhetoric without having considered very deeply whether his students understand the nature of right and wrong (*Gorg.* 459d–60a). Thucydides, on the other hand, emphasized that democratic debate was always put at risk by the rivalry between speakers, the ignorance of impressionable crowds, and the tendency of individuals to pursue their own interests as opposed to those of the city. For example, Diodotus, an otherwise unknown speaker, highlights the justified fear any speaker must experience in presenting his views to the citizenry (Text 26).

---

26. If anyone is suspected of corruption, but nevertheless gives the best advice, we begrudge him the alleged profits to such an extent that we deprive the city of the clear benefits he has to offer. It is an established principle with us that good advice frankly offered is no less suspicious than bad advice. As a result, it is as necessary for the speaker pushing through awful measures to win over the people by deception, as it is for the speaker with good advice to lie in order to be considered trustworthy. (Thuc. 3.43)

He pinpoints the problems of civic trust and leadership that might be intrinsic to democratic deliberation. Diodotus' rival Cleon lambasted the Athenian audience for their role in corrupting deliberation. According to Cleon, Athenians had become mere "spectators of speeches, rather than citizens deliberating about the city" (Thuc. 3.38).[38]

Thucydides was not alone in emphasizing the deficiencies of democratic deliberation. His near-contemporary Herodotus reported that the Athenian Assembly was easily deceived by self-interested speakers, such as Aristagoras of Miletus (5.97). And, more similar to the cases in Thucydides, Herodotus shows that the demos' greedy desires sometimes affected their sound judgment, as when they made an expedition with Miltiades to Paros in order to get rich quick (6.132). The structure of democratic debate left Athens's Assembly open to criticism along such lines, because democracy depended on the free expression of conflicting ideas, the turmoil and instability of ongoing debate, and the participation of all citizens whether rich or poor. But, whereas democracy represented argumentative conflict as a political and epistemological virtue, its critics seized upon it as the source of radical democratic misjudgment.

Thucydides' key point was that democratic rhetoric and deliberation were no substitute for precise knowledge about history and about prevailing political and military realities. In any realistic politics, *ergon* – just the facts – must take priority over *logos* – mere words. This strongly held conviction, however, does not make Thucydides' critique of democracy a simple one. Oligarchs, too, often made bad decisions, as did the Melians in their highly imprudent decision to resist Athenian power. Sometimes, moreover, the Athenian democracy could get it right, in Thucydides' view, as when the Athenians decided, overriding a previous decision, to spare the lives of most citizens of Mytilene, and merely to execute the leaders of the Mytilenian revolt from Athens. Both morally (as in this case) and practically (as in their acquisition of the empire), democratic success raised a large question for Thucydides' criticisms.

If democracy was addle-brained and greedy, and if the Assembly often made bad decisions, then how did the Athenians achieve such startling success in the real, competitive world of Greek politics? To this question, Thucydides offered an interesting answer: that (somehow) outstanding leaders rose to the summit of politics and led the people, willy-nilly, to do the right thing for the city. Under Pericles, for example, Thucydides says that Athens was a "democracy in name only, but in fact it was governed by its first man" (2.65). Athens could succeed, in Thucydides' view, only as a sort of monarchy in disguise. (Note that one of Thucydides' ablest modern interpreters and translators, Thomas Hobbes, read Thucydides as an avowed monarchist.) For this reason, Athens's success does not undermine Thucydides' criticisms of democracy as a system, because the system itself cannot guarantee that a new Pericles will arise or even be recognized as an outstanding leader. Rather, on Thucydides' account, Athens's post-Periclean leaders tended to be selfish, unpatriotic, and more concerned to outdo their political rivals than to advise the city well. Thus, despite his own evocation of Athenian brilliance in his funeral oration (2.36–45), Pericles himself can be criticized for failing to understand his own significant place in the democratic system. In Thucydides' view, at least, democratic ideology narrowed the horizons even of the most outstanding democratic leader.[39]

Socrates and Athens

Socrates' critique was multi-layered and rather different. In the trial of Socrates as represented by Plato, Socrates cross-examined Meletus, one of his prosecutors, about the charge that he had corrupted the youth. In response to Socrates' questions, Meletus asserted that the laws and the ordinary citizens educated the young in positive ways, whereas Socrates harmed them. To this Socrates rejoined that only experts, not the mass of ordinary citizens, were capable of improving horses; isn't the same true, by analogy, of improving human beings (25a–c)? His argument implies an objective conception of human flourishing analogous to the flourishing condition produced in horses by expert trainers.

More importantly, his argument also expresses antipathy toward democratic decision-making. This *technê* argument, or argument from expertise, was a common one in the Socratic arsenal; Socrates worked *from* expertise in a recognized human endeavor (i.e., horse breeding), to the murkier issues of the human soul. Xenophon and Plato alike provide numerous notices that Socrates used the *technê* argument to criticize the democratic Assembly. In Plato's *Protagoras*, for example, Socrates argued that virtue is knowledge, and knowledge is available only to the few, if to any at all. His argument criticizes the democrats' self-confident claims to knowledge or prudence, not to mention virtue (Text 27).

> **27.** I observe, then, that when we meet in the Assembly, when the city must undertake some building project, we send after architects and consult them about our projects; and when we are concerned with shipbuilding, we send for the shipbuilders, and similarly with all other things, whatever they think can be learned and taught. . . . But when it is necessary to deliberate about the administration of the city, then a builder stands up to advise them about these things, or a smith, or a shoemaker, a merchant or ship's captain, rich or poor, well-born or not, and no one rebukes these men . . . on the grounds that they did not study anywhere, or that they had no teacher. (Socrates, in Plato, *Protagoras*, 319b5–d5)

Similar arguments are expressed by Xenophon's Socrates (e.g., *Memorabilia* 1.2.9, 3.1.4–5, 3.7.5–9). It is plausible to ascribe this type of argument, in its essentials, to the historical Socrates, even if we are uncertain as to the precise contexts in which he deployed it. For Socrates, provided that experts are available, they – and not the demos or its orators (cf. *Gorg.* 455b–c) – should be consulted on all important political matters. This view directly contradicted the democracy's conventional ideas about education – as expressed in Protagoras's myth, in Athenian oratory, and in the responses of the democratic prosecutor Meletus. How, then, did Socrates view himself in relation to democracy – and, equally important, how was he viewed?

Later in the Platonic *Apology*, Socrates presented himself as the benefactor of the Athenian demos. He compared the demos to a horse and himself to a gadfly who spends his days stirring up the demos and upbraiding it (30e), so as to improve the Athenian citizenry morally (cf. 31b). The demos needs improvement because it is lazy (30e), cowardly (34e–35b, 38d–e), greedy, and misguided (29d–e). At his trial, therefore, Socrates presented himself as an ameliorative critic of democracy who used his considerable gifts to teach the highly imperfect Athenians where their true interests lay. (Again, of course, this might be a useful rhetorical stance to adopt while on trial.)

This did not mean that he himself claimed the knowledge he thought necessary for the full achievement of virtue. Rather, he saw himself as more enlightened than his fellows, in as much as he knew that he lacked wisdom of the greatest and most important things (i.e., ethical truths), whereas his fellow citizens were unaware of their ignorance. Taking into account Socrates' attitude toward law, and toward the ethical well-being of his fellow citizens, we might conclude that Socrates was an ameliorative critic who tried to inspire the Athenians to see the full implications of their ideals, and to live up to them. If we view Socrates as having lived an exemplary life on fundamentally Athenian premises, then I think we can see why his life and thought had such a claim on his fellow citizens. They did execute him, true, but they could not ignore him.

Socrates' desire to improve his fellow citizens must not mask the potentially radical implications of his political ideas. He rejected the Athenians' standard approach to civic education; he rejected the democratic claim to wisdom; and he refuted all interlocutors who thought they could offer a convincing account of virtue or of their own lives. Socrates found democracy to be a highly defective form of government. Scholars have argued, though, that this critical position is softened by Socrates' belief that attaining moral truth is impossible for human beings. In that case democracy might be a reasonable solution; or, at least, it might be more costly than it is worth to try to change democracy.[40]

I think we should reject this view. Socrates always sought after wisdom and assumed that epistemological progress was possible. He thought, moreover, that it was possible to find greater and lesser degrees of approximation to wisdom. Socrates himself is an example of someone who, in his own view, achieved a higher degree of enlightenment than his contemporaries; and his discussions would have been futile unless he believed that he, and others, could learn something valuable from them. Therefore, even if human beings can never acquire full moral expertise, it would seem reasonable for Socrates to endorse granting political power to those with a greater, rather than a lesser, degree of moral enlightenment.

We might ask why Socrates did not, in that case, pursue a more active political life, in the hopes of improving the city through ameliorating its public institutions. During the trial of the Arginusae generals, at least, Socrates took a public stand against what came to be widely acknowledged as an unjust procedure. Why didn't he do more of the same at other times – for example, when the Athenians were voting on the execution of the Mytilenians, or on their expeditions to Melos or Sicily, or on their gruesome attacks on Scione, or on the proposal to crucify the Samian rebels? And, moreover, why did he not work to reshape democratic institutions altogether, in accordance with his beliefs about moral progress? On his own account, the Athenian polis would have been better off if he or his friends had somehow won political power and tried to reform the demos' character so as to prevent, or at least limit, its tendency to commit injustice.

His own answer was resolutely pragmatic: no one who opposes democracy and tries to prevent injustice can escape with his life. "The man who truly fights on behalf of justice, even if he intends to stay alive only briefly, must remain a private citizen and not enter public life" (*Apology* 31e–32a; cf. 32e). Socrates believed that he could improve the Athenians' character more successfully by engaging in private conversation – as we see him doing in Plato and Xenophon – than by undertaking political, much less revolutionary, action. He may have been right. No antidemocratic thinkers could argue that the Athenians were unsuccessful at achieving their objectives, wrongheaded as they may have been. If Athenian democracy was nearly unstoppable, then Socrates' calculation may have been reasonable. He would have reduced his salutary moral impact if he had rashly entered politics, only to be "eliminated" by those with a material stake in the status quo. Compatibly with this response, Socrates also persuasively redefined the "political" so to as to claim, sincerely, that he himself was the only true politician in Athens (*Gorg.* 521d; cf. "Plato on Rhetoric and Order in the *Gorgias*" in chapter 6). By this he meant that he was the only citizen to put forward arguments designed not to flatter or gratify his fellow citizens, but rather to make them better.

Others might take a different view. Consider, for example, Socrates' refusal to participate in the execution of a certain Leon of Salamis, when ordered by the 30 Tyrants to fetch Leon from his home. Socrates says that though he could have been executed for disobeying, he did not follow orders but simply went home (*Ap.* 32c–e). He cited this as an example of his integrity; Socrates' integrity under pressure is a leitmotif of the accounts of Plato and Xenophon. Characteristically, Socrates stressed that he lived up in action to what he had always said in his conversations: "Then again I showed not only in words but also in action that death is, to put the matter very directly, of no concern to me at all; but it means everything to me not to do anything unjust or unholy" (*Ap.* 32d). A point of lesser interest is that Socrates (who adamantly affirmed the law) did not obey a command of the prevailing authorities; but this apparent inconsistency can be explained if we assume that he did not recognize the 30 oligarchs as a legitimate political authority. More importantly, though, why did Socrates fail to take a public stand against this command? Why didn't he leave the city in protest in order to join the democratic resistance?[41]

Socrates might again reply that he could do more good alive than dead; that there was effectively nothing he could do to stop the execution of Leon; and that joining the resistance was too risky, in light of his god-given mission to rouse and improve the Athenians like a gadfly. But none of this is convincing. Lesser intellects might be attracted to the straightforward idea that true moral heroes show heroic concern for others and stand by their convictions to the death. That is what we can observe in heroes such as Jesus Christ and Martin Luther King. As it is, Socrates' stance on the Leon of Salamis affair is too self-serving for his own moral good. Or, to put it more charitably, Socrates took a reasonably courageous stand in refusing to follow the Tyrants' orders, but he did not show himself to be a moral hero – a status that both Plato and Xenophon claimed for him.

In this light, consider also Socrates' attitude toward the Athenian empire. Athens's imperial subjects felt unjustly burdened by the demand for tribute and by the Athenians' interference in their domestic politics (cf. "Debating Athenian Imperialism" in chapter 5). The Athenians themselves may have recognized and worried that their empire was (at least to some extent) tyrannical and unjust. Socrates, though, is frequently said to have served courageously and patriotically in the Athenians' foreign wars. He himself apparently considered this service a sign of his courage, sense of honor, and obedience to Athenian officials. The Athenians might have argued that their empire was just or necessary or both – and Socrates might have agreed. He might also have figured that he had to serve in order to defend Athens; and, after all, he had been commanded to fight by Athenian laws to which he owed obedience, unless he could persuade the demos to change them.

Yet, in his account of the Leon of Salamis episode, and frequently elsewhere, Socrates makes much of his unwillingness to harm others. Even if Socrates could argue that he fought to defend the city, on just grounds, he still had to confront a set of thorny questions. I do not think he ever did so. Was his military service not in aid of Athenian imperialism, which was an expression of the Athenians' acquisitiveness and lust for power? By serving on campaign, did he not thereby promote in his fellow citizens all the baser human instincts which he set himself against throughout his entire life? Did he not convey the wrong message by risking his life in order to strengthen the Athenian Empire? That was not a good way to care for the souls of either foreigners or his fellow citizens. And surely higher laws against harm should have militated against his obeying the human laws promoting imperialism.

For all his justified criticism of democracy on ethical and intellectual grounds, therefore, Socrates too can be criticized for failing to live up, maximally, to his own ideals. It was not for this reason, of course, that the Athenian jury condemned him. Rather, their verdict resulted much more from the atmosphere of anger and suspicion that characterized the city in the late fifth century. Socrates was a crank, yes, but he was executed because he was an *untimely* crank. At the end of the war, contemporaries found Socrates' influence on Critias, Alcibiades, and others to be worthy of serious punishment; thus, in the *Memorabilia*, Xenophon took pains to reduce the impact of Socrates' supposed "teaching" of these individuals (cf. the report in Text 28).

28. Did you, men of Athens, then execute Socrates the sophist, because he was shown to have been Critias' teacher, one of the thirty men who destroyed the democracy . . . ? (Aeschines 1.173)

In an Athens less wracked by defeat, suffering, plague, and all the moral quandaries raised by recent re-evaluations of *nomos* and *phusis*, Socrates' fellow citizens might have found him more amusing and less threatening. Athenians should be praised for allowing Socrates the freedom to pursue his conversations publicly for so long. Equally, they should be criticized for executing a man (even if not a hero) who lived his life committed to the laws and dedicated to improving his fellow citizens.

chapter 5
Imperialism

Imperialism is often discussed as a peculiarly modern phenomenon. Marxists, in particular, tend to view imperialism as the outgrowth of late capitalism – sometimes as a development leading to the rise of a global proletariat (cf. Lenin's *Imperialism: The Highest Stage of Capitalism*, 1916). In this chapter, however, we explore ancient Greek conceptions of imperialism, on the assumption that this term can usefully be applied to pre-capitalist societies. The ancient discussions can help to draw us back from the rigidity of modern analyses and focus our attention on the human passions, political contexts, and ethical consequences of imperialism. Here, too, questions of just distribution were connected to the ethical evaluation of virtue and vice, and both were enveloped in wider discussions of which political systems tended best to sustain imperialism. The most enlightening approach to the ancient discussions can be found, as often, at the end of the classical period.

Aristotle Analyzes Imperialism

In one of his later works, the *Politics*, Aristotle warned of the threat militaristic states posed both to others and to themselves. The threat to others is easier to understand. In Aristotelian terms, it consists in enslaving those who are not naturally fit for slavery. Such a practice would seem to be the height of injustice, recognizably so even to imperialists, since even imperialists demand just treatment from others, particularly their fellow citizens. Thus, from the perspective of justice, Aristotle noticed a contradiction in imperialism: "But many people appear to think that despotic rule is statesmanship, and they are not ashamed to act toward others in ways they would never consider just or advantageous to themselves; for, among themselves, they seek just governance, but in relation to others they have no concern for justice" (*Pol.* 7.2.1324b32–6). Aristotle was astonished by the Greeks' lack of impartiality. They did not regularly apply to others the standards they demanded for themselves. Their lack of impartiality, in fact, was a sign of their willingness to be unjust. In most philosophical treatments, ancient or modern, justice requires impartiality or it is nothing.

The less obvious problem with imperialism is that it threatens the health of domestic politics. It teaches citizens to value those qualities of character that lead to acquisition, to the greatest influx of material goods (7.14.1333b5–29). This wrongly gratifies the baser passions of the citizens. It thereby leads them away from the pursuit of noble activities such as peaceful political cooperation or philosophical contemplation of the truth. Moreover, at the limit, such an education of citizen desire leads to the hazardous belief that individual citizens ought to strive to win enough power to rule over their own cities (7.14.1333b32–3). By observing his city's behavior abroad, the citizen learns that aggressive behavior is rewarded; consequently, he begins to believe that aggression within the polis, rather than discussion, is a healthy form of politics. This, in turn, leads to unjust hierarchy, and even to tyranny, within domestic politics, which makes the city incapable of defending itself. Citizens tend to defend a city in which they receive due respect, not one that forces them to work for the good of a tyrant.

Yet the problem remained that all cities need to defend themselves. They must make a significant cultural investment in persuading citizens that patriotic self-sacrifice is a good thing, and that courage on behalf of the polis is a cardinal virtue. But courage itself is imperialistic among the virtues – it tends to override the claims of justice and self-restraint, on the grounds that such peacetime virtues would have no application or *raison d'être* without soldiers to defend the polis courageously. Left to its own devices, courage tends to trump the other virtues. Combine this with the self-promoting tendencies of most states, and you end up with a pugnacious citizenry fighting expansionist campaigns in the name of self-defense. That, in a nutshell, explains the particular aggressiveness of city-states in the ancient Mediterranean, particularly the three great imperialists Sparta, Athens, and Rome. Such an ideology was elaborated in Machiavelli's very particular reconstruction of Republican Rome in his *Discourses* (ca. 1517). In the imperial polis, courage became the citizens' virtue *par excellence*. Isocrates, for example, went so far as to assert that the gods brought about (the Persian) wars out of admiration for the natural bravery of the Athenians, in order to grant such bravery its due of glory (Isocr. 4.84). The Greeks found war both emotionally exciting and intellectually compelling. The cities' cultural investment in producing a defense force had ramifications that went well beyond defense.

Many contemporaries, however, found this investment, at least in its classical Greek form, to be destructive. Later in this book, we shall see how Plato, in particular, tried to displace the contemporary politics dedicated to courage and imperialism and to establish his own utopian politics based on transcendent knowledge. For now, though, it is enough to say that Plato and Aristotle recognized the Greek culture of imperialism as a problem. In the *Laws* Plato criticized states such as Sparta for making courage their supreme virtue when it should rank fourth in order of importance (630d–631d). As the "footstool of the virtues," courage must find meaningful direction from other, higher-order values such as justice. Aristotle found that the Spartans and others like them had begun to distort courage by undervaluing the virtue itself as compared to the material goods and honors that derived from it. The very success of the Spartans' imperialism turned their bravery into a vice – according to Aristotle.

These late classical critiques focus attention on the two basic questions raised by imperialism for Greek political thought. First, how and why might interstate aggression be called unjust? The obvious answer – that it is unjust to take from others what is rightly theirs – must give way to a more searching examination of how ancient Greek thinkers understood international relations, justice between states, and the ethics of warfare. To grapple with these issues, we must examine not only the ethics of such questions, but also the ancient thinkers' views on how and why expansionist drives arose in the first place. The imperialists' self-justifications, which we will also explore, might ring disturbingly modern to us. Second, what are the effects of imperialism? Plato and Aristotle proposed that imperialism both expressed and encouraged excessive desires, and that successful imperialism led to enervating luxury, decadence, and materialism. Thus, whatever virtues might have been instrumental to the imperial agenda, they were at once distorted beyond recognition, or even destroyed, in the process of achieving imperial aims. As in their analysis of internal politics, Greek political thinkers focused on justice and the virtues, or rather on injustice and the vices, in interstate relations, and they made meaningful connections between foreign policy and domestic political health.

Definitions and History

In this chapter imperialism refers to the systematic attempt to annex territory and to acquire control over others, with the goal of maintaining that power in the future, and to the long-term benefit of the conquering state.[1] This rules out ordinary raiding expeditions or simple conquest: Xenophon's fictitious king Cyrus of Persia recognized the difference (Text 1).

> **1.** We must not therefore be careless or move on to enjoying the pleasures at hand. For winning an empire is a great accomplishment, I think, but it is still greater for the one who has taken an empire to preserve it. Often the one who merely displays boldness can take an empire, but it is impossible for the conqueror to hold onto what he has taken without moderation, self-restraint, and a great deal of care. (Cyrus, in Xenophon, *Cyropaedia*, 7.5.76, cf. 8.7.7)

Imperial power can assume many forms: taking possession of land, compulsory military service, tribute, interference in domestic politics, denial of an autonomous foreign policy, establishing garrisons, and so forth. Since imperialism is a term used to criticize others, the key is that the subjects of imperialists are unwilling followers, who lack the basic good of self-determination, whether politically, militarily, or economically.

It is useful to evoke the Aristotelian distinction between tyrants and monarchs, for we will find that in Greek thought imperialism was foreign policy in the tyrannical mode. Aristotle argued that kings ruled by law over willing subjects, for the good of the subjects themselves, whereas tyrants ruled lawlessly over unwilling subjects for their own pleasure (*Pol.* 3.14.1285a16–29, 5.10.1310b31–1311a8; cf. Isocr. 8.91). Kings ruled justly, nobly and advantageously for their subjects, because they were outstanding in virtue; and tyrants the opposite, on all counts (*Pol.* 3.17.1287b36–1288a6). Sometimes, for reasons we will explore, subjects explicitly used the tyrant metaphor to describe imperialists, and other times not; but, either explicitly or implicitly, imperial states acted like tyrants in that they exploited their subjects for their own good, without their consent. There is no need to stumble over the terminology of monarchs and tyrants, however, if we recognize that sole rulers could call themselves monarchs and present themselves as genuine statesmen – and still be pejoratively labeled "tyrants" by those they oppressed.

Granted, oppression itself is a judgment call. There were ambiguous cases, as well as self-interested denials of tyranny and debates about how far exploitation went or could go. But the subjects' own perspective was significant because their consent, or lack thereof, was one – perhaps *the* – crucial indicator of imperialism. Although some have argued for the appropriateness of the Greek term "hegemony" (*hegemonia*), instead of imperialism, the only people to gain from such an ideological label are imperialists, then and now. "Hegemony" would have implied "leadership" to a Greek, and thus it could only be a self-serving ideological mask.[2] The Greeks had no native term that corresponds precisely to "imperialism"; their word for this exercise of power was *archê*, which means "the first place or power," or more simply "rule." The usefulness of "imperialism" as a rubric lies in its capacity to accommodate various forms of state-based exploitation, while focusing attention on the maintenance of power and the reduction of others' freedom. The bluntly evaluative term, however vague it may be, is what we need.

In the era just before the Persian Wars, the philosopher Heraclitus wrote that "War is the father of all and the king of all, and some he reveals as gods, other as men; some he makes slaves, others he makes free" (*DK* 22 B 53). The subsequent two centuries would illustrate the truth of that claim in ways that were probably unintended by its author.[3] For in 490 BC armies of the Persian King Darius squared off against the Athenians and Plataeans in the plain of Marathon. The Greeks were victorious. Their victory led Darius's son Xerxes to undertake a full-scale campaign against Greece, which culminated in Greek victories over the Persians at Salamis (480 BC) and Plataea (479 BC). The Persians were eventually driven from the

Aegean Sea altogether at the Battle of Eurymedon (ca. 466 BC). From the first, the Greeks recognized these confrontations as battles over the freedom and slavery of their people. But they surely did not foresee the consequences of Athenian leadership in these wars. For the Persian Wars led to further wars, but this time within the community of Greek states. The Athenians acquired leadership of the Greek alliance against Persia in 478 BC, but then turned their allies into imperial subjects until the end of the fifth century (404 BC). They were followed, in turn, by the Spartan imperialists, who were then followed by Philip of Macedon. The Eastern Mediterranean saw a succession of empires in the classical period. War, specifically imperialistic war, had truly become the father of all; each time it emerged, contemporaries saw their freedom and slavery hanging in the balance.

It was and is difficult to establish a firm basis for ethics or law between states. Among modern theories, the long-dominant "Realist" school of international relations maintains that morality, obligation, and justice are not useful conceptual tools for analyzing interstate affairs. States, acting as "quasi-individuals," pursue their own self-interests in accordance with the prevailing "realities of power."[4] This modern view derives ultimately from Thucydides' *History*, where Athenian speakers argued that human nature drives states to seek domination. Invoking justice is a last-ditch strategy of the weak (Thuc. 1.76). Realism – in its classic Thucydidean, Machiavellian, and Hobbesian forms – has traditionally maintained precisely such a pessimistic view of human nature. This holds true even for moderate realists, who argue that morality, though worthy of consideration, is negotiable: in extreme circumstances, or in acts of self-defense, states might override morality, albeit perhaps with regrets.[5]

Although policy has often been based on such prudential considerations, other political thinkers maintain that we have obligations to those beyond our own borders. The trouble is how to frame positive arguments for such obligations. Arguments might be centered on impartiality as a principle of global justice; or on the cosmopolitan ideal of respecting all human beings as persons with special "capabilities"; or on our shared interest in maintaining a pluralist world order, or a global environment habitable by human beings.[6] Perhaps most interesting for our purposes, though, are attempts to extend liberal (especially Rawlsian) principles of distributive justice to the international world. The global world puts these principles at risk because they were originally designed to explain our intuitions about individual societies considered as cooperative ventures for the common good. Many question whether states, too, can be understood on that model. The classical Greeks had interesting approaches to such questions, because they envisioned themselves as both united culturally and separated politically. That combination of diversity within unity led to novel – even arresting – arguments about ethics, character, human nature, prudence, and justice within the Hellenic and the wider Mediterranean worlds. Greek political thinkers discussed not only ideal interstate relations, but also, even more importantly, non-ideal worlds and their constraints as well as their opportunities. They focused on such questions because of their implicit belief that war was an endemic feature of the human condition, whether people wanted to believe it or not (Text 2).

> **2.** All these things have been provided for us with a view to war, and the lawgiver, as I see it, had war in mind when he organized our institutions. It is also likely that he set up communal meals since he saw that all men, when they go off to fight, are forced by the circumstances to eat together in order to protect themselves. Indeed, he seems to me to have recognized the folly of ordinary men who do not know that they are constantly engaged in war against all other cities for their entire lives. (Cleinias, in Plato, *Laws*, 625d7–e7)

This must have seemed, to them, true by observation.

Ancient Greeks undoubtedly saw themselves as a "panhellenic" community, united by shared religion, language, and custom (Text 3).

> **3.** Nowhere on earth is there so much gold or land outstanding for its beauty, that we would take it in return for willingly medizing [going over to the side of or acting like a Mede or Persian] and enslaving Hellas. For many powerful considerations keep us from doing so, even if we wanted to: first and most important are the statues and houses of the gods that have been burnt and demolished. We must avenge these sacred possessions to the greatest extent possible and not come to an agreement with their destroyers. And, moreover, we

must take into account the Hellenic nation, which has the same blood and uses the same language, and holds in common the shrines of the gods and sacred rites and shared customs. It would not be right for the Athenians to betray these. (Hdt. 8.144.1–2)

Greeks subscribed to norms of reciprocity and cooperation between states; their elite often had strong ties of "ritualized friendship" (*xenia*) with the elite of other states; and they were used to forming military alliances to ward off enemies. Sometimes sub-groups united along ethnic lines: Ionians with Ionians, Dorians with Dorians, and so forth. But these were fragile coalitions that could break apart as soon as more compelling interests became visible. All these associative features can be seen in the *Iliad* – the founding text of Greek conceptions of "international politics." Archaic and classical Greeks also shared ritualized "rules" of warfare, which included a formal declaration of war, safe passage for heralds, the granting of truces to recover the dead, and so on. There was a powerful basis for viewing Greeks as members of the same community.

Even so, despite the longstanding analogy between individual and polis, classical Greek cities acting internationally did not always consider themselves subject to intra-polis ethical standards. A bright line separated those within the polis group from those without.[7] This had been true since the time of the Homeric epics. Homeric heroes won glory and prestige from successfully raiding neighboring territories, though they subscribed, at least in principle, to well-defined canons of justice and self-restraint at home. Solon, too, railed against aristocrats who treated their fellow Athenians like foreign enemies, even as he exhorted the Athenians to "thrust off disgrace" by recovering nearby Salamis, which they had once annexed. The cosmopolitan ethic of treating all human beings alike came to Greece only late in its history (see "New Directions," "The Politics of Cynicism?" and "Stoicism and Epicureanism" in chapter 8). *Mutatis mutandis*, classical Greeks accepted a brand of Cicero's restricted cosmopolitanism, according to which we have special obligations to our city-states, which co-exist with thinner obligations to those of the same "nation," and still thinner obligations to humankind generally (*De Officiis* I.50–8). Nevertheless, unbridgeable distinctions were often made between Greeks and those non-Greeks they called *barbaroi* (barbarians). Whatever lines Greeks might draw to suit the occasion, Aristotle was right: impartiality was not typically part of interstate ethical thinking.

Monarchic Imperialism

Freedom and slavery, West versus East, the succession of empires – these were the major themes of Herodotus's history of the Persian Wars. And it is by turning to the concrete details of historical writing that we can, I think, best come to understand Greek thinking about imperialism. On this topic, especially, philosophical inquiry must be chastened by attention to historical detail. Herodotus's avowed goal in writing his history was to commemorate the glory of Greek and Persian actions (1.1). He operated within the Homeric tradition of celebrating the military exploits of warriors.

But dedication to the glories of war contributes to war's status as the father of all. War could be downright addictive (Text 4).

> **4.** Although they had previously been more cautious than others in regard to such things, they [the Spartans] were such lovers of warfare and risk-taking, that they did not keep their hands off either their allies or their own benefactors. (Isocrates 8.97).

The pressures to go to war, to expand, and to acquire more territory were particularly strong in the kingdoms of the Near East. Herodotus viewed individual passions as a key motive for imperialism: a succession of kings, including Croesus, Cambyses, Darius, and Xerxes, not to mention others, had insatiable cravings for acquisition. They wanted the wealth and power, as well as the prestige, brought by endless expansion. Their own freedom consisted in the ruthless exploitation of their subjects and in the unlimited acquisition of further territory. Freedom, in other words, was for them the freedom to rule tyrannically over a subject population of, in effect, slaves. This way of representing Persian rule reflects Greek ideology, but it contains a certain amount of truth. Although Herodotus was not a system-building theorist of human nature, his work offered a compelling, and disturbing, picture of how people actually behaved, and why.

Herodotus, moreover, analyzed how the imperialistic passions of individuals were promoted by particular cultural values, practices, and institutions. For Herodotus was too complex to believe that expansionist drives could originate simply in the desires of individuals. No: he showed that imperialism is a phenomenon of cultures.[8] Planning his campaign against Greece, Xerxes indicated the pressures a young king might experience when confronted by the history of his own people (Text 5).

> **5.** Well then, as for the accomplishments of Cyrus, Cambyses, and my father Darius, and as for the peoples they acquired, no one needs to tell you: you know it all. But as for me, ever since I took this throne, I have been paying careful attention to how I might avoid falling short of those who came before me on the throne, and to how I might avoid adding less power to the Persian empire. (Hdt. 7.8.a)

Xerxes' confrontation with history boldly illustrates that national ethos is built upon narratives and historical memory, both of which can, in the right (wrong?) circumstances, lead to imperial aggression. In Persia, as throughout the ancient Mediterranean, these pressures were driven by conceptions of masculinity – kings, and even their subordinates, had to live up to the aggressive images of manliness and "courage" that were traditional in their cultures (3.120, 3.134); otherwise, they would be viewed as weak and lacking in ambition. In the minds of these hyper-aggressive kings, even the gods were supposed to sanction and promote imperialism (7.8). Wars inspired by religion were not only a phenomenon of the Middle Ages; they resulted, in classical antiquity, from the tight interweaving of religion and politics.

If monarchs were pressured to expand, then a question remained as to whether monarchs made good imperialists. The late fifth-century Hippocratic author of the treatise *Airs, Waters, Places* found that subjection to a tyrant enervated a people and sapped them of courage (Text 6).

> **6.** Wherever people are not their own masters and do not rule themselves, but are under tyranny, they have no reason to train for war, but every reason not to appear warlike. For the risks are not the same for them: under tyrants, warlike men are likely to be compelled to go to war for the sake of their masters, to endure hardship, and

> to die far from their children, their wives, and all others who are dear to them. And whatever noble and brave deeds they do serve only to strengthen and advance their tyrants, while the men themselves reap only danger and death. (Hippocratic *Airs, Waters, Places*, 16, tr. Gagarin/Woodruff)

This view, which was reiterated by Herodotus (5.78), was often combined with the quasi-racial prejudice that Asians were simply born to be cowards, perhaps because of Asia's mild climate. Herodotus was ambivalent on this issue: he showed Cyrus and Darius successfully expanding Persia and remarked on the personal courage of Xerxes' picked troops. However, he mostly denigrated the Persian troops for fighting out of fear of punishment, which, to him, made them less capable of succeeding at imperialism. According to Herodotus, the Persians fought under continual surveillance and sometimes had to be whipped into battle, whereas the Greeks fought out of self-respect, a sense of honor, commitment to freedom, and obedience to impartial law.[9] That is why Xerxes discovered at Thermopylae that his army contained "many followers, to be sure, but few real men" (Hdt. 7.210).

Herodotus was therefore pointing to inherent (in his view) features of monarchy to argue that monarchs do not make successful imperialists. He pursued this idea at a theoretical level in his so-called Constitutional Debate, in which the Persian Otanes, a champion of popular government, criticized monarchy for the characteristic vices of envy and arrogance (3.80). Though set in Persia, this debate undoubtedly reflects Greek political thought. Envy, Otanes says, results from the monarch's fear of excellence among his subjects, which causes the character of his subjects to deteriorate; arrogance, on the other hand, arises because of an excess of wealth and other advantages (3.80). Monarchs typically develop these vices in the course of their tenure: absolute power at least *tends* to corrupt absolutely. And the monarch's character has everything to do with the political success and military strength of his regime. A character in Xenophon's *Cyropaedia* revealingly points out that the wicked Assyrian king hates not so much those who wrong him, as those who appear better or more virtuous than he is. Therefore, he ends up with vicious, defective citizens, who are increasingly incapable of defending either the king or themselves (5.4.35–6).

Such accounts of monarchic infirmity found parallels in many other texts and settings. Aeschylus' *Persians* (472 BC), for example, celebrated the Greeks' superior rationality and courage as the basis of their victory at Salamis. The play drew attention to the Persians' lack of free speech, to Xerxes' unaccountability, and to the consequent failures of Persian foreign policy. This lifted the critique of monarchic character to the level of a systematic attack on the monarchic system. In the fourth century, Demosthenes asserted, in a similar vein, that "dynasties" ruled by a few men often produced cowardly citizens because they failed to distribute the rewards of courage fairly – because, in turn, they had not, like democracies, established effective canons of social shame (60.25–7). Elsewhere, he said that Philip of Macedon hogged all the imperialistic glory for himself, reserving rewards for toadies at court who delighted in drinking binges and lewd dancing (2.15–20). This made him a less effective imperialist, as did the fact, as Demosthenes saw it, that free constitutions tend to distrust their neighbors governed by tyrants, who were usually expansionist (1.5). Tyrants not only create dissatisfaction within their own polities, but also provoke hostility from other states. Isocrates too believed the Persians incapable of manly virtue, because ordinary citizens were trained to be servile, officials failed to respect equality or value patriotism, and everyone had to humiliate himself before the king; this made the Persians treacherous and cowardly (4.150–2). Notice that all of these analysts tried to weave together, in tight causal chains, the monarch's own character, the political system itself, the monarch's creation of individual and social vices, and his tendency to isolate himself internationally. Clearly, much of this is informed by the democratic quest for self-definition and superiority. But, if the democrats' arguments for the value of freedom and equality had merit (cf. chapter 3), then there must be a kernel of truth to the idea that tyrannies undermine their imperialist ambitions from within.

Negative stereotypes of the Persians and other "barbarians" help to explain much of Greek political self-definition in the fifth century, but these stereotypes did not correspond to the Persians' success in expanding their empire or to their continuing power in Mediterranean politics. However, after the fall of Athens's fifth-century empire, political thinkers began to re-assess the merits of monarchic imperialists, both from a prudential and an ethical standpoint. Entrenched democrats such as Demosthenes remained hostile to monarchs,

such as Philip of Macedon, but they came to appreciate their effi-
ciency and used it in arguments designed to arouse fear and anger
among their fellow citizens (Text 7; cf. Dem. 18.235).

> **7.** For Philip is solely in charge of all things, both open and secret,
> and he is at the same time general, ruler, and treasurer, and he
> himself is always with his army; this gives him a distinct advantage
> in conducting military operations swiftly and at the right time.
> (Demosthenes 1.4)

But others explored the possibility of successful imperialism led
by enlightened monarchs. This was the theme of Xenophon's *Cyropaedia* (*Education of Cyrus*) of the 360s BC. Xenophon's principal
interest here – as in other works, such as the *Agesilaus* and *Anaba-
sis* – was leadership, or, more precisely, what sort of leader could
establish a stable and effective government over other men (1.1.1–
3). For he saw that instability was inherent in political life, since
"men form conspiracies against no one more than those whom
they perceive trying to rule them" (1.1.2). Cyrus, however, was a
unique ruler, he says, in that he ruled over willing subjects because
of his knowledge and virtues. We might speculate that, in inventing
such an ideal ruler, Xenophon (along with Isocrates, as we shall
see) was dreaming principally of political stability in the chaotic
world of fourth-century Greece (cf. chapters 4 and 6).

To become a successful imperialist, Cyrus first developed the
virtues of kindness, benevolence (*philanthrôpia*), courage, self-
control, and foresight. Xenophon patiently shows how each of
these virtues contributed to Cyrus's conquest of most of Asia. He
first illustrates Cyrus's capacity to develop a base of support among
his own people. With great political prudence, Cyrus rearranged his
ancestral Persia so as to reduce the importance of entrenched hierarchy and to maximize equality of opportunity.[10] Even the ordinary
citizens of Persia were given an opportunity to carry the heavy
armor formerly reserved for the upper classes; and it was decided
by popular demand that rewards and praise were to be distributed
solely on the basis of merit (2.3.4–16). Cyrus's central insight was
that leaders best motivated their troops through showing kindness
and friendship to them, and through understanding their own
interests better than the troops did themselves (2.4.10).

Having won quasi- "republican" support from the Persians, Cyrus proceeded to expand his sway through military conquest, through capable diplomacy with the Assyrian defectors Gobryas and Gadatas, and through making his subjects prosper more completely than they could have imagined under their former masters. His self-control enabled him and his Persians to avoid the weakness and passions brought on by self-indulgence and to reward his other friends and followers appropriately (4.2.42–6; cf. 1.6.45). In short, he was an ideal ruler for both acquiring an empire, holding on to it, and making it prosperous (8.7.7), and this impression lasts throughout the work.

Even so, Xenophon invites his readers to ponder the limitations of Cyrus's life and legacy. The most arresting source of such doubts is the work's final chapter (8.8), in which, immediately upon the great king's death, Cyrus's successors quarrel, the old morality falters, and the empire begins to crumble. Although older commentators once considered this final chapter corrupt, because it strikes such a dissonant note with Cyrus' death-bed scene (8.7), it is more reasonable to interpret it as raising doubts about monarchic succession and imperialism. Machiavelli, one of Xenophon's most careful readers, raised the same problem: virtuous kings are often succeeded by less worthy sons, so that kingship often turns into tyranny (*Discourses*, 1.2; cf. Polybius 6.8–9).

But Xenophon also suggests that imperialism itself is partly to blame. Even Cyrus was unable to persuade the Babylonians to obey him willingly. Therefore, he was forced to resort to ignoble tactics to maintain his own power – such as cultivating a bodyguard of eunuchs, wearing make-up to appear more imposing, and enlisting a veritable army of spies to search out potential rebels. Moreover, when Cyrus returns to his native Persia, his wise father Cambyses expresses concern that he will bring his imperialist self-aggrandizement into Persia itself (Text 8).

8. But if you, Cyrus, carried away by your luck at present, try to rule the Persians, like the rest, out of greed, or if you, my fellow citizens, begrudge him his power, and try to deprive him of it, I assure you both that you will deprive one another of many good things. (Cambyses, in Xenophon, *Cyropaedia*, 8.5.24)

His advice raises questions about Cyrus's capacity to rule the other nations for their benefit, rather than his own. Perhaps the underlying thought was that even the wisest and most virtuous kings can only accomplish limited good through imperialism, human nature being what it is. Not only do kings like Cyrus have to contend with wicked subjects –those whom Machiavelli would call "men as they are" – but they must also contend with the insatiable desires that the gods have implanted in all human souls, including royal ones (8.2.20).[11]

Isocrates had a very different understanding of the prospects of monarchic imperialism. He maintained that the troubles of fourth-century Greece could be solved by a panhellenic crusade against the barbarian Persians. After essaying the possibility of joint Athenian and Spartan leadership of such a venture in his *Panegyricus* (380 BC), he concluded, in his *Address to Philip* (346 BC), that Philip would be Greece's best leader. Throughout these works, his chief concern was to define the nature of good leadership, or, put differently, to ask what justifies a claim to leadership in the international world (4.21–2, 98–9). Note that his task was different from Xenophon's, because in the Greek world, as opposed to that of Asia, sole rule was an object of suspicion rather than a first postulate of civic flourishing. Examining Greek history with a broad lens, Isocrates argued that individual "great men" – such as Alcibiades, Conon, Dionysius (5.58–5), Agesilaus (5.86–7), Heracles (5.109–15), and Agamemnon (12.76–83) – have played, and therefore could now play, a critical role in transforming Greek politics.

Isocrates was aware of the moral ambiguities (to view them charitably) associated with some of these figures, but he judged that Philip of Macedon could rival their brilliance and effectiveness while showing due respect to all Greece. This judgment was based on the behavior of Philip's ancestor Perdiccas, who founded the Macedonian kingdom on the basis of a unique insight: whereas Greeks cannot tolerate sole rulers, other nations, such as Macedon, cannot flourish without them (5.105–8). Therefore, to succeed in international politics, Philip must persuade the Greeks to stop fighting each other, and compel the barbarians to submit to Greek rule; words and deeds must be applied as suitable to each case. Moreover, Philip must combine his well-known intelligence with courage, piety and loyalty, if he truly wants success. Again, considering the career of Philip's son Alexander, we might question the likelihood of these qualities being passed on to the next generation. Alexander was a profoundly successful conqueror, but a hopeless statesman (cf. Plutarch *Moralia* 207D for the Roman emperor Augustus' recognition of this point).

Obviously Isocrates viewed Philip's possible conquest of the Persians in a positive light: he wrote that it would enable Philip to rival Heracles "in the character of his soul, in benevolence, and in his good will toward the Greeks" (5.114). Isocrates saw manifold goods coming to Greece from imperialism: the liberation of Ionian Greeks, the rehabilitation of Greek self-respect, the foundation of cities, the settlement of disruptive mercenaries, security for mainland Greece, justified glory for Philip, and revenge for past wrongs. He also recognized that Greek poverty could be assuaged by the fabulous wealth of Persia. (He was apparently not as worried as others that an influx of wealth would degrade the Greeks' character, though the reasons for his optimism are not entirely clear.) In other words, Isocrates viewed imperialism as a source of peace and concord – within the Greek world. However, he made almost no attempt to justify the (to us) obvious harm such policies would wreak on the Persians themselves. In part this was unproblematic, to him, since he envisioned future wars as wars of revenge: the Persians had been the first to enslave the Ionians, attack Greece itself, destroy Greek temples, and so forth. But, more deeply, Isocrates believed that barbarians were naturally aggressive and antagonistic toward others, while Greeks nurtured an eternal hatred of the Persians, based on ingrained natural hostility (4.157–9; cf. Dem. 21.48–50). This natural enmity was highly susceptible to a religious interpretation. Inflate rhetorically as needed (Text 9).

9. Those who want to remain on good terms with the gods and who are also committed to their own self-interest – whom should they attack? Should they not attack those who are both their enemies by nature and their ancestral foes – who have, moreover, acquired an extraordinary amount of wealth and yet are least able to defend what is theirs? (Isocr. 4.184)

Natural Superiority?

Natural differences, then – this was Isocrates' moral justification for the monarch's expansionist ventures. The basic idea of Greek superiority had wide currency in classical culture; hence Isocrates' belief, no doubt, that his arguments would be persuasive.[12] Plato, for example, argued that decisive differences separated Greeks and barbarians. Therefore, military conflict with barbarians was entirely different from that within the Greek community (Text 10).

> **10.** Then we shall say that when Greeks make war on barbarians and barbarians on Greeks, they are hostile by nature, and that their conflicts must be called war; but when Greeks fight with Greeks, we shall say that they are friends by nature and that in such a situation Greece is sick and suffering from civil strife, and that their conflicts must be called civil wars. (Plato, *Republic* 470c5–d1)

Aristophanes represented non-Greeks as slavish, unintelligent, inferior, and ridiculous figures. In Euripides' *Iphigeneia at Aulis* (produced ca. 405 BC), the title character insisted, "Mother, it is right for Greeks to rule over barbarians, and not barbarians over Greeks; for barbarians are slaves, while the Greeks are free" (1400–1). This type of attitude, which was based on a particular view of nature, eventually led to the self-serving idea that enslaving the Persians was good, not only for the Greeks, but also for the Persians themselves.

Such ideas helped to inform Aristotle's theory of "natural slavery." Aristotle's argument was not often made explicit by other Greeks: why should the (superior) Greeks worry about the welfare of (inferior) Persians? Or, perhaps, since the vast majority of people throughout history have recognized the fundamental sameness of all human beings (Text 11), Greeks simply could not address the question explicitly without seeing themselves in a repellent light.

> **11.** For no single thing is so similar to another, so equal, as we all are to one another. But if corrupt habits or empty beliefs did not twist and turn our weak minds wherever they began, no one would be more similar to himself than all of us are to all. And so, whatever the

definition of human being is, one definition applies to all – which is enough of an argument that there is no difference in mankind. (Marcus, in Cicero, *Laws*, 129–30)

In short, Aristotle's argument was that since some people (read: Persians) were naturally suited to slavery, because of their intellectual weakness, they could live more flourishing human lives under the rational supervision of a (Greek) master (for further discussion, see "Nature in the *Politics*" in chapter 7). Even in the classical period, however, such attitudes did not go unchallenged. In reviewing previous opinions on slavery, Aristotle himself mentions that some maintain that slavery exists purely by convention, i.e. law, and force – specifically, that slavery results purely from defeat in war. Even Aristotle agreed that, in those cases at least, slavery was contrary to nature, since there is no relevant natural difference among human beings that would justify enslaving war-captives. According to Aristotle, though, this confusion results from nature's own inability to enact its purposes fully in each case. True, rational Greeks can wrongly become slaves; that is no argument against slavery as such, but rather merely against its illegitimate application (again see "Nature in the *Politics*" in chapter 7).

For the historian of political thought, Aristotle's counter-arguments lend credibility to the existence of an important group of theorists who questioned the legitimacy of slavery in principle, not just in practice. The "abolitionist" sentiment underlying their views survives in a single fragment of the sophist Alcidamas (ca. 370 BC): "The deity gave liberty to all men, and nature created no one a slave."[13] A compatible sentiment, moreover, was expressed in a fragment from Antiphon's fifth-century *On Truth* (Text 12), which emphasized our shared human vulnerability to luck.

12. The laws of nearby communities we respect and honor, but those of communities far away we neither respect nor honor. In this we are barbarous toward each other, when by nature we are all at birth in all respects equally capable of being both barbarians [i.e. foreigners] and Greeks. We can examine those attributes of nature that are necessarily in all men and are provided to all to the same degree, and in these respects none of us is distinguished as foreign

> or Greek. For we all breathe the air through our mouth and through
> our nostrils and we laugh when we are pleased. (Antiphon DK 87 B
> 44, tr. Gagarin/Woodruff)

The sophist Lycophron, finally, drew attention to the "luck of the draw" in relation to high and low birth (Aristotle fr. 91 Rose).[14] Such comments on the luck of birth might constitute the basis of an attack on the institution of slavery. Classical Greeks articulated the basic rudiments of universal rights without drawing out the consequences.

Debating Athenian Imperialism

As we have seen, the Greeks' reflective examination of imperialism began with analysis of a Near Eastern kingdom and was elaborated straightforwardly in relation to other kingdoms. The ordinary Greek polis did not engage in imperialism. Only three Mediterranean poleis – Sparta, Athens, and Rome – did so to any significant degree. In the formative period of Greek political thought, in the late sixth and fifth centuries, imperialism was something that non-Greeks (i.e., Persians) did to Greeks. Traditional Greek warfare was border warfare without significant conquest of territory, much less stable administration over foreign lands. Therefore, imperialism was first characteristic of tyrannical monarchs, and only afterwards, as we will see, of classical Athens, with its lethal combination of a powerful navy and radical democracy.[15] It is worth speculating that the Greeks were able to reflect so richly on imperialism because it was something foreign to the Greek world; it was something brought in by outsiders, rather than something a polis engaged in. By contrast, when it comes to a practice or concept already embedded in their culture, such as slavery, classical Greeks were much less insightful.

However debatable the enslavement of barbarians might have been in the Greek view, Greeks were generally opposed, at least in principle, to the enslavement of other Greeks. Examining imperialism within the Greek community, therefore, brings us closer to modern discussions of imperialism and international relations. What laws or code of ethics, if any, govern interstate relations in cases where mutual obligations are recognized? Often explorations of such issues are retrospective: they provide ex post facto justifications of imperialism, centered on ideas of liberation, introducing civilization or enlightenment to others, protection from outsiders, and (again) natural rights or laws of domination. For example, the Spartans notoriously proclaimed that they attacked the Athenian Empire in order to liberate the Greeks, and then proceeded to establish a harsh empire of their own. Herodotus illustrated, more importantly, that Greece's first large-scale, "internal" empire – that of fifth-century Athens – arose in the wake of the Hellenic defense against the Persians. Although Herodotus praises the Athenians' self-sacrifice, leadership, courage, and dedication to Greek liberty during the Persian Wars, he remarks that they connived to usurp the military command from Sparta once the Persian threat was over (8.3). Throughout the fifth century, Athens used its record of virtuous leadership to justify its imperialism within Greece.

Herodotus was one of the first thinkers on record to criticize Athenian imperialism.[16] Just before his remark about Athenian usurpation, Herodotus had praised the Athenians for giving up their claim to command the Greeks at sea. Their generosity was especially consequential, he says, since "civic conflict is worse than external war fought by a like-minded people to the same degree as war is worse than peace" (8.3). This "panhellenic" viewpoint provided a framework for Herodotus to represent Athens' relations with other Greek states as analogous to civic relationships within the polis. Imperial Athens was, to Herodotus, the successor to the Eastern imperialists. But its behavior was even more susceptible to criticism because of its previous benefactions to the Greeks and because of its high-minded rhetoric of rejecting Persian enticements, remembering Greek kinship, and liberating all Greeks (cf. 8.144). In Herodotus' view justice meant principally being satisfied with one's own goods and not behaving acquisitively toward those of others. For the Athenians to exact tribute from other Greeks, therefore, was both unjust and nearly treasonous (cf. 6.42). It was also highly imprudent, because, Herodotus thought, cities and kingdoms rise and fall in regular succession, and prosperity never lasts long (1.5). Thus an oracle originally intended for the Persians appeared, ominously, to apply also to the Athenians: "Bright Justice (*Dikê*) will quench powerful Greed (*Koros*), the child of Arrogance (*Hubris*)" (8.77). In Herodotus's narrative, this religious prediction had an explanation based on both historical factors and human nature as Herodotus conceived of it.

Herodotus showed that Eastern despotism made for unsuccessful imperialism, but, ironically, Persian culture also encouraged imperialism as a sign of the king's merit. Putting these interpretations together, Eastern despotism is inherently self-destructive. Athenian democracy, by contrast, produced courageous citizens who were capable of imperialism. In Herodotus' reconstruction, however, Athenians succumbed to the character defects of their own leaders. This could not have occurred had not the ordinary Athenians been ignorant of their own genuine self-interest. Herodotus' account of Themistocles brings out these points clearly. A brilliant, energetic, and successful leader at Salamis, Themistocles showed his true colors after the Greek victory in 479, when he exploited his command of the Greek fleet to extort money from a number of small Greek islands (8.111–12). Herodotus says that he was always greedy to get more money (8.112). But the Athenians followed him and other acquisitive leaders because they were capable of being deceived (1.60, 5.97) and because they loved money (6.132) as much as their leaders (6.125). This, unfortunately, was the real and eventual, if unintended, meaning of Miltiades' exhortation to Callimachus before the battle of Marathon (Text 13).

13. It is now up to you, Callimachus, either to reduce Athens to slavery or to make the city free and to leave behind for all future men a memorial that surpasses the one left by Harmodius and Aristogeiton. . . . All these choices belong to you and depend on you; for if you agree with my proposal, then your country will be free and your city the first of all Greek cities. (Hdt. 6.109)

For the Athenians, being first and free meant having the power to rule over other Greeks – and using it.

In making such arguments, Herodotus adopted the stance of the "wise warner," like certain deposed kings in his own story, such as Croesus, who came to "learn through suffering."[17] Thus he did not depict Athens's downfall (indeed, Athens had not fallen by the time he wrote in the 420s!), but rather provided a subtle analysis-cum-condemnation of the Athenians' domestic and foreign policy choices. To him, the Athenians' excessive desires were imprudent as well as unjust, because luxury, a consequence of imperialism, tended to sap the fighting strength of those who indulged in its pleasures. As Cyrus explained in the work's conclusion, self-indulgence makes men subjects rather than rulers (Text 14).

14. Cyrus said that soft regions tend to produce weak men, since the same land typically cannot grow both wondrous fruit and brave warriors. The Persians saw the point of this and went away, yielding to Cyrus's good judgment. They chose to live in a poor land as rulers rather than to farm rich plains as the slaves of others. (Hdt. 9.122)

But Herodotus did not stop there in criticizing Athenian imperialism. Rather, he put forward the Athenian Solon himself as a moral advisor to would-be imperialists. Asked by the rich Croesus to identify the happiest man on earth, Solon named the (otherwise unknown) Athenian Tellus, who had sufficient wealth, a prosperous city, healthy children and grandchildren, and courage enough to die for his city (1.30). On the basis of such considerations, Solon advised Croesus to consider what was suitable to life as a whole, and to acquire goods appropriate to the station of human beings, not gods, animals, or tyrants – or acquisitive imperialists. For Herodotus, such was precisely the Athenians' problem: they lacked understanding of the ingredients of a good and flourishing human life, even if they were successful at imperialism.[18] This criticism was developed at great length by Plato in the *Gorgias* (see "Plato on Rhetoric and Order" in chapter 6; cf. Isocr. 8.83–5).

What did the Athenians have to say for themselves? No modern political thinker would justify imperialism, but the Athenians' views might disturbingly resonate, not so much with modern political philosophy, as with modern rhetoric and policy analysis. Throughout the century, the Athenians tried to capture the memory of the Persian Wars for their own imperial advantage. They were constantly making historical arguments against the rival claims of other poleis such as Sparta and Corinth (Hdt. 7.139; Isocr. 4.98). Athenian traditions insisted, indeed, that the reputedly brave Spartans wanted, foolishly and out of fear, to stake their hopes in the Persian Wars on walling off the Peloponnese, which would have resulted in disaster both for themselves and for the other Greeks (Isocr. 12.51; 4.93; Lys. 2.44–6). The Spartans eventually aided the Athenians, as everyone knew, but again only from fear (Thuc. 1.74) and when forced by shame at the Athenian example (Isocr. 5.97). These arguments had historical merit, but the Athenians found their fellow Greeks slow to accept the conclusions they drew from them.

Their conclusion was that it was reasonable for Athenians to maintain "leadership" of the Greeks after the Persian Wars. What was the motive of such leadership? Early on, revenge against the Persians was a credible motive, or perhaps leading a panhellenic crusade into Persia. Either way, the Athenians could have maintained their leadership without tyrannizing over the others. The language of alliance had more traction in this situation. By the last quarter of the fifth century, however, the Athenians had worn out their welcome. Resistance to Athenian imperialism was not uncommon (Text 15).

15. These revolts were principally caused by the subjects' failure to pay tribute or to provide ships and sometimes by their military desertion. The Athenians were strict in exacting the tribute and they caused their allies pain, since they employed force against cities that were not accustomed or willing to suffer hardship. And in other ways the allies were no longer pleased to have the Athenians rule them; the Athenians no longer took the battlefield on an equal basis, and it was therefore easy for them to bring rebels back into the alliance. (Thuc. 1.99.1–2)

During the Peloponnesian War, for example, the Spartans successfully exploited "freedom" and "liberation" as slogans to motivate secession from the Athenian Empire and to inspire loyalty to themselves. The Athenians' subjects made appeals both to liberation and to Spartan manhood in soliciting help from the Spartans (Thuc. 3.13). Thucydides depicted the Mytilenians, citizens of a powerful subject-polis, as emphasizing the problem of inequality. In a speech in Thucydides, for example, the Mytilenians analyzed the Athenians' tyrannical behavior as a violation of the equality that should obtain between allied states (Thuc. 3.9–14). Having seen the Athenians enslave their other "allies," the Mytilenians feared for their own independence, since the Athenians had successfully built up their own strength on the basis of tribute, divided the allies' loyalties, and come to resent dealing with Mytilene on the basis of equality (Thuc. 3.11). Thucydides put the Mytilenians' concerns into a theoretical register, but his critical perspective on Athens was undoubtedly shared by many of the subject states themselves. Clearly the Athenians were not leaders governing for the good, and with the consent, of the governed.

Arguably, it was primarily the allied elite, not the allied demos, who so resented Athenian rule. The "Old Oligarch" said as much in the course of arguing that the Athenians won allies by installing democracies in their subject states (Text 16).

> **16.** About the allies, they sail out and lay charges against them, as it appears, and they hate the "worthy," since that know that it is necessary for the ruler to be hated by the ruled, and if the wealthy and "worthy" are powerful in the allied cities, the empire of the Athenian people will be of very short duration. Therefore, they disenfranchise the "worthy," and confiscate their property, and exile and kill them, but they strengthen the worthless. (Old Oligarch 1.14)

Note again the contemporary resonance of such tactics. It may have been true that most ordinary citizens of Athens's subject states simply wanted peace, order, and democracy, and that they willingly gave up political autonomy, and paid tribute, to secure these goods. Moreover, a few allies stuck with the Athenians through their military defeats in Sicily (413 BC). But, even if the empire was popular to this extent, it was still morally objectionable that the Athenians ran a systematic protection racket, profited themselves, disadvantaged their subjects, and reveled in the irresistible joys of power. This is why, when the Athenians re-established a "hegemony" in the fourth century, they set up a charter clearly explaining that it would differ from the fifth-century empire in granting autonomy and property rights to the allies (378/7 BC; Text 17).[19]

> **17.** Let it be voted by the People: If anyone wishes, of the Hellenes, or of the barbarians who are living on the mainland, or of the islanders, as many as are not subject to the King, to be an ally of the Athenians and of their allies, it shall be permitted to him to do so, remaining free and autonomous, living under whatever constitution

he wants, neither receiving a garrison nor having a governor imposed upon him nor paying tribute, but he shall become an ally on the same terms as those on which the Chians and the Thebans and the other allies did. ("Charter of the Second Athenian Confederacy," Harding 35 = *IG* II² 43, tr. P. Harding, *From the end of the Peloponnesian War to the battle of Ipsus*, Cambridge, 1985)

From the perspective of political thought, there were two problems with Athenian imperialism – injustice and imprudence.

Athens's subjects, for obvious reasons, cared more about the injustice they thought they were suffering. Cries of "unfairness" must have been a common feature of the subject states' rhetoric; that would help to explain the Athenians' repeated attempts to justify themselves and to reassure themselves that they were on the right course. The allies' complaints obviously derived from a concern with justice and equality. As we have seen, the Greek view of justice depended in essence on the idea of equality: justice meant that equal things – material goods, honor, respect – had to be distributed to equal people. The issue of injustice was bound to arise because of the way the Athenian Empire had developed. The Athenians had established themselves as leaders of the panhellenic coalition against Persia – or, in other words, as leaders of a voluntary association promoting a well-defined, publicly acknowledged, and shared conception of the common good. They and their allies interpreted the Athenians' leadership of the Greeks by analogy with an individual's leadership of his fellow citizens within the polis. That analogy made sense of the Mytilenians' evocation of equality and it may have had some hold on the Athenian imperialists themselves (Thuc. 1.77). Interestingly, however, this panhellenic language itself came back to haunt the Athenians because, as they became more openly imperialistic, they violated the equality that had once, at least theoretically, obtained within the alliance. Their manifest injustice therefore gave rise to criticisms that exploited the language of slavery.

Our knowledge of the Athenians' responses to such charges is limited by the absence of contemporary, fifth-century speeches delivered in Athens as the empire was being expanded and defended, and as the Athenians grew ever more fearful of losing power during the Peloponnesian War. At least within Athens, politicians and public speakers publicly took for granted the justice of Athenian rule over others; there was little room for public criticism of the Athenians' general foreign policy objectives. Our surviving fifth-century sources – primarily Thucydides, Aristophanes, and the Old Oligarch – mostly depict the Athenians as united in their belief that they deserved to rule, that other Greeks benefited from their leadership, and that fear of others compelled them to seek domination.[20]

Fourth-century literature offers a detailed set of self-justifications for Athenian imperialism. The funeral oration composed by Lysias in the 390s provides a window into the self-justifications that appealed to popular Athenian audiences in the fourth century. In particular, this funeral oration and literary works that were perhaps influenced by it illustrate the sorts of arguments that had currency with the Athenian demos. These arguments had remarkable staying power (cf. Isocr. 4.74). Both Lysias and Isocrates of course had their own specific, contemporary interests in mind in their speeches and pamphlets. As we saw in "Evidence and Sources" in chapter 3, though, we can use the less problematic fourth-century sources for democratic ideology to trace lines of democratic thinking back into the more problematic fifth-century sources, such as Thucydides.[21] This is a plausible approach, but we must keep in mind the caveat that Thucydides' own literary, ideological, and didactic purposes are ever present in the speeches he presents. In addition to searching out and analyzing the Athenians' self-justifications, we will also be attuned to Thucydides' own presentation of such matters.

Lysias' *Funeral Oration*, probably written in the 390s, is a key text for our purposes. Lysias' presentation in this speech is generically consistent with other known examples of this genre.[22] Orators giving a speech on this occasion typically begin with the mythical history of Athens and then move on to an idealized description of more recent historical events, all the while describing the city's justice, generosity, pity for the weak, prudent leadership of the Greeks, and so forth. The culmination of this "history" of the city is praise of those who recently fell in battle, particularly for their way of living up to the ideals exhibited by their ancestors. The funeral orations, as a genre, provide a wonderful table of the political virtues as they apply to the city, and they were obviously meant as an education to the survivors.

Lysias expatiates at great length on the Athenians' unique claims to responsibility for the Greek victory over the Persians in the

Persian wars – a point that Athenian patriots had to emphasize in a world where responsibility for the victory was always in dispute (cf. Hdt. 7.139). By contrast, he criticized the Peloponnesians for their cowardly decision to wall off their homelands during the last part of the Persian invasion (2.44–6). This "Athenocentric" history of the Persian War period helped Athenians justify the claim that they deserved to "lead" the other Greeks during the fifth century. Next came the extraordinary representation of the Athenians' empire. The Athenians saved their allies from civic strife and compelled them to live on a basis of equality within the cities, rather than as slaves to the rich (Lys. 2.55–6). Thus, through their imperialism, the Athenians put their allies' politics on a more just and stable footing. The Persian King conceded some of his land when he saw the Greeks' strength united under Athenian leadership; Athenians protected and led the other Greeks. (One can also see such standard ideas reflected in Plato's satirical funeral oration, the *Menexenus* [242a–b, 244c].) The Athenians' loss in the naval battle at Aegospotami (405 BC), Lysias says, ultimately enabled the Persians to overpower many Greek cities and to drive Greece as a whole into a state of fear and slavery (2.58–60). The point is that the Greeks were much better situated with the Athenians in charge.

In other fourth-century funeral orations, the story is much the same. For example, Demosthenes said in his own funeral oration of 338 BC that, after the Persian Wars, the Athenians prevented other Greeks from exhibiting *pleonexia* – a vice that involves greed, self-aggrandizement, and injustice. The Athenians, he says, always fought on the side of justice and risked their lives for the sake of the Greeks' welfare (60.11). Elsewhere, Demosthenes reiterated that the Athenians were not naturally suited to pursue *pleonexia*; rather, their habit was to prevent imperialists from threatening the freedom of others (8.41–2). These points are striking because in the fifth century *pleonexia* was a common term used by critics of Athenian imperialism. Clearly fourth-century Athenians were sensitive to criticism of their imperialism and made every effort to justify themselves and to distance themselves from any ethical criticism of their leadership.

Such ideas were elaborated in unparalleled detail in Isocrates' *Panegyricus* and *Panathenaicus*. These were political pamphlets written in the fourth century for an elite readership, though they appear to incorporate many sentiments that would likely have appealed to a broad range of Athenian citizens. In these works Isocrates celebrated Athens's civilizing force, its establishment of democracies, its provisions for Hellenic security, and its encouragement of Hellenic prosperity (Text 18).

> **18.** In return for these benefits, if they had thought about it even a little, they would have been right to be grateful to us. For we took over their cities – some of which had been altogether ruined by the barbarians, others of which had been ravaged – and we led them to the point where, though they gave a small part of their possessions to us, they had no less than those Peloponnesians who pay no tribute at all. (Isocr. 12.69)

According to Isocrates, Athenians wanted to be military leaders not tyrants (5.80), they granted their allies freedom, they encouraged their growth and flourishing, they set up democracies, they established colonies for protection (5.103–7; cf. 12.48, 53, 67), and so on. Xenophon, however, gleefully reported that when the Athenian Empire was on its last legs in 405 BC, the Athenians "reckoned that there was no deliverance for them except through suffering the same things they had inflicted on others; they had mistreated people of small cities, not in order to avenge themselves, but through arrogance and for no other reason than their alliance with Sparta." (*Hellenica* 2.2.10). Having read Thucydides' presentation of the Melian dialogue (Thuc. 5.84–116; cf. "Thucydidean Imperialists Revisit *Nomos* and *Phusis*" in chapter 4), one might be inclined to agree with Xenophon.

Against this background, we are in a better position to interpret the Thucydidean representation of Athens's self-justifications. In Thucydides' text, the situation is much more ambiguous than we find in the fourth-century funeral orations and related works. In domestic conversations about imperialism, for example, prominent Athenians in Thucydides' text appear to have recognized moral ambiguities, only to override them through claims of utility, glory, and the welfare of Athens. In speeches reported by Thucydides, for example, Pericles admitted that acquiring an empire may have been unjust, but he argued that the Athenians would put themselves in grave danger if they attempted to give up their empire (2.63.2). He also declared, "By our daring we have forced every sea and land to be accessible to us, and everywhere we have established eternal memorials of our evil and our good" (Thuc. 2.41.4). The Thucydidean Pericles openly acknowledged the moral ambiguities of Athenian imperialism. It is unlikely that the historical Pericles could have acknowledged such ambiguities in public – and yet it is credible that Athenians recognized a possible moral problem with imperialism, because they constantly needed reassurance that their imperialism was legitimate (cf. Isocr. 4.100).[23]

We can gather some sense of their attempts to reassure themselves from Thucydides' depiction of the Athenians' speeches abroad.[24] Thucydides reports an Athenian speech given at Sparta before the war started (1.73–8). The Athenian ambassadors *say* that their aim is not to justify themselves so much as to make the Spartans think carefully before entering a possibly unnecessary war. But the speech is shot through with self-justification, and we can observe in it many of the rhetorical stances familiar from the fourth century. The envoys recall Athenian leadership and courage during the Persian Wars and claim chief responsibility for the Greek victory (1.73–4). They also report that their "allies" had voluntarily chosen them to be leaders, when the Spartans declined to help their fellow Greeks finish off the war against Persia (1.75; cf. Isocr. 4.72). These were stock themes in the Athenians' self-justifying repertoire, as we know it from the fourth century. The Athenians also emphasized the advantages they bestowed on others, their relative moderation, and thus their worthiness to rule (Text 19).

19. We have done nothing surprising or contrary to human nature by accepting an empire when it was given and not letting it go. We have been overcome by the three greatest things: honor, fear, and self-interest, nor did we first begin to act this way. It has always been the case that the weaker are kept down by the stronger. Also, we think we are worthy of our empire, and you thought so, too, until now, when you have taken your own self-interest into account and used the justice argument. To this day, no one given the chance to gain something by force has preferred such arguments and so kept himself from taking more. (Thuc. 1.76)

One might wonder what sort of voluntary choices are possible when an armada is sitting in the harbor, but imperialists commonly emphasized their worthiness to "lead" (cf. Xen. *Cyropaedia* 1.1.3–4, Lys. 2.47; Isocr. 4.71–2, 4.99–100). Finally, the Athenians stress their mildness as compared to the Spartans, in that they established impartial jury-courts to hear cases involving allies and Athenians (Thuc. 1.76–7; cf. Isocr. 12.56–7). It is plausible to believe that Athenians of the fifth century had developed such a repertoire of self-justifications. One confirmation of this point is that, in the fifth century, Athenian tragedy was full of scenes in which Athenians were bearers of justice, enlightenment, and civilization to other, implicitly less humane cities (for fourth-century treatment of similar themes, cf. *Menexenus* 244e).

It is eerily fascinating to hold up the Athenians as a mirror of modern democratic rhetoric. If Athenian self-absorption seems transparently repellent, then what are we to think of the democratic rhetoric produced by post-Cold War America? One scholar has described this rhetoric as follows:

Much of the rhetoric of the "New World Order" promulgated by the American government since the end of the Cold War – with its redolent self-congratulation, its unconcealed triumphalism, its grave proclamations of responsibility – might have been scripted by Conrad's Holroyd: we are number one, we are bound to lead, we stand for freedom and order, and so on. No American has been immune from this structure of feeling, and yet the implicit warning contained in Conrad's portraits of Holroyd and Gould is rarely reflected on since the rhetoric of power all too easily produces an illusion of benevolence when deployed in an imperial setting.[25]

The comparison with modern America lends credibility to Thucydides' representation of Athens as crudely self-justifying. This is true even if we believe that, elsewhere, Thucydides highlighted the morally questionable aspects of Athenian imperialism for his own literary and didactic purposes.

At least in Thucydides' text, the Athenians' self-justifying sentiments co-existed with other discussions that utilized the language of pure *realpolitik*. Their most chilling, and least persuasive, argument was that they had done nothing contrary to human nature in accepting an empire when it was given to them. Human nature drives the strong to rule the weak. On the face of it, this sounds like a theoretical justification drawn from sophistic thinking about *nomos* and *phusis* (cf. *"Nomos* and *Phusis"* in chapter 4). The Spartans would have done the same, they say; so would the Melians or anybody else with enough power (1.76, 5.105). "The gods, in our opinion, and men, as we know clearly, are always driven by natural necessity to rule over anyone they have in their power" (5.105). Such speculations assumed both a pessimistic view of human nature and an amoral vision of relations among states. By human nature these Athenians would have understood the passions of fear, envy, greed, ambition, and so forth. They turned their belief in the primacy of these passions into a general law of imperialism that favored the strong (Text 19).

Because of the evidently sophistic overtones of this argument (cf. *"Nomos* and *Phusis"* in chapter 4), it is possible that some such formulation could have been developed by the Athenians in the late fifth century.[26] This must remain an open question. But, given our general knowledge of public rhetoric (cf. the analysis of American rhetoric quoted above), and of the Athenians' tendency toward self-justification, it is more likely that such arguments represented a Thucydidean "spin" on Athenian imperialism. To Thucydides, the Athenians exhibited a practical ethos that the "sophists" found clever ways to theorize and justify. These arguments, or some such arguments, Thucydides might have said, are what the Athenians *had* to have in mind in pursuing their ruthless imperialism. Thucydides put these speeches into the mouths of Athenians, in other words, in order to teach his readers what the Athenians' real motivations were, insofar as he could discern them.[27]

By bringing up fear as a central motivation (Text 19), the Athenians at Sparta argued very interestingly that imperialism was a sort of compulsion or necessity driving states such as their own. Fear and compulsion characterized not the victims, but the imperialists themselves. That is a significant reversal of the typical picture. And it is a complex reversal. For it was not only that human beings were driven by materialistic or honor-loving passions. Rather, the perception that others, too, were driven by these passions made fear one of the primary engines driving politics altogether. According to Thucydides, for example, it was inevitable that Sparta would start a war against Athens because the Spartans feared the continued growth of Athenian power (Thuc. 1.23). Ironically, perhaps, the Athenians' tyrannical rule over the other Greeks meant that they were constrained, as a matter of self-protection and freedom, to hold on to their tyranny – or so the speakers represented by Thucydides argued (Text 20).[28]

> **20.** You do not see that you hold an empire that is a tyranny over unwilling subjects who are constantly plotting against you. They do not obey you because you do them favors while harming yourselves, but rather because of your superiority in strength – not their goodwill. (Cleon, Thuc. 3.37).

Sometimes this idea was transformed into an argument that, at this point in their political evolution, the Athenians could not, under threat of slavery, reckon up, like household stewards, how far they wanted their empire to extend (Thuc. 6.18); their only salvation, in other words, lay in the endless pursuit of self-aggrandizement.

This vocabulary of constraint, necessity, and natural fears is typical of war hawks then and now. Fear certainly has the capacity to galvanize a population to political and military action. Even if Thucydides himself wanted to emphasize the importance of fear, then, this is a credible sort of vocabulary to attribute to Athenian leaders during the tense years of the Peloponnesian War. It speaks volumes about both the fears and ambitions to which citizens are susceptible. But it says something even more important about the role of politicians who encourage hawkish agendas to divert attention from domestic problems, to create artificial unity, or to secure their own positions. That, at least, was a criticism that could be leveled against Athenian politicians during the Peloponnesian War (Text 21).

> **21.** "You desperate farmers, if you want to hear how Peace was lost, listen to what I say. First, Pheidias, who was in trouble, laid hands on her. Then Pericles, fearing that he might share his friend's bad fortune, and afraid of your naturally ferocious ways, before suffering anything terrible himself, he set the city on fire, throwing in a small spark of the Megarian decree; and he blew up such a great war that all the Greeks everywhere were crying from the smoke. And when the first vine began to crackle against its will, and the wine-jar, struck by anger, kicked another jar, there was no longer anyone who could stop it, and Peace disappeared." (Aristophanes, *Peace*, 603–14)

Final Thoughts

What, then, is the relationship between democracy and imperialism? For Herodotus, as for other critics of Athenian democracy, the Athenian demos could be duped by its leaders into expanding its power over the other Greeks. It was possible to look upon Athens's leaders as the engine driving Athenian imperialism. Thucydides modified these arguments by suggesting that democracy helped to unite the demos and its leaders in a self-conscious, and largely successful, imperialistic coalition.[29] He argued that (literal) tyrants did not make good imperialists because they had to spend too much money and energy on self-protection at home (1.17). Democrats solved the problem of greed and ambition within the city by developing well-founded mutual trust and concord among themselves, and by channeling their acquisitive passions outward against the other Greeks. As a point of historical fact, the Athenian democracy was strikingly successful at doing this.

Thucydides, however, added to his representation of democratic imperialism yet another layer of interpretation. In Thucydides' interpretation, the Athenians had developed a national ethos conducive to imperialism; he put a speech to this effect into the mouths of the Corinthians at Sparta (Text 22).

> **22.** And, for the city's sake, they treat their bodies as though they belonged to others altogether, whereas they treat their minds with special care, in order to do something for the city. And if they have plans in mind, but do not accomplish them, they suppose that they are thereby deprived of what belonged to them, while whatever they go after and acquire, they consider trivial compared to what they will do in the future. . . . We could accurately sum it up by saying that their nature is such as not to allow themselves or anyone else any quiet. (Corinthians, Thuc. 1.70)

The Corinthians presented the Athenian character as instilled by nature, but this speech also draws attention to the Athenians' political construction of a patriotic ethos which consisted in their willingness to sacrifice themselves for their city. We saw in chapter 3 that such a tendency toward self-sacrifice was inculcated by the Athenians' democratic education. Thus, in Thucydides' interpretation, nature, culture, and history all contributed to the formation of the Athenians' imperialistic character. The democracy liberated the citizens' energy because they all shared in the material rewards and glory of empire. Even the lower classes could enjoy the dividends of conquest. Their naval power made them highly untraditional in both the speed with which they could suppress far-flung rebellions and in their capacity to withstand ravaging and siege. Democracy created a novel type of power whose very existence, to some extent, depended on the material gains made possible by empire. Thucydides' interpretation is a striking and compelling vision of democratic imperialism.

To Thucydides, of course, imperial Athens was not impervious to criticism, either on the grounds of injustice or on those of vice and imprudence. The Athenian statesman Cleon, in Thucydides' representation, criticized his democratic audience for being too compassionate, too decent, and too indulgent in the pleasures of hearing clever arguments – all of which, he said, put imperial states at risk (Thuc. 3.40). Thucydides himself agreed, at least, that the democracy was too shortsighted and self-indulgent to expand successfully without the leadership of great men such as Pericles. Pericles provided rational guidance and self-restraint, thereby bestowing upon the democratic polis virtues that it did not naturally possess. After his death, Thucydides said, faulty leadership led to a reduction in the city's power (Text 23).

23. Those who came after him were more equal in relation to one another, and each one of them strongly desired to be first among them; and so they began to manage the city's business in such a way as to gratify the people. In such a great and imperial city, this led to many mistakes, and in particular to the expedition against Sicily. (Thuc. 2.65)

(For similar criticisms of the post-Periclean leadership, see Isocrates' speech *On the Peace* [355 BC, 8.121–33].) Thus, Thucydides criticized Athens not so much for injustice as for its imprudent handling of the war after Pericles' death. This is one point where Thucydides' criticisms appear to be unpersuasive. The empire continued intact for almost 30 years after Pericles' death – not to mention its successes before Pericles became a dominant leader!

Plato, on the other hand, reverted to the Herodotean "influx of wealth" critique. At the end of his dialogue *Gorgias*, his character Socrates criticized the democratic leadership, including Pericles, for gratifying the demos' materialistic desires (Text 24).

24. Callicles, you are now doing the same thing: you praise men who have entertained the Athenians sumptuously and feasted them on what they desired. And they say that these leaders made the city great. But they do not perceive that it is bloated and decaying underneath because of those early leaders. For, without regard for moderation or justice, they have filled the city with harbors, dockyards, walls, tribute payments, and other such nonsense. When, therefore, a fit of weakness comes, they will allege that their contemporary advisors are responsible, but they will praise Themistocles, Cimon, and Pericles – the ones who are in fact responsible for their troubles. (Plato, *Gorgias*, 518e1–519a7)

By contrast with Thucydides, Plato saw Pericles as simply one more leader who "pandered" to the demos' lowest instincts and appetites. Either way, the democracy could be criticized for its vices and imprudence even by those who recognized that it had achieved its own imperialist aims. Both Thucydides and Plato concentrated on the vices of character that, they believed, corrupted (or embodied the corruption of) the democratic polis.

It is illuminating to compare Athenian imperialism with the short-lived imperialism of fourth-century Sparta, since Sparta was typically considered an exemplar of virtue. After the fall of Athens's fifth-century empire, Sparta developed an Aegean empire of its own. (Of course, as the Athenians liked the remind them, the Spartans had been imperialists of a sort in the Peloponnese from the eighth century onward; for their annexation of Messenia, and leadership of the Peloponnesian League, see "Sparta and the Politics of 'Courage'" in chapter 2.) Sparta was well known as the most stable of Greek regimes, in part because of its famously "mixed" constitution: kings, elected "ephors," a council of elders, and a citizen assembly provided checks and balances on one another (cf. Polybius 6.48–50). Machiavelli saw that such a constitution suited a land-based power with the limited military objectives of defense (*Discourses* 1.6; cf. Polybius 6.49–50). For Machiavelli, at least, Sparta could not establish a successful empire because of its rejection of immigrants and, consequently, its small population (*Discourses* 2.3).

Classical Greeks argued, by contrast, that Sparta's rigorous cultivation of virtue, especially of courage, was well suited to its exceptional military power. However, many also argued that Spartans, as imperialists, did not live up to the traditional ideals that had made Sparta great, and in particular that the influx of wealth corrupted long-standing Spartan virtues (Xenophon, *Constitution of the Spartans*, 14; Isocr. 8.95–6, 8.103). More importantly, the Spartans violated justice, sold out the Ionian Greeks to Persia, and became a universal object of hatred (Isocr. 4.110–18, 8.97–102). Their injustice led to civic strife and profound suffering in many Greek cities, notably Athens (Xen. *Hellenica*, 2.3–4). This is a sharp notice to find in Xenophon, who ordinarily praises Sparta for its cultivation of discipline and justice. He made the point even more sharply by portraying his fictitious Persian Cyrus, by contrast, as calming civic strife through imperialism (*Cyr.* 7.4.1–7). Political criticisms of vice and injustice therefore extended beyond monarchies and democracies to that constitution, the Spartan, which many Greeks found to be the most virtuous. The criticisms were remarkably similar across the board.

A different account of the consequences of imperialism, however, could be found in Athenian popular forums. Aristophanes and Euripides made warfare a central topic in a number of their plays. Although they did not theorize imperialism as such, their presentation of warfare and its consequences helped to form the political imaginations of Athenian citizens who voted for nakedly imperialist ventures. Like Thucydides, Isocrates, and Plato, these playwrights made the point that imperialism is based on military force and violence. As a result, imperialism often brings suffering, as well as power and material benefits, to the home population.

Several of Aristophanes' plays – including the *Acharnians* (425 BC), *Peace* (421 BC), and *Lysistrata* (411 BC) – dramatized the suffering caused by Athens's continuous warfare and illustrated the manifold benefits of peace. The title-character Lysistrata, for example, organized a panhellenic coalition of women in order to stop the fighting between Athens and Sparta. To do so, she staged a "sex-strike" and oversaw the women's take-over of the Athenian Acropolis. The play advanced interesting criticisms of Athenian men and their political rhetoric: under the guise of protecting their city and families, the men consumed resources in order to pursue the ultimate male dream of conquest. Strikingly, Athenian tradition maintained that the early Athenians (men, of course) had founded their political order through defending the city from imperialistic Amazons (Lys. 2.4–6)! Aristophanes asserted rather that the manly pursuits of war were gradually destroying *Athenian* women and households. The Athenians' narrow-minded pugnacity was thereby revealed as immature, adolescent, and misguided. The men were unable to grasp the importance of their families, the benefits of peace, and the significant common ground they shared with the Spartans. Note that Isocrates, the fourth-century panhellenist, argued in *On the Peace* that peace, not unjust war, brings the only truly praiseworthy advantages. Therefore, warfare should be pursued only in order to protect or promote peace.

It is ironic to observe that, in the *Lysistrata*, only Aristophanes' women, and not real men, were capable of panhellenism. Why would this be the case? The answer may be that the men had too much at stake in going to war: their self-image as men, and the justification of their exclusive political power, rested on their capacity to defend the city. Men derived benefits from going to war that were unavailable to the women who stayed home. Aristophanes was suggesting, perhaps, that such benefits did not contribute to the welfare of the city, or, for that matter, even to the men's own self-interest, properly understood. This challenged the prevailing ideology that warfare brought men to manhood and taught them useful skills; a Euripidean character's statement to that effect was shown to be signally mistaken (Text 25).

> **25.** Helen suffered hardship not because she wanted to, but because of the gods. And this was of very great benefit to Hellas; for being inexperienced in arms and fighting, the Greeks learned how to be men. Association teaches mortals everything. (Menelaus, in Euripides, *Andromache*, 680–4)

Athenian men needed an altogether different understanding of their principal virtues, if they wanted to pursue the benefits of peace. This, however, does not mean that Aristophanes was a peacenik. His plays were meant to provide a check on excessive pugnacity, without recommending that warfare be avoided at any cost. Aristophanes arguably wanted his fellow citizens to hit the golden mean between a tame pacificism and rampant imperialism.

Euripides' war plays are susceptible to a similar interpretation. By reflecting upon them carefully, the Athenians could come to appreciate the costs of warfare to themselves and to their subjects. In plays such as *Trojan Women* (415 BC), for example, Euripides staged the appalling aftermath of the Greek sack of Troy. Amidst a great deal of understandable lamentation for sexual depredation, the loss of children, and the destruction of temples, the prophetic Cassandra insightfully interprets the costs of the Trojan War even to the successful Greeks (Text 26).

> **26.** Hunting down one woman and one passion, Helen, the Greeks lost innumerable men. And their clever general lost what he held most dear for the sake of what was most hateful to him, giving up the pleasures of his own children for the sake of his brother's wife – all this despite her having been carried off with her consent, not by force. When they arrived at the banks of the Scamander, they began to die, though they had not been deprived of their land's boundaries, nor of their fatherland with its high towers. And those whom Ares chose, they did not see their children, and they were not shrouded in burial-robes by their wives' hands, but they lie dead in a foreign land. Similar things happened to those at home: wives lost their brave husbands, and died as widows, while others, now childless, died in their homes after raising their children in vain. (Euripides, *Trojan Women*, 368–81)

Whatever an Athenian audience thought of the justice of the Greek expedition to Troy, it was impossible to view the suffering of these women without a certain amount of sympathy. In the Assembly, the Athenians continued to be hard-nosed realists. Their bellicose policies showed few signs of becoming more peaceful. Athens wasn't often on the lookout for politicians who just wanted to give peace a chance. But at least the Athenians had heard and processed such criticisms of war – another sign of the democracy's capacity to accept self-criticism.

It is impossible to measure the effect such theatrical experiences had on Athenian citizens, who continued to vote for wars of imperialism. It may be that such comedies and tragedies moderated the tendency toward violently angry responses and helped Athenians step back and view their own self-interests more clearly. That, at least, appears to have happened in 427 BC, when the Athenians at first voted to execute the entire male population of (rebellious) Mytilene, and then had a change of heart and reconsidered the issue.[30] They spared most of the men, but still executed roughly 1,000 of the conspirators. They distributed most of Mytilene's agricultural land to Athenians (Thuc. 3.36–50). That, perhaps, was *their* interpretation of the golden mean. It does not meet our ethical standards by any means. But neither this disconnect, nor our knowledge of Greek history and political thought, prevents *us* from reading Euripidean and Aristophanic plays as urgent calls for peace. Our golden mean is different from that of Athens; our checks on violence and anger are properly more substantial than those of Athens; and, therefore, these dramatic explorations of imperialism, war, and peace, should have a different effect on us. If they do, then we might be misreading the plays to excellent effect.

chapter 6
Fourth-Century Revisions

The death of Socrates was a signal event in Plato's life. But the revolution of the Thirty Tyrants was a watershed in everyone's life (cf. chapter 4, Introduction; "*Nomos* and *Phusis*"). Athens had never witnessed such bloody civil strife. The violence and greed of the Thirty arguably stemmed from the ideological fanaticism that characterized the last three decades of the fifth century. With the Peloponnesian War over, however, with Socrates dead, with the Athenian Empire gone, and especially with the recent experience of the bloody junta, political thought began to take, almost had to take, new directions. By contrast with the bitterly critical late fifth-century discourse on democracy, fourth-century thinkers advanced novel positive ideas about nondemocratic forms of government. These thinkers idealized monarchy in particular, but they were also attracted to aristocracies modeled on traditional lines – for example, that of Sparta, and that of (a largely imaginary) "ancestral" Athens. For the most profound thinkers, Plato and Aristotle, the new traditionalism provided a basis for constructing radical visions of the political future.

During the Peloponnesian War, the Athenians' long-term strategy (cf. chapter 4, "*Nomos* and *Phusis*") devastated Greece's economic infrastructure, reduced manpower reserves, and made civil war common. Xenophon dramatized such problems in his history of the Greek world (*Hellenica*) from 411 to 362 BC. The moral centerpiece of this work was the programmatic account of the Thirty Tyrants.[1] In Xenophon's presentation, these tyrants had established an anti-polis. Led by Plato's cousin Critias and his uncle Charmides, and backed by the Spartans, the oligarchs executed political opponents, indulged their greed for gain, and banished scores of democratic citizens. Their need to pay the Spartan garrison forced them to confiscate property in order to maintain power – which cast them, in Xenophon's view, in the worst possible light (Text 1).

> **1.** [Once the Thirty had seized the arms of ordinary citizens,] since they knew they were now able to do whatever they wanted, they killed many out of hatred and many others for their money. In order to be able to pay the garrison, moreover, they thought it best for each of their number to arrest a resident alien, to execute their victims, and to confiscate their property (*Hellenica* 2.3.21)

Even Plato, originally an oligarchic sympathizer, later viewed the democratic fifth century as a golden age by comparison (*Epistle* 7.324d4–8). Like Thucydides' excursus on Corcyra, Xenophon's set piece detailed the corruption brought on by civil war and the vices of unworthy rulers. Xenophon's narrative is filled with such conflicts between polarized groups of democrats and oligarchs. The Peloponnesian War left a legacy of political infighting that demanded better political solutions.

To use a common Platonic metaphor, the body politic was sick and needed physicians who could restore political health. How to do so, when the so-called nobility had established a reign of terror in 404–3 BC? This was the problem that demanded a solution. The pious answer was that rulers had to exhibit both the traditional virtues of character – self-restraint, justice, courage, and piety – and the intellectual virtues of wisdom, foresight, and practical intelligence. But there were two problems: first, aristocrats in power empirically confirmed that power corrupts; second, the Athenian democracy had successfully taken charge of the aristocratic virtues. After expelling the Thirty Tyrants, Athenian democrats drew up, and largely adhered to, an amnesty agreement that forbade public recollection of past wrongdoing. As a sign of democratic moderation, the amnesty was a triumphant moral victory. Xenophon, Isocrates, and Plato could only turn to theory. But the Athenian democracy could legitimately lay claim to the traditional political virtues. The argument that aristocrats exhibited such virtues more reliably than their "inferiors" had been exposed as snobbish and false.

As a result, the theorists had to rehabilitate aristocratic politics through emphasizing the connections between individual talent, ethical education, and the constitution. To establish lasting political health, cities needed talented individuals, education, and institutions that would discourage abuses of power. Many saw monarchy as a panacea; others looked to properly constituted institutions. But Isocrates summed up the matter best when he said that the "soul (*psuchê*) of the city is nothing other than its *politeia*" (7.14). *Politeia* normally means "constitution," or the distribution of offices and power. But Isocrates showed that *politeia* must also be construed broadly. It includes not only the institutional distribution of power, but also the community's ethos, including its goals, values, and educational strategies. Emphasizing character and constitution enabled fourth-century thinkers to develop a more sophisticated body of thought than traditional aristocrats were capable of. Isocrates' pointed equation of *psuchê* with *politeia* was a first move in the effort to reconfigure the traditional relationship between ethics and politics.

The Ancestral Republican "Solutions"

In the *Areopagiticus* (ca. 355 BC), Isocrates idealized an "aristocratic democracy" in which the most virtuous and wisest men held the principal offices but did not conceive desperate desires for power. The demos had the authority to elect magistrates and to hold them accountable (7.26–7). The laws and customs of this "ancestral constitution" (cf. *Antidosis* 232) made the people pious, just, and friendly toward one another. Isocrates was careful to intertwine his explanation of the citizens' good character with the constitutional structure of the imagined early republic. The key was that the aristocratic Areopagus Council supervised the citizens' behavior and saw to the maintenance of "good order" (*eukosmia*, 7.37). According to Isocrates, not only children, but also fully formed adults, needed a continuing education in self-restraint and proper deportment. By contrast with ordinary democratic discourse, therefore, Isocrates argued that citizens became virtuous not because of democratic laws, practices, or rituals, but rather because of the ethical habits they learned from the city's leading men (7.39–40). These habits were enforced by vigilant supervision and, if necessary, by swift and just chastisement. The Areopagus saw to the community's piety, security, civic friendship, and patriotism. The result of this inculcation of civic virtue was unanimous dedication to the community. This was a powerful contribution to the idealized aristocratic self-image in the wake of the corrupt "aristocracy" of 404 BC.

One of Isocrates' chief concerns was to show that this ancestral constitution achieved justice. To make this argument, Isocrates probed the ordinary conception of equality and judged it inadequate (Text 2).

> **2.**   Above all, they governed the city well because they knew that of the two recognized types of equality – one distributing the same to all, another distributing to each his due – one was more useful. They rejected the one that esteems the noble and the worthless alike, on the grounds of its injustice. They chose the one that honors or punishes each according to his merit, and they used this principle to govern the polis. They did not choose their magistrates by lot from all citizens, but rather they chose the best and those most suited for each particular duty. For they expected that the other citizens, too, would be of a similar character to those who administered their political affairs (Isocr. 7.21–2)

According to Isocrates, there were two kinds of political equality: one based on merit, another based on the citizens' status as free adult men. (These "two kinds of equality" were often described in mathematical terminology – the merit-based form being called "proportional" or "geometric" and the simpler form being called "arithmetic".)[2] This distinction represented a positive response to democratic equality. The antidemocratic argument was simple, traditional, and powerful. Honor and power ought to be distributed to each according to his merit – not according to his status as a free man. Achilles had once used a similarly "meritocratic" argument to condemn Agamemnon's unjust greed (cf. "Achilles, Agamemnon, and Fair Distribution" in chapter 2). By contrast with Protagoras, therefore, Isocrates emphasized the differences among citizens rather than their (rough) similarity. "Proportional equality" enabled Isocrates to justify hierarchy by appealing to properly understood equality. (Note, by contrast, that freedom never became a positive oligarchic value, because what mattered to oligarchs was a status-conscious hierarchy, not inclusive political participation or the freedom to live life as one pleased.)[3] In the light of proportional equality, then, justice required that only a few virtuous citizens, or even a single remarkably virtuous individual, hold power.

In the *Areopagiticus*, Isocrates also used utilitarian arguments to promote aristocratic rule. It was not only that aristocrats deserved power; rather, and more importantly, the city would be better off if they were in charge. Isocrates wanted to show that aristocrats could govern the polis most nobly (*arista*) and most wisely (*sôphronestata*); both adverbs have aristocratic overtones. He criticized contemporary democracy for its political vices, which originated in the citizens' misunderstanding of key values. They wrongly viewed "self-indulgence as democracy, violation of the law as freedom, frank speech as equality, and freedom to do anything and everything as happiness" (Isocr. 7.20). Democrats had taken their meritorious values to unhealthy extremes, because they lacked the supervision of superiors who could keep them "centered." To correct this situation, Isocrates argued, the right people must be in control. As the Athenians' ancestors recognized, the citizenry at large would exhibit the same ethical characteristics as the magistrates who were in charge (Isocr. 7.22). It turns out, then, that those in charge (and not the *politeia* itself) will be the architects of the citizens' character. Perhaps imperceptibly, Isocrates slides from arguing that the *politeia* shapes the citizens' character, to arguing that the character of the powerful – i.e., the best men – educates the lower classes. This move put Isocrates on a slippery slope. The same held true for other fourth-century thinkers who followed suit.

Isocrates' aim, then, was to promote an aristocratic paternalism that would guarantee discipline, patriotism, and order. Yet his proposal is unsuccessful because he provides no structures to ensure the reproduction of a virtuous aristocracy. Was there any plausible reason to believe, in the fourth century, that if aristocrats were back in power – say, in the Areopagus – then they would govern in a spirit of patriotism and self-restraint? How could Isocrates guarantee that the demos would recognize men of virtue and so elect them to office? With what knowledge could the Areopagus securely identify civic virtue in practice? The only assurance Isocrates can offer is a flimsily conventional account of how best to educate the young in virtue (7.43–9). But, if that had been enough, then how did Athens arrive at its current state of corruption? Isocrates' work brings to light the tension between relying on the *politeia* – on the system itself – to produce political health, and relying on the character of individuals who happen to be in power.

Polybius provided the most authoritative statement of the need to rely on the *politeia* for successful reproduction of a healthy political culture. Writing in the second century BC, he analyzed Rome's rise to imperial greatness as a function of its "mixed constitution." For Polybius, the best constitution mixes elements of kingship, aristocracy, and democracy, because inherent in each simple form were characteristic vices that led to instability. By contrast, a mixed constitution, such as one could find at Sparta or Rome, embodied a state of dynamic equilibrium and a system of checks and balances (Text 3).

> **3.** Lycurgus, foreseeing these problems, did not establish a constitution that was simple or of a single form, but he joined together all the excellent and distinctive features of the best constitutions, in order that no part could grow excessively large and turn into its related vice, but, with the power of each balanced by the others, no one of them could lean forward in any way or sink. (Polybius, 6.10.6–7)

Whoever happened to be in office, the system itself provided its own safeguards and sources of self-restraint. The result was that change would be measured, cautious, and prudent. Meanwhile, individual vices, should they emerge in the public sphere, would be tempered by the self-interest of other "branches" of the government. This type of system depends on the wisdom of the lawgiver or the "framers" and does not demand significant faith in the virtue or educability of individuals. It may indeed imply a pessimistic view of human nature because all individuals need to be checked and balanced by the structure of constitutional government.

Of all the classical Greek states, Sparta came closest to Polybius' recommended model. And it held pride of place as a long-term republican constitution for many centuries. Alongside Rome, for example, Sparta was held up for high praise as a durable and prosperous republic in Machiavelli's *Discourses*. Already in the fourth century, Xenophon's *Constitution of the Spartans* proclaimed the virtues of Sparta's social and political institutions. But his "constitution" centered more on character than political structure. According to Xenophon, the legendary Lycurgus inculcated the virtues, especially self-restraint, through a rigid educational system (Text 4).

> **4.** He observed that where only volunteers take care over virtue they are not sufficient to strengthen their fatherlands, so he forced everyone, as a matter of public policy, to practice all the virtues at Sparta. Therefore, just as private individuals who practice are superior in virtue to those who do not concern themselves with it, so also is Sparta, not surprisingly, superior in virtue to all other cities, since Sparta alone makes the pursuit of nobility a matter of public concern. (Xenophon, *Constitution of the Spartans*, 10.4)

Xenophon illustrates that the Spartan constitution is balanced by a mixture of kings, a council of elders, an assembly of citizens, and democratically elected magistrates known as ephors. His chief aim, however, was to explain the wisdom of the lawgiver in providing for the proper education of desire. It was as if all the elements were in place, but there was as yet no systematic theory weaving together character and institutional design in order to restore the aristocratic order.

Xenophon's own work shows that such a theory was needed: contemporary Spartans, he says, signally failed to live up to Lycurgus' ideals. "Now they exert themselves," he bitterly declares, "much more in seeing how they will exercise power than in figuring out how to be worthy rulers" (14.6). The lawgiver had developed an irresistible war-machine through his educational practices. But the Spartans, he says, took their originally admirable love of glory to an unhealthy extreme. Their military victories, and eventually their imperialism, led them to abuse and destroy the virtues that had once made them successful. Other authors joined Xenophon in criticizing Spartan militarism and imperialism. As Plato would later point out, the Spartans valued only one part of virtue – courage – which is, as it happens, the least significant part of virtue. They had no idea how to use their military capacity to promote a peaceful and healthy political life. Polybius, differently, suggested that the Spartans were unsuccessful imperialists in the long run, because Lycurgus' system had not taught them how to supply themselves adequately so as to maintain and extend their conquests abroad; Rome was a far more successful imperial power

(6.48–50). Finally, as even contemporary Athenians recognized, Spartan self-restraint and courage were bought at a high price: the sacrifice of individual freedom to an extent unimaginable elsewhere in Greece. Xenophon's admiring examination of ancestral Sparta did little to rehabilitate what was, even to contemporary Athenians, much less to us, a rigid dystopia.

The Monarchic "Solution"

Beyond such republican nostalgia, another important focus of fourth-century political thought was the optimistic turn toward monarchy. Alongside their republicanism, Xenophon and Isocrates elaborated theories of monarchy. The fourth century was a time of casting about for solutions to Greece's numerous political, social, and economic troubles. The uniquely strong and wise individual was a tempting possibility. No elaborate constitutional design would be necessary if properly educated and supremely powerful individuals came to power and put their energies in the service of the common good. Isocrates praised and exhorted Evagoras, Nicocles, and Demonicus in his "Cypriot" orations; and in other works he cultivated Philip of Macedon and Archidamus of Sparta. Xenophon held up for admiration the virtues of King Agesilaus of Sparta and the fictional King Cyrus of Persia. Plato traveled to Sicily and tried unsuccessfully to educate the sole rulers of Syracuse. Later, in his *Statesman*, he argued that the only constitution deserving of the name was that of a single monarch with confirmed political expertise – all other constitutions being merely corrupt shams. The major question was how to produce the best man.

There were precedents for optimistic thinking about monarchy. The Homeric epics offered fully developed narratives highlighting the virtues and vices of single rulers (cf. chapter 2, "The Elitist Response"). The *Odyssey*, in particular, represented Ithaka as completely dependent for its welfare on the leadership of Odysseus, who, Telemachus tells the Ithakans, "once was the ruler among all of you here, / and he was like a kind father" (*Od.* 2.46–7). The status of ruler as savior was similarly embedded in traditional narratives of early kings and lawgivers. King Theseus of Athens, for example, was credited with purging the countryside of myriad plagues, killing the Minotaur and freeing Athens from paying tribute to King Minos of Crete, not to mention achieving the union of Attica with a political center at Athens (Plutarch, *Theseus* 8–25). Early lawgivers, too, such as Lycurgus of Sparta, were credited with transforming disordered cities into homes of individual virtue, political stability, and military power.

These traditional ideas were first theorized by Darius in Herodotus's "Constitutional Debate" (Text 5).

> **5.** Nothing is better than the rule of the single best man. He would govern the people flawlessly because of his good judgment. And he would keep secret, to the greatest extent possible, his plans to confront his enemies. (Darius, at Hdt. 3.82.2)

Darius's argument was that monarchy was both best and inevitable: best, provided that a wise and honest leader could be found; and inevitable, because oligarchy and democracy, he says, devolve through infighting into chaos, from which political health must be restored through the emergence of a single ruler. But Darius's interlocutors recognized the dangers of such concentrations of power. Otanes emphasized the monarch's envy and arrogance, both of which stemmed from his inability to wear his power lightly. For Otanes, monarchs typically could not resist the joys of power or withstand the sight of another's success. If we think back to Agamemnon, or to the rulers of Hesiod's polis, then we recall that such criticisms of oppressive rulership had equally deep roots. Fourth-century thinkers rejuvenated both sides of the monarchic equation by illuminating monarchy's positive and negative potential.

The most interesting point among many, for us, is that monarchs were often imagined as solving problems through uniting Greece's military forces in panhellenic expeditions against the "barbarians" (cf. "Natural Superiority" in chapter 5). Their powerful leadership could put an end to warfare between Greek cities and to civil strife within those cities. The former theme is more prominent in Isocrates' appeals to Philip of Macedon. For Isocrates, Philip was well-positioned to act as panhellenic leader because "other men with good reputations were governed by their cities and the laws, and they could do nothing other than what was commanded" (5.14). Although Athenian speakers like Demosthenes might view Philip as a menace, Isocrates placed his hopes in Philip's ability to produce concord among the warring Greek states through military leadership. It was above all the monarch's freedom that gave Isocrates hope.

Slightly different thoughts animated Xenophon's admiring biography of the Spartan King Agesilaus. Among his many virtues, Xenophon says, Agesilaus was politically intelligent and courageous enough to establish harmony in the faction-ridden cities of the former Athenian empire (*Agesilaos* 1.37–8). He was the model of a patriotic and law-abiding monarch who worked within the Spartan constitution. Xenophon's praise of Agesilaus' patriotism includes many examples of his unwillingness to harm the other Greeks and of his persistent vision of uniting Greeks in the fight against the Persians (*Agesilaos* 7.1–7). Either way, such accounts of the monarchic "solution" were very different from those of early modern theorists. In the *Leviathan* (1651), for example, Thomas Hobbes hoped for a monarch who could hold the elite in check so as to produce security for ordinary people. The drive to make monarchs into panhellenic crusaders was a highly distinctive cultural idea.

Amidst such vividly imagined ideals, Isocrates also drew attention to the need to educate monarchs. There would always be worries that Otanes was right. Absolute power might have harmful effects on the king's soul. In *To Nicocles*, Isocrates remarked that, as supremely powerful individuals, monarchs need education more than anyone else. Yet others approach them only obsequiously and so fail to admonish them or to teach them anything (2.3–5). In a monarchy, the king's character is crucial to establishing a healthy politics, but the very position of the king seems to militate against his receiving a proper training in character. Therefore, Isocrates exhorts his addressees to master themselves and their desires above all (Text 6).

> **6.** Rule over yourself no less than over others, and consider this your most royal attribute: that you are the slave to none of the pleasures, but instead you have mastery over your own desires more than over the citizens. (Isocrates, *To Nicocles*, 29)

Through self-mastery kings will be able to devote themselves to the common good and to serve the people – both of which are crucial to the longevity of the regime. But Isocrates expressed anxiety over whether a public-spirited king could reliably be created.

Such anxiety led Isocrates and Xenophon alike to imagine that kings themselves would come to appreciate the potential unhappiness in their own positions. Even voicing such an idea might have a positive effect on those with tyrannical aspirations. Because power corrupts, Isocrates says, monarchs have historically led unenviable lives – which makes people wonder whether private life might not be better after all (*To Nicocles* 5). That worry was the central theme of Xenophon's odd inquiry into tyranny, the *Hiero*. In this fictional dialogue between Hiero of Syracuse and the poet Simonides, Hiero explains all the difficulties of living as a tyrant – for example, that the tyrant's friends and subjects never love him freely but only through compulsion. True consent and mutual respect were impossible because of the overwhelming force commanded by the tyrant. Simonides provided the solution: the tyrant must use his wealth to enhance the beauty and power of the city, he must reward those citizens who contribute to the common good, and he must develop kindness and generosity as his principal virtues. Xenophon offered no recipes for how to achieve these noble ideals. But he provided some sort of response to the worries that one-man rule evoked in his contemporaries. Single rulers had to avoid tyranny at all costs, for fear that they would harm not only their subjects, but also themselves.

Plato's "Solutions"

Plato fits coherently within the movement to establish connections between constitution and character. But his work was also shaped by his vehement reactions against the sophists and against the unreflective banality of ordinary thinking. Like many conservative theorists, Plato started with a critique of his own political culture. He claimed to be the sophisticated doctor providing, first, a diagnosis of observed culture and, second, a "cure" – which, in his case, amounted to the revolutionary proposal that philosophers should rule. In the event, we might conclude – to adapt the words of the Roman historian Livy – that fourth-century politics could not endure either its own vices or the medicines that would cure them (cf. Livy, *Preface*, 9).

First, two preliminary points about Plato's relationship to politics and history. Some interpreters of Plato – notably, later Platonists – have held that Plato's interest in politics was superficial. They argue that his political ideas were mere "window-dressing" for his exploration of metaphysics, epistemology, and ethics.[4] I reject this view for three reasons. First, like other Greek thinkers, Plato found that ethics could only be understood in a political context. For better or worse, the polis provided an education in character for its citizens. Their ethical development depended largely on the norms of their political culture. Second, our view of a "political" Plato receives strong confirmation from Aristotle's critique of Platonic politics in Book 2 of the *Politics*. Aristotle, for one, took Platonic politics seriously. Third, Plato made three trips to Sicily (388 BC, 367 BC, and 361 BC), presumably in order to re-found Syracusan politics on a philosophical basis. He discussed the trips in the (probably authentic) *Epistle 7*. Plato had a significant interest in politics and political thought.

The other point concerns Plato's place in this book as a whole. I have argued that students of ancient political thought must approach ancient texts from both a historical and a normative standpoint. The ancient authors both responded to "local" circumstances and conceived ambitions that went beyond their specific historical contexts. The same approach can be applied, in essentials, to Plato. But Plato was an exceptionally imaginative figure. He thought himself out of his local circumstances to an extent unthinkable for most writers. Therefore, it makes sense to approach his work largely from the philosophical and normative perspective, so as to avoid unacceptably "flattening" it out. The proper methodological balance is always difficult to achieve. But we can hardly go wrong in making every effort to respect Plato's own formidable philosophical ambitions.

Criticizing Contemporary Politics

Plato diagnosed contemporary culture as highly susceptible to skepticism and disorder. Unlike Xenophon, however, who criticized specific events, regimes, and agents of the past, Plato's starting-point was ethical interpretation. At the end of *Republic* Book 7, he sketched a psychological history illustrating the likelihood that unreflective traditionalists, no matter how talented, would end up as lawless skeptics in the contemporary world. Young people grow up learning principles of good behavior from their families. As a result, they tend to resist bodily and other temptations in favor of acting nobly. But then a sophist poses difficult questions: What is the noble? What is the fine? What is the good? And the young man is unable to justify his traditional beliefs in the face of counter-arguments. His natural response to such difficulties, Socrates says, is to "conclude that the noble is no more noble than the shameful, and likewise in the case of what is just and good and whatever else he held in the highest esteem" (538e). He becomes disordered. He comes to have no firm ethical convictions and no way to justify traditional precepts. He is susceptible to skepticism or relativism or worse. The citizens of classical Greece could not, in Plato's view, avoid such a "plunge" without developing deeper ethical understanding.

Plato's dialogues suggested, worse still, that even traditional morality was corrupt at the core. In the *Republic*, for example, Socrates indicates that traditional ethics shares basic (and harmful) beliefs with leading "immoralists" such as Thrasymachus (Text 7).

> **7.** I think we will say that poets and storytellers are wrong about the most important things in human life: they say that many unjust people are happy, while the just are miserable, and that injustice pays if it goes unnoticed, while justice is another's good and harmful to oneself. (*Rep.* 392a13–b4)

In other words, ordinary citizens acquired from the traditional educators, i.e. the poets, Thrasymachean cynicism about justice. Such corruption is deeply embedded in contemporary politics; it did not result from the teachings of those latecomers, the sophists. Rather, the demos itself is the greatest sophist. The citizenry as a whole inculcates ethical values into the souls of emerging citizens, so as to reproduce themselves in the next generation (Text 8).

> **8.** When, I said, many of them sit together in the assemblies, the law-courts, the theaters, army camps, or some other common meeting place shared by the many, and they find fault with some things that

are said or done, with a great uproar, while they praise others, excessively in each case, shouting out and making loud noises, the rocks and the surroundings echo in response and provide a doubly loud din of blame and praise. In such a situation, what will be the condition of the young man's heart, as they say? What sort of private education will resist this, and not be washed away by such blame and praise, and go, carried down the stream wherever it might take him, so that he will say that the same things are noble and shameful as these do, and he will conduct himself as they do, and be the same sort of person? (*Rep.* 492b5–c8)

Sophists simply reflect the moods and appetites of the powerful democratic beast. They have no account to offer of concepts such as the just, the beautiful, and the noble, other than what they know will gratify the demos's basest desires.

Plato's criticisms culminated in the *Republic*'s memorable allegory of the Cave. This image enabled Socrates to describe the condition of unenlightened, i.e. ordinary, human beings. The allegory compares ordinary people to chained prisoners in a cave, constrained to watch shadows flit about on the wall before them. They enjoy their condition, resist being liberated, and center their lives on discussing the shadows, their noises, and their movements. Plato condemned the world of unreflective moral belief as a world of shadows far removed from the truth. Since moral opinions were typically inherited from poets, from drama, and from sophistically trained orators, Plato used this image to attack the entire self-contained culture of belief that surrounded him, all in one blow. Conventional belief (including the sophists' pretentious articulation of it) was a prison whose inmates were doomed to live out an ugly, unenlightened life that no one, upon reflection, would choose for himself.

Plato's powerful critique of ordinary morality is most apt if seen in the context of democracy. The free circulation of opinions between leaders and demos created a vicious feedback loop in which leaders become the flatterers of demotic desire. They simply handed back to the demos whatever it wanted to hear. Undoubtedly these criticisms stemmed from Plato's diagnosis of imperial Athens. Citizens such as the greedy and ambitious Alcibiades learned the lesson of the city all too well: that justice is weak and foolish and that it is a law of nature that the strong will rule wherever possible. Athenians didn't need to learn these lessons from the sophists. According to Plato, though, the sophists cemented these ideas and provided a superficial theoretical grounding for them. Plato thus assaulted the Protagorean and democratic justifications for democracy. Democratic deliberation was a cognitive trap, for Plato, rather than a method of achieving practical wisdom. Plato convincingly reinterpreted democratic public dialogue as (1) motivated by greed and narrow self-interest and as (2) trapped in a cave-like world of unreflective, and often questionable, ethical belief. Thus democracy could not achieve the political goal of ensuring its citizens' well-being.

Plato on Rhetoric and Order in the *Gorgias*

These criticisms come through powerfully in the *Gorgias*. At first glance, this dialogue explores the role of rhetoric in politics. Through the discussion, however, Socrates' interlocutors come to understand a key Platonic point. To investigate rhetoric is also to explore the nature and ends of political debate, the aspirations of political leaders, and the relationship between politics, ethics, and philosophy. Through several conversations, it emerges that orators and rhetorical teachers do not understand the ends which rhetoric is meant to serve. They unreflectively take over their aims and desires from their culture. Gorgias' student Polus, for example, argues that the skilled speaker has nearly dictatorial power. He can kill anyone he chooses, banish others, and confiscate property (466b–d). Polus argues that the instrumental power to satisfy one's desires is a very great good. His model is Archelaus of Macedon, a dictator and usurper who, though full of vices, is nonetheless very happy – according to Polus. And, he says, everyone in Athens would agree, except Socrates.

The stage is set, therefore, for an exploration of how, and to what ends, the polis educates the individual. Socrates' strategy is to show that the ostensibly political topic, rhetoric, has considerable implications for the ethical well-being of the individual. His questioning reaches its climax in his conversation with Callicles. A hard-core immoralist, Callicles rejects Socrates' use of conventional "shame" to trip up Polus. For Socrates had defeated Polus through securing his agreement that wrongdoing is shameful, and therefore harmful to the agent's soul. Callicles, however, distinguishes between conventional justice and what he calls "natural justice" (cf. "The Challenge of Thrasymachus and Callicles" in chapter 4). For Callicles, shame, justice, equality, and other democratic values, are tools used by the weak to constrain the strong. They have no existence apart from this conventional use. On the other hand, powerful men deserve, as a matter of natural justice, to take as much as they can get. Callicles outlines his ideal in a succinct and arresting statement (Text 9).

> **9.** This is what is noble and just according to nature, and I will say it to you now with perfect frankness: it is necessary for one who intends to live correctly to allow his desires to be as great as possible and not to control them, and to be ready and able to satisfy his enlarged appetites through courage and intelligence, and to fill himself full of whatever he happens to desire. (*Gorgias* 491e6–492a3)

He emphasizes the instrumental use of courage and intelligence to enable the strong man to satisfy his enlarged appetites. With help from Socrates, he clarifies this position further: the "strong" are not those with the most physical power (that would be the demos as a collective body), but rather a class of naturally intelligent and courageous men, a certain sort of elite.[5]

Callicles' ideal would have had a primitive attraction for most Greek men. Callicles advanced, in a more sophisticated form, the ideals that Agamemnon had once promoted.[6] The strong, the powerful, and the intelligent can and should take as much as possible because they deserve it, as a matter of fairness. Callicles is explicitly putting forward a theory of justice centered on his belief in the extreme natural inequality of human beings. To Socrates, though, this position re-fashions the very mistake he has pinpointed throughout the dialogue. The instrumental use of power (whether rhetorical, intellectual, physical, or otherwise) cannot be called decisively good or bad, until we examine the ends it targets. For him, that claim holds true at both individual and social levels. Callicles is drunk with the fantasy of power, but he has no clear conception of what power is for.

Pressed on this point, Callicles argues that power is valuable because it enables a man to win pleasure. He resorts to his culture's ill-defined hedonism because he has not adequately explored how he should live – nor, it is implied, has anyone else in democratic Athens.[7] Socrates shows, though, that such hedonism can easily conflict with Callicles' admiration for courage and intelligence. For example, a coward, or even a passive homosexual, Socrates says, might win more pleasure than Callicles' "strong man." The sequence of the argument shows that Callicles, like his simpler counterparts Gorgias and Polus, and like the democracy as a whole, also pursues a conception of his good that he does not truly understand.

Socrates frames his investigation of the ends of rhetoric with reference to democracy and imperialism. For example, he calls Callicles a lover of Demos; he twice compares Callicles to Alcibiades, Athens's imperialist leader; and Callicles says that he admires the old-time architects of the Athenian empire, such as Themistocles, Cimon, and Pericles. Because of his emphasis on courage, intelligence, and endless acquisition, then, we might interpret Callicles as embodying the Athenians' imperialist ideals. He does closely resemble the Athenians as represented by Thucydides. More precisely, Callicles has imbibed Athenian ideals and then reinterpreted them in a philosophically powerful way. Callicles' emphasis on natural justice made him slightly different from the Athenian imperialists represented by Thucydides. For Thucydides' Athenians, nature drove men, as a matter of observable fact, to take as much as possible. Nature led the strong to rule the weak wherever possible. For Callicles, by contrast, it was a matter of *justice*, not simply power, that certain individuals should satisfy their enlarged appetites.[8] Callicles had been educated all too well by the experiences of democracy and imperialism. Such is, I think, the significance of Socrates' profound reflection on the democratic leaders' necessary adaptation of themselves to the character of the demos (Text 10).

10. If you think, Callicles, that anyone at all will give you some such *technê* as this, which will make you very powerful in this city, though you are (for better or worse) unlike the constitution, then you are wrong. For you must be not an imitator of the constitution, but naturally like these men, if you intend to make significant progress toward winning the friendship of the Athenian demos, or,

> indeed, that of Demos the son of Pyrilampes. Whoever, then, will make you most like these men, will turn you into a politician – which you want – and, moreover, into an orator. For each one delights in words that are spoken consistently with his own character and detests the contrary. (*Gorgias* 513a7–c2)

Strikingly, Callicles aspires to turn this education back against the demos itself. He hopes to rule over ordinary citizens tyrannically. His aspirations indicate that the democracy educates its aristocrats badly and imprudently, if its imperialist ventures fostered such hatred of the system itself (cf. "Debating Athenian Imperialism" in chapter 5).

Callicles was a threat to the democracy that democracy itself had generated. But was Callicles also a threat to himself? Were his ideals intrinsically wrongheaded? That was more difficult to demonstrate. In order to illuminate the issues involved, Socrates develops an analogy between physical and psychological health. This is a crucial argumentative step, because of the difficulty of clearly grasping what is good for the soul. Socrates proposes to move from the better known case of physical health, to the less clear case of psychic health. It is a strategy Plato would employ again and again. In this case, the analogy enables Socrates to argue persuasively that the soul does have a condition of health; that such a condition can and must be rationally accounted for by a recognized art; and that psychological health, like physical health, is an objective fact, not a subjective judgment. To flesh out these points, Socrates argues that just as trained and knowledgeable doctors care for the body, so too must trained and knowledgeable political leaders care for the soul (Text 11).

> **11.** I am saying that there are two arts for these things (body and soul) which are two. The art set over the soul, I call political; the one set over the body, I am not able to give you a single name for; though the care of the body is one thing, I declare that it has two parts – physical training and medicine. In the art of politics, corresponding to physical training there is legislation, and corresponding to medicine there is justice. (*Gorgias* 464b3–8)

Socrates' position is sharply different from modern conceptions. It is unclear whether we should accept the analogy of soul to body, or whether we should view the soul as amenable to expert guidance and treatment, as the body can be trained and cared for by physicians. Such an analogy is deeply antithetical to the liberal traditions of modernity. Modern traditions tend to value the greatest individual freedom compatible with equal freedom for others. Modern liberal philosophers abhor the view that individuals are defective and in need of therapy from recognized experts or, worse, from the state. Can one endorse modernity's robust commitment to individual freedom and also accept that psychological health is objective and objectively knowable?

This would be an awkward combination of views. The very awkwardness, I think, has often led to the belief that an individual's good is a subjective matter, that happiness and lifestyle are up to the individual. Nevertheless, one might simultaneously value freedom and accept that individual good is objective, provided that one values freedom and individual dignity over an externally imposed lifestyle that was said to be good. (I do not consider here the additional complication that one might believe both that the individual's good is objective and objectively knowable, and that no one in fact knows what is good for the individual.) Perhaps the argument would be, first, that the dignity of ordinary human adults depends on their self-direction, their willingness and ability to live their lives from within, and to make their own decisions for themselves. We tend to see self-direction as having an intrinsic moral importance. The value of self-direction might therefore override the imposition of "psychological health" from external sources. Secondly, we could argue from the likely *consequences* of imposing a lifestyle or choices on individuals. Forcing an unwilling adult to do "what is good for him," from the outside, is unlikely to yield the desired result. For example, the state would be unwise to mandate attendance at the opera for purposes of elevating the citizenry, since the likely result in most cases (including my own) would be boredom and resentment, rather than edification.

Plato rejected such arguments as misguided and harmful. Why should citizens not be guided in their behavior if such guidance might lead to better results? Socrates uses his examination of Callicles to explain what those "better results" might consist in. To render his conception of the human good plausible, Socrates provisionally argues from another analogy – the analogy of crafts. Architects, shipbuilders, and so forth aimed to create a harmonious, self-consistent, and organized product. Similarly, trainers and doctors give order to the body and arrange it in its correct proportions (504a). By analogy, then, the healthy condition of the soul will consist in order, proportion, and regularity. It is just such a condition of health that the good orator must aim to inculcate in the citizens (Text 12).

> **12.** And the name for the states of organization and order of the soul is "lawful" and "law," which lead people to become law-abiding and orderly, and these are justice and self-control. . . . So this is what that skilled and good orator will look to when he applies to people's souls whatever speeches he makes as well as all of his actions. (*Gorgias* 504d1–7, tr. Zeyl)

Order results from discipline, symmetry, and proportion and so produces health and beauty.

Through his quest for order, Plato began to justify the view that politics had to be a philosophical subject, consisting in knowledge of what is good and bad for human beings. Only a "philosophical politics" could promote the properly understood welfare of the citizens. From Socrates' perspective, even the late, great politicians of Athens, such as Pericles, were panderers who gratified the demos. They satisfied the demos's desires for ships, dockyards, harbors, and so forth, without attending to the welfare of the citizens' souls. Because the demos is the ultimate source of democratic authority, democracy is doomed to promote pandering leaders who must parrot back to the demos its own wishes. Democracy's simple premise is the ruthless promotion of demotic desire, independent of the good. For Socrates, on the other hand, the real statesman, properly understood, is the doctor who best cares for the human soul. The good doctor's care will result in the harmonious arrangement of the soul's parts. This arrangement will lead to psychological health and to the soul's possession of justice, moderation, and every other virtue (504). Socrates' negative vision of democracy, along with his account of what constitutes a true statesman, enables him to make the otherwise extraordinary claim that he alone is a statesman in Athens (Text 13).

13. I think I am one of the few Athenians (to avoid saying I am the only one, though I am the only one of those now living), to put my hand to the true art of politics and to practice politics – in so far as I speak with a view not to flattering others, but to what is best, and not to what is most pleasant. I am not willing to take your advice seriously, to practice "such clever things," and I will not have anything to say in my defense at a trial. (Socrates, at *Gorgias* 521d6–e2)

Without such a philosopher in charge, the soul will arrive at a horribly disfigured condition, out of harmony with itself and ugly to all onlookers. This is the point of Socrates' final myth in the *Gorgias*, but it would not be surprising if most readers had hoped for a fuller explanation of the harmonious soul than they actually find there. Ethics and politics were intertwined for Plato, but, as the myth shows, Plato was recalibrating the equation in order to emphasize the importance of the individual soul.

The Priority of Reason in City and Soul: Plato's *Republic*

To arrive at his conception of psychic order, Socrates must move from physical order to the idea that virtue is the orderly condition of the soul. He does not justify such a move in the *Gorgias*; he does not explain, further, why psychological health leads to the social virtues (after all, a physically healthy body can be used for good or bad purposes). Nor, in that dialogue, does he offer an account of the healthy political culture that might act as a counterpart to the diseased democratic culture. How, then, to create a culture which reliably produces ordered souls – a culture which does not, in other words, rely on the extraordinary and necessarily incomplete efforts of a superhuman figure such as Socrates? And how to fill in the blanks left open by Socrates' vague description of the soul in the *Gorgias*? Crafting the right political culture, and the right education for individuals, became the tasks of Plato's *Republic*. In this great work, Plato explored the ethical and political implications of order, harmony, and coherence in a more profound way.

Plato set this dialogue in fifth-century Athens. He saw Athenian democracy as a culture that had lost ethical coherence. Socrates' main interlocutors are Glaucon and Adeimantus, Plato's brothers and aristocratic Athenian citizens. They endure Thrasymachus' declaration that justice is "another's good" and therefore harmful to oneself. They also listen avidly to Socrates' dialectical triumph over Thrasymachus, but they remain unconvinced. They say that they constantly hear Thrasymachean ideals recommended in fifth-century Athens (the *Gorgias* shows us why that was the case) (cf. "The Challenge of Thrasymachus and Callicles" in chapter 4). They desperately want Socrates to put their faith in justice on a deeper philosophical footing.

For the sake of argument, the brothers assert that we are all greedy and ambitious by nature. The weak devised a social compact to limit the aggression of the strong. They therefore educated citizens to abide by their values – justice, equality, and so forth. But, if anyone had a ring of invisibility, such as the mythical Gyges, he would certainly use it to satisfy his own appetites without hesitation. How, then, can we maintain that justice really benefits its possessor, since typical human behavior tells a different story? Since Socrates addresses chiefly these interlocutors, we can infer that Plato has reined in his ambitions.[9] He could not convince Callicles. Now it appears impossible to convert the Thrasymachuses of this world to the moral point of view. Nonetheless, it is possible to explain and justify justice to those so disposed – and thereby to deepen their moral aspirations and political commitments. We should always be asking who is the audience of the political thinkers we study.[10]

Although Socrates singles them out for praise as the sons of Ariston (367e–368a), which might suggest that their upbringing in the family is responsible for their commitment to justice, the origin of that commitment is never fully explained. This hints at what we already know from the case of Callicles: that democracy's production of just individuals is random and uncertain. If politics is responsible for producing just individuals, then Socrates needs to develop a novel politics that can reliably achieve proper moral goals. This thought lies behind Socrates' argumentative strategy. To explain the benefits of justice, Socrates establishes an analogy between the polis and the soul. This strategy brings home the close connection of ethics and politics. Socrates justifies his approach by observing, empirically, that cities derive their ethos from the individual characters of the inhabitants, and vice versa. Although the brothers ostensibly left politics out of account, Socrates asserts that justice and happiness can be achieved only in the right sort of polis.

The city–soul analogy enables Socrates to utilize the better known circumstances of civic life to illuminate the obscure workings of the human soul. It was obvious to contemporaries that justice within the city was good for the city. The city's harmony and well-being depended on basic agreement about what constituted the just distribution of power, honor, and material goods. Without such agreement, as we have learned from Thucydides and Xenophon, the city could never flourish. Therefore, it was intuitively plausible that justice promoted social health. Riotous desires and untoward aggression *within* the city were unhealthy; conversely, justice *within* the city enabled the city to flourish. If Socrates can, accordingly, find a way to explain justice *within* the human soul, then he can explain why, similarly, justice will enable the individual's soul to flourish.

This strategy solved a problem for Socrates. Justice is ordinarily considered a social virtue – a virtue we exhibit in relation to others. Socrates uses the city–soul analogy to suggest that justice could be understood simply within the soul, without worrying in the first instance about others.[11] This enables Socrates to concentrate, as in the *Gorgias*, on the order and healthy condition of the soul as such. But he shows awareness that focusing on such questions also requires him to imagine politics differently.

Therefore, Socrates' analogy is not simply an *ad hoc* argumentative strategy. There is a deeper point. Socrates' shift from "social justice" to justice in the soul indicates that he is transforming the very concept of justice that he was originally asked to explain. The reason for his shift is that justice looks and feels different for the ignorant, on the one hand, and the properly educated, on the other. Only the properly educated can appreciate, understand, and enjoy the benefits of justice. Proper education, however, requires a correspondingly supportive political culture. The contemporary Athenian culture distorts the minds of its citizens to such an extent that they regard justice as worthless and injustice as profitable. All their intuitions have gone wrong. Their intuitions are so far gone that they view justice as an inconsequential sequence of irritating rules and compulsory requirements such as paying one's taxes. They cannot see that justice is a flourishing condition of the soul. With the right political culture in place, however, individuals could grow to appreciate the nature and benefits of justice, and to see it as consisting in a properly ordered soul – a soul that mirrored the order of the cosmos. If the *Gorgias* illustrates how wrongheaded political education can produce the disordered soul of Callicles, then the *Republic* shows how the education offered by an ideal polis can establish order in the souls of its leading citizens. The city–soul analogy helps to show how, and why, ethical and political flourishing go hand in hand.

Briefly, Socrates' argument is that justice in the city consists in an ordered arrangement of its classes (rulers, warriors, and producers) – which results from the broad consensus that those with knowledge should rule the polis for the good of the whole. Similarly, Socrates argues, the soul's good consists in the ordered arrangement of *its* "parts" – reason, spirit, and appetite – all of which "agreed" that reason should rule with wisdom for the person's overall good. This much is accomplished by the end of Book 4. In Books 5–7, Socrates fleshes out the city's political structure and deepens our understanding of reason's ruling with knowledge. We come to see that reason's rule in the soul requires, for Socrates, philosophic knowledge of the ordered structure of the cosmos as a whole. This deepens the conversation about order and proportion in the *Gorgias*, but the basic line of thought is continuous. Then, armed with such knowledge, Socrates and his friends investigate the psychological and political problems that result from various types of disorder in the soul (Books 8–9). The formal argument is concluded when Socrates triumphantly proclaims that the philosopher is 729 times happier than the tyrant. The final book seals this conclusion with a myth of the afterlife.

Throughout this work, Plato elaborated the themes of the preceding tradition of Greek political thought. First, his educational theory emphasized the development of virtue as crucial to both individual happiness and political health. He argued that ethics should not be viewed from the perspective of rules or individual acts. Rules and actions could lead only to a hopelessly incomplete and ambiguous approach to ethical questions. Rather, Plato emphasized the good of the agent's soul as the proper starting-point of ethical (and political) thinking. Second, politics and ethics were closely allied, in that proper political arrangements helped produce flourishing and socially acceptable individuals, while virtuous individuals contributed to the justice and soundness of the political culture. Third, he agreed that political inequality must be justified by appeal to relevant differences among citizens. In this case, a rigid political hierarchy had to be established on the basis of the rulers' knowledge of the truth. To make the case for such an arrangement, Plato implicitly utilized the principle of geometric equality. He supported this principle with a metaphysical theory that pervades his politics. On all three counts, Plato was engaged with contemporary politics, but he also used his "local" responses to develop theories that have turned out to be of globally historical importance. I deal with these three points in turn.

Educating Citizens in the Classical Context

The ideal polis, Callipolis, is premised on an educational system that properly trains citizens' appetites and drives for honor (Books 2–3). In other words, the system trained the two lower parts of the soul: the "spirited" part, which is the source of our desires for honor, our anger, our proper self-respect, and our sense of shame; and the appetitive part, which drives us to satisfy our bodily and other materialistic desires. Socrates argues that the poets, who were the traditional educators, wrongly strengthen these parts through their narratives and plays. For example, he says, Homer depicted Achilles as avaricious in taking gifts from Agamemnon and a ransom from Priam in exchange for Hector's corpse (390e). To the extent that Achilles was a cultural hero, this depiction trained citizens to esteem the love of money and to overvalue (objectively unimportant) material goods. Similarly, in relation to "spirit," the warriors of Callipolis must be trained to be neither overly aggressive nor too soft. Through musical and literary education, they will be trained to be friendly to their fellow citizens and appropriately harsh to outsiders. Above all, their sense of honor has to be squared with the demands of justice and due respect for others.

In concentrating on how to reshape these two "lower" psychic impulses, Plato implicitly commented on the chief drives promoted by contemporary culture. Material acquisitiveness was an obvious feature of imperialistic cities and of their citizens. "Spirit," or *thumos*, had been the central value of Greek men since Homer. But, far from inspiring men to act honorably, it could make them act like aggressive dogs, by leading them to identify, wrongly and imprudently, with inflated ideas of self-importance, anger, pride, and ambition. As Thucydides had once pointed out (3.82), the primary causes of civil war in the fifth century were excessive acquisitiveness (*pleo-nexia*) and unrestrained ambition (*philotimia*). These two impulses drove badly educated individuals to violate standards of justice in order to win more (or, rather, too much) wealth and honor for themselves. They were motivated by an objectively false concep-tion of what is good for human beings and why. In Plato's view, "immoralism" was inscribed into the souls of all Greek citizens, by virtue of the wrongheaded political values of the broader culture.

In Books 8–9, Socrates explores the political consequences of overvaluing spirit and appetite, and undervaluing reason. These books describe the imperfect constitutions – timocracy, oligarchy, democracy, and tyranny. Each imperfect constitution arises through the misdirected impulses originating in either the spirit or the appetite of the inhabitants. These books advance Plato's critique of contemporary Greek politics. But they deepen that critique by illustrating the pathologies of soul that characterize ordinary citi-zens of each constitution. They also suggest that disordered desires for honor and material goods tend to destabilize states with faulty educational systems. Politics in the existing cities tends to be a whirlpool of incongruent drives and desires, in which moral and political coherence is out of the question. And thus the key to political health is to establish a proper education for all citizens.

Politics and Ethics

Putting his educational theory to work in the ideal state required Socrates to overhaul existing politics. This is the second point – the reshaping of politics to create the conditions for ethical flourishing. First of all, the rulers – who turn out to be the philosophers – must "supervise the storytellers" (377b). In other words, the city relies on government-imposed censorship to train the citizens correctly. This provision might not be repellent to modern citizens if applied exclusively to children. But Socrates intends to drive poets out of Callipolis altogether, because their traditional stories are harmful – sometimes because they are false, sometimes because the truth itself is harmful. (There is one qualification: Socrates does "allow in" poets who sing hymns to the gods and heroes provided that their rhythms and content are carefully supervised. Callipolis can have poetry workshops, but their point will be not be to inspire "creativity"; it will be to encourage writers to decorate "beneficial messages" in the right way.)

Second, in order to cement the hierarchy of classes in the city, Socrates proposes to educate all citizens by using what he calls a "noble lie." From birth onward, the rulers must teach all citizens that the three classes of the city – economic producers, warriors, and rulers – have metals in their souls – iron or bronze, silver, and gold, respectively. The classes are arrayed in a divinely ordained natural hierarchy, which must be maintained if the city is to stay healthy. Justice in the city, in fact, consists primarily in each class doing the work it was ordained to do, and in not rebelling against the naturally just rule of the golden class. We have still to explain why a ruling class of philosophers should, in Socrates' view, be in charge of Callipolis, but let us step back to consider the revolutionary character of these educational proposals.

The censorship and educational provisions, among others, led Karl Popper to categorize Plato as an enemy of the "open society," as a theorist of totalitarianism. Whatever the contested term "totalitarian" means, Popper was right to see Plato as hostile to individuality, freedom, and pluralism. But, by contrast to standard "totalitarian" regimes, such as the fascist states of the World War II era, Plato had serious philosophical justifications for his political hierarchy, censorship, and social control of individualism. However disturbing we might find his provisions, it was not, for him, simply a matter of the rulers' seizing power for their own benefit. First, his rulers do not rule in their own interests, but rather in the city's interest. And, indeed, they are legally forced, against their inclination, to rule "patriotically" in the city rather than to pursue their first love: philosophy. Second, Plato viewed his conception of the Good as overriding freedom, respect for individual human preferences, private life, and other democratic values. In modern terminology, he valued the good over the right – and by "good" he intended the "good of the city," not the good of any particular citizens or groups.

Some of the more unlikely proposals put this concern for the good to the test. For example, Socrates plans to establish the ideal polis by "rusticating" those over 10 years of age – that is, "sending them to the country," with the ominous implication that they will be disposed of there. The (Platonic) good clashed with such free-doms and privileges as were accorded citizens in Athenian democracy – and much more so, in modern democracies. Popper was one-sided in his critique, to be sure, but, to the extent that we value private freedom and individual choice, it is hard to be completely out of sympathy with his views.

Plato's other political stipulations were equally radical. First, the guardians of the city would be forbidden to own property privately. This provision was supposed to create unity and dedication to the common good (Text 14).

> **14.** For them alone of the city's inhabitants, it will not be right to handle or touch gold and silver, or to go beneath the same roof as it, or to wear it as jewelry, or to drink from silver or gold cups. And so they will save themselves and they will save the city. But if they ever acquire private property – land, houses, or money – they will be household managers and farmers instead of guards, and they will become hateful tyrants instead of the allies of their fellow citizens. (*Republic*, 417a–b, Tr. Grube, rev. Reeve, adapted)

Plato's worry was obviously that those with power would abuse it for the sake of their own profit. Such abuse was characteristic of historical Greek aristocrats, such as the Thirty Tyrants of Athens. Plato's rulers would be institutionally forbidden to own property and therefore less likely to fall prey to materialistic urges. As we will see, greed was also a particular concern of the Platonic *Laws*.

Second, Socrates argues that women and children must be possessed in common and that women, like men, must be trained to be rulers. Instituting a policy of "everything in common" was Socrates' attempt to secure civic harmony in the topsy-turvy, stasis-ridden world of classical Greek politics (note Aristotle's criticisms of this provision in chapter 7). Through these provisions, Socrates elevated women to a status far beyond what they experienced in the historical Greek polis. He argued, appealingly to us, that there was no relevant difference justifying the exclusion of women from political power.

But his feminist sympathies were not deep. He made clear that, in his view, women are weaker and less competent than men in every area of life. And his provisions on women and children were linked to an abhorrent plan to institute eugenics. His elaborate plan involved a rigged sexual lottery in which attractive, athletic men and women were to be given state sanction to have sex and reproduce. Others would mysteriously lose the lottery and be denied the pleasures of sex and reproduction (could such a lottery really work in practice? If the handsome athletes won nearly every time, things might look suspicious, and it is notoriously difficult to impose celibacy . . .). Sexuality and the denial of family life are thus other areas in which the "totalitarian" label might be applied to Plato, in that his arrangements provided for the state's "total control" of intimate details of the lives of citizens. Even so, we should be clear where to draw the line in criticizing Plato. It has been argued, for example, that he did not respect the subjectivity or individuality of women – central concerns of modern feminism – but notice that he did not respect those features of men, either.[12] He promoted his conception of the good at the expense, altogether, of what we would call individual rights or freedoms.

Philosophical Rulers

Socrates' most important political innovation was his provision that philosophers must rule. Without this provision, he argues, justice in the polis can never be established. Socrates "clears the deck" by showing that contemporary ridicule of philosophers is misplaced. In fact, he argues, many so-called philosophers deserve ridicule rather than the honorable title of philosopher. They are either useless cranks or, worse, men with good natures and intelligence who have been corrupted by the misguided education of cities as they are. The problem is compounded by the tendency of ordinary people to fail to recognize true philosophers. True philosophers too often seem to be out-of-touch, other-worldly stargazers. And that is precisely the characterization that Plato's argument refutes.

True philosophers, as Plato shows, are more in touch with reality than ordinary people. Plato establishes the grounds for his political hierarchy, with philosophers as rulers, by appealing to the philosophers' knowledge of Reality. This is Reality with a capital "R" because Plato identifies what is "really real," not as the world of particular things known to the senses, but rather as the world of intelligible ideas known to the intellect. To give an account of his metaphysics and epistemology in the *Republic*, not to mention elsewhere, is beyond the scope of this book, but three points should be noted.

First, knowledge is the basis of Plato's distinction between genuine rulers and those sophists and politicians who do not deserve political power. As Socrates says, politicians of his time pay careful attention to the "passions and desires of a big, powerful beast," i.e. the demos (493a). They render that beast's convictions back to it during political gatherings, since they have no rational account to offer of what is "noble or shameful, good or bad, just or unjust"; they simply say whatever suits the beast's desires (493b). By contrast, philosophers do have a reasoned, articulate account of these ethical concepts. Their political program derives from their knowledge of objective ethical facts about the world.

Second, their knowledge covers not just the everyday particulars of earthly experience, but also their understanding of what Plato calls "forms."[13] There is no proper theory of forms in the *Republic*, or anywhere else that we know of. As far as we can reconstruct the concept, forms explain at least why particular things take on aesthetic or moral attributes in specific circumstances. For example, the Form of Beauty explains fully what beauty is and why things are beautiful; and things are beautiful, moreover, by "participating" in the Form of Beauty. The forms bear the predicates "beautiful," "just," and so forth in an unqualified way, by contrast with particular things, which bear these predicates uncertainly and in a qualified way. Knowledge of the forms therefore provides intellectual depth to the philosophers' understanding of particular things; it helps make sense of the deep realities underlying the quotidian world. As a result of their knowledge of forms, philosophers can deliberate about political questions on the basis of profound understanding of the moral structure of the world. In the rapidly evolving world of practical politics, they alone can distinguish the just from the unjust, the prudent from the foolish, the honorable from the shameful, and so forth – and they can explain why their distinctions hold water. (It is perhaps a limitation of Plato's account that he does not distinguish between practical and theoretical wisdom, as Aristotle was later to do.)

Third, at the climax of their training, the rulers achieve an understanding of the Form of the Good.[14] Socrates never directly describes this elusive concept, but it emerges that the Form of the Good is imagined as a deep coherence in the structure of reality. The Good is a cosmic principle of order that makes the other forms intelligible and real. It also accounts for their being good. For example, it is through its coherent relation to the other forms (say, of temperance, piety, and courage) that the form of justice, and thus the virtue of justice, is good. It is, moreover, only by coming to understand the Good that philosophers can produce a healthy polis and a flourishing citizen body. Since they understand the ordered structure of the universe, they will naturally desire, or so Plato thought, to reproduce that order in their own souls, in the souls of others, and in the Callipolis as a whole. Plato's conception of the Good is thus an extension of Socrates' appeal to order in the *Gorgias*. Socrates had rejected Calliclean self-seeking on the grounds that it creates disorder in the soul. In the *Republic*, the Good consists chiefly in harmony and "order" (*kosmos*). The just man desires to arrange his soul so as to reflect this cosmic order. Therefore, through the metaphysics of the *Republic*, Plato put Socrates' rejection of Callicles on a firmer footing. He also began to imagine the ordered polis as a reflection of the divine order of the universe.

Through appeal to their knowledge of the Good, Socrates justifies the philosophers' governance of Callipolis. By analogy, the proposed political hierarchy also helps explain why reason and its striving for the truth must be granted priority in the soul. The reasoning part of the soul governs desire and spirit with wisdom, for the good of the whole person. This is the deeper meaning of Socrates' representation of justice as a form of psychic health. Reason aligns the parts of the soul so as to reflect the ordered structure of the cosmos (500b–c). This psychic order is meant to be obviously desirable to its possessor. Furthermore, although it goes well beyond the "garden variety" justice that Glaucon and Adeimantus were worried about, it nevertheless motivates those with ordered souls to perform just actions. The philosophers' chief desires will henceforward be intellectual – a sort of erotic striving to gain the truth (490a–b). Other sorts of desire will, in turn, tend to wither away (485d–e). Gazing upon the ordered structure of the *kosmos* enables the philosopher to grasp the goodness of order and to devote his energies to producing such order in himself and in the polis. He simply, and properly, loses interest in the desires of the soul's other parts.[15]

We can see why certain interpreters have understood Plato as chiefly a philosopher of ethics, epistemology, and metaphysics rather than politics. It is worth insisting, though, that his other interests were embedded in and responsive to political culture. In the *Republic*, even so, politics is never an end in itself. Rather, it is a means to establish institutions that promote ethical development and happy lives for individuals. Perhaps one might be tempted to say that the *Republic* has no politics, because there is no political negotiation or compromise, no true public sphere, no need to hash things out "in the middle" of the city (as the Greeks would say). What would be involved, for example, in the "citizenship" of the non-philosophers? Is the translation "Republic" for the Greek *Politeia* therefore misleading? It is hard to imagine, one could perhaps argue, a politics worth the name in a polis where most citizens live in darkness in a different world from the decision makers. But this line of thinking relies on too narrow a conception of politics. Plato's *Republic* imagines the rulers' exercise of power for the good, and with the consent, of the governed, and it outlines specific institutional arrangements to achieve that good. The dialogue represents politics as a form of aristocratic governance that is based on knowledge and that seeks the welfare of the governed.

Even so, this line of thinking brings up an important question for the society of Callipolis. What political and social implications does Plato's description of philosophical knowledge have for the non-philosophers of Callipolis?[16] If desire is a "beast that assumes every shape" (588e), in need of being restrained, and worthy of suspicion but not respect, then is the political position of the producers equally wretched? On the most charitable reading, Socrates' argument does not so much imply disgust and contempt for the appetitive part of the soul, as the belief that appetite stands in need of supervision and therapy if it is to be maintained in a healthy condition. For example, Socrates argues that the just individual must "supervise the beast with many heads like a farmer, nourishing and taming the gentle ones, but stopping the savage ones from growing" (589b).

This account implies that although the appetitive desires are given priority in the producers' souls, the producers nonetheless live as temperately and as moderately as possible, because of the rulers' supervision of them. They live in the cave and are unable to appreciate or enjoy the benefits of morality for the right reasons.

Even so, they are incomparably better off under the rulers' therapeutic eyes than they would be in any other regime. At least in Callipolis they are likely to behave appropriately and not to harm others through injustice. As Aristotle would later put it, they perform just acts but not *as* the just man would perform just acts. Nonetheless, their performance of virtuous acts and their citizenship in the Callipolis make their lives more orderly, temperate, and just, and thus more reflective of the ordered structure of the *kosmos*, than could possibly be the case otherwise. This might go some distance in allaying the concern for the non-philosophers. Still, Socrates' persistent emphasis on quashing desire makes one disturbingly anxious on behalf of the producers, since they correspond in the state to the desiring part of the soul.

Instructively, such worries do not arise in an explicitly comparable work of political theory, Cicero's *Republic*. Cicero's work forces readers to recognize what they may have forgotten. Plato's Callipolis has no history, no rich culture, and no time-honored institutions which ground the people's loyalty, establish cohesion, inspire patriotism, and motivate respect for justice and the common good. Like Polybius, Scipio (who guides Cicero's dialogue) regards the pure constitutions as intrinsically unstable; therefore, he says, a mixed constitution is best. Mixed constitutions diffuse equality widely throughout the citizenry and have no "alter-ego" into which they can be transformed (as monarchies, for example, can be transformed into tyrannies, or aristocracies into oligarchies) (1.69).

The main point, however, is that the Roman republic has displayed its merits over time and is the best constitution in practice. It is a true republic, with free-wheeling politics; and, as Book 2 shows, it has a long history of negotiating settlements, refining values and virtues, working to develop a shared culture, and inculcating a dedication to the republic. Rome's republic, therefore, is truly "the property of the public" (3.43). The Ciceronian counterpart shows that Plato's republic is a very different beast with a great deal of explaining to do. It will, by contrast, have difficulty motivating real people to join the citizen ranks; its "noble lie" is a thin substitute for real history; and its laws and decisions will not really be the property of the public. Only a few citizens, the philosophers, will have ownership of the public even as they (perhaps unrealistically; cf. chapter 7 for Aristotle's thoughts) are prohibited from owning private property.

Platonic Political Philosophy after the *Republic*

We know independently that the *Laws* is Plato's last work; it was unpublished at the time of his death. There is good reason to believe, too, on stylistic and thematic grounds, that the *Statesman* is part of a group of dialogues that should be associated with the same period as the *Laws*. Thus it is fair to say that two major works of Platonic political philosophy postdate the *Republic* and were probably written in the last two decades of Plato's life: *Statesman* and *Laws*.[17]

In these works, we see significant continuity with, but also differences from, Plato's earlier political dialogues. The most important continuity, perhaps, is Plato's emphasis on expertise or knowledge as the single most important criterion for proper rule. (In the *Statesman* this expertise is called *politikê epistêmê* or *politikê technê*; we will explore shortly what this expertise consists in). Proper rulers know what is best and utilize their knowledge and power for the improvement of the citizenry. This emphasis on the ruler's expertise corresponds to Plato's persistent, often devastating, criticisms of existing constitutions – particularly democracy. Thus, despite recent arguments, later Platonic political philosophy is not friendly to democracy. There continues to be a "sliding scale" of value among human beings. To put it crudely, some human beings, particularly those capable of understanding and of progress in virtue, are superior to others – craftsmen, farmers, and slaves.

This observation leads to a significant break with the earlier dialogues. For in the ideal cities of these two dialogues, being capable of significant progress toward virtue is the key criterion of citizenship. Unlike the *Republic*, these dialogues suggest that even non-philosophers can achieve considerable levels of understanding and virtue. Their achievement in this respect naturally improves their lot in life; they are much better off than the producers and warriors of the *Republic*. The hitch is that all those incapable of virtue – including any kind of "producer" – are to be excluded from citizenship entirely. In these dialogues, in other words, Plato redraws the boundaries of citizenship to exclude all those incapable of progress in virtue.[18]

The Eleatic Visitor, who directs the conversation of the *Statesman*, emphatically argues that there is only one "correct" constitution, all the others being worthless imitations (Text 15).

> **15.** As long as they [expert statesmen] use knowledge and justice and preserve the city and make it better to the extent they are able, we must say that this is the only correct constitution . . . As for all the others we are discussing, we must say that they are not legitimate, indeed that they are not really constitutions, but imitations of this one. (*Statesman* 293d8–e4)

The dialogue as a whole consists in a laborious effort to separate out the statesman, by virtue of his political expertise, from others, such as doctors or sophists, who might claim to be the proper supervisors of the human community. The Visitor says over and over that every such "claimant" other than the statesman is a charlatan or a magician – an expert in deceptive persuasion. He thereby draws a bright line between the expertly governed ideal constitution and all the rest. This dividing line, which is based upon the statesman's political knowledge, enables the Visitor to construct a profound critique of all existing constitutions.

In particular, the Visitor bluntly rejects the Protagorean belief in the collective wisdom of the demos. Even in such a trivial pursuit as the game of *petteia* (possibly a type of backgammon), he argues, we find very few experts. And thus, even fewer still can acquire expertise in politics (292e–293a). But, democrats could respond, public deliberation produces a sort of enhanced practical wisdom that can issue only from transparent, dialectical exchange among equals, in which citizens willingly revise their opinions and submit their ideas to the scrutiny of others. The Visitor has a particular reading of the assembly which tries to defuse such arguments. He offers a quasi-genealogy which purports to explain how the "second-best," i.e. incorrect, constitutions have come to exist.

In his view, citizens in the assembly (in either democracy or oligarchy) distrust experts and imprudently offer opinions about subjects with which they are unfamiliar (cf. 298a-e). Therefore, unenlightened citizens make laws that dictate, quite ignorantly, how, when, and why the arts are to be practiced. Any kind of scientific or ethical research thereby becomes nearly impossible. Inevitably, this leads to a decline in human civilization generally – to the corruption of the arts, the elimination of research, and the impossibility of expanding human knowledge. The "second best" constitution keeps the ignorantly framed laws rigidly in control.

No originality is allowed. This picture of the corrupt constitutions of Greece includes a pointed reference to the democracy's execution of Socrates – a pioneer in the furtherance of human creativity and knowledge (Text 16).

> **16.** And therefore it will be necessary, furthermore, to establish a law for all these cases, if anyone is found investigating the art of piloting a ship or seafaring, or health and truth in the art of medicine, or the effects of hot and cold winds, contrary to the written law, or making clever inquiries into anything whatever in such matters. First we must not call him a doctor or a pilot but rather a stargazer, some idle sophist. Then, any citizen who wishes to do so, can hale him before a jury-court on the grounds that he is corrupting other, younger men and persuading them to apply themselves to seamanship and medicine, not lawfully, but so as to govern ships and the sick with sole authority. And if he is shown to be persuading either younger men or older men against the laws and the written rules, then we must punish him with the most extreme penalties. (*Statesman* 299b2–c5)

Socrates has become a symbol pointing beyond his own life to the spirit of human creativity hampered by existing polities. Thus, the Protagorean picture was not only hopelessly optimistic, but also wrongly supportive of constitutions and laws that lead inevitably to human decline.

The Visitor takes the opportunity to explore the problematic role of law in existing constitutions. Everyone would be better off, he says, if a quasi-divine statesman ruled with political expertise. (Note that the ideal city of the *Statesman* has laws, in fact, but they are based upon, and secondary to, the statesman's knowledge.) Laws are a blunt and over-rigid set of guidelines drawn up to govern, albeit clumsily, the diverse and unpredictable experiences of real human beings. They are always too general; they always miss subtle differences; and, in any event, they must always be interpreted by imperfect human agents in order to be applied to particular cases. In case he should ever be found, the expert would naturally revise his own (expert) laws in the light of changing circumstances. Ordinary people, though, are in a predicament: they have no intellectual basis on which to ground their changes to law, and yet they have no reason for faith in existing laws which they or other non-experts have made. Contrary to prevailing views, then, law provides no reason for optimism about the health of existing constitutions. Even so, despite the inadequacy of existing law, the Visitor hastens to add that rigidly law-bound constitutions are healthier than other, lawless constitutions, which tend to be controlled by the machinations of deceptive politicians.[19]

The Visitor's point about lawless and lawful polities can be generalized. His crucial idea is that there is but one correct constitution as opposed to all the rest. Ordinary constitutional distinctions – few versus many, rich versus poor, force versus consent, and lawful versus lawless – are insignificant by comparison. Plato shows a deep awareness of the contemporary classification of constitutions along such lines. His formulations are similar to those found in Aristotle's *Politics*; either he influenced the young Aristotle in the Academy, or he learned from his prodigious student across the seminar table.[20] Plato's own chief comment, however, is that the entire discussion is nearly worthless, since the true criterion of constitutional "correctness" is the knowledge of the ruler. If government is not guided by such knowledge, then *any* distribution of power is bound to be wrong, along with any (trivial!) distinctions such as that between force and consent.

The question of force and consent raises disturbing possibilities. The statesman is in principle justified in using force to found the correct city, to maintain its political health, and to reform individual citizens. For example, the Visitor argues that the statesman will, if necessary, purge the city by banishing some, executing others, and sending out colonies "like swarms of bees" (293d–e)! He will also use force, where necessary, to help individuals make ethical progress. The statesman is (as in earlier dialogues) said to be analogous to a doctor ministering to his patients. Accordingly, the Visitor argues, forcible treatments are justified provided that they contribute to the patient's health – whether he consents or not (Text 17).

> **17.** If, therefore, someone does not persuade his patient, but correctly understands the medical art, and he forces either a child or some man or woman to do what is better, contrary to the written rules, what will be the name of his forcible treatment? Won't it be anything rather than a disease-producing mistake contrary to the

> medical art? And wouldn't the patient being forced to do what is better be right to say anything about the case except that he has suffered an unhealthy misuse of the art at the hands of the doctor who forced him? (*Statesman* 296b5–c3)

Therefore, Plato still subscribes to the spirit of paternalism we have met throughout his work. As we will see, however, he moderates this approach in the *Laws*. In his last work, the Athenian distinguishes between slave and free doctors in order to clarify the role of persuasion in statesmanship. He explains that slave doctors do not give an account of their patients' illness or of their treatment, whereas free doctors interview their patients, come to understand the illness, rationally explain a treatment plan, and institute a regimen for health with the patient's consent (720a–e).[21] Can we harmonize these ideas? What is Plato's stance on the citizens' relation to the expert governor?

The answer to such questions depends on the status of ordinary citizens in these works. In both works, I would argue, Plato introduces an important change from the *Republic*. Now, instead of having three classes of citizens with producers on the bottom, Plato defines the citizenry more narrowly, as "the community of the virtuous."[22] The new system of the later works is based on different ideas about the citizens' intellectual capacities. In the *Statesman*, the Visitor says, achieving virtue will depend upon implanting in the citizens' souls "a really true and fixed opinion about what is noble, just and good, and their opposites" (309c). The Visitor's description of true, securely fixed opinion identifies a significant awareness of moral truth – an awareness ultimately grounded in the statesman's own knowledge of the truth. In the *Statesman*, Plato has upgraded the status of "opinion," not of course to the level of philosophical knowledge, but to the level of significant, reasoned awareness of important truths about human life.[23]

We find a similarly positive assessment of the citizenry of the *Laws*. As free citizens, they have sufficient reasoning capacity to understand and be rationally persuaded by the lawgiver; that is the point of the analogy with slave and free doctors. In the *Laws*, the Athenian Stranger also argues that his imagined citizens are like puppets of the gods – they are tugged by powerful emotions, but also have a rational cord that they must obey. In the form of this "golden, holy" cord, the citizens possess reason, "the common law of the city" (645a). As we shall see, their status as free, and by some description virtuous, citizens depends on their rationality and their capacity to be persuaded by the reason of the laws.

Therefore, even though the statesman has a free hand, in principle, to encourage his citizens' ethical development by force, nonetheless the ideal in both works is that he will rationally persuade his citizens to act virtuously. Such persuasion would both be a sign of respect and show recognition of the citizens' genuine capacity to make moral progress.

In the *Statesman* specifically, then, what will political life look like? Rather than democratic deliberation (cf. "Democratic Deliberation" in chapter 3), there will be political officers who aim to carry out the statesman's plans. Beyond the statesman himself, there is little to differentiate citizens from one another. Therefore, most citizens will presumably hold office at one time or other, though the nature of most offices is left undefined. There are, however, three important offices – those of general, judge, and orator. They have specific areas of expertise and to some extent act on their own initiative, independent of the statesman-ruler. For example, the orator works in concert with the ruler to persuade citizens to do what is right (304a). He helps citizens develop their own independent understanding of the just, fine, and noble, as these concepts pertain to particular laws or political decisions made by the statesman. He is a teacher of the citizens. And so his art is far removed from democratic oratory, or from democratic deliberative exchange, but he at least demonstrates that Plato found the citizens described in the *Statesman* to be worthy of respect. This orator practices something like the "true" oratory mentioned in the *Gorgias*, but here his speeches are clearly informed by, and subordinated to, the statesman's political expertise (whereas in the *Gorgias* even leaders such as Aristides the Just – a good man, yes, but not in possession of political knowledge as defined by the *Statesman* – could practice the true oratory; cf. *Gorgias* 526b).

Whatever the nature of the citizens' participation, however, this constitution is not a "democracy" even though all citizens participate. For this "ideal" city is controlled hierarchically by the authoritative political expertise of the statesman. As a result, it lacks the freedom and negotiation characteristic of democratic politics. We have already seen, indeed, that to the Visitor democracy is an imperfect constitution, a mere shadow of the single correct constitution. Through their education, natural intelligence, and capacity for virtue, the ideal citizens will lead a notably virtuous life and thereby flourish under the statesman's supervision. Thus, the statesman's city is different from democracy in two ways related to the intellect. First, the ideal city's laws and customs are grounded in the statesman's singular expertise. Second, the statesman provides that the citizens, as individuals, will have a much more robustly reasoned account of their beliefs than, according to the Visitor, democratic citizens could possibly attain. Both differences help to make the ideal citizens much more virtuous than citizens of a democracy could ever hope to be, in Plato's account.

How does the king promote the ethical flourishing of the citizenry? This is another way of asking, In what precisely does the statesman's political expertise consist? What relationship, if any, does it have to the knowledge possessed by the philosopher-rulers of the *Republic*? Toward the end of the dialogue, the interlocutors define political expertise as the art that controls all the other arts used in the state, as well as the laws, and that supervises everything in the city and correctly "weaves" everything together (305e2–6). It is the knowledge that enables rare experts to direct, manage, and care for human beings, not through carrying out practical duties, such as leading armies into battle, but rather through identifying the appropriate times and circumstances for the practical arts to be applied (305c10–d4). It is a kind of knowledge particularly concerned with identifying the "right opportunity to act" (*kairos*). This directive knowledge enables the statesman to command generals, orators, and judges, as well as other subordinate experts, to apply their skills at certain times, and not at others, and in certain ways but not others. Moreover, it produces political health in cities, as the weaving metaphor implies, by relating citizens to one another appropriately, by enabling them to overcome their potentially unhealthy innate proclivities, and by correctly entrusting practical decisions to the right people, in the right way, and at the right time.[24] In the *Statesman*, politics consists in the statesman's education of citizens in how to go on together with others whose natural tendencies are different from their own – and in the decision-making practices that this educated citizenry habitually carries on.

Insofar as the statesman's political expertise consists in understanding the proper relationships between other arts, and the proper timing for the application of other arts, his knowledge is a kind of second-order expertise. It enables him to employ the specific expertise of the orator, the general, and the judge in the right way, at the right time, and for the right reasons. The idea of a second-order expertise is familiar from Plato's *Euthydemus*, where, in a short passage, Socrates argues that the art of politics (or kingship) consists in knowing how to use the products of other arts, in such a way as to make citizens wise and good (288e–292e). (The *Charmides* also explores the possibility that such a second-order knowledge, a "science of science," exists and asks what benefits, if any, it confers on human beings; cf. 166c–175e). The *Euthydemus* leaves readers uncertain as to how, precisely, the political art will make citizens wise and good, except by educating them to become aware of guiding ethical and political truths (292d–e). The *Statesman* gives a more specific answer to this question, one that takes advantage of the longstanding Platonic concern to establish order in the soul.[25]

According to the Visitor, the king must, like an expert craftsman, "weave together" everything in the city in the best way possible. The Visitor observes that in cities there tend to be those with a natural proclivity toward courage, and those who incline toward moderation. The first group is more aggressive and hotheaded, while the second is non-confrontational and accommodating. Because of their natural inclinations, these types tend to come into conflict with one another in the polis – a conflict that the Visitor describes as "a disease" most inimical to politics (307d). The Visitor is emphatic that through education the citizens must come to share in both courage and moderation. Whoever is incapable of uniting these apparent opposites in the proper way will be killed, banished, or thoroughly disgraced (309a). Because of their intelligence and firmly grounded opinions, all citizens of the ideal city will unite courage and moderation and be capable of understanding (with sound, though not complete, reasons) how, when, and why to pursue peace and accommodation or confrontation and war, as the case may require. The citizens go beyond their natural tendencies so as to deliberate with others unlike themselves.

Normally, Plato would not endorse the idea that parts of (genuine) virtue could come into conflict. After all, "courage" would not really be courage if it did not (say) square with the requirements of justice. It is arguable that the Visitor raises this question in order to explain more certainly how knowledge or right opinion helps to make the virtues of distinct areas of life coherent and consistent. His point is that the statesman must, above all, see to it that such moral coherence is woven into the fabric of the citizens' lives, through training of character and intellect. This mandate leads to particular political proposals to ensure the unity of apparently opposite virtues: for example, naturally courageous types must marry into the families of the naturally moderate, and types with opposite proclivities must serve together on boards of magistrates, so as to "balance" each other's natural tendencies. The statesman, in Plato's account, enables his citizens to live the best life possible through providing for the most complete ethical education of which they are capable. There is no incompatibility, therefore, between Plato's account of the rulers' knowledge in the *Republic* – which is knowledge of the Forms and especially of the Form of the Good – and his account of the statesman's expertise. In order to educate citizens in what is fine and just, to make them both courageous and moderate, and to unite them politically through "weaving," the statesman's directive activities will have to be informed by the knowledge which Plato ascribes to the philosophical rulers of the *Republic*.[26]

The statesman's project of weaving together virtues in the soul so as to create order and coherence furthers the earlier project of establishing an orderly soul. Already in the *Gorgias*, many of the central ideas were in place. The biggest problem with Callicles, according to Socrates, was the lack of harmony in his soul. He was out of sync with the *kosmos* of the universe. But Socrates' account of psychic health was vague and incomplete. In the *Republic*, Plato developed his emphasis on order by fleshing out the relationship between order and the Good. He also illustrated why knowledge of the Good, and therefore order, were central to the individual's attainment of psychological health. The philosophical elite exhibited the highest order of soul possible, through likening their own psyches to the order they witnessed in their philosophical contemplation. In the *Statesman*, we find another development of Platonic thinking about order. In this work, order finds special application in the souls of the citizenry at large. Through the expert "weaving" of the statesman, the citizens achieve an ordered balance of virtues in the soul, as well as possessing good reasons for valuing and trying to maintain such order. Plato is therefore more optimistic about the life-prospects of non-philosophers than he had ever been, but the new boundaries of citizenship cause many would-be citizens to be altogether excluded from the goods of political life.

Plato's last and longest work, the *Laws*, develops many of the themes found in the *Statesman*. To get a handle on this complex work, it is helpful to begin near the end. Having sketched the foundation of a state he calls "Magnesia," the Athenian Visitor argues that states must be founded in order to achieve a single purpose or end – virtue. Every citizen of Magnesia, he has argued, must work with great effort to achieve goodness and "the excellence of soul that befits a human being"; nothing else, not even the state itself, must compromise this goal (770c–e). Most contemporary states, by contrast, exist in order to further the aims of a particular faction or to produce wealth or to promote excessive freedom (Text 18).

> **18.** And it is no wonder that often the standard of justice, in the eyes of some, is that certain people will rule in the city, whether they happen to be better or worse men, whereas for others the standard is that they will be wealthy, whether they are enslaved or not, and others are driven by the desire for a life of freedom. (*Laws* 962d9–e4)

Achieving political health therefore requires clarity as to the nature of virtue. In particular, he says, it requires the rulers to understand that virtue is a unity even though it might be called by different names (courage, restraint, justice, wisdom) in different circumstances. Even at the level of its terminology, this part of the conversation is reminiscent of earlier Platonic ideas about the forms. To translate this conversation into the earlier terminology, the rulers of Magnesia (or at least some of them) must understand that which is truly good and virtuous, in an unqualified sense. They must grasp the forms. Then, they must craft their legislation so as to promote and exemplify their knowledge of the good.

The *Laws* therefore subordinates politics to philosophical knowledge, for the sake of achieving virtue in the polis. This work departs from earlier discussions, however, in its emphasis on theology as the key to establishing a suitable politics. His constitution, the Athenian says, should properly be called a "theocracy" after the god who is really in charge of it (Text 19).

19. Best of men, you really do have a share in constitutions, but the ones we named just now are not constitutions, but ways of managing cities that are ruled over and enslaved by certain parts of themselves, and each one gets its name from the ruling power. But if it is necessary to name the city on some such basis, then we should call it by the name of the god who really does rule over sensible men. (*Laws* 712e9–713a4)

The Athenian explains the "bedrock" of his theology in Book 10. Atheism, he argues, is a form of mental disease and corruption. It is promoted by thinkers who believe that the world arose from nature and chance rather than a purposeful intelligence. Human law is, from this perspective, a trivial convention; and "what is fine by nature is one thing, while what is fine by law is another" (889e). Readers cannot help recognizing that the Athenian is holding up Calliclean ideas to scrutiny, for the purpose of disproving them. Such a strategy is typical of this work: embedded within profoundly novel arguments is a re-playing of prominent themes from earlier dialogues, integrated into a brilliant and persuasive whole.

The Athenian's own theological argument sketches a metaphysics that gives priority to the soul over matter. Among other interesting points, though, most important for us is his development of what we might now call "natural law" (Text 20).

20. In particular, he should defend the law itself and art as existing by nature or as being not less real than nature, if at any rate they are the offspring of intelligence, as a true account reveals – an account such as you appear to me to be offering, and with which I agree. (*Laws* 890d5–8, spoken by Cleinias)

Human legislation is set up as a reflection of the divine law, which is expressed in the ordered motions of the *kosmos* (cf. 690b–c). Human law imitates the justice of the laws of the universe that are ordained by a providential and superlatively just and virtuous being. The ruling body must be capable of contemplating the orderly movement of the stars, since these are controlled by reason (*nous*), which gives order to the entire universe (966e). Elsewhere, the Athenian suggests that physics and astronomy are sub-fields of theology (822a–c)! Understanding this and other theological points is the key to the knowledgeable governance of Magnesia. Legislation must be crafted with one eye on the reasoned order of the universe, and the other on the political world of becoming. In fact, making a point that the Stoics were to build upon at great length, the Athenian argues that "as much immortality as is in us, we must manage our houses and our cities both publicly and privately in accordance with this, naming this share of reason 'law'" (713e–714a). Such theories were the Greek legacy to the Christian natural law tradition best exemplified by Aquinas. As often, Cicero was the "filter" through whom this legacy was transmitted (Text 21).

> **21.** The origin of justice must be derived from law. For law is a force of nature, it is the rational intelligence of a wise man, it is the measure of justice and injustice. . . . And therefore, since nothing is better than reason, and since reason exists in both human beings and in god, the first association between human beings and god is found in reason. However, those who share reason, also share right reason; since this is law, we human beings must also be considered allied with the gods in law. (Marcus, in Cicero, *Laws* 1.19, 23, Tr. Rudd, adapted)

Like the city imagined in the *Statesman*, Magnesia is also a "community of the virtuous."[27] All citizens must strive to fulfill their potential to achieve virtue. Though being in charge of private farmsteads, they are legally discouraged from participating in the practical management of their farms. To create a citizenry capable of virtue, moreover, certain "purges" (as the Athenian puts it) will be necessary, to weed out potential troublemakers, often the poor (735a–736c).

Some of the governmental structures that guide the city to virtue are left unclear. But the crucial point is brought out in the Athenian's description of the "Nocturnal Council," as Magnesia's governing council is called. This august body is to consist of priests, the ten senior "Guardians of the Laws," the minister of education, and select younger associates, in their 30s, who will retire when they reach the age of 40. Since this council is charged with broad oversight of the city's laws and affairs, some of its members will naturally receive a sustained philosophical education. This gives them deep insight into the laws of the city. Others, in particular the younger associates, however, will not be philosophers. They will achieve a significant degree of virtue without attaining philosophical knowledge. Thus, as the Athenian points out, there will be intellectual distinctions within the group – as befits, we must recognize, the hierarchy of old and young (Text 22).

> **22.** Having observed these things, the lawgiver will set guardians over all his laws. They will make sure – some with wisdom, others with true belief – that intelligence binds together all these provisions in such a way that they are clearly based upon self-restraint and justice, not wealth or ambition. (*Laws* 632c4–d1)

The Council is not equivalent to the body of philosophical guardians described in the *Republic*, but it emphasizes the thesis that Plato consistently adhered to throughout his career. Politics must be directed by philosophy or it is nothing.

Politically speaking, therefore, the *Laws* is basically similar to the *Statesman*: philosophical rulers, with genuine knowledge of the "oneness" of virtue, beauty, and so forth, will guide the state with wisdom, while the other citizens, on or off the Council, will be capable of acting well in the practical world, and of articulating good reasons for their ways of acting. All of the citizens will be of essentially the same character, and all deserve respect for their progress toward virtue – like the citizens of the *Statesman*. Since the younger associates on the Council must retire at age 40, it is clear that this expected "turnover" will spread political knowledge and virtue widely in the city.[28]

The *Laws* does, however, draw out in vast detail a topic largely unexplored in the *Statesman*: namely, the role of law in the best state. Whereas the *Statesman* concentrated on criticizing (existing) law, the Athenian explains that laws can serve several purposes in the community of the virtuous. First, once the basic principles are settled, they provide largely immutable standards of behavior for all citizens for the duration of the community. They can be changed only through the unanimous vote of all citizens. But if they genuinely reflect the divinely ordained order of the *kosmos*, then they will provide an exemplary guide to human action.

Second, and perhaps more important, the Athenian provides that laws are not to be mere prohibitions. Rather, they are to be prefaced by "persuasive preambles" that explain the reasons for right action, exhort citizens to live up to their nature as virtuous human beings, and encourage them to overcome the human susceptibility to moral weakness. As in the *Statesman*, the citizens of the *Laws* merit and properly receive reasoned explanations of laws and public guidelines. This helps them act in a more deeply virtuous way than would otherwise be possible, because they come, through the laws and their preambles, to understand why they should act as the law tells them to. Their understanding, in turn, ensures the legitimacy of the government in the eyes of the governed. The city is founded on consent – a principle the Athenian emphasizes throughout the conversation (e.g., 684a–b).

Third, the laws will practically embody the wisdom and experience not only of the original legislator, but also of successive legislative guardians. These guardians are expected to develop the body of law through interpretation in the light of evolving circumstances.

There is no philosophical inconsistency between *Statesman* and *Laws* on the subject of law. Rather, they concentrate on different aspects of legislative authority in existing cities and in the ideal cities being founded. But the Athenian takes a dimmer view of the *Statesman*'s recommendation that authority should be concentrated in the hands of a single expert. In his review of previous constitutions (Book 3), he recommends a republican or "mixed" constitution, in order to rule out the corruption necessarily (he says) brought on by absolute power. This sort of corruption is not contemplated in the *Statesman*. In his last work, therefore, Plato makes more modest claims for the moral integrity of those he wishes to put in positions of leadership. The *Laws* opts for a philosophical version of the "republican solution," whereas the *Statesman* chooses a philosophically informed "monarchic solution." Most readers will find the former option more plausible.

The Athenian's more modest claims raise the question of ideal versus actual in the *Laws*. Is the Athenian putting forward utopian political theory? Is Magnesia a practicable city, or an ideal one, or something in between? In larger terms, what sort of ambitions on behalf of politics in the human world is it appropriate for a lawgiver or a theorist to have?

In the *Republic*, Socrates had insisted that Callipolis was a practicable, if highly unlikely, constitution. At the original founding of
Magnesia, Cleinias says that he has been chosen, with nine colleagues, to found a colony in Crete. In the present conversation,
therefore, he proposes constructing an imaginary community, "as
though we were founding it from the beginning"; he emphasizes
that the initial "foundation" of Magnesia is to be undertaken at
first only in speech (702b–e). Then, in his discussion of property
distribution, the Athenian remarks that he would like to describe
the ideal society, then the second and third best, in case all of them
can be of use to future legislators, who must adapt their choices to
the prevailing conditions (739a–b). However, he recognizes that
absolute community of property, and therefore unity, is absolutely
ideal and worthy of the gods or their children. But, since such
perfection is impracticable for human beings, the interlocutors
agree to focus on the "second-best" state, in which 5,040 plots of
land are distributed. These are farmed by individual households,
but should be considered the property of the state. This arrangement is obviously not ideal, in the Athenian's terms, but it does
approximate to the ideal. The Athenian explains that the "legislator" ought to describe in detail which provisions he really considers
ideal, and then, only afterwards, concern himself with establishing
which are possible or impossible in practice (745e–746d). This is
the practice he follows in establishing provisions for sexual behavior, too (841a). In short, then, this work represents utopian political
thought, but with an eye fixed more firmly on human weakness
and the susceptibility to corruption than in the *Republic*.

The Athenian's reduced ambitions (so to speak) correspond to
the striking emphasis he places on inculcating self-control in all
citizens. It is notable how often and insistently he returns to this
theme throughout the work, particularly in connection with the
need to avoid material greed and self-indulgence. In dealing with
topics as diverse as homicide (870a) and military training (831c–d),
the Athenian reviles the human tendency to indulge in acquisitiveness (Text 23).

23. The most important source [of voluntary homicide] is lust
ruling over a soul that has been made wild by desires. Such cravings
are usually directed toward the object of most men's greatest and

> most powerful passion – wealth, which, through nature and harmful lack of education, gives rise to countless insatiable desires for unlimited acquisition. (*Laws* 870a1–6)

Therefore, in his general preamble to the proposed legislation, the Athenian proclaims that all citizens must "honor" their souls first after the gods, then their bodies, then their material possessions (726a–728c).

The idea of "honoring" the soul appears to refer to what we might call living with appropriate self-respect.[29] The soul-honoring, or self-respecting, individual will avoid indulging in pleasure, will not preserve his life at any cost, and will feel disgust at the excessive acquisition of material wealth. Those who lack self-respect in this sense are made wretched, even if they escape legal punishment. (In Plato's theory (*Laws*, Book 9), punishment *should*, in fact, serve to cure the wretched, on the Socratic assumption that no one harms his own soul intentionally; again notice the connections with *Gorgias*.) On the other hand, living in a virtuous and self-respecting way produces pleasure and happiness, because self-respect maintains the soul in a condition of health, whereas vice is harmful. Again, the themes of *Gorgias* and *Republic* are revisited, but in such a way as to make a genuinely happy life available to all ordinary citizens of Magnesia.

There are numerous features of this ambitious work that are beyond the scope of the present book. In view of the next chapter, however, it is worthwhile to point out the respects in which this work appears to anticipate Aristotle's ethics and politics. First, and most important, the emphasis on the community of the virtuous is crucial to Aristotle's own best constitution in *Politics* 7–8. Plato anticipates, in fact, the Aristotelian idea that there are two kinds of good human life – the theoretical and contemplative, on the one hand, and the practical life devoted to politics and ethical virtue, on the other.

Second, Plato's method of consulting the past and considering the rational opinions of others is similar to Aristotle's standard "data method" of approaching ethical and political questions. In short, the philosopher considers carefully what people generally think about an ambiguous question, and then proceeds to rationalize and harmonize the best available insights. In Book 3, for example,

Plato looks to other constitutions (real or imaginary) to reflect upon the best means to found a state – which is similar to Aristotle's examination of other political theories and constitutions in *Politics* 2. Or, at an ethical level, Plato considers current thinking about slavery in order to figure out the best method of handling slaves in Magnesia (776b–778a).

Finally, the Athenian insists upon the "mean" between pleasures and pains as the appropriate ethical target for virtuous individuals (792c–e). He also says that the wise man will try to hit that target through listening to "right reason" (*tois orthois logois*, 696c9–10). This anticipates Aristotle's discussion of virtue in the *Nicomachean Ethics*. It should go without saying by now that Aristotle explicitly takes the discussion of virtue to be the preliminary study for any good legislator or politician.

chapter 7
Aristotle's Political Thought

Born in 384 BC, Aristotle did not witness the upheavals of late fifth-century politics. He was not an Athenian citizen. In the realm of ethics and politics, however, he is nonetheless best viewed as continuing the project outlined in the late Platonic texts. This is a heterodox view to the extent that Plato and Aristotle have traditionally been considered divergent in their philosophical approaches. As Raphael's *School of Athens* indicates, Plato looked upward to the heavens as the source of truth, while Aristotle emphasized empirical research in the world we know. This might be true enough for the Plato of the *Republic*. In the *Laws*, however, Plato elevated the political function of law, emphasized blending the "pure" regimes, used a method of exploring common opinions, and offered a practical political agenda. In all of these ways, Aristotle's political thought bears a distinct resemblance to Plato's. Moreover, Aristotle's division of constitutions takes the Platonic classification (*Statesman* 291d–292a) as its starting-point. Aristotle provided, therefore, a novel synthesis and development of Greek traditions that Plato had refashioned in the preceding generation.

Our interest in Aristotle, however, is not merely historical, much less antiquarian. It is possible to read Aristotle as a contemporary,[1] as a philosopher whose insights into the human condition and specifically into politics can deepen our current political understandings, enrich our political vocabularies, and force us to rethink our own modern preconceptions. By examining politics through an Aristotelian lens, we can look more deeply into the causes and constituents of political health and come to identify the possibility of political consensus amidst the diversity of modern life. In particular, Aristotle's politics poses a powerful challenge to modernity's characteristic endorsement of subjective theories of the human good and human happiness. For Aristotle, human beings have a nature that provides (admittedly rough and imprecise) guidelines about human well-being. Human "flourishing" can be correctly or incorrectly described at a certain level of generality, whatever individuals may happen to think about their own welfare. Individuals can and do construct misguided interpretations of their own well-being. At the same time, as we shall see, Aristotle provides no rigid or authoritarian or even detailed guidelines as to how human beings should live; such questions, as he often points out, cannot be answered with great precision or exactitude. General reflections in this realm, he says, are true only "for the most part." Even so, Aristotle's conception of nonrelative standards can help modern citizens communicate with others not only within their own cultures, but also outside them. Finally, Aristotle's political thought provides significant resources in explaining democratic deliberation and justifying its value. Aristotle is both anti-subjective and broadly sympathetic to ordinary people.

Aristotle outlined his *Politics* in the final section of the *Nicomachean Ethics* (Text 1).

1. Then, on the basis of the collected constitutions, let us examine what sorts of things preserve and destroy cities, and what sorts of things preserve and destroy each type of constitution, and for what reasons some cities are well governed and others badly. Once we have examined such things, perhaps we might see in general which constitution is best, and how each might be best arranged, and with which laws and customs. (*EN* 10.9.1181b17–22)

The *Politics* has a twofold program – to ameliorate existing constitutions and to describe the best constitution.[2] To Aristotle the two prongs of this inquiry are closely intertwined. In order to discover which constitution is best, the philosopher must investigate practically what works and what fails in constitutions as they are. In this passage, specifically, he refers to his school's well-known collection of 158 "constitutions" – i.e., analyses of constitutions of the Greek cities. The only one of these that survives is the *Constitution of the Athenians*, a work that resulted from wide reading and historical research (albeit not in the modern sense), informed by Aristotelian political theory. It provides a much more careful historical account than anything comparable in Plato's works – for example, the Athenian's "history" of constitutions in *Laws* Book 3, or Socrates' presentation of the "devolving" constitutions in *Republic* Books 8–9. Aristotle's method of combining historical analysis with normative theory is especially clear in his treatment of widely admired existing constitutions, such as those of Sparta, Crete, and Carthage (*Politics* 2.9.1269a29–2.11.1273b26), and in his engagement with the political legacy and thought of historical figures such as Solon. It is particularly useful to examine Aristotle both within his historical context and from the perspective of his normative theory.

His combination of the analytic and the evaluative makes Aristotle's project considerably more complex than previous accounts. He outlined his philosophical aims with great precision in a famous programmatic section of the *Politics* (4.1.1288b10–4.2.1289b26). He aspired to understand

1   what constitutes the best constitution;
2   what constitution is generally acceptable and generally preferable for most actual cities;
3   which sort of constitution is most suitable for the different kinds of citizenry that exist;
4   how constitutions might be established; and
5   what causes constitutions to be preserved and destroyed.

This last objective required him, as he thought, to enumerate the different types (and even subtypes) of constitution, so that we find a great deal of historical detail about existing constitutions throughout the work. Aristotle had general beliefs about the best form of constitution and human life, and these emerged in no small part from his sympathetic approach to politics as he observed it.

This explains why he applies the term polis more generously than Plato had done, for example, in the *Statesman*. According to Plato's Eleatic Visitor, non-ideal constitutions are not worthy of the name. For Aristotle, by contrast, a wide variety of human partnerships – of a certain size, and with other common features – count as real poleis with real constitutions, even if they make mistakes about what is good for them. (Note, though, that Aristotle too excluded certain actual constitutions: for example, democracies where the untutored demos, and not the law, has final authority: cf. 4.4.1292a4–1292a38.) Holding this view did not commit Aristotle to relativism: he recognized important differences between good and bad, healthy and diseased constitutions; but it did imply considerable respect for, and interest in, constitutions as they are.

Civic Conflict, Emotion, and Injustice: Observing the Polis as It Is

Aristotle recommended starting with empirical observation before moving on to theory. So it makes sense for us to begin, too, with the obvious concerns faced by political actors in fourth-century Greece. Aristotle was concerned particularly with civic conflict. Aristotle's interest in civic conflict locates him coherently within the fourth-century framework established in chapter 6. He devoted Book 5 of the *Politics* to this subject and built his analysis on a basic political premise articulated earlier: "Justice is the political good, and this consists in what is of common advantage" (3.12.1282b16–18). When there is a failure of justice, or rather when citizens perceive such a failure, rightly or wrongly, then conflict ensues. In other words, the key motivation driving citizens to civil war was the perception of injustice (whether correct or incorrect).

Aristotle looked carefully at the citizens' political opinions, character, and emotions to discern the sources of such perceptions. Aristotle contends that constitutions arise with general agreement that justice consists in giving equal things to equal people, i.e. that justice is proportional equality (5.1.1301a27). But constitutions-as-they-are typically fail to realize this kind of equality, because different sub-groups tend, wrongly, to generalize equality in one area of life to equality in all areas of life. For example, democrats believe that, because they are all equally free men, they are therefore equal in every politically relevant way (they thereby turn proportional equality into arithmetic equality, cf. "Mapping out the Problem" in chapter 4); oligarchs, by contrast, believe that they are unequal in every politically relevant way because they have more wealth than others. Thus, Aristotle theorized civic strife as a defect of constitutions that do not adequately promote equality and thereby produce injustice (Text 2).

2. They (democracy and oligarchy) all have something just, but, speaking without qualification, they are mistaken. Therefore, when they have a share in the constitution that conflicts with the conception of justice each side has, they fall into civil conflict. (*Pol.* V.1.1301a35–9)

Note Aristotle's traditionality: from the unstable politics of Agamemnon's army, to Thucydides' Corcyraeans, to Xenophon's imploding polis, the key to *stasis* was the question of justice, understood as a form of proportionally equal distribution of goods and honors.[3]

What creates civic stability, however, is not only (actual) justice, but also *consensus* as to what constitutes a just distribution of goods in a polity and, in particular, consensus about the just distribution of political power. Citizens tended, in Aristotle's view, to regard the common interest too narrowly and as partisans. They lacked a generous and enlarged perspective on politics. Even when they are not intentionally selfish, most people are incapable of taking an enlarged view, because, as Aristotle puts it, "Most people judge badly about their own affairs" (3.9.1280a15–16). Thinking too highly of oneself is for Aristotle a common human failing, as are suspicion of others, envy of others' good fortune, and the inability to appreciate the value of generosity. To pinpoint his concerns, Aristotle says that most people share Thrasymachus' view of justice as "another's good," and therefore, he implies, they condemn it as foolish (*EN* 5.1.1130a3–4, 5.6.1134a35–b6). The consequence is that most existing constitutions turn out to be democracies or oligarchies. These are constitutions in which citizens take a narrow view of self-interest. Either the numerous poor or the wealthy few end up winning the game of power that appears to be at the heart of real-world politics. Since few have ever imagined, much less witnessed, healthy politics, it is not surprising that many understood the goal of politics to be the domination of others. What he saw made Aristotle believe that many individuals and poleis are incapable of achieving happiness (7.13.1331b39–1332a7).

Aristotle developed such views by observing specific events. For example, in describing how constitutions change, Aristotle recalls that "in Chalcis the demos with the nobles removed Phoxus the tyrant and immediately took hold of the *politeia*" (5.4.1304a29–31). In virtue of other, similar "case studies," Aristotle concluded that emotions and self-assessments often played a major role in causing revolution (Text 3).

> **3.** In general, one must not forget this: those responsible for increasing the city's power, whether private citizens, magistrates, tribes, or, generally, any part or any multitude whatever, set in motion civil conflict. For either men envious of their honors will start the strife, or they will not wish to remain on equal terms with others, out of a feeling of superiority. (*Pol.* V.4.1304a33–8)

As experience showed, most actual citizens were driven by the desire to avoid dishonor and material loss, by ambition and greed, by anger at others' (presumptively unjust) prosperity, by indignation at others' arrogance, and by fear. Aristotle's theoretical interest in justice and equality was intimately related, in practice, to the powerful emotions that shape political life. Thus, in turn, his interpretation of politics depended on views about psychology. The importance of envy, anger, feelings of superiority, resentment, and so on show that the proper understanding and education of character were crucial to maintaining political stability. One of Aristotle's most important contributions to political thought was his understanding of emotion.

Aristotle's *Rhetoric* helps us to understand the nature of political emotion. According to Aristotle, the emotions have a cognitive or intellectual dimension. They depend on the agent's values, beliefs, perceptions, and desires. Aristotle therefore disagreed with previous (and, again, subsequent) philosophers who accepted a sharp distinction between emotion and intellect. (Incidentally, cognitive psychologists and contemporary philosophers have come, more and more, to endorse Aristotle's view.)[4] Aristotle held both that emotions are intentional (i.e., they are *about* something) and that they embody judgments of particular situations.

His discussion of anger is particularly illuminating. For Aristotle, anger was a typical and healthy reaction to dishonor (Text 4).

> **4.** Let us then define anger as a longing, accompanied by pain, for a real or apparent revenge for a real or apparent slight, affecting a man himself or one of his friends, when such a slight is undeserved. (*Rhet.* 2.2.1.1378a, tr. J.H. Freese, *Aristotle: The Art of Rhetoric*, Loeb Classical Library, Cambridge, Mass., Harvard University Press, 1926)

Anger wells up in individuals when their status is publicly questioned or contested in areas that the individual cares about. For example, a warrior cares especially about the conduct of war and becomes infuriated when he feels, rightly or wrongly, that he has been insulted, or that his status has been unjustly threatened, in relation to war. The key point is that anger is a strong reaction against (perceived) injustice. On the other hand, instead of getting angry, individuals tend to accept without question what they view as just (2.3.15). Because our principal concern is to be treated as we subjectively think we ought to be treated, questions of emotion, character, equality and justice were intertwined in Aristotle's theory.

From the tenor of this analysis, it sounds as though Aristotle, in his guise as a "real-world" theorist at any rate, was writing in the tradition of the "Old Oligarch" and others for whom the polis was by nature a battleground. In particular, civic conflict appears to be an expression of nearly intractable problems. How can we identify justice in the polis? Is anger, which originates in subjective appraisals, a good index of unfairness in distribution? Is a *just* distribution merely that distribution which happens to satisfy all concerned parties – or can people be wrong about their own and others' self-interests even if they are satisfied with the status quo? Or is there, perhaps, a quasi-Platonic objective standard, an "Archimedian point," to which we might appeal?[5]

It turns out that, unlike the Old Oligarch, Aristotle is guardedly optimistic about the possibility of healthy transformation in the real world. The desire for justice is a positive, healthy human characteristic that leads, in the right circumstances, to political stability and concord. But human beings need to be better educated in what constitutes justice in specific circumstances – or, rather, in how to reason practically from the world of bewildering particulars to decisions and norms of distribution that create fairness and equilibrium within the polis. Human beings have the innate capacity to live well, provided that they are educated properly, treated humanely, raised in security, and thereby enabled to make good choices about how to live. Aristotle's standards of justice and the good life come, however, not from Platonic Forms, or from any religious authority, or any other type of extra-human source. Rather, they come from a particular – though again purposefully vague and imprecise – understanding of human nature.

Exploring What Ought To Be: Aristotle's Naturalism

Politics and *Nicomachean Ethics* work together to say what the best human life is and to say what the best political life is (*EN* 1.2.1094a24–b11, 10.9.1179b31–1181b24). The key to Aristotle's view of individual flourishing and political health is his naturalism – his theory of human nature, function, and purpose. Some readers have viewed this theory as providing, therefore, a rich and determinate account of what constitutes the best life for members of the human species. Aristotle's interest in the world of biology, zoology, and other life sciences is well known. It is tempting to view Aristotle's approach to human beings, by analogy, as biological – examining, classifying, and making judgments about human beings as a special type of animal species.

Aristotle's approach to human beings, however, cannot be precisely similar to such scientific methods. Convention and culture are distinctly important in human life, as are complex human language and the possibility of creating a shared history in human communities. In trying to understand the nature of human beings, therefore, Aristotle had to take into account the complex beliefs and practices of diverse human communities. He collected the "data" of myths, narratives, laws, and so forth as raw materials from which to derive an understanding of the characteristic and healthy behavior patterns of human beings. Aristotle's conception of human nature, therefore, did not provide an external vantage-point from which human lives could be evaluated, much less one rooted in the metaphysical realm of Plato's forms. Rather, Aristotle's was a philosophical and evaluative analysis starting from this-worldly appraisal of different types of human choices and lives.

For all that, he was offering nonrelative, nonsubjective ethical and political evaluations. He observed and made general judgments about human beings and their healthy or unhealthy conditions. Upon reflection, this approach is similar to our approaches to the raising of children, our friendships, and our basic thoughts about emotional well-being. In conversations about such matters, for example, we might argue that self-respect is a basic human good – as are internal self-consistency, the lack of shame, the ability to take pleasure in one's work, and so forth. We assert these arguments as generally true, full-stop, whatever anyone might think. Such judgments, indeed, are characteristic of psychotherapy and psychiatry – areas in which no practitioner would question the value of such basic goods for human beings. Judging from our everyday practices, we already find good reasons to endorse Aristotle's method.[6]

Note that, for Aristotle, our general reflections on human nature are always marked by the use of practical reason (see below, "Aristotle on the Good Life," for further discussion of the different intellectual capacities). When we discuss a polis or an individual, we are not applying technical scientific reasoning; this is what is implied by Aristotle's discussion of ethics and politics as a practical science.[7] Practical reasoning is what enables us to apply the theory of human nature to individual cases. Our generalizations, accordingly, are acceptable only "for the most part," not across the board. Our practical reasoning about particular cases enables us to see that the specific ways in which basic values are worked out in an individual case will vary greatly depending on circumstances.[8] We make allowance for accidents, luck, contingency, and individual differences. Aristotle makes the same point by introducing the case of physical health: Milo, the professional wrestler, obviously and understandably requires a different diet from ordinary people (*EN* 2.6.1106a36–b7). So too with the ethical, emotional, and psychological realms. Marked as it is by practical (not theoretical) reasoning, Aristotle's explanation of individual and political well-being is flexible enough to accommodate diversity while also promoting a nonrelative conception of what is good for human beings and political cultures.[9] This approach differentiates Aristotle from Plato, who did not clearly distinguish between the practical and theoretical functions of the intellect.

Aristotle on the Good Life

Aristotle laid out the substance of his theory of human well-being in the *Nicomachean Ethics*. This treatise was, as we saw in the Introduction, a preliminary study for legislators. Aristotle's method comes through clearly in the opening pages. Aristotle argued that if we reflect upon our lives, and observe human beings living well and living badly, then we should recognize that it is in our interest to make every effort to give our lives coherence as a whole. (Notice the continuity between this view and that of Socrates in the Platonic *Gorgias*: "Plato on Rhetoric and Order in the *Gorgias*" in chapter 6.) We ought to aim at one ultimate goal or end (*telos*). More precisely, we ought to recognize the existence of such an aim, understand its content, and organize our lives accordingly. Observation shows that disorganized or random lives tend to be unsuccessful. But how do we determine the content of such an aim?

Aristotle started with what people say. This is an obviously quotidian approach, but that is its great strength. It is plausible and matter-of-fact. And it turns out to yield important results. Everyone agrees that the chief life-goal is *eudaimonia* – "happiness," or, better, "human flourishing." But what is involved in leading a flourishing human life? Canvassing common opinions, and subjecting them to scrutiny, led Aristotle to rule out pleasure (which we share with animals), money (which is a means to an end, not an end in itself), and honor (which depends too much on the opinions of others). To tackle the key questions about the human good, Aristotle believed, we need a clearer "anatomy" of the human soul. Only such an investigation will yield information about the distinctive activities and excellence of human beings. What, specifically, is good for human beings and not for (say) horses, flowers, or gods? *Eudaimonia* will, as Aristotle put it, consist in the activity of the soul exhibiting a distinctively human excellence (*EN* 1.7.1098a16–17).

By observation, again, Aristotle judged that the soul has a "nutritive" part, which we share with animals and plants; a desiring part, which is capable of obeying rational commands; and a rational part, which has both practical and theoretical orientations (*EN* 1.131102a26–1103a3). Understandably, our highest and most distinctively human part is the rational. Within the rational part, the contemplative element is superior to the practical. In Aristotle's view, therefore, the highest form of human life is that devoted to contemplation of unchanging (e.g., scientific or mathematical) truths. The activity of the theoretical intellect is most divine for human beings; it, more than anything else, elevates us and makes us as happy as we can possibly be (Text 5).

> **5.** We must not agree with those who advise us to think human thoughts, since we are human, or to think mortal thoughts, since we are mortal, but instead we must become immortal, in so far as it is possible, and do everything for the sake of living in accordance with the best thing in us; for even if it is small in size, it far exceeds all other things in power and in value. . . . As a result, the activity of the god, which is far superior in blessedness, would be contemplative. And whatever human thing is closest to this is most conducive to happiness. (*EN* X.7.1177b31–1178a2; X.8.1178b21–4)

A second-best – happy, yes, but not the happiest – life will be one restricted to the practice of moral virtue, which is governed by the practical intellect. This is the life of moral and political excellence, one that exhibits justice, courage, moderation, and the other virtues of character (*EN* 10.8.1178a9–b7). The practical intellect enables individuals to administer politics, to govern themselves, to exhibit the virtues, and to reason about the changing world around us. As its name implies, the excellence of this part of the soul has a practical, often political orientation (Text 6).

> **6.** The option that remains, then, is that it is a true and reasoned disposition fit for action in relation to things that are good or bad for human beings. . . . Therefore, we think that Pericles and others of that sort have practical wisdom, since they are able to discern what is good for themselves and for other human beings. (*EN* VI.5.1140b4–6; VI.5.1140b7–10)

As we have seen, Plato did not distinguish between the theoretical and practical intellect. Aristotle's distinction helps explain his respect for non-philosophers. Like Plato in the *Statesman* and

Laws, Aristotle provided for a relatively broad citizen-body in his best polis. His distinction between theoretical and practical intellect helped strengthen the foundation of this provision. Before we turn to Aristotle's best polis, however, we must specifically explore his conception of nature in politics.

Nature in the *Politics*

Aristotle classified the polis as a species of *koinônia* – an "association," a "partnership," something held in common. In Book 1 of the *Politics*, he applied his naturalistic theory to such partnerships in several memorable theses:

1 the polis exists by nature (1.2.1252b30);
2 man is a political animal (1.2.1253a2–3); and
3 the polis is naturally prior to the individual (1.2.1253a25–26).

All three ideas are alien to modern ways of thinking; Hobbes, for one, explicitly rejected all of these ideas on the grounds that the state is the product of "Art" and that citizens are by nature fearful of one another.[10] Aristotle's main point is that human beings can flourish if they are citizens of a polis, through practicing the virtues of social life, and perhaps through contemplation – but not if they do not. He made this point very strongly. Someone who is by nature without a polis is not human: he is either inferior to us or he is a god. It is not enough simply to live in the polis as a non-citizen; carrying out the functions of citizenship enables individuals to exercise irreplaceably important moral and intellectual virtues – specifically, justice and other social virtues, and practical reasoning.

Aristotle offers a robustly political definition of the individual. The sentiment resembles that of Solon in the sixth century BC ("Archaic Athens and the Search for Justice" in chapter 2). What does Aristotle's formulation imply? He recognizes, of course, that individuals could survive outside the polis, in principle, but such extramural individuals would be imperfect, useless, or corrupt, much like a severed foot or hand that exists independently of the body that had once given it meaning and purpose. Aristotle's political definition of the human individual is a general application of the principle that the whole is prior to the part (1.2.1253a18–19) – which, in this case, implies that the part's purpose is to contribute to the good of the whole. On the face of it, this might be thought to have disturbingly totalitarian implications. The state appears to claim the individual as its own; the individual's good is found, it seems, to consist in contributing to the state's welfare (cf. 1.4.1254a9–10, 1.6.1255b9–15).

Clearly, however, Aristotle did not intend his theory to have such implications. His legislators were supposed to order the polis in such a way as to provide for the good of the citizens, as individuals, and not simply for the state as a collectivity. The analogy with hands and feet – or, as he says, with an isolated chess piece – is not precise. The polis provides the context, education, and institutions in which the human good might be achieved, but it does not altogether resemble an organism whose limbs and inner organs are citizens.[11]

Aristotle defuses any problematic totalitarian implications by viewing the polis as a community consisting of stable, hierarchically embedded sets of relationships. Aristotle contends that the polis, so described, arises on the basis of distinct roles first established within the household and the family. These distinct roles are hierarchical in a particular way. They are based on the association of a "ruling" element – i.e., the male head of household, who rules the family through his practical reason – and the "ruled" elements – the women, children, and slaves – whose lives are better off, Aristotle asserts, through being guided by the householder's prudence (1.2.1252a24–b1). The lives of both rulers and the ruled are considerably improved when we observe the proper hierarchies, because the welfare of rulers and ruled is intimately connected in the household and in the city. Thus, in Aristotle's theory, our (self-) interests are invested in others within the family and the polis; these others and their interests are aspects of ourselves, and their welfare is integrally tied to our own flourishing, and vice versa. In Aristotle's conception, therefore, the polis is not an organism consisting of citizen-limbs, but rather a community of relationships in which an individual's good is relationally linked to the good of others within the household and within the city. This implies interdependence rather than totalitarianism.

How distinctive, in Aristotle's view, were political communities? For Aristotle, other animals, too, are called "political" – bees, cranes, and other animals that had a basically "social" existence.[12] What, if anything, differentiates human beings or makes their polis-partnerships species-specific? Aristotle responds to this question by further defining what is distinctively human about polis-partnerships. Human beings are, Aristotle contends, political in a higher degree than other social animals, in that they are furnished with the faculty of language. Their political associations have a unique complexity and sophistication – one might almost say "dignity" – derived from their moral perceptions and conversations, which language makes possible (Text 7).

> **7.** Speech is for the purpose of making clear the advantageous and the harmful, and so also the just and the unjust; for this is peculiar to human beings in comparison to the other animals: having the perception, uniquely, of what is good and bad, just and unjust, and the other things; and partnership in these things makes a household and a city. (*Pol.* I.2.1253a14–18)

The human being, however, is not a political animal simply by virtue of using signs to convey meaning. It is possible to use language in a brutish way and for evil ends. Rather, the unique dignity of human politics, properly understood, derives from the ethical conversations which language makes possible. Such conversations are the forum in which we exercise our practical intellects, and they are the means through which we take a critical perspective on the lives we are already leading. They help make the polis, and our lives, better in very practical ways. But more importantly they help us become more self-conscious in our pursuit of human flourishing.

Aristotle's points about language and morality can be interestingly applied within discussions of modern politics. In the modern world, cross-cultural and cross-ethnic contact, respect, and tolerance are often charged political issues. Human linguistic capacities arguably enable human beings to discuss, and even provisionally to determine, standards of virtue and appropriate behavior across cultures, provided that suitable efforts at translation are made. Our capacity to discuss the virtues and vices in language can be utilized not only within a particular city or nation, but also across national and ethnic boundaries.[13] And there is reason to think that human experience has enough in common – e.g., scarce resources, the fear of pain or death – to make such conversations useful, meaningful, and helpful to our politics.

For example, a large part of human nature is our experience of *need*. Language helps us to formulate questions about how to meet our natural needs for food, clothing, security, and so forth. Naturally these questions first arise in the household; they are not the atomized reflections of individuals. Rather, they arise, for all of us, in the shared experience of natural needs within the household. By extension, such natural needs become questions for the larger communities of which households are a part. Through language we can map out areas of common experience, and common difficulty, which are susceptible to further explanation and even to possible solution. By developing a longstanding claim about human linguistic distinctiveness, Aristotle provides conceptual resources, and even hope, to modern political agents aiming to pursue tolerance through emphasizing the shared elements of our humanity. At the same time, however, Aristotle's emphasis on language and moral conversation also helps us to recognize our differences across cultures and the possible limits to our shared understandings. Language maps out areas of common *and differing* experiences. Universality applies only "for the most part." The recognition of similarity and of the limits to similarity is also crucial to pursuing tolerance when cultural contact is at issue.

On what grounds does Aristotle argue that the polis itself is natural? After all, human and specifically political development lack the consistent achievement of flourishing that one finds in normally developing species of plants and animals. Why are there so few flourishing poleis in the real world, and so many flourishing oak trees?[14] Provisionally, the answer to the first question is that forming political partnerships is, as we can observe, a characteristic human behavior. Aristotle offers something of an evolution from household to village to city in the first book of the *Politics*, but he does not provide an account of a founding moment – akin, for example, to a social contract (he mentions founders, but only rarely). In his account, he is describing what human beings typically do. And this description turns out to play an explanatory role in his account. Through living in the polis, human beings achieve their condition of flourishing as human beings. In this context, the major differences between human beings and oak trees are that human beings make choices in establishing their partnerships, that they intentionally and self-consciously develop conventions, and that they utilize language in striving to pursue the good life in common. They must help nature attain its purposes. Our greater faculties of choice and self-development make our achievement of flourishing riskier, and yet potentially greater.

One of humanity's most important techniques of pursuing the good life, therefore, turns out to be convention.[15] Accordingly, Aristotle's flexible naturalism can be read as a response to previous debates within Greek political thought, specifically the *nomos–phusis* controversy (see "*Nomos* and *Phusis*" in chapter 4). Against thinkers like Callicles, Aristotle argued that the polis – along with its laws and conventions – exists by nature. Aristotle thereby provided a way to eliminate the sharp line between natural and conventional justice. By doing so he also defused the general argument that "nature" implied the bestial, the lawless, the unjust, and so on. The consequence of his argument was profound. His argument elevated the status of "convention," but without turning him into a legal positivist. He respected convention as such but tried as much as possible to improve particular conventions.

Aristotle on Slavery

One problematic issue related to nature and convention was slavery. It is in the context of his discussion of the "natural" household, village, and polis that Aristotle's infamous theory of "natural slavery" can be found (1.4–7). The master–slave relationship is one of the hierarchical relationships within the household, and Aristotle's thinking about slavery is rooted in his theoretical vision of the household. To Aristotle, it was crucial to grasp and put into practice the proper hierarchy, with a view to promoting the welfare of all parties concerned. Aristotle sets up his discussion by drawing attention to a dispute: some think that slave ownership is identical with household management, statesmanship, and kingship, whereas others hold that there is no natural distinction between master and slave, and therefore no justice in the institution (1.3). Aristotle's own position on slavery is complex but worrying. He does not say outright that there is no such thing as natural slavery. In fact, he says the opposite: "Therefore, some are clearly free by nature, others are slaves by nature, and to these slavery is both advantageous and just" (1.5.1255a1–3). The best polis, as he describes it, will have slaves working the land, and it is presumably a just polis – so here again Aristotle's view appears firm. What reasons could he have had for thinking that natural slaves exist and that the condition of slavery is (or would be) good for them?

Aristotle's argument derives from the familiar Aristotelian idea that throughout nature there are ruling and ruled elements. Their relationship is both necessary and beneficial (1.5.1254a22). So too, he implied, with human beings. Some human beings, he asserts, are deficient in practical reason (1.13.1260a12). They are naturally subject to those with the deliberative faculties to guide them. They stand in the same relation to their superiors as a part to the whole – or as the body to the soul; and therefore the good of the slave consists in contributing to the good of the master (1.6.1255b9–15). For this argument to work, the gap between master and slave must be very wide, akin to the qualitative difference between soul and body or human being and animal (Text 8).

> **8.** All those that differ from others as much as a soul differs from the body and a man from a wild beast (and those whose function is the use of the body are in this condition, and this is the best thing that comes from them), these are slaves by nature, and it is better for these to be ruled by this kind of master, as it is also in the other cases mentioned. For the man who is capable of belonging to another is a slave by nature . . . the one, that is, who shares in reason just to the extent of apprehending it but not having it himself. (*Pol.* I.5.1254b16–23)

Aristotle's empirical observations create problems for his argument. One major problem with presuming a qualitative gap between master and slave is that Aristotle's "natural slaves" are capable of apprehending reason. In that respect, at least, they are not like bodies or animals. They are more like desire in relation to reason – in which case they should be regarded as citizens under the political rule of a statesman or monarch (1.5.1254b2–23). Another problem with the argument is that, as Aristotle explains, nature often does not succeed in marking a clear physical distinction between slaves and free men (1.5.1254b27–1255a1). We are left, in practice, to make judgments about the murky conditions of each individual's invisible soul. It is easy to go wrong. Nature might have provided us with the wherewithal to make correct judgments. Third, Aristotle argues that admonition rather than command should be applied to slaves; masters should not deprive their slaves of explanations (1.13.1260b5–7). This recommendation again suggests that slaves are not mentally deficient in the strong way needed to support Aristotle's argument. Fourth, Aristotle argues that masters cannot be friends with their slaves as slaves, but they can befriend their slaves as human beings (*EN* 8.11.1161a30–b6). It is unclear what this last point could amount to, other than serious ambivalence as to the existence of slaves by nature. Finally, Aristotle argues that citizens of the best polis should hold out freedom as a reward for slaves (7.10.1330a31–3), and we are told that Aristotle emancipated slaves in his will (D.L. 5.14–15). Apparently, therefore, Aristotle's picture of natural slavery is not deterministic or fixed, if "natural" slaves can justly be freed.[16]

Slavery is one area – perhaps *the* one area – where Aristotle's empirical observations conflict sharply with his theoretical conclusions. Admittedly, Aristotle makes his position more plausible by recognizing that slavery is often unjust in practice. For example, those with respectable intellects and virtuous characters might be enslaved in war, in which case their enslavement would be unjust. Aristotle also tries to soften his case by arguing that natural slaves are better off when they are subject to the guidance of a master. But these palliatives did not undo the damage caused by his theory either to his own politics or to later slaves, as in the American South, whose masters utilized Aristotelian arguments to justify this institution.[17]

We might confine ourselves to four observations about Aristotle's theory. First, and most important, it is worth considering whether one damages the cause of liberty even by engaging with such arguments. Engaging with the argument might be like trying to prove to a racist that some underprivileged groups do, indeed, deserve the right to vote. Such engagement concedes too much of the playing field.[18] Second, like modern racist ideology, Aristotle's theory is based on bad science, prejudice, and faulty deductions. He is at least honest enough to recognize and point out his short-comings and ambivalence to his readers. Third, it may be that Aristotle's theory influenced the military and political behavior of his student Alexander, who utilized Macedonians and Greeks to govern the cities of conquered Asia and placed indigenous peoples firmly in the underclass. Plutarch reports that Aristotle encouraged Alexander to lead the Greeks, but to act as a master toward barbarians: that is, "to care for the Greeks as though they were friends and family, but to behave toward the barbarians as though they were animals or plants" (*Moralia* 329b). Such a connection must remain speculative. However, it makes a certain amount of logical and historical sense, especially when we consider that Aristotle possibly alluded to Alexander in his discussion of absolute kingship (*pambasileia*, cf. 3.16–17).[19] Fourth, Aristotle's own best polis, as we shall see, relies for its food production and other necessary "ingredients" on an underclass of serfs or slaves who are not part of the citizen-body. Aristotle's repellent theory appears, therefore, to be integral to his account of the best polis.

Polis and Citizenship in General

To understand Aristotle's view of the best polis, we must be familiar with his understanding of citizenship and the constitution (*politeia*). Aristotle distinguished between properly political and merely "necessary" elements of the polis. Even though the polis has a variety of elements – citizen males, resident aliens, women, children, and slaves – only citizens share in the deliberative and judicial functions of the city (3.1.1274b38–1275a33). Different regimes specify various requirements for citizen status. Generically, though, citizens will be those with a "share" in the *politeia*, in that they control its decision-making and administration of justice. Aristotle thus offers our most precise definition of the polis as a "citizen-state." More specifically, citizens share in the *politeia*, i.e. the city's "constitution" or "way of life." In our discussion of Isocrates' *Areopagiticus* ("The Ancestral Republican 'Solutions'" in chapter 6), we saw that *politeia* refers to much more than the legal and power-sharing arrangements established by a "constitution."

To describe a *politeia* fully, as Aristotle says, one must identify both its distribution of offices and power-sharing arrangements, and, more importantly, the end or aim of the constitution as a whole (Text 9).

9. A constitution is an arrangement concerning offices in cities, describing by what means they are distributed, and what body has authority over the constitution, and what is the end or goal of each community. (*Pol.* IV.1.1289a15–18)[20]

The distribution of power is straightforward: in democracies, all free adult men have political power; in oligarchies, all free adult men who meet a certain property qualification have political power; in aristocracies, all virtuous men, and so forth. Describing the "aim" or goal of the constitution is murkier. Different constitutions value certain principles and ways of life over others: the key values might be freedom, wealth, virtue, military might, and others. For example, a city such as Sparta exists, according to Aristotle, in order to make war and to win power over others. Therefore, its entire way of life – its values, its honors and rewards, its educational system – will be directed toward the supposed good of developing courage and winning wars. The same holds true in democracies (which are devoted to freedom) and in oligarchies (which are devoted to acquiring wealth).

This description does not commit Aristotle to relativism, even if an entire polis holds to the same opinion. We can criticize the ends to which a polis devotes itself. In Aristotle's view, for example, the key imperfection of the Spartan system is its overvaluing of a single aspect of virtue – courage. This goal makes Spartans more impoverished, in human terms, than they should be. Human life holds out rich possibilities that the Spartan focus on war obscures. But Aristotle is not contemptuous of the Spartan constitution, nor does he unrestrainedly criticize ordinary constitutions that are devoted to life itself, or to other values, rather than to the good life as he conceives of it. He is sympathetic with ordinary human aims, which, as he reiterates constantly, usually contain at least a grain of sense or truth (Text 10).

> **10.** Above all, living well is the goal for both communities and individuals. But people come together and establish political communities also for the sake of life itself. For perhaps there is some part of goodness even in mere life itself, provided that the hardships of life are not excessive. It is clear that, though they endure substantial suffering, most men cling to life, since there is some element of health and happiness in it, and a natural sweetness. (*Pol.* III.6.1278b23–30)

His friendliness to the ordinary is one of his most significant, transforming, and appealing attributes.

What he *cannot* imagine is that the polis would be neutral as to its citizens' ends. He vehemently rejects the view of the sophist Lycophron, who argued that the law should act merely as a defensive covenant, as a source of protection against unjust acts. For Aristotle, that would turn the political association into a mere alliance (3.9.1280b6–12). The cardinal principle of liberal political theory would hardly have seemed "political" at all to Aristotle. The same holds true, as we will see, for "social compact" theories such as that of the Epicureans. Even in ordinary settings, Aristotle held a thick conception of the role of politics in an individual's life. His conception derived from his view of the polis as natural – a view that itself was rooted in his theory of the household. For Aristotle, the polis could never be, like an alliance, either artificial or instrumental or temporary.

Aristotle's Best Polis

Aristotle describes the best polis chiefly in books 7–8 of the *Politics*. The key to understanding Aristotle's best polis is his view that although the polis "comes to exist for the sake of living, it exists for the sake of living well" (1.2.1252b29–30). In other words, like the household and village, the polis grows out of the necessity for human beings to satisfy their daily and recurrent needs, such as the need for food or shelter. Every polis needs inhabitants who are "necessary" for the city's (physical and biological) existence – whether these are slaves or various types of citizen laborers, including farmers, who produce goods for the city. In the best polis, these inhabitants cannot be citizens because, Aristotle thinks, they cannot "practice the things related to virtue" (3.5.1278a20–1). Aristotle's belief was that manual labor stunts moral growth and thereby limits the development of virtue in all those who must help to provide for the daily recurrent needs of human life (Text 11).

11. It is necessary to consider mechanical whatever task, art, or education makes the body or soul or mind of free men useless for the employment or practice of excellence. (*Pol.* VIII.2.1337b8–11)

The good life of the citizens was therefore, for Aristotle, parasitic upon slave-producers, because it required leisure for politics and contemplation. Leisure has always been great work if you can get it.

The best polis is dedicated to the good life as described in the *Nicomachean Ethics*: that is, the good life of moral and intellectual excellence. The *telos* of the constitution must be the cultivation of goodness in character and intellect (Text 12).

12. Let this much be assumed right now, that the best life for both individuals separately and cities in common, is the life of virtue supplied with enough provisions to make it possible to have a share in virtuous actions. (*Pol.* VII.1.1323b40–1324a2)

The citizenry, therefore, will exclude those who are unable to develop the virtues of these parts of their souls. Like the citizenry imagined in the Platonic *Statesman* and *Laws* (see "Platonic Political Philosophy after the *Republic*" in chapter 6), therefore, the citizenry of Aristotle's best polis would also consist only of the virtuous. Obviously his citizens, like those of the Platonic Magnesia, will devote themselves to ruling and being ruled in turn, and some of them will turn to philosophy, since they are freed from producing the daily necessities of life. Unlike Plato, however, Aristotle devoted considerable attention to the potential for conflict between those

with practical political orientations and those with more substantial philosophical commitments (7.2–3). Such potential for
conflict reflects a basic lack of clarity as to which life – the ethical
or the contemplative – is best. This political problem did
not arise for Plato because he did not emphasize the distinction
between practical and philosophical wisdom. Aristotle must convince each claimant to goodness that both practical and philosophical orientations have enormous value for the city and its
citizens.[21]

Conflict arises because politically engaged members tend to view
philosophers as idle and inactive, whereas philosophers tend to
view the politically active as aiming at tyranny over others. Aristotle
recognizes that each criticism contains a grain of truth (7.3.1325a23–
34). In particular, he says, constitutions such as those of Sparta and
Crete (note again Plato's similar worries in *Laws* Books 1–2) give
credence to the idea that political action tends to be devoted to the
unjust conquest of others. Such an impoverished view of the active
life is abhorrent in itself and also imprudent: conquest-oriented
states destroy themselves because they do not train citizens to enjoy
the activities of peace. Instead, they instill in citizens the desire for
mastery over their fellow citizens, just as the warlike city seeks
mastery over other cities (7.14.1333b29–35).

Conversely, the life of inaction, it is said, and Aristotle seems to
agree, can never be intrinsically praiseworthy or preferable to the
life of action. What both sides need to see is that, on the one hand,
the active life of politics, construed as a life of ethical virtue, brings
about great nobility in the polis; and, perhaps more importantly,
the life of theoretical contemplation must be considered "active"
in the relevant sense. Philosophical speculation is a form of active
and intense intellectual engagement. If the life of contemplation
were not a substantial activity of excellence, then, Aristotle argues,
how could we admire the life of god, which is pure activity, and
purely intellectual activity at that? (Text 13).

13. For god and the cosmos would hardly be in good condition
otherwise, since they have no activities outside those internal to
themselves. (*Pol.* VII.3.1325b28–30)

Even if conflict erupts, however, Aristotle's best polis should be able to avoid the widespread *stasis* of the fourth-century polis. Civic trust should ultimately prevail because of the citizens' shared education and sense of purpose. Moreover, material benefits are distributed justly and in such a way as to ensure the well-being of all citizens. Conditions would be such as to defuse conflict before it became too serious. And citizens would be educated to be friendly to one another, to know one another's characters, and to have roughly similar ethical values.

What does such a polis look like in practice? The best polis is an "association of equals" (7.8.1328a35–7), that is, of equal citizens who rule and are ruled in turn, who administer justice, who make political decisions, who fight for the polis, and who take over the products of the laborers and use them for the city's good. (Aristotle entertains the possibility that a single individual will be so far superior to others that it would be just and prudent for him to rule as a king [3.13–17], but he considers this possibility highly remote when dealing with Greek people [7.14.1332b12–35]. This surely affects the recommendations he might have made regarding Philip or Alexander's leadership of the Greeks.) This polis is self-sufficient for living life both practically and morally. In order to avoid conflict between citizen and non-citizen groups in the polis, the rulers must also have the capacity to use military force if necessary. At the limit, only those with force can ensure that the constitution will survive. According to Aristotle, therefore, since nature makes younger men physically strong and older men wise, it is both prudent and just to make the younger citizens warriors, the older ones political office-holders, and the very old priests (7.9). This constitutes a just distribution in the sense of giving to each age group its due, that is, a share in the constitution that is proportional to its abilities and to its potential contribution to the common good. The common Aristotelian principle of "ruling and being ruled in turn" (cf. 7.14.1332b25–7) is therefore based, in the best case, on the difference between an older group of rulers and a younger group of the ruled. This hierarchy again reflects, and is built upon, the hierarchy between old and young first encountered in the household.

Unlike the philosopher-rulers of Plato's Callipolis, all of Aristotle's citizens will own property privately (7.9.1329a17–26). (There will also be public property, of course, some devoted to the gods, some dedicated to paying for the common citizens' meals.)

The provisions for private property in particular were established for important ethical and political reasons. First, each individual should hold one lot near the frontiers of the city, and one lot near the center (7.10.1330a9–25). The reason for this, according to Aristotle, is that it will produce greater civic solidarity in the face of external enemies; everyone will have an equal interest in defending the outlying regions, and presumably similar sentiments about going to war altogether. This provision has the effect, in other words, of "randomizing" territorial allegiance, so that particular local interests will not adversely affect the deliberations of the city altogether. Moreover, it provides the citizens with access to various types of "local knowledge." The spread of knowledge and communication throughout the city advanced Aristotle's project of making his citizenry not a casual group of indifferent individuals, but a body of citizens unified by trust, shared goals, and friendship (Text 14).

> **14.** With regard to giving judgments about justice, and to distributing offices according to merit, it is necessary for citizens to know one another, and what sort of men they are, since wherever this does not happen, the distribution of offices and the giving of judgments deteriorates. (*Pol.* VII.4.1326b14–18)

(There are interesting parallels between Aristotle's provisions and the actual constitutional arrangements of Cleisthenic Athens, which united in practice citizens from throughout the unusually large territory of Attica. Furthermore, the provisions might make a person wonder, as has at least one modern political theorist, why territorial representation exists in modern democracies and whether it is an institution worth maintaining.[22])

Second, and more important, the ownership of property was crucial to the citizens' ethical development and well-being. This point comes through clearly in Aristotle's criticisms of previous thinkers in Book 2 of the *Politics*. Plato's *Republic* was a particular target in this book. The chief difficulty with common possession of property, initially at least, is that people tend to neglect what is common. They genuinely apply their energies only to what they call their own (2.3, 2.5.1262b39–1264a1). Moreover, people often get into disputes when they hold property in common, so that lack of private ownership would reduce the level of civic cooperation and harmony. At a deeper level, however, private property enables the citizens to be generous and public-spirited. The ideal constitution ought to make citizens so disposed that they will want to use their property to contribute to the welfare of others and to promote the common good. If property is wholly held in common, therefore, then generosity, not to mention temperance, will become impossible. As Aristotle shows in his critique of Phaleas of Chalcedon, another theorist, his belief that private property will provide the "raw materials" of virtue depends on his own citizens' properly educated desires: they must want neither too little nor too much (2.7.1266b26–31).[23]

Partly because Book 8 is unfinished, we have only vague impressions of citizen education and civic life in this polis. One key principle, though, is that all activities will be directed toward, and derive meaning from, their contribution to the goods of leisure and peace. As Aristotle says, the legislator must establish arrangements that reflect this ordering: "War is for the sake of peace, work for the sake of leisure, and necessary and useful things for the sake of what is fine" (7.14.1333a35–6). Aristotle's criticism of contemporary militarism is tied to his theory of the virtues. Both necessary activities such as war and the peaceful life of politics and philosophy have their own distinctive virtues. Courage, for example, is particularly necessary when the city is at war and is therefore a prerequisite of enjoying a life in the polis devoted to goodness. Temperance, on the other hand, is easy to achieve during the straitened circumstances of war, but is particularly necessary within cities whose residents enjoy an abundance of material satisfactions. And so on with the other virtues. Because of Aristotle's emphasis on the relationship between ethics and politics, it is regrettable that his detailed educational program has not survived. From what we can surmise in *Politics* 8, it appears as though he proposed utilizing a traditional education in tragedy and the arts, after careful thinking through of what such things might teach us.

In part the virtues must be developed through the city's physical and institutional arrangements. For example, the territory must be plentiful enough to enable the citizens to live a life of liberality, but not so abundant as to promote extravagance. Moreover, the provisions for owning property are intended, in part, to promote courage in meeting external attacks. But the primary way of promoting a virtuous citizenry is through education, and it is in education that the legislator must be attuned to the conclusions reached in the *Ethics* about the make-up and healthy development of individuals. In the ethical treatises, Aristotle's goal, as he stated over and over, was not merely to articulate a conception of goodness, but more importantly to make men good (*EN* 2.2.1103b27–9). That goal helps us grasp the intimate connection between Aristotelian ethics and politics. The statesman and legislator must arrange the polis so as to enable his citizens to flourish. To do so properly, he must understand the ethical and intellectual make-up of individuals, and he must see to it that his citizens receive an education that will enable them to attain the ends which nature has ordained for human beings.

Let us note, above all, that Aristotle's description is thick but vague.[24] It describes ethical and political life at an appropriate level of detail – i.e., the imprecise level of which the subject naturally admits. Aristotle's ideals were also provisional and revisable. They were meant to draw readers into the conversation and to provide some development of thought in areas worth looking into. The resulting picture has many attractions. It is certainly meant to be achievable in the real world, even if it has never in fact been achieved. Legislators educate citizens at state expense. They provide individuals with the wherewithal – materially, educationally, emotionally, and ethically – to make good choices about how to live. No citizens "fall through the cracks." Conversely, all citizens participate in the great human goods made available by political, or in some cases philosophical, activity. The crime rate is very low. Citizens live in basic security and with a sense of ongoing welfare. Children are well cared for, as are the elderly. The city is meant to provide most of the things we would all want for our children and our family members – a good index of nonrelative human value, by Aristotle's lights. Note that all of these human goods are established without reference to particular cultural traditions. The best polis is meant to be good for all human beings, and it looks like a promising candidate in that regard (for further reflections, see chapter 9).

Is this polis' political health bought at too high a price? Modern Western citizens could never accept that the citizens' leisure and well-being should be founded on slave labor. That is too high a price. To "translate" Aristotle's ideas into a form that would be acceptable today, we would need to imagine a (non-slave-owning) society in which work is shared fairly and workers of all sorts are viewed with sympathy and treated with dignity. As we will see in considering the Epicureans' ideal community, the problems of ordinary economic production – the production of food and other daily recurrent necessities – will always be with us, as will the need to care for the sick, the very young, and the elderly.[25] The protracted leisure Aristotle wants to provide for his citizens will be impossible if we decide, as we certainly should, to devise ways to distribute such quotidian work more fairly and sympathetically. The fair distribution of such work is one of the keys to establishing a just society. If philosophical and political leisure is necessarily tied to rigid injustice in the distribution of social work, then the so-called goods of such leisure are not worth having.

We might also wonder whether Aristotle's polis is not claustrophobic. For example, he offers detailed guidelines for when men and women should marry (ages 37 and 18 respectively), based on his beliefs about their own physical development and the likelihood that their offspring will be healthy and male. He strictly regulates procreation, which he calls a "public service" (7.16.1335b28–9), and forbids the rearing of deformed children. Even if the polis is to be arranged to promote the welfare of citizens, Aristotle emphatically defines the individual as a citizen, as a political being (Text 15).

15. At the same time, we must not consider any one of the citizens to belong to himself, but rather we must consider all to belong to the city, since each is part of the city. (*Pol.* VIII.1.1337a27–9)

He held a strongly political vision of how most individuals should spend their time and energy. And his case for the human good might not be strong enough for us to want to give up our rich private lives in favor of his thoroughly public conception of what is good for us.

Political Possibilities in Existing Cities

With Aristotle's description of the best constitution in mind, as well as his account of civic conflict, we might approach existing politics again through the entryway of justice. Aristotle uses the concept of justice in a variety of ways in his ethical and political works. In Book 5 of the *Nicomachean Ethics* Aristotle distinguished between "universal justice" and "particular justice" as dispositions of individuals. "Universal justice" encompasses all the virtues, such as courage and generosity, insofar as individuals exhibit them toward others and in social contexts. Universal justice drives people to abide by the law and to serve the common good. "Particular" justice is a part of universal justice and consists in fair-mindedness in distributing goods and in meting out punishment. It was specifically opposed to the acquisitive behavior characteristic of badly-educated individuals. These are the terms in which Aristotle described the best sorts of citizens and individuals.

As we have seen, however, Aristotle was also interested in people and constitutions as they are. Cutting across these conceptions of individual justice, therefore, was "political justice," which refers to justice relative to the different existing constitutions. Citizens might often behave in ways that were endorsed by the laws and constitution of the city in which they lived, and Aristotle was willing to explore this sort of behavior as a type of relative justice. In a democracy, for example, a poor farmer might justly participate in deliberation in the assembly, whereas in an oligarchy or aristocracy his political participation would be unjust. Aristotle correctly observed that the term "justice" (*dikaiosunê*) was used in widely different ways throughout the Greek world (Text 16).[26]

16. Similarly, the things which are just not by nature but by human agreement are not everywhere the same, since constitutions also are not the same. But the best constitution by nature is everywhere the same. (*EN* 5.7.1135a3–5, tr. Ross, rev. Urmson, in Barnes, ed., *The Complete Works of Aristotle*, adapted.)

This observation, however, did not lead him to abandon the search for the correct and best account of justice. The poor democratic farmer might justly vote in his own city, and he might thereby help to promote and preserve the existing constitution; but this did not mean that his possession of voting privileges was just without qualification. Aristotle's nonrelative standards of justice, as embodied in his best polis for example, indicate that he could take a critical perspective on justice as understood in the existing constitutions. We should understand his conception of "political justice," therefore, as a sign of his sympathetic awareness, as an analyst of the real world, that different political regimes promote (or ought to promote) conceptions of justice that will make them healthier and more capable of surviving, even if those conceptions of justice are not fully correct.

Justice without qualification was, therefore, not simply embodied in the positive, existing law of Greek communities, even if Aristotle was willing to explore "political justice" relative to the existing constitutions. Positive law could, in Aristotle's view, go wrong in two ways. First, it could fail to correspond to or support the aims of the existing constitution. This would be a legal error relative to the constitution. Second, if the constitution itself were unjust, then the laws would be "rigged" in favor of the rulers and would thereby deviate from correctly described standards of justice (3.10–11).

Such reflections enable Aristotle to make a crucial, and highly original, distinction within the traditional concept of "good government" or "orderliness" (*eunomia*) (Text 17).

> **17.** Therefore we must assume that obeying the established laws is one type of good government (*eunomia*), while another type occurs when the laws being obeyed have also been laid down well (for it is possible to obey even badly made laws) (*Pol.* IV.8.1294a4–7)

Eunomia in the sense of obedience to the laws might be a good and stabilizing force, even in imperfect or "deviant" constitutions; but a deeper sort of "orderliness" can be found only if the laws themselves genuinely promote human flourishing. Existing law must itself be judged by the standards of Aristotle's nonrelative, and independently described, account of justice. Only a theorist such as Aristotle could have maintained his nonrelative standards alongside such a flexible, and largely tolerant, exploration of existing constitutions.

Aristotle's account of political justice and *eunomia* helps us understand how he could show an interest in existing constitutions while also maintaining a critical distance from them. In exploring existing constitutions, Aristotle aims were modest. He aspired to help Greek city-states establish political stability, and to do so he emphasized justice – particularly justice in the distribution of goods and power. But he also understood the limits of justice if justice was not supported by the citizens' friendship with and sympathy for one another. While justice is indeed the key to establishing political stability, it cannot be identified or exemplified in particular cases – from the distribution of offices to court judgments – unless it is informed by the citizens' sympathetic relationship with one another. Citizens must be bound, for Aristotle, by a relationship of civic friendship (*philia*). Civic friendship builds consensus and thereby makes the criteria of justice more obvious.

In general, however, citizens, or "share-holders" in the *politeia*, do not necessarily view one another sympathetically. They do not necessarily agree on the nature of politics itself. They do not often share the same conception of what politics is about, altogether, or, to put it differently, of why polis-partnerships formed in the first place, and what they are really for. Short of establishing the best constitution, then, what could be done in practice to contain the stresses and pressures created by such disagreements?

The Best Constitution in Relation to Existing Conditions

Aristotle offered a response to this question in his account of the best practicable constitution. What is the best that we can do, right now, given the existing conditions of the Greek polis? Alongside his other ambitious projects, Aristotle also proposed to describe the best constitution for the majority of human beings and cities in the Greek world as it was in his day (Text 18).

18. What is the best constitution, and what is the best life for most cities and most men, not judging by a standard of excellence beyond ordinary individuals, or by a standard of education which requires considerable good fortune in nature or equipment, or by the standard of the constitution of our prayers, but rather aiming at the life which most people can share in and the constitution which most cities can share in? (*Pol.* IV.11.1295a25–31)

The best practicable constitution allows for a certain amount of conflict, but not to such a degree as to render political life impossible. Aristotle called this constitution "polity" (*politeia*), or simply "constitutional government." To give a rough description of its features, Aristotle again had recourse to his ethical works.

Aristotle's account of the "polity" is marked by his traditional picture of moral and political virtue. His focus is on the mean: ethically speaking, he says, "the life dedicated to the mean (*to meson*) is necessarily the best life, i.e. the mean that each individual can achieve" (4.11.1295a37–9). Similarly, he argues, the best practicable constitution will be that in which the "middling" group – i.e., the group with moderate property, in between the rich and the poor – holds power and rules for the common good. Stated in this way, Aristotle's rather quick and easy transition from individual virtue to political well-being might appear to be an illegitimate "slide." But Aristotle grounds his theory in well-defended propositions concerning the moral character of the middle group.

First, he argues, the excessively beautiful, strong, well-born, and rich are arrogant and tend to be contemptuous of their inferiors. The poor, on the other hand, are weak and prone to committing petty crimes. Only the middle group enjoys moderate wealth, which makes them neither too grasping nor fearful that others might desire to steal their possessions. To cap these arguments, Aristotle quotes the Archaic poet Phocylides: "Those in the middle have many excellent things; I want to be in the middle in the polis" (4.11.1295b34). It is striking that Aristotle summons up the long-standing "middling" ideology promoted by Hesiod, Solon, Phocylides, and other archaic poets, so as to explain and confirm his own theory of the best practical constitution (cf. "The Egalitarian Response" in chapter 2). The traditionalism of his approach resulted in large part from his readiness to endorse the respectable opinions of his culture.

Second, Aristotle views the middle group as more amenable to listening to and following rational argument than the other groups. This novel idea goes well beyond anything found in archaic poetry. Aristotle's reasoning is left implicit. But his idea appears to be that only the middling group is capable of ruling and being ruled in turn, as equals, whereas the others are either too domineering or too abject and slavish. It is characteristic of the middling group, therefore, that it neither avoids office nor pursues it eagerly (4.11.1295b12). Those in the middle respect equality and timely rotations of political power, because they alone have learned self-respect and respect for others. Therefore, they will be likely to engage in genuine political exchange and debate. Consequently, they will be open to being persuaded by their fellow citizens, if they hear good arguments worthy of making them reconsider their views. Their generally well-developed ethical character will encourage them to listen to and be persuaded by rational argument.

This is a highly innovative argument for the value of educating citizens in modest circumstances, and attempting to instill in them ordinary virtues, self-respect, and tolerance for others as well as the capacity for forming friendships. Aristotle's underlying idea is that such citizens will be capable of managing disagreements peaceably, through their capacity to debate political issues in public and to come to reasoned resolutions and compromises. In this constitution, publicly expressed disagreement might be healthy for politics if it defuses tensions and helps to produce more prudent decisions; recall that Athenian democrats made the case for democratic deliberation on largely similar grounds ("Democratic Deliberation" in chapter 3). For Aristotle, then, a willingness to listen and a citizen's "persuadability" quotient went a long way to defusing the extreme emotions that drove violent reactions to conflict. Thus, in describing the best constitution in existing conditions, Aristotle again had recourse to his penetrating theory of emotion and persuasion as expounded in the *Rhetoric*.

Finally, Aristotle argues, "middling" constitutions are less susceptible to faction than either democracy or oligarchy. The reasons for this are again implicit. Part of the reason is obviously pragmatic. In cases where faction seems likely to break out, the large middling group will be stronger than both rich and poor, and so capable of quashing any untoward or selfish behavior. Or, if this is impossible, at least the middling group will be stronger than either rich or poor singly, so that by combining with one or the other in times of upheaval it will prevent the destruction of political life. The problem, though, is that truly middling constitutions have only existed rarely, in Aristotle's judgment, because more powerful cities, such as imperial Athens, tend to promote the rise of either democracy or oligarchy. Aristotle shows detailed appreciation of the ways in which external politics can decisively shape domestic politics (cf. chapter 5). In principle, however, the middling group helps to quiet the competitiveness that typically characterizes relations between rich and poor. And it is precisely that competitiveness – which often turns into hostility – that accounts for the constitutional variety that Greece historically witnessed.

Classification of Constitutions

By contrast with the practically best constitution, constitutions as they are feature citizens who aspire to hold office continuously for the sake of self-enrichment (3.6.1279a13–15). Thus Aristotle begins his classification of constitutions. From the outset he strikes a note of pessimism. His basic classificatory distinction is between constitutions that promote the narrow self-interest of the rulers and constitutions that promote the common good (3.6.1279a17–21). The latter type, which he calls "correct," also involve the consent of the governed, whereas the former, "deviant" constitutions typically lack the consent of the governed. (For Aristotle's interesting reflections on political deception, see 4.12–13, where Aristotle argues that no real benefit can come from deceiving the people in order to win short-term advantages.) Within the two camps can be found ruling bodies consisting of one, few, or many citizens (3.7). The distinction between "correct" constitutions and "perverted" or "deviant" constitutions turned on whether the rulers (whether one, few, or many) ruled in order to promote the common interest or in order to satisfy their own interests (3.7). The correct constitutions were kingship, aristocracy, and "polity"; their perverted counterparts were tyranny, oligarchy, and democracy. Even if the latter ruled according to law, they should not thereby be considered "correct," since the laws themselves had to be laid down in accordance with the existing constitution; and if the constitution is deviant, then so too will its laws be distorted (3.10–11).

Aristotle fleshes out his classificatory scheme with a mass of historical detail. Because most constitutions in his day were either democracies or oligarchies, however, he focused most of his energy on these two "deviant" forms. He went far beyond previous theorists in recognizing the subtle variations of type within the generic forms "democracy" and "oligarchy." For example, democracies could have a (low) property qualification or none at all; democracies could be ruled by law or by the everyday decrees of the citizen assembly; or they could theoretically allow all men of free birth to participate in politics, but practically rule it out since the poorer classes have no leisure; or they could provide payment for the poor to participate; and so forth (4.4, 4.6). He also made the important observation that in practice and in ethos oligarchies are defined chiefly by giving power to the rich (who usually happen to be few), whereas democracies are defined chiefly by giving power to the poor (who usually happen to be numerous) (3.8). In other words, what matters about oligarchy is that the rich rule, the rich are valued for their wealth, and the city directs its energies toward the acquisition of wealth; whether the rich are few, moderately sized, or numerous is contingent and unimportant for the city's political ethos. This novel interpretation derived from Aristotle's willingness to test his abstract classification against the empirically observable reality – and to value the latter, in this case, as making more sense.

The Power of the Masses

The varieties of constitution are numerous. For our purposes, however, Aristotle's detailed exposition is less important than his sympathetic reflections on actual, ordinary constitutions. These reflections prove to be a counterpart to his suspicion of human beings as they are, in constitutions as they are. Aristotle suggests that granting the ordinary citizens deliberative and judicial power makes a certain amount of sense, because, even if they lack the nobility of the rich and well-educated, their insights might add up to more than the perceptions of the few (3.11). This will not work for every citizen body, he says, since some may be too debased to contribute to the common good, but it might work with certain moderately large groups. But is this optimistic idea not exposed to the Socratic objection that experts in each field – such as doctors or shipbuilders – ought to deliberate on relevant issues and vote in relevant elections?

Aristotle has two ways to defuse this appeal to the crafts. First, he insists that individuals as a group might recognize more of the truth than a tiny cadre of experts. As Aristotle recognizes, this point seems debatable, depending on the areas in which a decision is being made. For example, no group of non-experts will be better at "choosing a geometer" than professional mathematicians (3.11.1282a9). He would argue, though, that in other areas a group of interested and well-informed citizens could make more prudent decisions than "those who know" – in areas such as whether to go to war with a foreign country or how to distribute an unexpected windfall of cash. The difference is that the many gain in wisdom and prudence when they come together, as Aristotle explains in his "summation argument" (see "Democratic Deliberation" in chapter 3 with Text 11 of chapter 3). This sort of collective prudence does not apply to technical theory (such as geometry) or to the technical crafts; rather, it applies to matters of deliberation and is in the realm of practical reasoning – reasoning about what is true "for the most part." Aristotle adds to this optimistic picture a rather unsympathetic qualification: "When they come together, they all have enough perception, and mixing with the best men they benefit the polis, just as food, albeit impure, when mixed with pure food makes the whole dish more healthful than just a little pure food" (3.11.1281b34–8). As the metaphor of impure food indicates, his enthusiasm for the insights of ordinary people was important, but it was also limited. How delicious is a well-stocked banquet with a great deal of food – but much of it impure?

The second point, however, is even less controversial. Aristotle argues that in many (not all) crafts the best judge of the product is not the craftsman, but rather the user. The user of a house, for example, will judge the house even more intelligently than the builder. And the diner is better than the chef at assessing the quality of a meal. Aristotle again leaves the precise argumentation implicit. He implies, though, that ordinary citizens are, or can be, well informed in relation to using ships, public buildings, and public finances; in relation to fighting wars; in relation to participating in festivals; and so on, in relation to most things public assemblies make decisions about. Therefore, their perceptions should not be discounted on the grounds that they lack the capacity to make reasoned judgments. These are strong arguments against the anti-democratic philosophical tradition that Aristotle had inherited. They obviously share elements with the democratic ideology we considered in chapter 3. More strikingly, perhaps, they show Aristotle ascribing to democracy the "second-order" knowledge characteristic of what Plato had called the "science of science" – that is, the knowledge of how to use the products of productive crafts for the sake of the common good ("Platonic Political Philosophy after the *Republic*" in chapter 6).

Despite these similarities, however, Aristotle's account, more than the democrats', clarifies the differences between ancient and modern deliberative theories. Contemporary models of deliberative democracy interpret democratic politics as chiefly oriented toward enhancing our freedom, autonomy, and self-direction through shared "public reason." We have inherited the Kantian goal of legislating for ourselves in order to achieve freedom qua autonomy.[27] The Aristotelian approach is different along several dimensions. Aristotle's conception of public deliberation lacks the philosophical ambitions attributed by modern philosophers to public deliberation. Instead of achieving self-legislation and the transcendence of nature, the Aristotelian deliberative goal, rather, is pragmatic judgment and the development and use of practical reason. Thus, developing questions and provisional answers in common is useful not only pragmatically, but also educationally – in that participating in political deliberation helps individuals learn to exercise properly their intellectual and moral capacities. For Aristotle, deliberation not only instructs us in rational argumentation and evaluation, but also shapes our character so as to make us tolerant of others and of uncertainty, sympathetic to other points of view, and less dogmatic about our own ideas. These are substantial personal and political goods. Aristotle helps us see, in other words, what the rich possibilities of deliberation might be. Perhaps, for Aristotle, well-functioning democracies are not too different from the best practical constitution.

Equally sympathetic is Aristotle's argument that large groups are less susceptible to emotional decision-making than single individuals (Text 19).

19. When a single individual is overpowered by anger or some other such emotion, his judgment is necessarily corrupted; but, on the other hand, it is not easy for everyone to be angered and to miss the mark at the same time. (*Pol.* III.15.1286a33–5)

This was a staple of the theoretical tradition's worries about the vagaries of individual rule. At the same time, however, Aristotle's claim might be surprising. Thucydides' Cleon, for one, had lambasted the Athenian demos for being far too susceptible to emotions like pity, while Thucydides himself had implicitly criticized the democracy for indulging in its passionate desires to "get more" ("Thucydidean Imperialists Revisit *Nomos* and *Phusis*" in chapter 4 and "Debating Athenian Imperialism" in chapter 5). Moreover, Aristotle's *Rhetoric* purported to teach speakers how to move crowds emotionally, in accordance with well-informed rhetorical appeals. And, in the corpus of Athenian oratory, as we have often seen, speakers commonly appealed to the audience's emotions and simultaneously urged them to avoid emotional decisions in favor of their long-term self-interest. Aristotle's underlying idea is that large groups are better than small in general, but, to achieve even a moderate level of well-being, they must be well-educated, trained to exhibit virtue, and willing to observe limits, particularly those enshrined in healthy laws. Aristotle favored the large group over the single ruler, emotionally, only on condition that members of the demos are all free and law-abiding (3.15.1286a36–7).

Conclusion

Aristotle's approach sheds light on the possibilities and opportunities in political life, in ways that avoid the problems raised by modern debates between liberals, communitarians, civic republicans, and many others. He provides a rich, and often hopeful, picture of the ways in which human beings, working together, can develop nonrelative ethical and political ideals without appealing to religious authority or rigidly adhering to tradition. All human beings, as human beings, have natural needs – for physical subsistence, for education, for emotional development, for friendship. Rightly constituted, the polis can play an integral role in providing for such needs. The community will, in Aristotle's picture, receive in return well-informed, caring citizens. They will be capable of recognizing justice and realizing it in practice, and of restraining their desires to take too much, on the grounds that the good life for human beings must be found in exercising the virtues in common, not in private self-gratification. Despite its defects, much of Aristotle's theory is compelling and attractive. Suitably translated to modern politics, it can provide powerful resources for rethinking the shortcomings we find in our own approaches to political association.

chapter 8

Hellenistic
Political Thought

The rise of Macedon and the campaigns of Alexander changed Greek politics forever. Having attained the throne of Macedon in 360/359 BC, Philip II quickly transformed his kingdom into the eastern Mediterranean's dominant military power. He spent much of his career winning ascendancy over the Greek world, but his early forays to the east show that he had conceived much larger imperial ambitions by the time he died in 336. His son Alexander, who became king at the age of 20, proved to be a worthy successor. His conquest of Egypt, the Near East, and the former Persian Empire, along with his foundation of numerous "Alexandrias" in these regions, spread Greek culture to a previously unimaginable extent. On his death bed in 323 BC, Alexander reportedly granted his signet-ring – the symbol of his succession – "to the strongest" (D.S. 17.117.4). Even if this notice is the result of pure invention, Alexander laid down few guidelines for the succession to his throne, the administration of his kingdoms, and the sharing of power among his inner circle. As a result, roughly 50 years of bitter warfare followed, until the successors achieved relative international stability by establishing the "big three" kingdoms of the Hellenistic period: Egypt, Macedon, and Greater Syria (i.e., much of the former Persian Empire minus Egypt). The Hellenistic kings (known respectively as the Ptolemies, the Antigonids, and the Seleucids, after the founders of each dynasty) occupied center stage in the much larger post-Alexandrian world.

Contrary to traditional modern views, however, the dominance of these kingdoms did not spell the demise of the Greek polis. Civic life in the Greek cities continued to be vibrant and centrally important to Greek citizens. Epigraphic studies and reevaluations of the literary sources, Polybius in particular, have shown that Greek citizens continued to care deeply about their citizenship. They manned local militias, struggled to win political office, and educated the young in civic values. In foreign policy, of course, the autonomy of the Greek poleis was largely circumscribed. But many Greek cities had long experienced the condition of being subject to some sort of outside control, whether that of Athens or Sparta or Persia. To many Greeks, therefore, politics carried on largely as usual.

Because of the spread of Greek culture throughout the eastern Mediterranean and beyond, a major question for historians of this period is that of ethnic and cultural contact. Was there a "fusion" of civilizations, or is "colonialism" a more apt description of the relationship between Macedonians and indigenous peoples? Cultural contact had always been a central political question (cf. "Natural Superiority?" in chapter 5), but it assumes special importance for historians of this period because of the ancient traditions regarding Alexander's education and aims. It is possible to read Aristotle's *Politics*, particularly Books 7–8, as providing political recommendations for Alexander's organization of the new poleis of the East. Diogenes Laertius (5.22), moreover, reports that Aristotle wrote a work, merely a title to us, called *Alexander, or On Behalf of Colonists*. Through his conquests Alexander might have had the opportunity to establish an Aristotelian "community of virtue," with Greeks enjoying education, political roles, and leisure, and with non-Greek "barbarians" doing the productive work of agriculture and commerce – just as Aristotle had recommended in *Politics* 7–8.[1] Many ancient scholars, on the other hand, believed that Alexander aspired to create a "unification of mankind," rather than such a rigidly hierarchical politics (Text 1).

1. And indeed, the much-admired *Politeia* of Zeno, who founded the school of the Stoics, is directed toward this one chief point, that each of us should not dwell in cities or demes separated by their own codes of justice, but we should suppose that all human beings are fellow demesmen and fellow citizens, and our way of life and our order should be common, just like a herd that feeds together and is

nourished on a common pasture. This Zeno wrote, giving shape
to a dream or an image of a philosophical and well-ordered constitution, but Alexander put this idea into practice. (Plutarch, *De
Alexandri Magni Fortuna aut Virtute*, 329a–b)

The first interpretation must remain speculative, but there is
very little to justify the second: there was no unification of Greek
with Persian, Alexander's cities were dominated politically by
Macedonians and Greeks, and the hierarchies thus instituted persisted for centuries thereafter. Whatever the inspiration for his
political aims, Alexander was above all a political and military
pragmatist in search of glory. In the event, his conquests established a political and cultural framework for the eastern Mediterranean that would survive until the end of antiquity.

Alexander's conquests brought about extraordinary political
changes – the rise of monarchies, the enlargement of the known
political world, the relative insignificance of the classical polis, the
intensification of cultural contact. Such changes established novel,
indeed previously unthinkable, conditions in which political thinkers formulated their views. A major debate, in fact, has raged over
the implications of these changes for *ethical* developments in the
period. Traditionally, scholars had viewed the Hellenistic philosophical schools as deeply affected by the large and uncertain
Hellenistic political world. The traditional picture has held that
Epicureans withdrew from the polis and emphasized individual
pleasure and friendship; Cynics and Stoics invented the idea of the
"kosmopolis" (the "world-city"). Both, it was said, represented a
turn away from the ordinary world of politics, which, after the col-
lapse of the polis, could no longer be as satisfying as previously.

As many nowadays argue, however, such narratives do not
acknowledge the continuity of Hellenistic thought with previous
ethical and political ideas.[2] For example, the Hellenistic appeal to
nature as our guide in leading a flourishing life was also central to
Aristotle's ethics and politics. Additionally, Diogenes of Sinope (ca.
412–ca. 324 BC), the father of the Cynics, endorsed a particular sort
of cosmopolitanism already in the fourth century, on the grounds
that the traditional city-state and its laws and values were contrary
to nature. Finally, as we know from earlier chapters, the theories of
monarchy that appear so well suited to the rise of the Hellenistic

kingdoms do not represent a radical break with the theories of Herodotus, Xenophon, and Isocrates. The revisionist position appears to be very attractive.

Theory of Kingship

Despite its undoubted plausibility, however, the revisionist position should not be overstated. This becomes clear if we focus, as befits the present volume, chiefly on the political and the collective, rather than on the individual. The Hellenistic world was an enlarged world of seemingly limitless possibility. Members of the traditional elite, who had the leisure to study philosophy, also continued to play important political roles: in negotiating with kings, in promoting civic ceremonies and cults, and in engaging in diplomacy with other cities. They emphasized particular strands of the previous intellectual tradition – and not others – in order to make sense of the political continuities and discontinuities. Selection is itself a form of emphasis and interpretation, and an aid to making sense of changed conditions. For example, theories of kingship became more prominent than ever in a variety of rhetorical, historical, and imaginative genres. Demetrius of Phaleron, who governed Athens from 317 to 307 BC, once said to Ptolemy that kings ought to read the philosophical treatises on kingship, because "what friends do not dare to say to kings they write in books" (Stob. 4.7.27).[3] For obvious reasons, genres addressing the questions of kingship assumed increasing importance in this period.

Take, for example, the introductory section of a curious rhetorical work known as the *Rhetoric to Alexander*, of unknown authorship and preserved in the corpus of Aristotle's writings. As a whole, the work has the formally academic "feel" of the rhetorical treatise: it makes conventional moves such as dividing rhetoric into the traditional three categories (deliberative, epideictic, and forensic, 1421b9–10). It also instructs the orator on methods of argumentation, presentation, and their relationship to democracy and oligarchy. The opening address, however, purports to be a letter from Aristotle to Alexander. In all likelihood it reflects post-Aristotelian political thought. It exemplifies the rapidly evolving "mirror of princes" genre that was to become a staple of later antiquity and beyond. This genre developed fourth-century ideas found in

Xenophon and Isocrates, among others, but it is important that *these* strands of political thinking were developed, and not (say) the celebrated fourth-century discussion of *stasis*. It is helpful to read the Hellenistic exemplars of this genre both in relation to the preceding philosophical tradition and in connection with Alexander and the Hellenistic monarchs.

In its philosophical account of human reason as it relates to kingship and happiness, the letter goes well beyond what might be expected of an introduction to a rhetorical treatise. The letter recommends that the king should exert himself above all to order his mind, and his life, according to reason. Such ordering is of far greater importance than wearing splendid clothes or being physically attractive (1420a11–20). This point would have resonated with observers of the early Hellenistic kings. These kings were known for their ostentatious and dramatic public self-presentation, which included wearing fancy clothes made of the richest material (cf. Plutarch, *Demetrius* 41). The high-minded advisor to princes saw through the worthlessness of such competitive display and turned the king's mind to intellectual pursuits.

Through cultivating a well-ordered mind, he said, the king would provide an appropriate model for his subjects to imitate. Generally speaking, too, his prudence would provide advantages for his subjects. To make his deliberations effective, he must learn how to speak effectively and in a reasoned way. The letter's emphasis on reason and on reasoned speech is particularly important: because reason is distinctively human, the author argues, reason alone can provide for the well-being of humanity. It does so through teaching others ethical values that are suitable to human beings. On all of these points the connections with Plato and Aristotle are obvious, as are the reactions against prevailing trends in late classical and Hellenistic monarchy. Admittedly, the letter characterizes deliberation, not contemplation, as the most "godlike" of all human activities (cf. "Aristotle on the Good Life" in chapter 7 for Aristotelian reflections on our "godlike" contemplation), but this practical emphasis results from the rhetorical genre as much as anything else.

On the basis of his reasoned deliberation, the king should use rhetoric to educate his subjects and to improve their character and thus their lot in life. Royal rhetoric, properly used, becomes, in the author's presentation, the best guide to creating flourishing lives for the citizens of the Hellenistic kingdoms. We are not very familiar with the public speeches of the Macedonian and Hellenistic kings. But this letter recommends a style and set of motives that are, to a large extent, consistent with the kings' self-presentation in their rhetorically framed letters to Greek cities. Inscriptions on stone and Egyptian papyri preserve such letters from the kings to their subjects. Usually these letters are carefully crafted propaganda pieces designed to show off the kings as benefactors, deliverers of justice, and advocates of Greek freedom. The kings admitted competing with one another, true, but their ultimate goal, they claimed, was to ensure the welfare of their subjects, to restore cities that had fallen victim to natural disaster, and to be "zealous" on behalf of others. Occasionally, the kings could be terse, imperious, and threatening, although this style was adopted in order to bring aggressors back into line and, particularly in Egypt, to restore right relations between Greco-Macedonians and the indigenous population. Whatever their self-presentation, though, the kings aimed at creating flourishing conditions and well-being not for their subjects, but for themselves.[4] These dynastic overlords defined their kingdoms' "flourishing conditions" more in terms of wealth and power than "soulcraft."

It is in such a context that the letter makes a particular point of arguing that reason and well-argued speeches informed by sound deliberation must precede action. Demosthenes has once insisted on this in the fourth century (e.g., 60.17–18) and, despite its being obvious, this idea was worth emphasizing because Greek politics had traditionally valued deeds, especially military deeds, over words.[5] Nowhere was this hierarchy of action over thought more obvious than in the world of the Hellenistic kings, whose standard headgear included the wreath of the victorious athlete. This symbol was meant to imply that Hellenistic kings won authority not through inheriting power, but rather through ostentatious and daring accomplishments. Therefore, the author's apparently tedious emphasis on reason takes on special significance as an address to political leaders in a world where the rationally ordered soul must have seemed a quaint and outmoded ideal of the old Platonists (cf. chapter 6).

This focus on rationality leads the author to develop the familiar and longstanding discussions about the relation of enlightened monarchy to the rule of law. He is particularly concerned to distinguish the reasoned counsel of the king from the laws that govern democracy; he greatly values the former without disparaging the latter (Text 2).

> **2.** For it is strange that the one who is first in action should be obviously inferior to ordinary people in argument, even when he knows that, for those governed by a democracy, all matters are referred to the law, whereas for those ruled by a king, all matters are referred to reason. Therefore, just as the common law ordinarily directs self-governing cities to the best course, so too would your reason be able to guide your subjects along the most advantageous course. (*Rhetoric to Alexander*, 1420a17–26, tr. Forster, in Barnes, *Complete Works of Aristotle*)

Democratic law, he says, results from the consent of the community. But, according to his own premises, communities are better off being educated and enlightened by a rationally ordered monarch. Through the exercise of reason, the king himself furnishes a higher form of law for the community. This illustrates the superiority of the king's reason to positive law; compare the theory of Plato's *Statesman* on the hierarchy of political knowledge over law (cf. "Plato's 'Solutions'" in chapter 6). As a result, the king has special duties to develop a virtuous character and to live a rational life, since, in the transformed post-classical world, so much depends on single individuals who loom large over the eastern Mediterranean, not to mention over the laws and institutions of individual cities. The rational order of the king's mind rules out the arbitrary and selfish behavior that typically provoked anxiety about kings (cf. Polybius 6.10).

The author's emphasis on rational kingship was frequently reformulated by Hellenistic writers who tried to justify, and make sense of, the king's novel importance in the enlarged political world. One can see similar connections between kingship and rationality being worked out in other major political authors of this period, such as Polybius (6.6–7). But if the king supposedly embodied law for his subjects, then he was superior to positive law and so might tend to indulge in lawless acts, as one who was not necessarily limited by the law. One might worry about the king's arbitrary acts. Consider, for example, the theory attributed to Anaxarchus, an outspoken philosopher who traveled with Alexander on his campaigns. Plutarch records that Anaxarchus "consoled" Alexander after his brutal murder of his officer Cleitus by asking, "Do you not know that Zeus has justice and law seated by his side to prove that everything that is done by the ruler of the world is lawful and just?" (*Life of Alexander*, 52).[6] Plutarch comments that Alexander found consolation in this apparent license to act arbitrarily, but he adds that such ideas made Alexander, not surprisingly, more arrogant than ever. We can only imagine that such justifications became increasingly common as Hellenistic kingship became increasingly personal and arbitrary.

If the development of reason was central to the epistle to Alexander, then the development of virtue was central to another text in the same genre – the *Letter of Aristeas to Philocrates*. Again author and precise date are unknown, but judging by internal references the likelihood is that this letter was written in the mid-second century BC by an official in the Ptolemaic court at Alexandria.[7] The letter provides an obviously fictional account of the visit of 72 Jewish scholars to the court of Ptolemy II Philadelphus, for the purpose of translating the Pentateuch into Greek. Among other things, the letter describes a week-long series of banquets in which the king questioned the scholars on various facets of royal governance and character. It is in these conversations that the letter most resembles previous addresses meant to educate kings, and, at the final banquet, Ptolemy praises the learned men for giving him a full education in how to rule as a king (294). The conversations emphasize the traditional virtues of kingship: justice, moderation, benevolence (*philanthrôpia*), and piety. And so, we might think, the letter constitutes a traditional framing of new forms of cultural contact.

Two shifts of emphasis, however, are notable. First, the wise men repeatedly stress the importance of emotional self-mastery and control of the passions.[8] This theme had become crucial to ethical thought in the Hellenistic period, both in kingship treatises, and, as we shall see, in the formal philosophical schools. Such an emphasis made sense in context: if anger or fear had always been considered detrimental to politics, then it was especially crucial that the king, the most significant political figure, learn to channel his passions wisely and to eradicate them when necessary. Such themes were well known to classical Greeks (cf. our discussions of

Herodotus and Isocrates in "Monarchic Imperialism" in chapter 5), but again there is a new emphasis that makes sense in specifically Hellenistic circumstances. Second, each scholar suggests that the foundation of and source for virtue is God, in so far as human beings are the creatures of God and reach their fulfillment through God's guidance. This fusion of traditional Greek themes with ideas drawn from monotheism was unthinkable before the Hellenistic period. Even if Alexander's conquests had not led to a fusion of civilizations, nonetheless the *Letter of Aristeas* gives us a window into the possibility that contemporaries could powerfully and coherently synthesize ideas from different traditions.

Many other similar works are now mere titles – for example, the treatises on kingship penned by Aristotle's successor Theophrastus and by the Stoic Persaeus for the Hellenistic monarch Antigonus. However, the fifth-century AD anthology of John Stobaeus preserves fragments of kingship theories attributed to Pythagorean writers of mostly uncertain date. In all likelihood, they come from the Greco-Roman culture of the Roman principate, but I have chosen to include them here in order to illustrate how the Hellenistic theories were developed in detailed ways in later periods.[9] Though called Pythagorean, these texts are strongly Platonizing and also have much in common with the preface to the *Rhetoric to Alexander*.

Of chief interest for our purposes is their re-working of traditional comparisons and contrasts between kings and the law. Both "Archytas" and "Diotogenes" represent the ideal king as being "animate law" – that is, the living, god-like embodiment for his people of the eternal, divine, and unwritten law. He is the proper source for the positive law of communities, as he is also the standard by which local laws must be judged. In practice, these writers agreed, the king's embodiment of absolute law meant that his behavior, public measures, and general administration had to be most perfectly just (Text 3).

3. The most just man would be king, and the most lawful would be most just. For without justice no one would be king, and without law [there would be no] justice. For justice is in the law, and the law is the source [*aitios*] of justice. But the king is Animate Law [*nomos empsuchos*], or is a legal ruler [*nomimos archon*]. So for this reason he is most just and most lawful. (Stob. IV, vii, 61, tr. Goodenough, 65)

His virtuous behavior represented an imitation of cosmic order and harmony and itself stood as an object of imitation and emulation for his subjects. The Platonic echoes are obvious in these texts' emphasis on the harmony of the king's soul, which both imitates that of the cosmos and produces order and well being in his community. The connections with the *Rhetoric to Alexander* are also obvious. As we will see, moreover, there is considerable overlap with Stoic theories in all such passages. We are firmly on our way to Roman ruler-cult and to Aquinas' theory of natural law (Text 4).

> **4.** As stated above, a law is nothing else but a dictate of practical reason in the ruler who governs a perfect community. Now it is evident, granted that the world is ruled by divine providence, as was stated in the First Part, that the whole community of the universe is governed by divine reason. (ST. I–II, Q. 91, AA.1–6, tr. Baumgarth and Regan)

In analyzing the Hellenistic theories of kingship, we are tracing out the philosophical responses to the increasing tendency to deify Hellenistic kings and members of their families. The granting of cults and religious honors to generals and other leaders had occurred at least since the fourth century in the Greek world. Alexander frequently played upon his own claims to divinity toward the end of his life. In the Hellenistic period, the deification of kings had become a deeply entrenched part of civic life, as we can see from the effusive hymn sung by the Athenians to Demetrius "the city-sacker" (Text 5).

> **5.** How the greatest and dearest of the gods are present in the city; for the time has brought Demeter and Demetrius together here. She comes in order to celebrate the holy mysteries of Kore, while he comes with joy, suitably for the god, beautiful and laughing. He appears to be something august; all his friends are in a circle, and he is in the middle, as though his friends were the stars, and he the sun. Hail, son of the most powerful god Poseidon, and of Aphrodite! (Athenaeus, *Deipnosophistae* VI 253d–e)

The "Pythagoreans'" integration of such religious and political developments into the theory of kingship was a considerable achievement. The Hellenistic king was said to be "a copy of the higher king" and to be "on the one hand always intimate with the one who made him, while to his subjects he appears as though he were in a light, the light of royalty" (pseudo-Ecphantus, *On Kingship*).[10] Such intellectual trends are exotic compared to the traditional fourth-century concentration on the king's ethical and intellectual self-development. With the Hellenistic vision of kings as quasi-divine exemplars of virtue and order, we have come a great distance from the justice negotiated among rough equals in the archaic and classical polis. It was but a small step for Roman generals and emperors, even those who later converted to Christianity, to adapt such theories to their own rhetoric of power.

The Traditional Schools

The traditional Athenian philosophical schools continued to exist, but in a world of increasing, and increasingly sophisticated, philosophical rivalry. In the mid-third century BC Arcesilaus of Pitane became head of the Academy founded by Plato and turned it in the direction of skepticism. Prior to that transformation, however, thinkers continued to work in largely traditional Platonic veins. One good example of this trend is the pseudo-Platonic *Minos*, a third-century text, unfinished in its surviving form, which discusses the nature of law. The dialogue starts with Socrates' examination of his interlocutor's view that law is a political resolution or opinion of a particular city (314c). After a characteristic cross-examination, Socrates wins agreement to the idea that law, truly so called, cannot be unjust or harmful to the city; accordingly, law, properly understood, is not likely to be equivalent to the current or historical positive law of the Greek city-states, except in quite exceptional cases. To add weight to the distinction between the true law and most current laws, Socrates leads his interlocutor to point out that laws and customs differ throughout the Greek world. At the very least, therefore, not all current laws can be the equivalent of the true law; they cannot all be right on the essentials. Lawgivers in the world as it is get it wrong sometimes. As we saw in "Socrates and Nomos" in chapter 4, this general distinction between true law and positive law was highlighted in Plato's *Hippias Major.*

Armed with these insights, among others, Socrates argues that properly understood law is the discovery of the truth, or reality, no doubt the truth about what is good for the citizens, or specifically about what develops virtue in them. The discovery of "true" laws, characterized as such, is naturally seen to be of great value for citizens (315a, 321c–d). This characterization of true law leads the author to a typical Platonic stance. By analogy with experts in other fields of endeavor, the only person capable of drafting true laws is the expert, i.e. the king or lawgiver. The principal example of such a lawgiver is found to be King Minos of Crete, whose character and understanding imitate those of the god, and who, in fact, learned from Zeus himself how to make law an "education for virtue" (319a, 320b). The value of Minos's laws is demonstrated by their stability over the centuries; Crete has the most ancient laws of all Greek states, and "even now Minos's laws remain because they are divine" (318c). In Socrates' fantastic legal history, later generations have found no need to change what Minos got right in the first place.

In making such arguments, the author has lightly transformed certain Platonic ideas, particularly those found in the *Laws.* The city founded in the *Laws,* Magnesia, will be, properly speaking, a theocracy, just as Minos's law-code derived ultimately from Zeus and is said to be divine; and, like Minos's laws, Magnesia's laws will, once settled, remain fundamentally unchanged, if not absolutely immutable (cf. "Platonic Political Philosophy after the *Republic*" in chapter 6). (Even so, it has been pointed out, the earlier Platonic texts could not have endorsed the view that an actual lawgiver working in the trenches, Minos or otherwise, had lighted upon the ideal law-code; the ideal had always been an object of aspiration, not a practically attainable goal.[11]) Do such theories have any relationship to Hellenistic law and rulers? The author's reformulation of Platonic doctrine is largely compatible with the Hellenistic theories that envisioned the king as enjoying a specially favored relationship with the divine. After reading this work, a contemporary advisor to the royals might be excused for imagining that a Hellenistic monarch could achieve the same expertise as the character Minos. Even so, the ideal lawgiver, Minos, is represented as making laws for the virtuous governance of small Greek communities, rather than the enormous Hellenistic kingdoms. The author's outlook still reflects the vantage point of the "frogs around the pond," i.e. the traditional Greek city-states around the Aegean Sea, rather than one appropriate to the apparently limitless Hellenistic world.

Of the Aristotelian Lyceum we might tell a similar story of change and continuity. Some of Aristotle's successors designed kingship theories, while others continued to plow in the fields of constitution-theory for the traditional polis. Cicero was full of praise for Demetrius of Phaleron, traditionally considered a Peripatetic, for squaring a life of practical politics with the demands of substantial intellectual work (*Laws* 3.14). After being driven from Athens by Demetrius the "city-sacker" in 307 BC, Demetrius found a home in Ptolemy's court and is represented, by the *Letter of Aristeas*, as recommending the translation of the Hebrew Law described in that letter! The Peripatetics obviously found such various forms of political engagement highly suitable for philosophers.

Another traditional path was trodden by Theophrastus (d. 285 BC), Aristotle's immediate successor as head of the school, and a prolific author (cf. the titles listed by Diogenes Laertius, V.42–9). However, we have little more than titles of such works as *On Kingship*, *On the Education of Kings*, *Epitome of Plato's Republic*, 24 books *On Law*, *Of Legislators*, *Of Politics*, *Political Treatise dealing with Crises*, *Of the Best Constitution*, *Of Education*, and so forth. Still, Theophrastus' *Characters*, a short and humorous set of character profiles probably written around 319 BC, has survived intact and preserves an interesting portrait of, among others, the Oligarchic Man. This portrait is set squarely in the democratic city. The character is predominantly a critic of impoverished democrats, who are constantly looking for handouts and want more power than they deserve. Politically, therefore, he is hostile to democratic power. Conversely, though, the "oligarch" chiefly values the leadership of a single individual; he is said to recall only one Homeric verse – "The leadership of many men is not good; let there be a single leader" (*Iliad* 2.204, *Characters* 26.2)!

We can appreciate the tone of Theophrastus' humor only with difficulty, but it seems clear that he is looking back, with tongue in cheek, on the political conflicts of previous years, from the perspective of someone who knows just how trivial and ridiculous such "tempests" had become by his own day. "Oligarchs" had probably accommodated themselves to living amidst democrats reasonably well, but such accommodation was no longer at the center of political action in the age following Alexander. Despite his praise of sole rulers, the oligarch doesn't appear to realize that a Hellenistic monarch, or one of his lieutenants, might be just the answer to his dreams (or not, in the actual event). Even in the Hellenistic world, oligarchs still have their heads in the sand. Be that as it may, this portrait replays the persistent assumption that ethics and character are very much political matters for the traditional polis. That assumption was increasingly brought into question both by new political developments and by new and rival philosophical schools.

In the history of political thought, the Peripatetic Dicaearchus of Messene proved to be more influential than Theophrastus. For, as the Byzantine scholar Photius records (fr. 71–2, Wehrli), he elaborated a theory of the mixed, or "Dicaearchic," as it came to be called, constitution (Text 6).

6. The work comprises six books, in which he introduces another kind of constitution alongside those of the old writers, which he calls the "Dicaearchic." And he finds fault with the Platonic *Republic*, properly. They say that their constitution must be composed from the three kinds of constitution – royal, aristocratic, and democratic – with each constitution contributing the pure form to it, which would create that constitution that is truly best. (Photius Bibl. 37; Dicaearchus fr. 71 Wehrli)

The brief surviving notice shows that Dicaearchus envisioned the constitution as a mixture of elements of kingship, aristocracy, and democracy. This was not an entirely novel idea. The idea of mixing the pure forms first arose in the praise of Sparta in Plato's *Laws* and is compatible with certain ideas of "mixing" to be found in Aristotle's classificatory scheme. The reason Dicaearchus got credit for this idea may be that he "rescued certain ideas in Plato's *Laws* which had been overlaid by the *Politics* of Aristotle."[12] Moreover, in his own praise of Rome as a mixed constitution, Cicero, who knew Dicaearchus's text well, popularized the idea that Dicaearchus was responsible for an important elaboration of the theory.

Whatever the precise genealogy of the idea both prior to and after Dicaearchus, the theory of the mixed constitution became widely influential later in antiquity and seemed to be best exemplified by the political organization of Rome. As we have seen ("The Ancestral Republican 'Solutions'" in chapter 6), Polybius deserves credit for offering a detailed analysis of the Roman constitution in these terms. All the Hellenistic kings ultimately lost power to the self-governing republican citizens of Rome, whose constitution integrated the power of two executive consuls, an aristocratic Senate, and popular assemblies of all citizens. In this sense the "mixed" constitution drew on previous traditions in a strikingly forward-looking way. Republicanism survived the monarchic interlude, until it too was quashed by other monarchs – the Roman Emperors.

New Directions: Cynics, Stoics, and Epicureans

How were *individuals* supposed to react to the changed conditions of the Hellenistic world? The dominant philosophical schools of the period – Stoicism and Epicureanism – emphasized individual self-sufficiency, character development, and living one's life according to nature. This meant, too, living according to a single, rational plan with a single *telos* ("goal," "aim," "end") in view. For such theorists, the individual achieved happiness through establishing an undisturbed condition of soul (which the Greeks called *ataraxia*, or "tranquility"). This vision of individual flourishing did not necessarily imply, as is often thought, a turn away from politics. Rather, Stoics and Epicureans transformed the meaning of politics and political engagement in novel and compelling ways. The same can be said even of the most apparently apolitical group of philosophers, the Cynics.

The Politics of Cynicism?

Diogenes of Sinope (412/403–324/321BC), the father of Cynicism, was reportedly described by Plato himself as a "mad Socrates" (D.L. 6.54). Because of the variety and complexity of the source material, and the lack of any formal philosophical doctrine, it is difficult to describe Diogenes' philosophy in any detailed way. He did not develop a formal system, much less found a formal "school" – and in those respects he differed from the Stoics and Epicureans. The nonsystematic character of Cynicism made it attractive as a popular philosophy and, especially, as a way of life. It is important to read the source traditions about Diogenes and other early Cynics critically. Later Cynics made Diogenes into a literary character, and late biographical sources, in particular Diogenes Laertius, often interpreted fictional representations of him as providing the literal truth about his life. Even within his own lifetime, Diogenes was always being interpreted, represented, and caricatured for the particular literary and philosophical purposes of authors who found him to be a rich imaginative figure.[13] Moreover, there was a notable tendency in later traditions to magnify the connections between Diogenes and Socrates – and generally to interpret Socrates as a predecessor of various later philosophical schools.[14] And, finally, several key sections of Diogenes Laertius' life of Diogenes (VI.70–3) are strongly colored by Stoicism. At least in these important sections, the material attributed to Diogenes was Stoicized.[15] These considerations do not rule out all knowledge of early Cynicism, but they explain the need to be cautious.

The mad Socrates, Diogenes, developed different strands of Socratism in interesting ways. Diogenes' basic recommendation was "to deface the *nomisma*" – a Greek word ordinarily translated "coinage," but closely connected to *nomos*, or "law," "convention." Thus, Diogenes' slogan recommended abandoning conventions of all sorts as being inconsistent with, and indeed antithetical to, nature (cf. "*Nomos* and *Phusis*" in chapter 4). Therefore he was committed to a life of poverty, primitivism, and abstinence, as well as to the rejection of conventional social and political honors. Since any politics constituted a form of convention that, by definition, was not "natural," Diogenes was an anarchist. He rejected politics as it was practiced in his day, in favor of living what was, to him, an exemplary life dedicated to nature. "Defacing the currency" can be viewed as an anti-political slogan, but note that, for Diogenes, it represents a highly active form of negativity. Diogenes was out to prove the value of nature and the harmfulness of convention. His life was meant to be exemplary in that he wanted to teach his contemporaries how misguided their politics, and their lives, had become.

From the perspective of conventional society, of course, Diogenes was an outcast. His ethical commitments earned him the famous nickname the "Dog," because dogs were proverbially the most shameless of animals (the term "Cynic" derives from the Greek word for "dog"). According to the lascivious and sensational anecdotes preserved in the later tradition, Diogenes made a habit of flouting convention by masturbating or urinating in public, stealing from temples, dressing shabbily, and so forth. In part Diogenes' reaction to contemporary scorn was to embrace it with humor and a kind of comic nonchalance that is difficult to elicit from the (often) hostile source-tradition. His insouciance derived from his dedication to freedom and self-sufficiency. In the way he lived, he illustrated the value he placed on discipline, hard work, and self-mastery – all values that had always been deeply a part of Greek ethics (and politics). His model was the Greek hero Herakles. Therefore, despite the inevitable gap between Diogenes and most contemporaries, his way of life already had a claim on his fellow Greeks. Accordingly, through (and despite) his unconventional lifestyle, he tapped into his contemporaries' deepest ethical convictions in order to persuade them to abide by their own neglected ideals. He lived during the fourth century, so his ideals were by no means the product of the Hellenistic age. But it is easy to see why they would have been attractive to an age in which conventional politics were deeply unsettled by the conquests of Alexander and their aftermath.

Diogenes' thought – or at least what we know of it – had a power and coherence that one can appreciate within the context of classical Greek philosophy. He reacted to being an outcast not only by illustrating the humorous possibilities of flouting tradition, but also by developing penetrating philosophical responses. For example, he had an interesting and formally valid explanation of his tendency to steal from temples (Text 7).

---

7. This is an example of his reasoning: all things belong to the gods; but the wise are friends of the gods; and the possessions of friends are held in common; therefore, all things belong to the wise. (D.L. 6.37)

But, although he showed a mastery of rhetoric and logic, he rejected traditional *paideia* (education in culture), and so his philosophical arguments, such as they were, were shot through with sarcasm, irony, and humor. Diogenes illustrates how difficult it is to think oneself out of a tradition entirely, while still making every effort to have a claim on one's traditional contemporaries. It is impossible to be *completely* original, at least if one's originality is to have any meaningful purchase on its intended audience of contemporaries.

Such reflections lead us back to the question of whether Diogenes' way of life or thought can be construed as a form of *political* thought. Did he have any meaningfully positive ideals or did his "ideal" consist only in heaping scorn on the conventions, not to mention the people, around him? These kinds of questions come through particularly clearly when we keep his "predecessor" Socrates before our eyes. The answer, necessarily in brief, is that Diogenes' "defacing the coinage" amounted to anti-politics in that he rejected the standard Greek views of politics, but his individualism can be (very loosely) accommodated within the conception of "politics" proposed in the Introduction to this book. He took a notable stance on how power ought to be exercised and made clear the "fields of association and dissociation" to which he subscribed. He famously said, quoting lines of tragedy, that he was "without a polis, without a home, bereft of a fatherland, a beggar, a wanderer, living his life day by day" (D.L. 6.38). His "position," expressed in his mode of life, was that the individual's adherence to, and reliance on, nature superseded any political claims or obligations.

Most importantly, therefore, Diogenes promoted radical freedom for the individual – freedom from convention, the freedom to live according to nature, and the quasi-existential freedom from fear of life's hazards.[16] At the center of Diogenes' politics, accordingly, was robust individualism and self-sufficiency. Diogenes suggested that he learned from philosophy how to prepare himself for any twists of fortune (D.L. 6.63). He did not need the polis to educate him, to provide a meaningful life narrative for him, or to mediate between himself as individual and the larger world. He aspired to achieve the vaunted virtue of self-mastery not only in the sense of self-control but also, to the greatest extent possible, in the sense of controlling his own destiny. And he did so through hard labor, so much so that his hero was the laboring Herakles, who, he said, valued freedom above all (D.L. 6.71). His was more an existential than a political freedom, although his characteristic aspiration to live by nature meant that he was not so much a Zarathustrian self-creating hero as a rugged individualist striving to attain the state of human excellence and happiness as defined by nature.

It is in this context that his claim to be a *kosmopolitês* (citizen of the world) must be understood. A thoroughly anti-conventional attitude was embodied in this self-image (D.L. 6.63). He went further than Socrates in pledging his allegiance to all human beings, not those of a particular polis (he was reportedly an exile from Sinope). Diogenes' cosmopolitanism was negative; it consisted primarily in rejecting the polis. That is the point of the tragic lines quoted above and of others like them. For example, the Cynic Crates said that "a bad reputation and poverty were his fatherland, which could not be conquered by fortune" and that he was a "citizen of Diogenes, whom envy could not plot against" (D.L. 6.93).[17] Being a "citizen of Diogenes" is perhaps the most that can be said by way of identifying the positive outlook of Cynic cosmopolitanism. Patriotism for such a citizen would no doubt mean living as freely, unconventionally, and autonomously as possible.

How, precisely, might we compare and contrast the "mad Socrates" with Socrates himself? The main difference is that Socrates talked and behaved as he did in order to improve the polis. He encouraged his fellow citizens to live up to their own highest ideals. By contrast, Diogenes encouraged others to reject the polis altogether; improving the polis was not at issue for him. Socrates' allegiance to his fatherland, Athens, was expressed by his occasional participation in politics and in the city's foreign wars. His criticisms of Athens were not designed to encourage others to abandon politics altogether. Rather, he represented himself as the gadfly trying to rouse Athens' sluggish and complacent citizenry to honorable action. In all of these ways, Socrates differed considerably from Diogenes. Yet there is also reason to view Socrates as a "proto-cosmopolitan"; his moral mission arguably extended to all human beings, not only to his fellow citizens.[18] In this sense, and to this extent, Diogenes' own brand of cosmopolitanism can legitimately be considered an outgrowth of Socrates' moral mission. But we should keep in mind that although Diogenes continued to live in the city, and to conduct his dramatic "teaching" there, he aspired to sever his identification with the politics of the city entirely, and that is something Socrates could never have done.

It is useful, moreover, to contrast Diogenes with the contemporary anarchist position, because both ancient Cynicism and modern anarchism emphasize, above all, the absence of political constraints upon the individual's pursuit of happiness. Modern anarchists believe that we have a "continuing obligation to achieve the highest degree of autonomy possible"; as a result, "there would appear to be no state whose subjects have a moral obligation to obey its commands."[19] The state cannot legitimately compel its citizens to carry out orders, although citizens may choose to abide by existing laws for prudential reasons. It is unclear whether an anarchist state, made up of voluntary "promise-keepers," could be coherently imagined.

There are important differences as well as similarities to be noted. Cynics differed from anarchists in that their basis for rejecting the laws of the city was their rejection of convention and their adherence to nature. Anarchists, by contrast, base their rejection of ordinary politics on their strongly Kantian beliefs about individual autonomy and self-legislation. In a loose sense, however, there is considerable overlap between Diogenes' dedication to freedom and the anarchists' rejection of coercive governmental control of any sort.

Diogenes' dedication to freedom was a chief priority for him. He was not willing even to countenance an organized state's intervention in order to protect or enable the freedoms he valued most. This was a courageous (if improbable) position in an ancient world where slavery was a real risk. To counter that risk, it helped that, in Diogenes' own view, he could be free, in the relevant psychological sense, even when enslaved, as numerous anecdotes about his own enslavement – and his insouciant responses to it – are meant to demonstrate. (Whether these anecdotes preserve anything historical is unclear.) Diogenes' perspective obviously had nothing to do with the modern concern to protect individual rights. His interest was more in pursuing a "natural" lifestyle, and in developing his character to be such that he would be capable of living naturally no matter what others were doing. Like Socrates, he had great confidence in his self-mastery and self-sufficiency, and in his belief that other human beings would be better off if they followed his example.

Stoicism and Epicureanism

If Diogenes' ideals were attractive to many in the early Hellenistic age, then it should occasion no surprise that Stoicism, one of the two leading Hellenistic schools, was built on the foundations of Cynicism, specifically as regards its political thought. The school's founder, Zeno of Citium (333–261 BC), reportedly studied first with the Cynic Crates and then started discussing philosophy at the Painted Porch (or Stoa) in Athens. He exhibited many of the Cynic virtues but also got rewarded for them by conventional society. Diogenes Laertius quotes an Athenian decree honoring Zeno with a gold crown for his virtue, temperance, and education of the city's youth (7.10–12). Known for his self-mastery, he imitated the Cynics ethically without rejecting certain of the privileges of civilized life. His philosophy, therefore, curiously mixed the conventionally respectable with the Cynic dismissal of convention. Either way, though, his political views, insofar as we know them, had nothing conventional about them.[20]

In Diogenes Laertius we have a clear statement of some of the contents of Zeno's *Republic*, the most important document of early Stoic political thought (Text 8).

8. Some people, including the followers of Cassius the Skeptic, criticize Zeno on many counts. First, they say that he declares the ordinary education to be useless, in the beginning of his *Politeia*. Second, that he says that all those who are not virtuous are foes and enemies and slaves and hostile to one another, even parents to their children, brothers to brothers, and relatives to relatives. Moreover, in the *Politeia*, he maintains that only the virtuous are citizens, friends, kindred, and free, so that, for the Stoics, parents and children are enemies: for they are not wise. And he decrees, also in the *Politeia*, that women are to be shared, and in the 200s, that neither temples, law courts, or gymnasia are to be built in cities. And about the coinage he writes in this way: "We should not think it is necessary to supply coinage for the sake of exchange or for foreign travel." And he commands men and women to wear the same clothing and not to cover any part of the body completely. (D.L. 7.32–3)

From this brief catalogue, drawn from an opponent's writings, we can recognize the debt Zeno owed to Cynic views. He rejects conventional education, distinctions between the sexes, family life, and ordinary public institutions in favor of virtue and the community of the virtuous. Zeno's unconventional works left a deep imprint on the early Stoa. In his own *Republic*, Chrysippus, another early adherent of the school, confirmed Zeno's commitment to Cynic antinomianism: he allowed for cannibalism and incest and found nothing wrong with dispensing with ritual purification and otherwise following the unruly habits of the animal kingdom (LS 67 F, 67 G). Again the *nomos/phusis* relationship reasserted itself, but in a much different form. "Free love," even with teenagers, was not ruled out. For the Stoics, the reason for such shocking provisions is that human beings must be governed by their rationality, which they share with the gods, and they must lead their lives in accordance with nature and the cosmos. Therefore, particular ethical decisions depend on the appropriate application of reason to particular contexts – and conventions often constitute miscarriages of rationality.[21] Like the Cynics, therefore, but with a more systematic and formal theory, the Stoics found in nature a basis from which to criticize and reject ordinary conventions.

But they had many more positive proposals to offer. Zeno and Chrysippus held that only the wise and good could properly be kings, public officers, or even citizens, since only they could truly understand what contributes to the city's welfare (D.L. 7.122). This is the most emphatically ethical description of a citizen body we have thus far seen. Zeno's *Republic* envisions an ordinary polis community of virtuous citizens ruled by rationally constructed law. Unlike the Platonic Callipolis, though, Zeno's ideal city was pervaded by Eros, the patron deity of "friendship and freedom," who provided harmony (*homonoia*) among citizens and therefore political stability (Athenaeus 561 C = LS 67 D). Eros implies local ties of affection that bind citizens to a particular place, a particular polis.[22]

Despite the links that Eros establishes with the local polis, however, Stoics regularly used political language to describe the structure of the cosmos and the gods' rule over the world. Such language – sometimes metaphorical, sometimes not – was particularly suitable to their theories of the cosmos, divine governance, rationality, and the law. As Cicero reports, "They think that the world is ruled by the power of the gods, and that it is, as it were, the common city and state of human beings and the gods, and each one of us is part of this world" (*On Ends*, 3.64). (Readers interested in pursuing later developments of the Stoic themes of cosmic order and political leadership will find a valuable treatment in the so-called *Somnium Scipionis*, or "Dream of Scipio," in Cicero's *Republic* 6.9–29.)

These ideas had important political implications within the system. From their theories of the cosmos, divine governance, and nature, the Stoics derived their well-known cosmopolitanism, which was inextricably tied to their conception of natural law (Text 9).

> **9.** The dwelling-place of gods and human beings, and the structured whole consisting of gods and men and the things that exist for their sake, is called the cosmos. For just as the city is called two things – both the dwelling place and the structure composed of its inhabitants along with the citizens, so too the cosmos is like a city composed of gods and human beings, with the gods as the rulers and human beings as their subjects. And they form a community with one another through sharing in reason, which is the law of nature; while all other things exist for their sake. (LS 67 L; *SVF* 2.528)

Their conception of natural law placed great emphasis on human rationality. In this context, the Platonic distinction between "true" law and conventional law resurfaced in the Stoics' emphasis on "true law" as "right reason, agreeing with nature, spread over all, constant, eternal" (Cicero *Republic* 3.33 = LS 67 S; cf. Cicero, *Laws* 1.23). Such ideas on law and politics exemplified the distinctively Stoic elaboration of the Platonic and Aristotelian tendency to identify the human with rationality – which was, to all of these philosophers, the key link between humanity and divinity.

The tendency to use political language to describe humanity and the world generally is related to the Stoics' ambiguous stance on the polis and cosmopolitanism. Zeno's political ideal suggests cohabitation in the same locale; other Stoics took up a different position on this question by suggesting that all virtuous men (and women) were allied in spirit and reason wherever they resided. This ambiguity divides Stoic thought throughout later antiquity. Cicero, for example, articulates a "soft" cosmopolitanism that encourages citizens to recognize special obligations toward those of the same locale, while nonetheless emphasizing shared human nature and rationality (*On Obligations* 1.50–8). Marcus Aurelius, on the other hand, one of the Roman Emperors of the second century AD, had stronger commitments to the welfare of all human beings as human beings. Perhaps Aurelius's political views reflected in some measure the increasing distance between the city of Rome itself, on the one hand, and the Roman emperor and the theoretical concept of the empire, on the other.

This ambiguity, however, did not play itself out in the Stoics' views on political participation in the polis as it is. Even in the early Stoa, Chrysippus argued, in his *On Lives*, that the wise man should participate in politics, if nothing hinders him, because he would thereby be most capable of promoting virtue (D.L. 7.121). Participating in ordinary civic politics, or advising a king, or even becoming a real king if the opportunity presented itself, was strongly encouraged, since the wise individual could thereby help others live in accordance with nature – and, in any case, he needed to eat (*SVF* 3.686 = LS 67 W).[23] This is a more conventional approach to virtuous behavior, and indeed to teaching others, than that of Diogenes the Cynic, and it perhaps squares with the civic approbation granted to Zeno. Stoicism understandably became an important and widely respected philosophy in the Roman Republic and Principate, which had established politics as the center of the Roman citizen's life. In Cicero's Stoic-influenced political thought, for example, nature drives men to act on behalf of the common good and it helps men to overcome ignoble temptations (*Republic* 1.1). No wonder, then, that later Stoics were sometimes embarrassed by the Cynicism of Zeno's *Republic*, so much so that they reportedly tested the dedication of students before giving them this provocative text (Clement *Miscellenies* 5.9.58.2 = LS 67 E). Not just any sunny-day Stoic could grasp the value of cannibalism for the good life!

Epicurus (341–271 BC), by contrast, incurred no similar embarrassment. Later Epicureans considered their school's founder to be a culture hero, a benefactor, a trailblazer in the history of human efforts to attain enlightenment. The evidence for Epicurean political thought is again scattered and often late. By contrast with Stoicism, though, Epicureanism underwent significantly less internal development, because Epicurus made every effort to make his own meanings clear and to summarize his doctrines in pithy aphorisms for his followers (D.L. 10.35–6). In reconstructing Epicurean political thought, however, the modern interpreter is challenged by a long history of uncharitably negative characterizations, ancient and modern. The Epicureans believed that the highest good, and the natural human good, is pleasure. It was easy, accordingly, to represent Epicureans as vulgar hedonists or selfish libertines even though Epicurus himself is said to have lived a simple and modest life, free of luxury (D.L. 10.11).

More importantly, Epicurus viewed the chief pleasure as tranquility, as freedom from disturbances caused by unnecessary fear (Text 10).

10. Possessing the greatest wealth does not do away with turmoil in the soul nor does it bring forth joy worth mentioning – nor do status and admiration from the many, nor anything else related to the causes of unbounded desire. (VS 81)

He took himself to be a philosophical liberator, not a slave to his belly. His argument was that by understanding nature properly individuals would be liberated from the fear of death and from the anxiety-driven desires to acquire wealth and conventional power. The proper understanding of nature could be acquired only by perception of, and reasoning about, the physical world.

In his physical theory, Epicurus held that the universe is made up of atoms and void – atoms that continually collide, form physical entities (like human beings), and then dissolve, simply to repeat the process all over again, and with no overarching purpose. He believed that all human beings, along with this world and its heavenly bodies, would one day be resolved into their component atoms. The contrasts with Stoic physics and ethics could not be sharper; equally, Epicurus' atomic theory constituted a rejection of Aristotle's naturalism, in particular Aristotle's purposeful, teleological account of nature. These differences had important ethical and political implications.

In the Epicurean analysis of law, justice, and the origins of society, the fundamental principle was, in fact, Epicurus's anti-teleological physics: it was impossible to look to nature as an authoritative guide, and so everything depended on utility, calculation, and necessity. Society was originally based on a "social contract" among neighbors who wanted neither to harm nor be harmed (*DRN* 5.1011–27). The most prudent members enacted laws on the basis of their rational calculations of utility; those with good judgment had no need of laws, while the imprudent and forgetful had to be frightened into behaving appropriately (Porphyry, *On Abstinence* 1.7.1–9.4 = LS 22 M). Justice and the other virtues were accordingly utilitarian: once recognized as useful to communities, they were widely praised and disseminated. Virtue was not, as previously, an excellence of the soul's nature, but rather a calculated means to achieve certain individual, and especially social, goals. (Even in the real world, Epicurus asserted, individuals should be just only because the fear of being caught creates psychological disturbance, not because injustice is intrinsically wrong or unhealthy [*KD* 35]; cf. the theories of Antiphon and Critias in "*Nomos* and *Phusis*" in chapter 4.) But, according to Epicurean "history," the eventual "evolution" of technology and human society was such that individuals sought more and more power and wealth for themselves. Competitiveness led, in turn, to violence and havoc within the community, not to mention the small-scale misery caused by individuals' inability to fulfill their wrongheaded desires. To counteract these problems, or to offer solutions, Epicurus could not rely on a prior theory of human virtue, or "excellence," to criticize existing conditions and imagine alternatives.

Instead, the school offered a telling psychological critique of ubiquitous greed and ambition (Text 11).

> **11.** In general, greed and the blind craving for status, which force wretched men to go beyond the bounds of what is right and, occasionally, as partners and assistants in crime, to struggle night and day with exceptional effort to rise to the summit of wealth: these ulcers of life are nourished principally by the fear of death. . . . Through the blood of their fellow citizens they manufacture wealth and greedily multiply their riches, heaping slaughter on slaughter. They cruelly find joy in the sad death of a brother, and hate and fear the tables of their relatives. (Lucretius, *DRN* 3.59–75)

Epicureans helped to make their own ideals attractive through illustrating graphically the bankruptcy of ordinary political life. In his great poem *On the Nature of Things*, Lucretius adapted Epicurean concerns to fit the bitterly divisive world of the late Roman Republic. But his primary point was true to orthodox Epicurean theory: fear of death makes human beings anxious. They compensate for their anxiety by storing up possessions and power, as though such "goods" could help them somehow diminish the inevitability of death. The fear of death therefore drives people to harm their neighbors as much as themselves, and in many political cultures, according to Lucretius, people turn to violence and civic strife in order to reduce their anxiety by satisfying their ambitions. Lucretius revisited the traditional subject of civil war in order to explain the importance of abandoning "politics-as-usual" altogether. The only way to achieve lasting tranquility was to leave the "rat race" to others.

Thus it was for good internal reasons that the Epicureans recommended withdrawal from the conventional polis. In his own work *On Lives*, Epicurus said that the wise man would not participate in politics, or rule as a tyrant, or become a Cynic or a beggar (D.L. 10.119). The politics we know had nothing to offer. Rather, the highest activity – the chief source of pleasure – was friendship: "Friendship goes dancing around the world proclaiming to us all to awake to the praises of a happy life" (*VS* 52).[24] Friendship could be most fully experienced in the remote setting of the Epicurean "Garden," as Epicurus' school was known, in absolute withdrawal from politics. The point of withdrawal was primarily to avoid the wrong-headed passions and ambitions of civic life, which limited the potential, Epicurus said, for experiencing tranquil pleasures with friends.

Fair enough: the Epicureans recommended withdrawal from the unhealthy polis as it was. But this recommendation could draw fire from those committed to politics as such, and especially from those who aspired to improve existing politics. To Cicero, for example, the Epicureans were cowardly and untrue to human nature, properly understood, which drives individuals to contribute to the public good (*Republic* 1.1–12). To this the obvious Epicurean response was that nature – i.e. atoms moving randomly through the void – has no such normative recommendations to offer human beings. But Epicureans faced another sort of problem that derives from their withdrawal from politics. Wasn't the Epicurean Garden parasitic on existing (and admittedly troubled) political communities? Epicureans might look with disdain on existing politics, but they certainly relied on their wider communities, and on non-Epicureans, to provide them with defense, food, and so forth. Accordingly, they looked like the worst type of "free riders" (cf. Plutarch, *Against Colotes* 1127a). Was this a devastating criticism, or did the Epicureans have a response?

Observe that, even in the existing polis, the Epicureans' withdrawal was not absolute: the wise man would participate in civic festivals (D.L. 10.120), and the wise would get involved and be helpful, Epicureans said, in emergencies. Moreover, Epicurus was reportedly so generous to his native land that he was honored with statues in bronze (D.L. 10.9). More importantly, the Epicureans could respond that existing politics needed to be reconstituted – and that their small communities of the virtuously withdrawn might point the way. Like Socrates and Diogenes the Cynic, though, they generally refused to participate in politics as usual or to endorse contemporary political values. Their lifestyle of withdrawal, like that of Diogenes the Cynic, might provide a model of tranquility and appropriate behavior for contemporaries. And in this way they could view themselves as engaging in a sort of "anti-political politics" that made more robust positive claims than the Cynics. Compared to the Cynics, the Epicureans practiced a recognizable, if unusual, mode of politics in the Garden.

Beyond this, however, they could also enumerate certain utopian political ideals, and the question is whether these ideals also helped the Epicureans respond to the charge that they were "free riders." The evidence for these ideals is late, but there are important points of intersection with what we know of Epicurus' own writings. In the second-century AD, for example, the otherwise unknown Diogenes of Oenoanda in Lycia commissioned an enormous public inscription designed to teach the world the healing doctrines of Epicureanism. One section includes a vision of the divine life to be enjoyed by the utopian community he imagined (Text 12).

12. Then in truth the life of the gods will cross over to men. For all things will be full of justice and mutual friendship, and there will be no need for walls or laws or any other thing that we fabricate

because of one another. But about the necessities of agriculture . . . such things will, as necessary, cut into the continuous
pursuit of philosophy. For farming provides the things that nature
needs. (LS 22S, Diogenes of Oenoanda, fr. 21.1.4–14, 2.10–14)

This simple life is consistent with Epicurus' view that "the wealth
of nature has limits and is easy to obtain" (*KD* 15). Although Diogenes of Oenoanda did, in several important sections, draw his
ideas from all over the eclectic philosophical culture of the high
Roman Empire, nonetheless his utopian ideal is recognizably Epicurean and thus provides us with a helpful starting-point for the
ideal Epicurean vision.

Diogenes describes a small agriculturally based community as an
ideal. Isn't a minimal state organization, however, required to
provide defense for this minimalist community? In particular, who
will protect the Garden from men and women who happen not to
have heard of Epicurus' doctrines, or who happen not to care? The
beginnings of an Epicurean response would be this: Epicurus himself
was deeply concerned with questions of security at both the communal and individual levels (*KD* 40), but of course his concern with
communal protection is predicated on the existing world, not the
Epicurean utopia. Epicurus held that hatred, envy, and contempt
were the three chief sources of one man's injustice toward another
(D.L. 10.117). The wise man would master these passions through
reason; equally, competitiveness and fear should, on Epicurean
principles, be ruled out through secure knowledge of nature (i.e.,
that "death is nothing to us"). This argument says that, given a
worldwide community of Epicurean sages, the small agricultural
community we are discussing should not have to worry about
defending itself.

But how optimistic were Epicureans about the universal human
capacity to achieve wisdom? Specifically, is it possible to rule out
the need for self-defense on the grounds that all human beings
could come to accept the truth of Epicurean doctrine? On this point
Epicurus was clear: individuals needed to have the right physical
constitution and cultural background in order to become wise in
an Epicurean sense (D.L. 10.117). Nationality and custom can be
changed. However, if certain bodily constitutions prevent the

development of wisdom, then perhaps the initial answer does not solve the problem. On this account, the vision of a worldwide community of Epicurean sages appears to be practically (if not theoretically) impossible.

If a small-scale Epicurean utopia were to be established, then, it would need a minimal protective apparatus to defend itself against the unenlightened hordes. Some sort of political and military bodies would be necessary to keep the utopian agricultural community free from external threats and from possible internal disturbance. And that means one of two things. Either the Epicureans would have to "sub-contract" these functions out to others, i.e. non-Epicureans, in order to live a good and uninterrupted hedonistic life – which looks parasitic, or the utopian community would need to take on these functions itself, in which case the work of economic production, political administration, and military defense would leave much less time for eating figs and having witty conversations with friends. The utopian vision does not appear to work very well. "Utopia" may be a good place ("eu-topia"), but in this case it is also "no place" ("ou-topia").

We can approach the question of practicability from another perspective. Won't caring for the daily necessities of life detract significantly from the pursuit of pleasure? And, conversely, wouldn't extensive political and economic institutions help to provide the economic (e.g., agricultural) surplus that would, in turn, create greater possibilities for leisure, friendship, and pleasure? Epicurus maintained that our natural needs are easily satisfied (though perhaps not so easily as the Cynics thought). But, as Diogenes of Oenoanda shows, economic production was a necessity. This poses a problem. The Epicureans were, very attractively to the modern mind, dedicated to equality – both of the sexes and of rich and poor. Because of his egalitarianism, Epicurus could not choose another type of "utopian" solution – namely that of Plato and Aristotle – which arranged for citizens to pursue a leisured life of fulfillment and for non-citizens to manage the necessities of production. But then what (non-parasitic) sense can be given to Epicurus' sanctimonious exhortation, "We must free ourselves from the prison of ordinary business and political affairs" (*VS* 58)? Even in the ideal Epicurean community, *somebody* has to occupy that prison, at least on a rotational basis, if primary physical needs are to be satisfied.

Epicurus' belief that our natural needs are easily satisfied is far-fetched and masks a certain impracticality. His belief shares elements with the Marxist vision of the final stages of economic development, i.e. communism. Let us be clear that Epicurus was a proponent of private property, believed the wise man should occasionally work to acquire money (e.g., at the court of a king), and made explicit provisions for the inheritance and use of his own property in Athens after his death. Like Marxists, however, the Epicureans appear to have developed an ideal in which utopian communities will enjoy an abundance of material wealth without the need for exploitation of any social sector. This is a noble ideal. But, if equality is maintained, and if humanity fails to engineer robots to carry out all menial tasks, then the ideal requires that everyone will have to do a considerable amount of tedious work. Human beings have never truly reconciled the entrenched need to do menial tasks with the understandable desire to live the good life – which, whatever else it involves, surely also involves freedom from such menial tasks; or at least it has never done so in an ethical way that respects the equality and dignity of all and refuses to be parasitic upon anyone.

Different, but equally interesting, is another point of contact between Epicureans and recent Marxists. Both share the view of justice as a "a remedial virtue, a response to some flaw in social life." According to many Marxists, "Justice, far from being the first virtue of social institutions, is something that the truly good community has no need for." Rather, friendship, caring, and love are supposed to take the place of, and indeed to supersede, the role of justice in ordinary politics. With such attitudes one might compare the Epicurean emphasis on friendship and the belief that wise men have no need of laws or justice. Such views run into a number of problems even beyond the question of practicality. For example, there can be conflicts between the requests or demands of two different friendships, in which case justice should be a consideration in finding a resolution. Moreover, justice provides standards by which to interpret the demands of friendship, even if those demands might encourage us to supersede questions of justice and rights.[25] Finally, the Epicurean sage might experience problems within his hedonistic theory when friendship demands painful sacrifices or even death (friendship in Epicurean ethics is a complex topic that could still profit from further consideration). Whatever the

Epicurean response to these specific questions, our consideration of Cynics, Stoics, and Epicureans leads us to a final large question. Are we better off embracing politics, or being suspicious, reserved political participants, or even rejecting politics altogether? That question is the subject of final reflections in the Epilogue.

chapter 9
Epilogue: The Question of Politics

It is striking that so few Greeks of the archaic and classical periods questioned the value of political engagement. For all the surviving complaints about politics as usual, it is rare to find individuals, much less schools, taking such extreme anti-political positions as the Cynics and Epicureans. In classical Athens, to be sure, Socrates and later Plato provided some sort of precedent for such views. So too did certain disaffected members of the Athenian elite known pejoratively as *apragmones*, or "those who stay away from politics." To deal with such opponents of politics, the wider culture used strategies of containment and exclusion. Either way, those opposed to engagement won little respect for their choices in mainstream society. Pericles, for example, sharply reprimanded "free riders" in the funeral oration reported by Thucydides. Throughout the Greek tradition, more importantly, the nonengaged were ignored and despised. Or, perhaps, those already ignored for socioeconomic reasons withdrew from politics on the grounds that it was unjust and unsatisfying.

Withdrawal from politics constituted a serious, if implicit, challenge to mainstream views, because, as I have argued, Greek political texts represented politics as the primary avenue to achieving social justice and as the chief forum in which the human virtues could be developed and displayed. The intensity of this challenge, however, was reduced by the saliency of these texts' critical stance toward politics in the world as it is. This stance could range from ordinary criticism of political opponents to criticism attacking constitutions as such (say, that of democratic Athens). But, even in their most critical mode, these texts represented politics itself as not only the problem, but also part of the solution. Everyone found politics inevitable and inescapable, but most people, most of the time, also found it pragmatically useful and personally meaningful.

Ancient Greece's consensus as to the value and significance of politics conflicts sharply with the prevailing views of modern democrats. No doubt, there is a superficial rhetoric of engagement or activism in modern democratic culture. It does not run deep. In modern democracies, for example, formal political obligations are few and thin; private life constitutes the most meaningful sphere of human activity; and politics is not only far removed from ordinary life, but also considered either boring or, occasionally, depressing. And the motivation to engage in politics is, as the evidence appears to show, generally lacking. These differences are multiplied by near-universal endorsement of the aims of *homo oeconomicus*, "economic man." In the modern world, economic man's lifestyle receives justification from a pervasive ideology: that rational self-interest (once called, more simply and accurately, "greed") fuels growth, dampens destructive ambitions, and educates us in the virtues of civility. Finally, in certain modern democracies, especially the United States, religion provides an autonomous sphere of activity and fulfillment. Because of these differences, the study of ancient Greek politics and political thought inevitably raises a question for us. Are we better off ignoring politics and pursuing wealth or private enjoyment or religious satisfaction (or, somehow, all of the above), or could we find more human satisfaction through revitalizing the possibilities of meaningful political engagement?

Let us be clear: we cannot go backwards in time, nor, perhaps, should we want to. Nobody could legitimately approve of a political culture, like that of the Greeks, which institutionalized slavery, subordinated women, incited citizens to violence and war, and over-valued hot-headed masculinity. Nonetheless, our intellectual travels in time make one thing, at least, palpable. Even when it exists, as it too rarely does, modern political life is dominated by fear – in part the fear of military attack, in part the fear of intrusion by a powerful state apparatus. On their own (limited) terms, these fears are justified. Military attack by foreign powers is an ever-present danger. Moreover, as Constant and others argued long ago (cf. "Democratic Conceptions of Freedom" in chapter 3), the unity and wholeness of the ancient polis might be bought at too high a price, in that excessive unanimity has the potential to reduce individual freedom and autonomy. Are such fears inevitably and intrinsically part of political life? Must such concerns lead us to the unambiguous celebration of privacy and subjective experience? Or do ancient Greek theory and practice provide evidence to the contrary?

Aristotle, for one, provides a description of a shared, peaceful political life that also respects autonomy and does not encroach on individual liberties. This is one area, at least, where Aristotle's theory draws heavily on the democratic traditions of Athens. In their public conversations about the city, the Athenians, like Aristotle, developed a "thick" but "vague" description of human flourishing (cf. "Democracy Ancient and Modern" in chapter 3).[1] In other words, they developed a flexible table of virtues that citizens publicly discussed, revised, and applied, in order to work toward plausible conceptions of living well. True, Athenian democracy remains too claustrophobic a culture for certain modern theorists, but, on the other hand, our (modern) fear of others has arguably made us agoraphobic.

The consequence has been our loss of worthwhile traits, and, in general, our loss of a sphere in which to develop virtues such as civic courage, political friendship, generosity toward our fellow citizens, and gratitude. There are distinctively political forms of such traits that cannot be reproduced in civil society or the workplace. Even more important, perhaps, is that we agoraphobes have begun to leave the fight for justice to others – which means to leave it in abeyance. By contrast, ancient Greeks recommended, implicitly or explicitly, developing the virtues of character so as to produce a just society. Naturally, as they were equally aware, just societies are hard, if not impossible, to establish. Even so, their political struggle to achieve justice is exemplary. Struggling to realize social justice is a worthwhile endeavor for "activists" and for others. Utopian ideals can provide inspiration and good reasons for going on together.

This epilogue is far from a brief pressuring individuals to be charitable or to work for the good of others. Nor is it a policy proposal. Rather, it is a psychological and political recommendation, and, as such, it is intentionally abstract. Modern individuals would be better off if they willingly developed their capacities for virtue and willingly, and politically, utilized their virtues in order to understand and realize justice. Virtue is not a stodgy Victorian weapon of abuse; it is, as any Greek would have said, human excellence. Thus, as I see it, the recommendation is ultimately derived from ancient Greek ethics and politics. It is certainly strengthened by the ancient example. The ancient Greeks offer us a third option, one that differs both from atomistic individualism and from claustrophobic communitarianism. The ancient, justice-seeking virtue politics should act as both a corrective and an inspiration. But it needs to be suitably translated to the modern world.

What would a properly constructed *dêmokratia* look like if it existed today, within our cultural parameters? Above all, I think, such a system would require that the state make substantial material, educational, environmental, and health-care provisions for all its citizens. *Dêmokratia* would be much more a social democracy than the impersonal "democracy" that typifies the politics of, among others, modern America. Citizens would participate in local politics. They would find it meaningful to articulate their views in public, to make efforts to persuade others, and to learn from others how to enlarge their awareness and their sympathies. They would have the leisure for such participation, because they would not be struggling to provide the everyday necessities of life for themselves and their families. The *dêmokratia* would be a responsible participant in the international community. It would abhor chauvinism of any kind. It would help people develop the civic virtues. More importantly, it would educate people to utilize their practical reason on their own behalf, so as to make their choices, and their lives, more autonomous, intentional, and self-directed. And in this way *dêmokratia* would expand the scope of voluntary action, thereby furthering our individual and collective realization of freedom. Although this description synthesizes Aristotelian and democratic ideals, it is not a mushy fantasy. It is simple, obvious, and achievable – and worth achieving.

Modern, self-respecting *dêmokratia* would abandon the parochialism of the ancient model. Until the rise of cosmopolitan theories, Greek political thought did not extend political values to the international community, or to outsiders within the polis. Such extensions are necessary in the modern world. Our practice lags behind. But in theory, anyway, we have rightly abandoned slavery and the belief in a hierarchy of "races" and sexes. In subscribing to our ideals of inclusion, we have, I think, been truer to the ancient democratic commitment to freedom and equality than the ancient

Greeks themselves. Even so, instead of the standard polis-centrism of the ancient Greeks, we must adopt a cosmopolitan form of caring for all human beings. We must extend our concern for and interest in others beyond the exclusive citizens' club. In doing so, it will be useful, and more than simply useful, to reconsider ancient Greek political thought as a stimulus to rejuvenating our own politics, and our own lives.

Bibliographic Essay

Note: My practice throughout the book has been to cite works with which I have directly engaged or from which I have borrowed in the endnotes. In cases where a work is cited only once, I give the full citation in the note unless the work figures prominently in the bibliographic essay. In cases where a work is referred to several times, I have noted it by short title and given a full citation in the bibliographic essay. Where works are cited more than once in the bibliographic essay, I give the full citation at first mention, and cite by short title thereafter. I have included in this essay works that have influenced my discussions along with works that students could benefit from consulting.

General

There are two well-known classics written in English in the subfield of Greek political thought: T.A. Sinclair's *A History of Greek Political Thought* (London, Routledge and Kegan Paul, 1951; 2nd edn., 1967) and Ernest Barker's *Greek Political Theory* (2nd edn., London, Methuen, 1918); both are remarkable treatments of the subject, and I have found them interesting to argue with throughout my writing of the present volume. With the publication of the *Cambridge History of Greek and Roman Political Thought* (Cambridge, Cambridge University Press, 2000), Greek political thought has once again emerged as a salient subfield in its own right. This multi-authored volume, co-edited by Christopher Rowe and Malcolm Schofield, proceeds chronologically and (mostly) author-by-author; like the earlier works, and like this one, it offers a wide-ranging account of political "thought" (not theory) from Homer through Late Antiquity. A thoughtful and more politically engaged account of many central figures can be found in J. Ober, *Political Dissent in Democratic Athens* (Princeton, Princeton University Press, 1998), which offers an explicitly historical reading of literature critical of democracy from the mid fifth century through Aristotle and beyond. A. Saxonhouse, *Women in the History of Political Thought* (Greenport, Praeger Publishers, 1985) provides a stimulating account of women in political thought from the political theorist's perspective. Since so much of Greek political thought is concerned directly with ethics, it is extremely useful to consult K.J. Dover, *Greek Popular Morality in the Time of Plato and Aristotle* (Oxford, Oxford University Press, 1974). For a provocative overview of contemporary political thought, on which I have relied throughout, see W. Kymlicka, *Contemporary Political Philosophy: An Introduction* (2nd edn., Oxford, Oxford University Press, 2002). On the history of the period 1200–479, R. Osborne's *Greece in the Making 1200–479 BC* (London, Routledge, 1996) provides an excellent introduction, pitched at a high level. On other specific periods, readers might consult O. Murray, *Early Greece* (2nd edn., Cambridge, Mass, Harvard University Press, 1993); A. Powell, *Athens and Sparta* (2nd edn., London, Routledge, 2001); and F.W. Walbank, *The Hellenistic World* (rev. edn., Cambridge, Mass., Harvard University Press, 1992).

I have consulted all of these works throughout the present volume. Readers will, I think, recognize both my debts to these works and my interpretative and methodological departures from them. I have not mentioned these works by title in the chapter-by-chapter notes, but I have found it impossible to write this book without standing on the shoulders of all of these predecessors and others. Obviously, full documentation – either ancient or modern – for the views taken in this book would require another volume in its own right, as would a serious attempt to "locate" my arguments within existing scholarly discussion. I have, therefore, confined myself to only the most important works whose views I have sometimes followed and always learned from. I have made every effort, furthermore, to limit this bibliographic essay to works that might be profitably consulted by students.

Journals

Students interested in following the major lines of development in Greek political thought will want to consult several leading journals in the field. The international journal *Polis* is specifically devoted to Greek political thought and publishes contributions from scholars across the relevant disciplines, with a generally historicist bent. *Political Theory* occasionally includes sections on ancient political thought and does so within an explicitly normative and modernist framework. The *History of Political*

Thought is a wide-ranging journal that covers all periods and publishes work by scholars who take a variety of methodological stances. The more specialized *Journal of the History of Philosophy* publishes on philosophy and political thought from a generally analytic and normative standpoint.

Translations

Students with knowledge of the Greek language can profitably consult the Oxford Classical Texts and the Loeb Classical Library for most of the authors and works referred to in this volume. Students without knowledge of Greek can still benefit from consulting the Loeb volumes, particularly if they wish to find accurate literal translations of most ancient Greek texts. The Oxford Classics translations are recommended, as are most of the standard volumes in the Penguin series. I would recommend the Penguin translations of Homer by Robert Fagles (*Iliad*, New York, Penguin, 1998 and *Odyssey*, New York, Penguin, 1999). On the *Iliad*, I would also recommend consulting R. Lattimore, *The Iliad of Homer* (Chicago, University of Chicago Press, 1951) and M. Hammond, *The Iliad: A New Prose Translation* (New York, Penguin Books, 1987). On lyric and elegiac poetry, the updated Loeb volumes of Gerber and Campbell are particularly good. A useful collection of sources in translation is that of M. Gagarin and P. Woodruff, eds., *Early Greek Political Thought from Homer to the Sophists* (Cambridge, Cambridge University Press, 1995). On the fragments of the sophists, see also the translations in R.K. Sprague, ed., *The Older Sophists* (Columbia, S.C., University of South Carolina Press, 1972). On Herodotus, see the Penguin translation of Aubrey de Sélincourt (revised by John Marincola) (Harmondsworth, Penguin, 1996). On Thucydides, see P. Woodruff, trans., *Thucydides on Justice, Power, and Human Nature* (Indianapolis, Hackett, 1993). On Plato, I would recommend the excellent and up-to-date translations in J. Cooper, ed., *Plato: Complete Works* (Indianapolis, Hackett, 1997); for our purposes, note especially the translations of the *Republic* (Grube, rev. Reeve); *Gorgias* (Zeyl); *Statesman* (Rowe); and *Laws* (Saunders). On Aristotle, readers should consult J. Barnes, ed., *The Complete Works of Aristotle*, 2 vols (Princeton, Princeton University Press, 1984). I have consulted these translations and often been influenced by them.

Introduction

On the longevity of Greek political ideas, see, among many others, E.M. Wood, "Demos versus 'We, the People': Freedom and Democracy Ancient and Modern," in J. Ober and C. Hedrick, *Dêmokratia* (Princeton, Princeton

University Press, 1996), 121–37; J.T. Roberts, *Athens on Trial* (Princeton, Princeton University Press, 1994). My conception of the political is indebted to D. Hammer, *The Iliad as Politics* (Norman, Okla., University of Oklahoma Press, 2002), which improves upon Rowe's introduction to the *Cambridge History* (above, "General"). I have also found it helpful to read C. Meier, *The Greek Discovery of Politics* (Cambridge, Mass., Harvard University Press, 1990) and M.I. Finley, *Politics in the Ancient World* (Cambridge, Cambridge University Press, 1983). One can learn much about justice and the political, and in particular about the need to refine our conception of what constitutes distributive justice, from I.M. Young, *Justice and the Politics of Difference* (Princeton, Princeton University Press, 1990). On the nature of the polis, see M.H. Hansen, "95 Theses about the Greek Polis in the Archaic and Classical Periods" *Historia* 52.3 (2003) 257–82; J.K. Davies, "The 'Origins of the Greek Polis': Where should We be Looking?," in L. Mitchell and P.J. Rhodes, eds., *The Development of the Polis in Archaic Greece* (London, Routledge, 1997), 24–38; and Cartledge, *CHGRPT*, 11–22. On the question of the distinctiveness of the polis, see C. Smith, "Servius Tullius, Cleisthenes, and the Emergence of the Polis in Central Italy," in Mitchell and Rhodes, *Development of the Polis*, 208–16.

The question of how to situate ancient political texts in their historical contexts is a contested one. I believe that, in order to understand ancient political texts properly, and to appreciate them fully, we must interpret them both historically and normatively. J. Ober, "Models and Paradigms in Ancient History" in *The Athenian Revolution* (Princeton, Princeton University Press, 1996) 13–17 is an interesting brief treatment of some issues involved; see also Ober, *PDDA*. On making ancient Greek ethics meaningful to contemporary discussions, B. Williams, *Shame and Necessity* (Berkeley, University of California Press, 1993) is now standard; for political analogues, see the essays in J. Ober and C. Hedrick, *Dêmokratia* (Princeton, Princeton University Press, 1996). P.J. Rhodes, *Ancient Democracy and Modern Ideology* (London, Duckworth, 2003) argues that normative readings tend to be driven by modern agendas, and therefore tend to misinterpret ancient evidence; I find this unhelpful, in part because it is an unfair characterization. On situating texts in their historical contexts, see, in general, D. LaCapra, *Rethinking Intellectual History* (Ithaca, Cornell University Press, 1983) and Q. Skinner, *The Foundations of Modern Political Thought*, 2 vols (Cambridge, Cambridge University Press, 1978); for the classical Greek context, see my *GICA*.

Kymlicka, *CPP* offers a good introduction to liberalism and communitarianism; J. Rawls, *A Theory of Justice* (Cambridge, Mass., Harvard University Press, 1971) and R. Dworkin, *A Matter of Principle* (London, Harvard University Press, 1985) are among the most notable works of contemporary liberalism, while M. Sandel, *Liberalism and the Limits of Justice* (Cambridge,

Cambridge University Press, 1982) and A. MacIntyre, *After Virtue* (2nd edn., Notre Dame, University of Notre Dame Press, 1984) represent divergent communitarian views.

On the possibility of utilizing insights drawn from ancient politics to help rethink modern politics, see, for example, J.P. Euben, J.R. Wallach, and J. Ober, eds., *Athenian Political Thought and the Reconstruction of American Democracy* (Ithaca, Cornell University Press, 1994); D. Allen, *Talking to Strangers: Anxieties of Citizenship Since Brown v. Board of Education* (Chicago, University of Chicago Press, 2004); P. Euben, *Corrupting Youth: Political Education, Democratic Culture, and Political Theory* (Princeton, Princeton University Press, 2001).

Archaic Greece and the Centrality of Justice

In general, K. Raaflaub's chapter of the *Cambridge History* (above, "General") provides an excellent overview of history and political thought in the period. My focus on justice should be read alongside the treatment of A.N. Snodgrass, "The Just City?" in *Archaic Greece* (Berkeley, University of California Press, 1980), 85–122 and H. Lloyd-Jones, *The Justice of Zeus* (Berkeley, University of California Press, 1971).

An interesting debate over ideology and institutions can be found in J. Ober, "The Nature of Athenian Democracy," in *The Athenian Revolution*, 107–22, who argues for the primacy of ideological history against the institutional focus of M.H. Hansen in, e.g., *ADAD*, 73–85.

The view of the archaic poet as a persona has been expounded most forcefully by G. Nagy: see especially his Theognis article cited in note 2 of this chapter. On the panhellenism of the archaic poetic traditions, see G. Nagy, *Pindar's Homer* (Baltimore, Johns Hopkins University Press, 1990). On general questions of orality, poetic persona, and for specific interpretations of archaic poetry, see several other important works by G. Nagy: *The Best of the Achaeans* (Baltimore, Johns Hopkins University Press, 1979); "Hesiod," in T.J. Luce, ed., *Ancient Writers* (New York, Charles Scribner's Sons, 1982), 43–72; and *Greek Mythology and Poetics* (Ithaca, Cornell University Press, 1990). On injustice, greed, and *hubris* in the *Iliad*, see Balot, *GICA* and N.R.E. Fisher, *Hybris* (Warminster, Aris and Phillips, 1992); on Homer and political thought in general, see K. Raaflaub, "Homer and the Beginning of Political Thought in Greece," *Proceedings of the Boston Area Colloquium Series in Ancient Philosophy*, 4 (1988) 1–25, and "Homeric Society," in I. Morris and B. Powell, eds., *A New Companion to Homer* (Leiden, Brill, 1997), 624–48. On Hesiod as a critic of prevailing behavior, see R. Martin, "Hesiod's Metanastic Poetics," *Ramus* 21 (1992) 11–33 and R. Lamberton, *Hesiod* (New Haven, Yale

University Press, 1988). On the character of the early polis, see the essays in Mitchell and Rhodes, *Development of the Polis*. K. Raaflaub provides a good overview of archaic poetry in the context of the early polis in "Homer to Solon: The Rise of the Polis," in M.H. Hansen, ed., *The Ancient Greek City-State* (Copenhagen, Munksgaard, 1993), 41–105. Concepts of Greek citizenship are helpfully explored by P.B. Manville, *The Origins of Citizenship in Ancient Athens* (Princeton, Princeton University Press, 1990). On hoplites, see, among many, H. van Wees, "The Development of the Hoplite Phalanx: Iconography and Reality in the Seventh Century," in *War and Violence in Classical Greece* (London, Duckworth and The Classical Press of Wales, 2000), 125–66.

On equality, and specifically the Thersites episode, see most recently S. Stuurman, "The Voice of Thersites: Reflections on the Origins of the Idea of Equality," *Journal of the History of Ideas* 65.2 (2004) 171–89. On equality as a concept, the classic treatment is B. Williams, "The Idea of Equality," in P. Laslett and W.G. Runciman, eds., *Politics, Philosophy and Society* (Oxford, Blackwell, 1962), 110–37. On the sociology of the early polis, and the concept of the "middling" farmers, see V. Hanson, *The Other Greeks* (New York, Free Press, 1995). On the "elitist" and "middling" paradigms, I have adapted the accounts offered by I. Morris, "The Strong Principle of Equality and the Archaic Origins of Greek Democracy," in Ober and Hedrick, *Dêmokratia*, 19–48; and L. Kurke, *Coins, Bodies, Games, and Gold* (Princeton, Princeton University Press, 1999). For criticisms of these accounts, and in particular their reading of the symposium as the site of anti-polis ideology, see D. Hammer, "Ideology, the Symposium, and Archaic Politics," *American Journal of Philology* 125.4 (2004) 479–512. W.G. Thalmann, *The Swineherd and the Bow* (Ithaca, Cornell University Press, 1998) argues for an aristocratic reading of the *Odyssey* on grounds somewhat different from my monarchic reading. A seminal contribution to the study of aristocratic thought in this period, and in others, is W. Donlan, *The Aristocratic Ideal in Ancient Greece: Attitudes of Superiority from Homer to the End of the Fifth Century B.C.* (Lawrence, Coronado Press, 1980). O. Murray has done much to promote the idea of the symposium as an anti-polis; see, for example, his "Sympotic History," in *Sympotica* (Oxford, Oxford University Press, 1990), 3–13, along with other essays in the same collection. On "fear of diversity" in classical political thought, see A. Saxonhouse, *Fear of Diversity* (Chicago, University of Chicago Press, 1992).

The best history of archaic Sparta remains that of P. Cartledge, *Sparta and Lakonia* (2nd edn., London, Routledge, 2001); on the Spartan "mirage" in later political thought, see E. Rawson, *The Spartan Tradition in European Thought* (Oxford, Oxford University Press, 1969). On the potential problems created by bellicose conceptions of courage, see J.B. Elshtain, *Women and War* (Chicago, University of Chicago Press, 1995); A.O. Rorty, "The Two Faces of Courage," in *Mind in Action* (Boston, Beacon Press, 1988),

299–313; J. Elster, "Norms, Emotions, and Social Control," in D. Cohen, ed., *Demokratie, Recht, und Soziale Kontrolle im Klassischen Athen* (Munich, Oldenbourg, 2002), 1–13. My reading of the Solonian crisis follows *GICA*, 58–98, with bibliography cited there. My understanding of liberal individualism is based chiefly on G. Kateb, *The Inner Ocean* (Ithaca, Cornell University Press, 1992).

Athens's Political Self-Definition

On the history of this period, Powell, *Athens and Sparta*, provides a readable and thoughtful introduction, with thorough attention to Thucydides. An extremely useful introduction to Athenian ideology and practice, relying particularly on the evidence of fourth-century oratory, is offered by M.H. Hansen, *ADAD*, 54–85, with bibliography.

Athenian ideology and political thought have been "growth industries" in recent scholarship. On equality and freedom as Athens's fundamental democratic values, Ober and Hedrick, *Dêmokratia*, is fundamental. The essays contained therein took as their foundation M.I. Finley's pathbreaking *Democracy Ancient and Modern* (2nd edn., New Brunswick, N.J., Rutgers University Press, 1985). There is still much of value to be found in A.H.M. Jones, *Athenian Democracy* (1957; reprint Baltimore, Johns Hopkins University Press, 1986). For an interesting effort to elicit democratic theory from Athenian political texts, see A. Saxonhouse, *Athenian Democracy: Modern Mythmakers and Ancient Theorists* (Notre Dame, University of Notre Dame Press, 1996) and C. Farrar, *The Origins of Democratic Thinking* (Cambridge, Cambridge University Press, 1988).

On the democratization of elite virtue, and on popular belief in the "wisdom of the masses," J. Ober, *Mass and Elite in Democratic Athens* (Princeton, Princeton University Press,1989) is crucial; D. Whitehead, "Cardinal Virtues: The Language of Public Approbation in Democratic Athens," *Classica et Mediaevalia* 44 (1993) 37–75 derives similar points from public inscriptions. Compare the (to some extent) contrasting but equally interesting views of N. Loraux, *The Invention of Athens: The Funeral Oration in the Classical City* (Cambridge, Mass., Harvard University Press, 1986).

K. Raaflaub, *The Discovery of Freedom in Ancient Greece* (rev. edn., Chicago, University of Chicago Press, 2004) provides a searching account of the development of freedom as an ideal, along with a careful analysis of ancient arguments for and against democratic free speech. For a general discussion of freedom, see I. Berlin, *Four Essays on Liberty* (London, Oxford University Press, 1969). On free speech, specifically, see now the essays in I. Sluiter and R.M. Rosen, eds., *Free Speech in Classical Antiquity* (Leiden, Brill, 2004). On democratic self-criticism, see Ober, *PDDA*; S. Monoson, *Plato's Democratic*

Entanglements (Princeton, Princeton University Press, 2000); and, related to this, on civic courage, see R. Balot, "Free Speech, Courage, and Democratic Deliberation" in Sluiter and Rosen, *Free Speech*, 233–59, with H. Arendt, *The Human Condition* (Chicago, University of Chicago Press, 1958). On the *thorubos*, see most recently J. Tacon, "Ecclesiastic *Thorubos*: Interventions, Interruptions, and Popular Involvement in the Athenian Assembly," *Greece and Rome* 48.2 (2001) 173–92. On the question of free speech as a "right" in the ancient polis, see D. Carter, "Citizen Attribute, Negative Right: A Conceptual Difference Between Ancient and Modern Ideas of Freedom of Speech," in Sluiter and Rosen, *Free Speech*, 197–220.

"Deliberative democracy" has become a major interest of many contemporary democratic theorists: for further thoughts, see A. Gutmann and D. Thompson, *Democracy and Disagreement* (Cambridge, Mass., Harvard University Press, 1996) and the essays in S. Benhabib, *Democracy and Difference: Contesting the Boundaries of the Political* (Princeton, Princeton University Press, 1996). On Strauss and Straussianism, S. Holmes, *The Anatomy of Antiliberalism* (Cambridge, Mass., Harvard University Press, 1993) provides a very negative assessment; for a positive view, see N. Tarcov and T.L. Pangle, "An Epilogue: Leo Strauss and the History of Political Philosophy," in L. Strauss and J. Cropsey, eds., *History of Political Philosophy*, (3d edn., Chicago, University of Chicago Press, 1987). Among many other works by Strauss himself, see especially *The City and Man* (Chicago, University of Chicago Press, 1964) and *Natural Right and History* (Chicago, University of Chicago Press, 1953). Another type of elitist theorist is R. Michels, *Political Parties: A Sociological Study of the Oligarchical Tendencies of Modern Democracy*, (1915; reprint New York, Free Press, 1962), which has been successfully refuted, for Athenian democracy, by Ober, *MEDA*. On trust and democracies, see the interesting essays in M.E. Warren, *Democracy and Trust* (Cambridge, Cambridge University Press, 1999).

On Democritean ethics and politics, I have learned from Barnes, *PP*, 530–35; J.F. Procopé, "Democritus on Politics and the Care of the Soul," *Classical Quarterly* 39.2 (1989) 307–31 with Procopé, "Democritus on Politics and the Care of the Soul: Appendix," *Classical Quarterly* 40.1 (1990) 21–45; C.C.W. Taylor, "The Atomists," in A.A. Long, ed., *The Cambridge Companion to Early Greek Philosophy* (Cambridge, Cambridge University Press, 1999), 181–204; Jorgen Mejer, "Democritus and Democracy," *Apeiron* 37.1 (2004) 1–9; and Farrar, *Origins*, 192–264.

For Protagoras' relationship to democracy, see Farrar, *Origins*, and C.C.W. Taylor, *Plato: Protagoras* (2nd edn., Oxford, Clarendon Press, 1991), along with E. Schiappa, *Protagoras and Logos: A Study in Greek Philosophy and Rhetoric* (Columbia, S.C., University of South Carolina Press, 1991) and G.B. Kerferd, *The Sophistic Movement* (Cambridge, Cambridge University Press, 1981). My account of the relationship between normative and natural equality was inspired by Williams' searching examination (see above, "Archaic"). P. Cartledge, "Comparatively Equal," in *Dêmokratia*, 175–85, and K. Raaflaub, "Equalities and Inequalities in Athenian Democracy," in *Dêmokratia*, 139–74, are both outstanding; see also the brief treatment in Hansen, *Athenian Democracy*, 81–5, which somewhat underestimates the importance of equality in Athenian democracy. On the rowers and their role in democracy, see B. Strauss, "The Athenian Trireme, School of Democracy," in *Dêmokratia*, 313–26. On reading Rawls' difference principle alongside Athenian democracy, see J. Ober, "Aristotle's Political Sociology: Class, Status, and Order in the *Politics*," in C. Lord and D.K. O'Connor, eds., *Essays on the Foundations of Aristotelian Political Science* (Berkeley, University of California Press, 1991), 112–35.

Criticizing Democracy in Late Fifth-Century Athens

A very good historical introduction to much of the material discussed in this chapter can be found in M. Ostwald, *From Popular Sovereignty to the Sovereignty of Law* (Berkeley, University of California Press, 1986). K. Raaflaub, "Contemporary Perceptions of Democracy in Fifth-Century Athens," *CM* 40: 33–70 offers a helpful overview of the sources. I have approached some of the themes of this chapter in *GICA*, 179–233. W.K.C. Guthrie, *A History of Greek Philosophy*, vol. 3, *Sophists* (on the Sophists and Socrates), (Cambridge, Cambridge University Press, 1971) has been a critical resource for my account and is still well worth consulting on all aspects of late fifth-century thought, as is Kerferd, *Sophistic Movement*. R. Wallace, "The Sophists in Athens," in D. Boedeker and K. Raaflaub, eds., *Democracy, Empire, and the Arts in Fifth-Century Athens* (Cambridge, Mass., Harvard University Press, 1998), 203–22, offers perceptive revisions of the standard accounts; Raaflaub's "The Transformation of Athens in the Fifth Century," in the same volume, pp.15–41, is a useful synthesis of historical and intellectual trends in the period. I have also made use of R. Winton's thoughtful contribution to the *CHGRPT*.

On aristocratic thought in the late fifth-century, see Donlan, *Aristocratic Ideal*; a Marxist perspective on such ideals can be found in P. Rose's provocative *Sons of the Gods, Children of Earth* (Ithaca, Cornell University Press, 1992). On the basic framework of "ameliorative" and "rejectionist" criticism, and on the Old Oligarch, see Ober, *PDDA*. For a still useful historical commentary on the Old Oligarch, see H. Frisch, *The Constitution of the Athenians* (Copenhagen, Nordisk, 1942). On the plague at Athens, see S. Hornblower, *A Commentary on Thucydides*, Vol. 1 (1991; reprint Oxford, Clarendon Press, 1997).

On the authorship of the *Sisyphus*, see M. Davies, "Sisyphus and the Invention of Religion ('Critias' TrGF 1 (43) F19 = B 25 DK)," *Bulletin of the Institute of Classical Studies* 36 (1989) 16–32. On the contested identity of Antiphon, I follow the "unitarian" position, which has been forcefully espoused by M. Gagarin, *Antiphon the Athenian* (Austin, University of Texas Press, 2002), a book that also offers interesting remarks on the sophists and rhetoric and on Antiphon's *Truth*.

On Thrasymachus and Callicles, R. Barney provides a thoughtful analysis in "Callicles and Thrasymachus," *The Stanford Encyclopedia of Philosophy* (Fall 2004 Edition), Edward N. Zalta (ed.), URL: <http://plato.stanford.edu/archives/fall2004/entries/callicles-thrasymachus/>. J. Annas, *An Introduction to Plato's Republic* (Oxford, Oxford University Press, 1981) is well worth reading, as is C. Kahn, "Drama and Dialectic in Plato's *Gorgias.*" *OSAP* 1 (1983) 75–121. The Anonymus Iamblichi is an understudied but crucial contemporary of these figures: see the seminal article of A.T. Cole, "The Anonymus Iamblichi and His Place in Greek Political Theory," *HSCP* 65 (1961) 127-63. On the relationship of Athenian imperialists to Callicles, see A. Saxonhouse, "An Unspoken Theme in Plato's *Gorgias*: War," *Interpretation* 11 (1983) 139–69.

The bibliography on Socrates is, not surprisingly, immense and always growing. A useful introduction for students is that of C.C.W. Taylor, *Socrates* (Oxford, Oxford University Press, 1998). My own position on recovering the historical Socrates tends to be skeptical. Guthrie, *Socrates*, lays out the evidence in entirety and makes helpful philosophical and historical comments, while T.C. Brickhouse and N.D. Smith, in *Socrates on Trial* (Princeton, Princeton University Press, 1989), and *Plato's Socrates* (Oxford, Oxford University Press, 1994) provide a penetrating philosophical interpretation of Plato's Socrates. The most important Socratic scholar of the last century has been G. Vlastos; readers can learn much from arguing with his Socratic essays. Cf., e.g., *Socratic Studies* (ed. M. Burnyeat, Cambridge, Cambridge University Press, 1994). In my use of Xenophon as a source, I have been influenced by the thoughtful assessment of J. Cooper, "Notes on Xenophon's Socrates," in *Reason and Emotion* (Princeton, Princeton University Press, 1999), 3–28, which rehabilitates the use of Xenophon's evidence, against many generations of scholarly neglect. On Socrates and *nomos*, the critical work is R. Kraut, *Socrates and the State* (Princeton, Princeton University Press, 1984); my reading of Xenophon's Socrates on law follows D. Morrison, "Xenophon's Socrates on the Just and the Lawful," *Ancient Philosophy* 15 (1995) 329–47. A. Nehamas, *The Art of Living* (Berkeley, University of California Press, 1998), reflects on images of Socrates from Plato to Foucault.

On *logos* and *ergon*, A. Parry, *Logos and Ergon in Thucydides* (1957; reprint, Salem, N.H., Ayer, 1988) is still the best single study. On this theme in the

Laches, see, for example, W.T. Schmid, *On Manly Courage: A Study of Plato's Laches* (Carbondale, Southern Illinois University Press, 1992), with bibliography cited there. On Eteocles in Euripides, *Phoenissae*, see Balot, *GICA*, with bibliography cited. On Protagorean relativism and democratic politics, see Guthrie, *Sophists*, and Farrar, *Origins of Democratic Thinking*. On relativism in general, and on Protagoras' self-refutation, I have followed D. Keyt and F.D. Miller, Jr., "Ancient Greek Political Thought," in G.F. Gaus and C. Kukathas, *Handbook of Political Theory* (London, Sage, 2004), 303–19 at 306–8. J. Waldron, "The Irrelevance of Moral Objectivity," in R.P. George, *Natural Law Theory* (Oxford, Clarendon Press, 1992), 158–87, helpfully explores questions related to "moral realism" from a modern philosophical and judicial perspective.

On Thucydides' treatment of democracy, see especially Ober, *PDDA* and H. Yunis, *Taming Democracy* (Ithaca, Cornell University Press, 1996). In addition to the Socratic bibliography listed above, see also G. Vlastos, "Socrates and Vietnam," in *Socratic Studies*, 127–33, for a criticism of Socrates' failure to act decisively on important occasions; and G. Kateb, "Socratic Integrity," in I. Shapiro and R. Adams, *Integrity and Conscience* (New York, New York University Press, 1998), 77–112, for a provocative reading of Socrates as a model of heroic individualism.

Imperialism

Students will find a good introduction to (especially modern) imperialism in G. Arrighi, "Imperialism," in W. Outhwaite and T. Bottomore, *The Blackwell Dictionary of Twentieth-Century Social Thought* (Oxford, Blackwell, 1993), 274–7. For a more thorough treatment of many of the same issues, see G. Arrighi, *The Geometry of Imperialism* (London, New Left Books, 1978). The classic essay by Joseph Schumpeter is still worth reading: see J. Schumpeter, *Imperialism and Social Classes* (New York, A.M. Kelly, 1974). For larger perspectives on imperialism, taking ancient empires into account, see M.W. Doyle, *Empires* (Ithaca, Cornell University Press, 1986), who relies on a popular definition of empire as "effective control, whether formal or informal" (p.30).

Students will find a helpful overview of realism, and other theoretical issues in the study of international affairs, in C. Brown, "International Affairs," in R.E. Goodin and P. Pettit, *A Companion to Contemporary Political Philosophy* (Oxford, Blackwell, 1995), 515–26. Students of ancient history can acquire an interesting perspective on realism and Thucydides from G. Crane, *Thucydides and the Ancient Simplicity* (Berkeley, University of California Press, 1998). For the ethics of war and peace, see the essays in T. Nardin, *The Ethics of War and Peace* (Princeton, Princeton University Press,

1996), along with M. Walzer's classic *Just and Unjust Wars* (3rd edn., New York: Basic Books, 2000). On justice and impartiality, see J. Rawls, *A Theory of Justice* (above, "Archaic Greece"); T. Nagel, *Equality and Partiality* (Oxford, Oxford University Press, 1991); B. Barry, *Justice as Impartiality* (Oxford, Clarendon Press, 1995). For an interesting effort to understand "realism" in ancient and modern contexts, see L. Johnson, *Thucydides, Hobbes, and the Interpretation of Realism* (DeKalb, Northern Illinois University Press, 1993). On cosmopolitanism and "capabilities," from a specifically feminist perspective, see M. Nussbaum, *Women and Human Development: The Capabilities Approach* (New York, Cambridge University Press, 2000).

One of the key components of most examples of imperialism is a certain aggressive conception of masculinity, which is typically linked to narrow and militaristic conceptions of courage. I have explored the dangerous potential of such conceptions of courage in "The Dark Side of Democratic Courage," *Social Research* 71.1 (2004) 73–106; see also W.I. Miller, *The Mystery of Courage* (Cambridge, Mass., Harvard University Press, 2000). Robert Louis Stevenson called courage the "footstool of the virtues"; for an interesting treatment of courage in modern liberalism, see J. Scorza, "The Ambivalence of Political Courage," *Review of Politics* (2001) 637–61.

Imperialism has not figured prominently enough in scholarly discussions of the Greek world, but see the seminal collection of P. Garnsey and C.R. Whittaker, *Imperialism in the Ancient World* (Cambridge, Cambridge University Press, 1978), and, for comparison, see W.V. Harris, *War and Imperialism in Republican Rome 327–70 BC* (1979; reprint, Oxford, Oxford University Press, 1985) as well as the essays collected in C. Champion, *Roman Imperialism* (Malden, Mass., Blackwell, 2004).

On Greek stereotyping of the Persians, see E. Hall, *Inventing the Barbarian* (Oxford, Oxford University Press, 1989). T. Harrison, *The Emptiness of Asia: Aeschylus' Persians and the History of the Fifth Century* (London, Duckworth, 2000) provides a provocative, if occasionally one-sided, treatment of Aeschylus' representation of the Persians. Specifically on Persian imperialism, see *GICA*, 99–108, with earlier bibliography cited there. On Xenophon's *Cyropaedia*, readers will find much of value, and much to disagree with, in the thought-provoking treatments of C. Nadon, *Xenophon's Prince: Republic and Empire in the Cyropaedia* (Berkeley, University of California Press, 2001) and W. Ambler, *Xenophon: The Education of Cyrus* (Ithaca, Cornell University Press, 2001), both from an avowedly Straussian perspective. See also the thoughtful work of J. Tatum, *Xenophon's Imperial Fiction* (Princeton, Princeton University Press, 1989) and D. Gera, *Xenophon's Cyropaedia* (Oxford, Clarendon Press, 1993); V. Gray provides a good, if notably traditional, treatment of Xenophon in the *CHGRPT*, 142–54. My treatment of the *Cyropaedia* is indebted to these works; Nadon, in particular, is useful for bringing out the connections with Machiavelli. On slavery and natural superiority, see Guthrie, *Sophists*, 155–63; P. Garnsey, *Ideas of Slavery from Aristotle to Augustine* (Cambridge, Cambridge University Press, 1996); and chapter 7 ("Aristotle"), with bibliography there. On the worry that arguing about whether freedom is a good thing might damage the cause of human freedom in general, see Kateb, *Inner Ocean*.

On Athenian imperialism, the classic historical treatment is that of R. Meiggs, *The Athenian Empire* (Oxford, Clarendon Press, 1972). A well-chosen selection of scholarly views can be found in L.J. Samons II, ed., *Athenian Democracy and Imperialism* (Boston, Houghton Mifflin Company, 1998). An excellent recent collection of essays dealing with related issues is that of D. R. McCann and B.S. Strauss, eds., *War and Democracy: A Comparative Study of the Korean War and the Peloponnesian War* (London, M.E. Sharpe, 2001), especially the essays of Raaflaub on Athens and Ober on Thucydides and realism. On Herodotus and Athens, see, among others, J.L. Moles, "Herodotus Warns the Athenians," *Papers of the Leeds International Latin Seminar* 9 (1996) 259–84. On the Athenians of Thucydides, see W.R. Connor, *Thucydides* (Princeton, Princeton University Press, 1984) with my *GICA*, 136–78. There is still much of value in J. de Romilly, *Thucydides and Athenian Imperialism* (Oxford: Blackwell, 1963). On imperialistic rhetoric, see E. Said, *Culture and Imperialism* (New York, Knopf, 1993). On Spartan imperialism, see P. Cartledge, *Agesilaos and the Crisis of Sparta* (Baltimore, Johns Hopkins University Press, 1987), chapter 6.

The relationship between Athenian drama and political decision-making is notoriously complex and hotly contested. K. Raaflaub, "Father of All, Destroyer of All: War in the Late Fifth-Century Athenian Discourse and Ideology," in McCann and Strauss, *War and Democracy*, 307–56, offers a searching treatment and an important set of parameters for the discussion. See also the important collection of essays in C.B.R. Pelling, *Greek Tragedy and the Historian* (New York, Oxford University Press, 1997) and the illuminating essay by S. Goldhill, "The Great Dionysia and Civic Ideology," in J. Winkler and F. Zeitlin, *Nothing to Do with Dionysos? Athenian Drama in Its Social Context* (Princeton, Princeton University Press, 1990), 97–129.

Fourth Century

After a long period of neglect, Isocrates has once again become interesting to historians and theorists. On Isocrates as a critic of democracy, see Ober, *PDDA*, chapter 5; on general features of Isocratean rhetoric and teaching in their social contexts, see Y.L. Too, *The Rhetoric of Identity in Isocrates* (Cambridge, Cambridge University Press, 1995). On the two kinds of equality, F.D. Harvey, "Two Kinds of Equality," *Classica et Mediaevalia* 26 (1965) 101–46; 27 (1966) 96–100 (corrigenda) is fundamental. On the politics and philosophy of monarchy, I have found J.K. Davies, *Democracy and Classical Greece* (2nd edn., Cambridge, Mass., Harvard University Press, 1993), chapter 10, helpful. There is little interesting work at present on political thinking about monarchy, but see L. Strauss, *On Tyranny* (rev. and expanded edn., New York, Free Press, 1991) for a provocative reading of Xenophon's *Hiero*; Gray in the *CHGRPT* offers interesting remarks on panhellenism and monarchy in Xenophon and Isocrates; compare also the useful remarks on panhellenism in J. Dillery, *Xenophon and the History of his Times* (London, Routledge, 1995), 41–58.

The best book-length introduction to Plato's *Republic* remains that of Annas, *Introduction to Plato's Republic*. On Plato's relationship to contemporary politics, I have learned from Ober, *PDDA*; C. Bobonich, *Plato's Utopia Recast* (Oxford, Clarendon Press, 2004); Saxonhouse, *Athenian Democracy*; S. Monoson, *Plato's Democratic Entanglements* (Princeton, Princeton University Press, 2000). There is still much of value to be found in A.W.H. Adkins, *Merit and Responsibility* (Oxford, Clarendon Press, 1960).

On the general interpretation of the *Gorgias*, see J. Cooper, "Socrates and Plato in Plato's *Gorgias*," in *Reason and Emotion* (Princeton, Princeton University Press, 1999), 29–75, and T. Irwin, *Plato's Ethics* (Oxford, Oxford University Press, 1995). H. Yunis, *Taming Democracy*, usefully brings this dialogue into conversation with Thucydides and helpfully points out its connections with the *Republic*. On the argument with Callicles, see C. Kahn, "Drama and Dialectic in Plato's *Gorgias*," *Oxford Studies in Ancient Philosophy* 1 (1983) 75–121. On the interpretation of Callicles' hedonism, I have also learned from R. Barney, "Callicles and Thrasymachus."

The secondary literature on the *Republic* is vast. In addition to the works already mentioned, see the overview of E. Brown, "Plato: Ethics and Politics in the *Republic*," *The Stanford Encyclopedia of Philosophy* (Summer 2003 Edition), Edward N. Zalta (ed.), URL = <http://plato.stanford.edu/archives/sum2003/entries/plato-ethics-politics/>. N.P. White, *A Companion to Plato's Republic* (Indianapolis, Hackett, 1979) remains helpful on many important issues, notably on the interpretation of the Form of the Good; see also C.D.C. Reeve, *Philosopher-Kings* (Princeton, Princeton University Press, 1988). Readers will find much to think about and argue with in R.C. Cross and A.D. Woozley, *Plato's Republic: A Philosophical Commentary* (New York, St. Martin's Press, 1964). The classic article on the city/soul analogy is B. Williams, "The Analogy of City and Soul in Plato's *Republic*," in E.N. Lee et al., eds., *Exegesis and Argument: Studies in Greek Philosophy Presented to Gregory Vlastos* (Phronesis Supplemental Volume 1) Assen, Van Gorcum, 1973), 196–206. On the importance of rational order to Plato's ethics and politics, see J. Cooper, "The Psychology of Justice in Plato," in *Reason and Emotion*, 138–49. On justice in the *Republic*, see, among many others, G. Vlastos, "The Theory of Social Justice in the Polis in Plato's *Republic*," in

D.W. Graham, ed., *Studies in Greek Philosophy*, vol. 2 (Princeton, Princeton University Press, 1995), 69–103.

Modern reactions to Plato's politics have varied widely. Popper's is only one of the best known: see K. Popper, *The Open Society and its Enemies*, vol. 1: *The Spell of Plato*, 5th edn. (Princeton, Princeton University Press, 1966). On "totalitarianism," see C.C.W. Taylor, "Plato's Totalitarianism," in R. Kraut, ed., *Plato's Republic: Critical Essays* (Lanham, Md., Rowman and Littlefield, 1997), 31–48. For two very different critical overviews of modern readings, see the ambitious study of C.H. Zuckert, *Postmodern Platos* (Chicago, University of Chicago Press, 1996) and now M. Lane, *Plato's Progeny* (London, Duckworth, 2001).

The *Statesman* and *Laws* have been increasingly important objects of study in the last 15 years. On the *Statesman*, C. Rowe, *Plato: Statesman* (Warminster, Aris and Phillips, 1995) is useful, as is Rowe's contribution to the *CHGRPT*, 233–57. On politics in this dialogue, I have generally tended to follow the account of J. Cooper, "Plato's *Statesman* and Politics," in *Reason and Emotion*, 165–91. See also C. Gill, "Rethinking Constitutionalism in *Statesman* 291–303" in C. Rowe, ed., *Reading the Statesman* (Sankt Augustin, Academia Verlag, 1995), 292–305 and M. Lane, *Method and Politics in Plato's Statesman* (Cambridge, Cambridge University Press, 1998). There is much work still to be done on the connections between the *Statesman* and democracy. The standard work on the *Laws* remains that of G.R. Morrow, *Plato's Cretan City* (Princeton, Princeton University Press, 1960), but see now the excellent study of Bobonich, *Plato's Utopia Recast*, which I have followed generally and in many particulars. Also worth reading are T.J. Saunders, *Plato's Penal Code* (Oxford, Clarendon Press, 1991) and A. Laks' contribution to the *CHGRPT*, 258–92.

Aristotle

There are numerous valuable and challenging introductions to Aristotle's political philosophy. The most recent is that of R. Kraut, *Aristotle: Political Philosophy* (Oxford, Oxford University Press, 2002), but it is well worth reading the account of R.G. Mulgan, *Aristotle's Political Theory* (Oxford, Clarendon Press, 1977). Pitched at the level of professional scholars is the fundamental collection of D. Keyt and F. D. Miller, Jr., eds., *A Companion to Aristotle's Politics* (Oxford, Blackwell, 1991); see also the older, but not outdated, collection of J. Barnes et al., eds., *Articles on Aristotle*, vol. 2, *Ethics and Politics* (London, Duckworth, 1977). The century-old commentary of W.L. Newman, *The Politics of Aristotle*, 4 vols (Oxford, Clarendon Press, 1887–1902) has never been superseded for a passage-by-passage interpretation of the *Politics*. T. Irwin, *Aristotle's First Principles* (Oxford, Clarendon Press, 1988) provides, among very much else, an important treatment of most key issues in Aristotelian ethics and political thought.

Aristotle has always been studied intensely, and contemporary political philosophers continue to find much of value in his work: see, for example, the essays collected in A. Tessitore, *Aristotle and Modern Politics* (Notre Dame, University of Notre Dame Press, 2002). For exemplary, and highly divergent, neo-Aristotelian thought, see A. MacIntyre, *After Virtue* (2nd edn., Notre Dame, University of Notre Dame Press, 1984) and *Whose Justice? Which Rationality?* (Notre Dame, University of Notre Dame Press, 1988) and M.C. Nussbaum, *The Fragility of Goodness* (Cambridge, Cambridge University Press, 1986); "Aristotelian Social Democracy," in Tessitore, *Aristotle and Modern Politics*, 47–104; "Non-Relative Virtues: An Aristotelian Approach," in M. Nussbaum and A. Sen, *The Quality of Life* (Oxford, Clarendon Press, 1990), 242–69; "Nature, Function, and Capability: Aristotle on Political Distribution," *Oxford Studies in Ancient Philosophy*, Supplementary Volume (1988), 145–83. For general discussion of Aristotelian thought in contemporary political theory, see J.R. Wallach, "Contemporary Aristotelianism," *Political Theory* 20 (1992) 613–41. B. Yack, *The Problems of a Political Animal* (Berkeley, University of California Press, 1993) also reflects interestingly on the Aristotelian understanding of community and justice in ways that are useful to modern theoretical projects.

Aristotle on political emotion has become an important topic in recent discussions: W.W. Fortenbaugh, *Aristotle on Emotion* (2nd edn., London, Duckworth, 2002) is the standard work. On anger in particular, see the wide-ranging study of W.V. Harris, *Restraining Rage: The Ideology of Anger Control in Classical Antiquity* (Cambridge, Mass., Harvard University Press, 2001). On Aristotle's *Rhetoric* and emotion, see the collection of A.O. Rorty, *Essays on Aristotle's Rhetoric* (Berkeley, University of California Press, 1996). On Aristotle's account of the virtues, see A.O. Rorty's other seminal collection, *Essays on Aristotle's Ethics* (Berkeley, University of California Press, 1980), along with W.F.R. Hardie, *Aristotle's Ethical Theory* (2nd edn., Oxford, Clarendon Press, 1980). On Aristotle's "dialectical" qualities, see T.W. Smith, *Revaluing Ethics: Aristotle's Dialectical Pedagogy* (Albany, State University of New York Press, 2001).

On the question of the best type of human life, according to Aristotle, controversy has raged for a very long time. An interesting place to start is with S. Broadie, *Ethics with Aristotle* (New York, Oxford University Press, 1991), and with J. Cooper, "Contemplation and Happiness: A Reconsideration," in *Reason and Emotion*, 212–36, which should be compared with J. Cooper, *Reason and Human Good in Aristotle* (Indianapolis, Hackett, 1986). See also R. Kraut, *Aristotle on the Human Good* (Princeton, Princeton University Press, 1989).

On Aristotle's naturalism, see the important treatment of F.D. Miller, Jr., *Nature, Justice, and Rights in Aristotle's Politics* (Oxford, Clarendon Press, 1995); note also Miller's lucid contribution to *CHGRPT*. On naturalism, and on the question of "rights" in general, see the review-articles of J. Cooper and M. Schofield, among others, in the special issue of *Review of Metaphysics* (49.4, 1996) devoted to discussion of Miller's book. See also G.E.R. Lloyd, "The Idea of Nature in the Politics," in *Aristotelian Explorations* (Cambridge, Cambridge University Press, 1996), 184–204; W. Kullman, "Man as a Political Animal in Aristotle," in Keyt and Miller, *Companion*, 94–117; and D. Depew, "Humans and Other Political Animals in Aristotle's History of Animals" *Phronesis* 40.2 (1995) 156–81. For a more political interpretation of Aristotelian "nature," which helpfully discusses Aristotelian teleology in relation to modern science, see S. Salkever, *Finding the Mean: Theory and Practice in Aristotelian Political Philosophy* (Princeton, Princeton University Press, 1990), 13–104.

On Aristotle's theory of "natural slavery," helpful works are P. Garnsey, *Ideas of Slavery*, 107–27; B. Williams, *Shame and Necessity*, 109–118; M. Schofield, "Ideology and Philosophy in Aristotle's Theory of Slavery," in *Saving the City* (London, Routledge, 1999), 115–40; and J. Frank, "Citizens, Slaves, and Foreigners: Aristotle on Human Nature," *American Political Science Review* 98.1 (2004) 91–104, which provocatively argues that Aristotle self-consciously undermines his "defense" of natural slavery by offering a thoroughly politicized account of nature.

With regard to Aristotle's best polis, I have learned much from D. Depew, "Politics, Music, and Contemplation in Aristotle's Ideal State," in *A Companion to Aristotle's Politics*, 346–80; on the constitutional form of that regime, see C.N. Johnson, *Aristotle's Theory of the State* (London, MacMillan, 1990). On Aristotle's criticisms of Plato, see, with caution, R. Mayhew, *Aristotle's Criticism of Plato's Republic* (Lanham, Md., Rowman and Littlefield, 1997).

Aristotle's response to democracy continues to provoke responses at many different points on the spectrum. On Aristotle's relationship to democracy, see Ober, *Political Dissent*; Saxonhouse, *Athenian Democracy*; J. Frank, *A Democracy of Distinction* (Chicago, University of Chicago Press, 2004); and S. Salkever, "The Deliberative Model of Democracy and Aristotle's Ethics of Natural Questions," in Tessitore, *Aristotle and Modern Politics*, 342–74. For the "summation" argument and related arguments, see J. Waldron, "The Wisdom of the Multitude," *Political Theory* 23 (1995) 563–84.

Hellenistic Political Thought

An outstanding collection of texts, translations, and commentary can be found in A.A. Long and D. Sedley, *The Hellenistic Philosophers*, 2 vols

(Cambridge, Cambridge University Press, 1987); for the sake of convenience, I have cited texts by their section number as well as by ancient author. For an overview of political thought in this period, see G.J.D. Aalders, *Political Thought in Hellenistic Times* (Amsterdam, A.M. Hakkert, 1975).

On the history of the Hellenistic period in general, see now A. Erskine, ed., *A Companion to the Hellenistic World* (Oxford, Blackwell, 2003), for an outstanding introductory survey of many relevant topics. On Alexander's conquests and the questions of cultural contact, see, for very different perspectives, W.W. Tarn, "Alexander the Great and the Unity of Mankind," *Proceedings of the Cambridge Philological Society* 19 (1933), 123–66 and E. Badian, "Alexander the Great and the Unity of Mankind," *Historia* 7 (1958) 425–55 (both reprinted in G.T. Griffith, *Alexander the Great: The Main Problems*, New York, Barnes and Noble, 1966). For more general overviews, with collections of ancient evidence and modern interpretations, see I. Worthington, *Alexander the Great: A Reader* (London, Routledge, 2003) and J. Roisman, *Alexander the Great: Ancient and Modern Perspectives* (Lexington, Mass., D.C. Heath, 1995). On the question of Alexander's conquests and their relation to Aristotle's ambiguous understandings of natural slavery, see Ober, *PDDA*, 342–51.

For discussion of the relationship between Hellenistic philosophy and the enlarged Hellenistic political world, see A.A. Long, *Hellenistic Philosophy* (2nd edn., Berkeley, University of California Press, 1986), 1–13; G. Shipley, *The Greek World After Alexander: 323–30 BC* (London, Routledge, 2000), 176–91. On philosophers, kings, and power, see Long's provocative "Hellenistic Ethics and Philosophical Power," in P. Green, ed., *Hellenistic History and Culture* (Berkeley, University of California Press, 1993), 138–56.

On kingship theory, I have been influenced by D. Hahm in *CHGRPT*, 457–76, as well as by the seminal article of E. Goodenough, "The Political Philosophy of Hellenistic Kingship," *Yale Classical Studies* 1 (1928) 55–102, and the useful treatment of F.W. Walbank, "Monarchies and Monarchic Ideas," in *Cambridge Ancient History* vol. 7, Part 1 (2nd edn., Cambridge, Cambridge University Press, 1984), 62–100. The *Rhetoric to Alexander* is too little discussed in modern scholarship: in addition to Hahm, see also Rowe in *CHGRPT*, 393–4; and Sinclair, *History of Greek Political Thought*, 254–5. Similarly with the *Letter of Aristeas to Philocrates*, on which see especially the fine work of M. Hadas, *Aristeas to Philocrates* (New York, Harper, 1951). On the pseudo-Pythagoreans, see, in addition to Goodenough and Sinclair, B. Centrone in *CHGRPT*, 567–75. The pseudo-Pythagorean authors are worth considering in this chapter because they show just how different the new world and its theories could become; they may well form part of a Roman imperial "common culture."

On the traditional schools, Shipley, *Greek World*, 176–82, provides a concise overview. On the *Minos*, see Leo Strauss's highly unconventional treatment in "On the *Minos*," in T.L. Pangle, *The Roots of Political Philosophy: Ten Forgotten Socratic Dialogues* (Ithaca, Cornell University Press, 1987), 67–79, along with Rowe, *CHGRPT*, 307–9. On Theophrastus and his relationship to Athens and Athenian political thought, see Ober, *PDDA*, 364–6.

There has been a good deal of interesting recent work done on Cynicism. The most interesting and optimistic interpretations are offered in several articles of J.L. Moles: see especially "The Cynics and Politics," in A. Laks and M. Schofield, eds., *Justice and Generosity* (Cambridge, Cambridge University Press, 1995), 129–58; "Cynic Cosmopolitanism," in R. Bracht Branham and M.-O. Goulet-Cazé, *The Cynics* (Berkeley, University of California Press, 1996), 105–120; and his contribution to *CHGRPT*, 415–34. In *The Cynics*, note also R. Bracht Branham, "Defacing the Currency: Diogenes' Rhetoric and the *Invention* of Cynicism," 81–104. On Socrates and the Cynics (and the Hellenistic schools generally), see A.A. Long, "Socrates in Hellenistic Philosophy," in *Stoic Studies* (Cambridge, Cambridge University Press, 1996), 1–34, and E. Brown, "Socrates the Cosmopolitan," in *Stanford Agora: An Online Journal of Legal Perspectives* 1 (2000): 74–87. On libertarianism and anarchism, see R. Nozick, *Anarchy, State, and Utopia* (New York, Basic Books, 1974); Robert Paul Wolff, cited in the notes; and R. Sylvan, "Anarchism," in Goodin and Pettit, *A Companion to Contemporary Political Philosophy*, 215–43.

On Stoic political thought, M. Schofield's recent work is the best place to start: see his *Stoic Idea of the City* (Cambridge, Cambridge University Press, 1999), and, more concisely, his contribution to *CHGRPT*, 435–56 (which also includes interesting remarks on Epicureanism). On Stoic political thought in context, a good study is that of A. Erskine, *The Hellenistic Stoa* (Ithaca, Cornell University Press, 1990). See also E. Brown's innovative treatment in *Stoic Cosmopolitanism* (forthcoming), along with Long and Sedley's commentary on the relevant passages.

Epicurean political thought has long, and unfairly, been neglected. Much that is relevant here can be found in P. Mitsis, *Epicurus' Ethical Theory* (Ithaca, Cornell University Press, 1988), which is especially helpful on friendship. See also A. Alberti, "The Epicurean Theory of Law and Justice," in Laks and Schofield, *Justice and Generosity*, 161–90. Some related themes are treated in M.C. Nussbaum, *The Therapy of Desire: Theory and Practice in Hellenistic Ethics* (Princeton, Princeton University Press, 1994) and J. Annas, *The Morality of Happiness* (New York, Oxford University Press, 1993), esp. 293–302.

Notes

Chapter 1 Introduction: How to Do Greek Political Thought

1   Cf. Rowe, *CHGRPT*, 6.
2   J.K. Davies, "Origins," and C. Smith, "Servius Tullius, Cleisthenes," helpfully remind us that polis forms of organization were not uniquely Greek and that Greeks borrowed from and interacted with their Mediterranean neighbors in developing their politics and other aspects of their social organization. For further explanation of the numbers in this paragraph, see Hansen, *ADAD*, 55.
3   Meier, *Greek Discovery of Politics*, 4; cf. also, Hammer, *Iliad as Politics*, 18–48.
4   Kymlicka, *CPP*, 1.
5   This phrase comes from G. Taylor, *Pride, Shame, and Guilt: Emotions of Self Assessment* (Oxford, Clarendon Press, 1985).
6   Finley, *Politics*, 52.
7   Cartledge, *CHGRPT*, 13.
8   Hammer, *Iliad as Politics*, 30.
9   Hammer, *Iliad as Politics*, 20–6.
10 Cf. Strauss, *The City and Man*, 6–11; Strauss, *On Tyranny*, eds. V. Gourevitch and M.S. Roth, rev. edn. (New York, Free Press, 1991), 22–8.
11 Williams, *Shame and Necessity*, 3–4. The preceding quotation is from Williams, 3.
12 Rowe, *CHGRPT*, 6.
13 For the distinction between moral and ethical, see B. Williams, *Ethics and the Limits of Philosophy* (Cambridge, Mass., Harvard University Press, 1985), 1–21.
14 For an interesting modern attempt to examine virtue in politics, see B. Honig, *Political Theory and the Displacement of Politics* (Ithaca, Cornell University Press, 1993). On virtue ethics, see, for example, R. Crisp, *How Should One Live?* (Oxford, Clarendon Press, 1996).
15 See A.W.H. Adkins, "The Connection between Aristotle's Ethics and Politics," in D. Keyt and F.D. Miller, Jr., *A Companion to Aristotle's "Politics"* (Oxford, Blackwell, 1991) 75–93.

16 I mean, of course, the "liberal" tradition of Locke, Mill, Constant, Berlin, and Rawls, which can be distinguished from the common sense of "liberal" as applied, for example, to the Democratic Party in the United States. See Kymlicka, *CPP*, 53–101.

17 See, for example, Sandel, *Liberalism*.

18 For a sense of the frustrations, see, for example, C. Taylor, "Cross-Purposes: The Liberal-Communitarian Debate," in N. Rosenblum, ed., *Liberalism and the Moral Life* (Cambridge, Mass., Harvard University Press, 1989), 159–82.

19 For a modern treatment of this connection, see, for example, P. Berkowitz, *Virtue and the Making of Modern Liberalism* (Princeton, Princeton University Press, 1999).

20 For similar arguments on Aristotle's best polis, see Nussbaum, "Non-Relative Virtues," and Nussbaum's other articles cited in the Bibliographic Essay, section on chapter 8.

Chapter 2 Archaic Greece and the Centrality of Justice

1   Kymlicka, *CPP*, 1.

2   See especially G. Nagy, "Theognis and Megara: A Poet's Vision of His City," in T.J. Figueira and G. Nagy, eds., *Theognis of Megara* (Baltimore, Johns Hopkins University Press,1985), 22–81.

3   Balot, *GICA*, 59–67.

4   See G.S. Kirk, J.E. Raven, and M. Schofield, *The Presocratic Philosophers*, 2nd edn. (Cambridge, Cambridge University Press,1983), 117–22, 193–4.

5   P. Vidal-Naquet, *The Black Hunter* (Baltimore, Johns Hopkins University Press, 1986), 15–38.

6   P.J. Rhodes, "Introduction," in Mitchell and Rhodes, *Development of the Polis*, 6–7.

7   For Heraclitus, similarly, injustice and inequality drew men's attention to the importance of justice (*DK* 22 B 23).

8   On this feature of Greek political life, see J.-P. Vernant, *The Origins of Greek Thought* (Ithaca, Cornell University Press, 1982).

9   On all aspects of the middling group, including their size and position in the polis, see Raaflaub, "Homer to Solon" and Hanson, *The Other Greeks*.

10 For the basic typology, and interesting developments of it as applied to archaic poetry and history, see Morris, *Archaeology*, 155–91 and Kurke, *Coins*, 6–37.

11 Balot, *GICA*, 70–3.

12 This is a generalized picture of the situation; there was diversity throughout Greece both in the chronology and types of development

of hoplite fighting. See Hanson, *The Other Greeks* and, on early hoplite warfare, van Wees, "Development of the Hoplite Phalanx."

13   For a helpfully critical discussion of archaic tyranny, and of Theognis and Alcaeus, see Osborne, *Greece in the Making*, 190–7.

14   Tr. D.A. Campbell, *Greek Lyric I: Sappho and Alcaeus* (Cambridge, Mass., Harvard University Press,1982), adapted.

15   Tr. Campbell, adapted.

16   See L. Kurke, "The Politics of *Habrosunê* in Archaic Greece," *Classical Antiquity* 11.1 (1992) 91–120.

17   For the general concept, see Saxonhouse, *Fear of Diversity*.

18   For a good concise treatment, see Raaflaub, *CHGRPT*, 37–48.

19   Elshtain, *Women and War*; Elster, "Norms"; Rorty, "Two Faces."

20   S. Houby-Nielsen, "Interaction between Chieftains and Citizens?" *Acta Hyperborea* 4 (1992) 343–74.

21   Tr. D. Gerber, *Greek Elegiac Poetry* (Cambridge, Mass., Harvard University Press, 1999), adapted.

22   Balot, *GICA*, 73–9.

23   Tr. Campbell, adapted.

24   E.K. Anhalt, *Solon the Singer: Politics and Poetics* (Lanham, Md., Rowman and Littlefield,), 72–9.

25   Anhalt, *Solon*, 108–10.

26   For a vivid expression of such ideals, see Kateb, *The Inner Ocean*.

Chapter 3 Democratic Political Thinking at Athens

1   On the establishment of democracy at Athens, see Ober, *Athenian Revolution*, 32–52, along with the debate between Raaflaub and Ober in K. Raaflaub, "Power in the Hands of the People" and "The Thetes and Democracy," and J. Ober, "Revolution Matters," all in I. Morris and K. Raaflaub, eds, *Democracy 2500? Questions and Challenges* (Dubuque, Iowa, Kendall/Hunt, 1998).

2   Others were not delivered at all but were rather meant as literary "display-pieces" and distributed in pamphlet-form for a readership; such speeches are especially characteristic of the large corpus written by Isocrates and datable to roughly 420–320 BC.

3   Ober, *MEDA*, 43–9.

4   The best study of the rhetorical nature of ancient historiography is A.J. Woodman, *Rhetoric in Classical Historiography* (Portland, Areopagitica Press, 1988).

5   On reading Thucydides' speeches, see especially H. Yunis, "Narrative, Rhetoric, and Ethical Instruction in Thucydides," in L.C. Montefusco, ed., *Papers on Rhetoric IV* (Rome, Herder Editrice, 2002), 275–86; and Yunis, "Writing for Reading: Thucydides, Plato, and the Emergence of

the Critical Reader," in *Written Texts and the Rise of Literate Culture in Ancient Greece* (Cambridge, Cambridge University Press, 2003), 189–212.

6   In these cases, I will give references to illustrate the parallels in language, ideology, and sentiment.

7   See Ober, *MEDA*, 43–9; Raaflaub, *Discovery*, 9–13, 166–81.

8   Hansen, *ADAD*, 313–19 usefully discusses motivation and participation in ancient Athens, as does R.K. Sinclair, *Democracy and Participation in Athens* (Cambridge, Cambridge University Press, 1988). On questions of motivation and participation in modern politics, see Kymlicka, *CPP*, 326, with references.

9   See especially Whitehead, "Cardinal Virtues."

10   Compare Nussbaum, "Non-Relative Virtues" on Aristotle's "thick" but "vague" description of human flourishing.

11   See especially Finley, *Democracy Ancient and Modern* and Ober and Hedrick, *Dêmokratia*.

12   For these and other references to this point, and brief commentary, see J. Rusten, *Thucydides: The Peloponnesian War, Book II* (Cambridge, Cambridge University Press, 1989).

13   For similar ideas in a variety of popular forums, see Soph. *Ant.* 182–90, Dem. 18.205, Lys. 21.24, with Dover, *Greek Popular Morality*, 301–6.

14   For a nuanced treatment of the question of personal freedom at Athens, from a slightly different perspective, see R.W. Wallace, "Law, Freedom, and the Concept of Citizens' Rights in Democratic Athens," in *Dêmokratia*, 105–119.

15   On Constant's understanding of the ancient polis, see S. Holmes, "Aristippus in and out of Athens," *American Political Science Review* 73 (1979) 113–28.

16   On "living as you like," see also Hdt. 3.82.2–3; Lys. 26.5; Aristotle, *Pol.*, 1317a40–b16; and the critical remarks of Plato, *Republic*, 557b–558c; Old Oligarch 1.10–2, with Raaflaub, *Discovery of Freedom*, 227–3; Hansen, *ADAD*, 74–8. Many, but not all, of these references come from critics of democracy, but I do not believe that this warrants the conclusion that private freedom was not a value prized by democrats themselves. Rather, it was both important to democrats and easy for critics to attack. On Pericles' funeral oration as reported by Thucydides, see Loraux, *Invention of Athens*.

17   For a concise discussion, see Hansen, *ADAD*, 76–7.

18   Cf. Wallace, "Law, Freedom, and the Concept of Citizens' Rights," 106–7, 114–17.

19   Kymlicka, *CPP*, 284–326 discusses such theoretical strategies in the context of modern citizenship theory.

20   See Nussbaum, "Non-Relative Virtues" for this formulation as applied to Aristotle.

21   In relation to speaking in public, Aesch. 3.220 interestingly qualifies this point by saying that democracies give their citizens the freedom to speak only when they want to and when they have something to contribute to the common good; Dem. 22.30 suggests that most people did not in fact exercise the privilege of addressing the Assembly; cf. Dem. 18.308, Thuc. 2.40, with Hansen, *ADAD*, 306–7; Ober, *MEDA*, 295–9.

22   I. Berlin, *Four Essays on Liberty*.

23   See Balot, "Free Speech," 236–42.

24   See Balot, "Free Speech,"; S.S. Monoson, *Plato's Democratic Entanglements* is particularly good on questions of deliberation and autonomy; and cf. Saxonhouse, *Athenian Democracy*, 59–86.

25   On criticisms of the democratic audience, see Balot, "Free Speech," 236–9; J. Roisman, "Speaker–Audience Interaction in Athens: A Power Struggle," in Sluiter and Rosen, *Free Speech*, 268–75.

26   Gutmann and Thompson, *Democracy and Disagreement*, 43.

27   Cf. Raaflaub, *Discovery of Freedom*.

28   On the "wisdom of the masses," see Ober, *MEDA*, 163–5; on several of the themes I have mentioned, see Strauss, *Natural Right and History*.

29   See especially K.J. Dover, "The Freedom of the Intellectual in Greek Society," in *The Greeks and Their Legacy: Collected Papers*, vol. 2 (Oxford, Blackwell, 1988), 135–58.

30   Tacon, "Ecclesiastic *Thorubos*."

31   Arendt, *Human Condition*, 36.

32   Arendt, *Human Condition*, 186.

33   See Ober, *MEDA*, esp. 15–16 and R. Michels, *Political Parties*.

34   M.I. Finley, "Athenian Demagogues," *Past and Present* 21 (1962) 3–24.

35   See, for example, Warren, *Democracy and Trust* and A.B. Seligman, *The Problem of Trust* (Princeton, Princeton University Press, 1997).

36   Balot, *GICA*, 197–9.

37   The standard treatment of non-Athenian democracy is E.W. Robinson, *The First Democracies: Early Popular Government Outside Athens* (Stuttgart, F. Steiner, 1997). Robinson maintains that other democracies existed before that of Athens, but the evidence for these other cases is questionable, often because it is late. For democracy to exist in the "full" sense in which classical Athenians would have understood it, all citizens, including the poor, must fully share in political power; for further clarification of this point, see the debate between Ober and Raaflaub (above, n.1). Athens was the first Greek city to achieve this integration of the poor.

38   Cole, "Anonymus Iamblichi" (see "The Challenge of Thrasymachus and Callicles" in chapter 4), though, has argued strongly that the Anonymus Iamblichi derives from Democritean thought; if so, we can gain a better sense, through the surviving excerpts of his work, of what Democritus' political thought was like.

39   Tr. Procopé, "Democritus on Politics – Appendix," 27.

40   On these points, see Mejer, "Democritus and Democracy," 3–5.

41   Farrar, *Origins*, 77.

42   For the basic accuracy of the speech as a representation of the views of the historical Protagoras, see the arguments offered by Schiappa, *Protagoras*, 145–8. For excellent remarks that complicate this attribution, see Farrar, *Origins*, 44–98.

43   On Protagoras's epistemological theories and their possible relation to democracy, see chapter 4.

44   Quoted in I. Morris, *Archaeology as Cultural History* (Oxford, Blackwell, 2000), 111; from R. Dahl, *Democracy and Its Critics* (New Haven, Yale University Press, 1989), 98.

45   On *isêgoria* (free and equal speech), see Hdt. 5.78; on equal protection under the law, see Dem. 51.11; on equality before the law, see Aesch. 1.5; Hansen, *ADAD*, 81–5 offers a concise and helpful treatment, citing a great deal of evidence; Hansen's treatment, however, differs from my own on the relationship between natural and normative equality. See also Raaflaub, "Equalities and Inequalities," 139–43.

46   Cf. Williams, "Equality."

47   For discussion, see Hansen, *ADAD*, 306–20.

48   On these points, see Raaflaub, "Equalities"; Cartledge, "Comparatively Equal"; and Strauss, "Athenian Trireme."

49   Rawls, *Theory of Justice*, 75; Ober, "*Polis* as a Society."

Chapter 4 Criticizing Democracy in Late Fifth-Century Athens

1   See Ostwald, *Popular Sovereignty*, 175–81.

2   See Wallace, "The Sophists in Athens."

3   On using Thucydidean evidence, see "Evidence and Sources" in chapter 3; it is important to recognize Thucydides' account of Corcyra as his own interpretation. His interpretation answered to important elements of the political and social realities and drew out features of those realities that were relevant to his didactic and political intentions.

4   On this topic in general, see Ober, *PDDA*, esp. 39–41.

5   For this typology, see Ober, *PDDA*, 48–51.

6   S. Holmes, *The Anatomy of Antiliberalism* (Cambridge, Mass., Harvard University Press, 1993), 3–4.

7   See especially Guthrie, *Sophists*, 55–60; Kerferd, *Sophistic Movement*, 111–30.
8   For a general account, see Guthrie, *Sophists*, 44–54; Kerferd, *Sophistic Movement*, 4–41.
9   J. Ober, "Thucydides, Pericles, and the Strategy of Defense," in J.W. Eadie and J. Ober, *The Craft of the Ancient Historian* (Lanham, Md., University Press of America, 1985), 171–88.
10 On the problems and issues involved, see Balot, *GICA*, 179–233.
11 For theoretical reflections on texts and their role in enabling or inspiring action, see Q. Skinner, "Some Problems in the Analysis of Political Thought and Action," in J. Tully, *Meaning and Context* (Cambridge, Cambridge University Press, 1988), 97–118.
12 Socrates is reported to have made a similar distinction between those who violate the laws of men and those who violate the laws of the gods; cf. *Xen. Mem.* 4.4.21. For a helpful discussion of Antiphon on law and nature, see Barnes, *PP*, 508–16. The first translation in this paragraph is adapted from Barnes; the second is Barnes'.
13 On the contested identity of Antiphon, I follow the "unitarian" position, which has been forcefully restated by Gagarin, *Antiphon*. On what is known of Antiphon's oligarchic sympathies and connection with the revolution, see Ostwald, *Popular Sovereignty*, 359–64.
14 Schol. Aesch. 1.39, tr. Levin, in Sprague, *Older Sophists*, 247.
15 See Barnes, *PP*, 451–8.
16 Barney, "Callicles and Thrasymachus."
17 For arguments that Callicles was a historical figure, see E.R. Dodds, *Plato: Gorgias* (Oxford, Clarendon Press, 1959), 12–15; Kerferd, *Sophistic Movement*, 52.
18 In rejecting the distinction between *phusis* and *nomos*, the Anonymus might be reflecting the ethical and political views of Democritus; see C.C.W. Taylor, "The Atomists," in A.A. Long, ed., *The Cambridge Companion to Early Greek Philosophy* (Cambridge, Cambridge University Press, 1999), 181–204; Mejer, "Democritus and Democracy," 8; Cole, "Anonymus Iamblichi."
19 Cf. *Gorgias* 488c–489d.
20 A similar view is taken by A. Andrews in A.W. Gomme, with A. Andrewes and K.J. Dover, *A Historical Commentary on Thucydides* (Oxford, Clarendon Press, 1945–81), vol. 4, 161. For a different reading, see Powell, *Athens and Sparta*, 182–6.
21 Ostwald, *Popular Sovereignty*, 431–45.
22 J. Cooper, "Introduction," in *Plato: Complete Works* (Indianapolis, Hackett, 1997), xiv–xv.
23 Cooper, "Introduction," xv–xvi.

24 See Cooper, "Notes on Xenophon's Socrates"; Nehamas, *The Art of Living.*

25 On the *Crito*, see especially Brickhouse and Smith, *Plato's Socrates*, 141–55; Kraut, *Socrates and the State*, 5–24; Ober, *PDDA*, 179–89.

26 For these arguments, see Morrison, "Xenophon's Socrates."

27 See Morrison, "Xenophon's Socrates" for discussion of these terms and for a helpful exploration of what the distinction involves.

28 Scholars have long debated whether mankind in general is supposed to be the measure of things, or individuals separately; what kind of subjectivist view this statement might represent; and whether the doctrine is to be applied to all evaluative and perceptual terms, or simply to certain terms (or categories), such as "just" and "beautiful," but not to others, such as "advantageous." For interesting discussion of the complexities involved, see Schiappa, *Protagoras*, 117–33; Guthrie, *Sophists*, 181–92; Barnes, *PP*, 541–53 (on various topics related to Protagorean relativism); Kerferd, *Sophistic Movement*, 83–110; Keyt and Miller, "Ancient Greek Political Thought," 306–8.

29 For a development of this possibility, see Farrar, *Origins*, 62–4, 75–7.

30 Keyt and Miller, "Ancient Greek Political Thought," 307–8.

31 See Barnes, *Presocratic Philosophers*, 541–53; M.F. Burnyeat, "Protagoras and Self-Refutation in Plato's *Theaetetus*," *Philosophical Review* 85 (1976) 172–85.

32 See Keyt and Miller, "Ancient Greek Political Thought," 306–7.

33 Keyt and Miller, "Ancient Greek Political Thought," 307–8; Taylor, *Plato: Protagoras*, 83–4.

34 Keyt and Miller, "Ancient Greek Political Thought," 306–8.

35 See especially Ober, *PDDA*, 52–21.

36 For a searching examination of rhetorical theories, see Barnes, *PP*, 516–22, 523–9, 541–53.

37 Tr. Sprague, *Older Sophists.*

38 Such criticisms of democratic debate were common in fourth-century oratory also; cf. Balot, "Free Speech."

39 Balot, *GICA*, 147–9.

40 Kraut, *Socrates and the State*, 194–244; see also Brickhouse and Smith, *Plato's Socrates*, 155–66.

41 For an interesting treatment of such questions, see G. Vlastos, "Epilogue: Socrates and Vietnam," in *Socratic Studies*, 127–33.

Chapter 5 Imperialism

1 See further Harris, *War and Imperialism*, 4.

2 For an interesting discussion of hegemony and some related issues, see J. Wickersham, *Hegemony and Greek Historians* (London, Rowman and Littlefield, 1994).

3   On the interpretation of this fragment, see Kirk, Raven, and Schofield, *Presocratic Philosophers*, 193–4.
4   Brown, "International Affairs," 515.
5   See the helpful discussion of D.R. Mapel, "Realism and the Ethics of War and Peace," in Nardin, *Ethics of War and Peace*, 54–77.
6   Brown, "International Affairs," usefully summarizes the arguments that have been developed at considerable length in the specialist literature and provides a helpful bibiography; on capabilities specifically, see M.C. Nussbaum, *Women and Human Development*.
7   Balot, *GICA*, 58–98.
8   Balot, *GICA*, 99–108; Said, *Culture and Imperialism*.
9   See E.G. Millender, "*Nomos Despotês*: Spartan Obedience and Athenian Lawfulness in Fifth-Century Thought", in V. Gorman and E. Robinson (eds.), *Oikistes: Studies in Constitutions, Colonies, and Military Power in the Ancient World Offered in Honor of A.J. Graham* (Leiden, Brill, 2002), 33–59.
10   On these and related themes, see Gera, *Xenophon's Cyropaedia*, 163–4, 176–7; Nadon, *Xenophon's Prince*, 39–40, 55–60 for a darker assessment; and Tatum, *Xenophon's Imperial Fiction*.
11   Cf. the conflicting assessments of Nadon, *Xenophon's Prince*, 139–46 and Gera, *Xenophon's Cyropaedia*, 280–300.
12   For a good introduction to the traditional Greek arguments based on natural Greek superiority, see R. Kraut, *Aristotle* (Oxford, Oxford University Press, 2002), 290–5; Guthrie, *Sophists*, 155–63.
13   Tr. Garnsey, *Ideas*, 75.
14   See Guthrie, *Sophists*, 152–5 at 153–4; Garnsey, *Ideas*, 75–8.
15   On the novelty of Athenian imperialism within the Greek world, see Raaflaub, *Discovery of Freedom*, 118–28; see in particular pp. 122–6 on the differences between Athenian imperialism and Spartan hegemony over the Peloponnesian League. It is perhaps worth noting the small-scale example of annexation-oriented imperialism in Sparta's annexation of Messenia in the late eighth century BC.
16   Balot, *GICA*, 114–35.
17   J.L. Moles, "Herodotus Warns the Athenians," *Papers of the Leeds International Latin Seminar* 9 (1996) 259–84.
18   Cf. B. King, "Wisdom and Happiness in Herodotus' *Histories*" (PhD, Princeton University, 1997).
19   On the thorny issues surrounding the popularity of Athens's empire, see, as an introduction, the texts and essays collected in Samons, *Athenian Democracy*, 241–79.
20   On these and related themes, see Raaflaub, *Discovery of Freedom*, 166–81.
21   This approach has been used effectively by Raaflaub, *Discovery of Freedom* and Ober, *MEDA*.

22 Loraux, *Invention* is the best discussion of the generic tropes of the funeral oration.

23 Raaflaub, *Discovery of Freedom*, 168.

24 On many of these points, see Raaflaub, *Discovery of Freedom*, 166–81.

25 Said, *Culture and Imperialism*, xvii.

26 Raaflaub, *Discovery of Freedom*, 335 n.14.

27 On Thucydides' didactic purposes in composing these speeches and putting them into the mouths of Athenians, see especially H. Yunis, "Narrative, Rhetoric, and Ethical Instruction in Thucydides" in L.C. Montefusco, ed., *Papers on Rhetoric IV* (Rome, Herder Editrice, 2002), 275–86; and Yunis, "Writing for Reading: Thucydides, Plato, and the Emergence of the Critical Reader," in *Written Texts and the Rise of Literate Culture in Ancient Greece* (Cambridge, Cambridge University Press, 2003), 189–212. Yunis' work makes clear how suspicious we ought to be of efforts to claim that the speeches were delivered as Thucydides presents them.

28 On the constraints of imperialism, see V. Wohl, *Love among the Ruins* (Princeton, Princeton University Press, 2002), 171–214.

29 Balot, *GICA*, 136–78.

30 On the emotional education provided by going to the theater, see M.C. Nussbaum, "Tragedy and Self-Sufficiency: Plato and Aristotle on Fear and Pity," in A.O. Rorty, *Essays on Aristotle's Poetics* (Princeton, Princeton University Press, 1992), 261–90.

Chapter 6 Fourth-Century Revisions

1 Dillery, *Xenophon*, 138–63.

2 See Harvey, "Two Kinds of Equality."

3 Cf. Hansen, *ADAD*, 76.

4 J. Annas, *Platonic Ethics, Old and New* (Ithaca, Cornell University Press, 1999).

5 Kahn, "Drama and Dialectic."

6 On Callicles in relation to the preceding tradition of Greek thought, see Adkins, *Merit and Responsibility*, 232–43, 266–81. At 238, Adkins made the memorable remark, "Scratch Thrasymachus and you find King Agamemnon" – which could have been applied to Callicles, and perhaps even more appropriately in light of Socrates' use of the (counter-)example of scratching an itch as a form of pleasure (*Gorgias* 494c).

7 Barney, "Callicles and Thrasymachus."

8 A. Andrewes in A.W. Gomme, with A. Andrewes and K.J. Dover, *A Historical Commentary on Thucydides* (Oxford, Clarendon Press, 1945–81), vol. 4, 183–5.

9   Ober, *PDDA*, 197–213.
10 B. Williams, *Ethics and the Limits of Philosophy* (Cambridge, Mass., Harvard University Press, 1985), 26–9.
11 Cf. Annas, *Introduction*, 153–69.
12 Annas, *Introduction*, 181–5; A. Saxonhouse, "The Philosopher and the Female in the Political Thought of Plato," *Political Theory* 4.2 (1976) 195–212.
13 For an introductory account, which I have largely followed here, see N.P. White, *A Companion to Plato's Republic*; for a more specialized treatment, see, among many others, Irwin, *Plato's Ethics*, 262–80.
14 On the Form of the Good, the philosopher-rulers, and justice, see for example, Cooper, "Psychology of Justice," and R. Kraut, "The Defense of Justice in Plato's *Republic*," in *Plato's Republic* (Lanham, Md., Rowman and Littlefield, 1997), 197–221.
15 See Cooper, "Psychology of Justice," Kraut, "Defense of Justice," and, for a different appreciation, E. Brown, "Minding the Gap in Plato's *Republic*," *Philosophical Studies* 117 (2004) 275–302.
16 This is an important question for Williams, "Analogy of City and Soul"; see also the interesting discussion in Bobonich, *Plato's Utopia Recast*.
17 Cooper, "Introduction," in *Plato: Complete Works*, xiii–xiv.
18 Bobonich, *Plato's Utopia Recast*, 412–17.
19 On law, see Rowe, *Plato: Statesman*, 15–18.
20 I owe this suggestion to Malcolm Schofield.
21 See J. Cooper, "Plato's *Statesman* and Politics."
22 Bobonich, *Plato's Utopia Recast*, 416.
23 For previous Platonic discussions of "opinion," cf. *Meno* 97a–99d, with Cooper, "Plato's *Statesman* and Politics," 182–4. As Malcolm Schofield has suggested to me, it is possible to view the *Statesman* as developing logically from the *Republic* in its definition of the citizen body, if we see the city of the *Statesman* as including only Callipolis' warriors and philosophers, and excluding the producers. The Callipolis' warriors have correct opinions that are said to be "dyed" into their souls and to exist, therefore, unshakably in their souls; cf., e.g., *Republic* 429c–430c. This is roughly comparable to the correct opinions of all citizens (excluding the statesman himself) in the ideal city of the *Statesman*.
24 This is the burden of Lane, *Method and Politics*.
25 I owe much here to conversations with Malcolm Schofield; cf. also Rowe, *CHGRPT*, 251–53; Lane, *Method and Politics*, 171–82.
26 Cf. Rowe, *CHGRPT*, 237–9.
27 Bobonich, *Plato's Utopia Recast*, 409–19.
28 Bobonich, *Plato's Utopia Recast*, 393–4.

29 On this concept, see M.C. Nussbaum, "Shame, Separateness, and Political Unity: Aristotle's Criticism of Plato," in A.O. Rorty, *Essays on Aristotle's Ethics*, 395–435.

Chapter 7 Aristotle's Political Thought

1 For this formulation, see J. Frank, "The Classical Greek World," forthcoming in *The Oxford Handbook of Political Theory*, edited by John S. Dryzek, Bonnie Honig, and Anne Phillips; cf. also Frank, *Democracy of Distinction*, 1–16.
2 For further discussion, see C. Rowe, "Aims and Methods in Aristotle's *Politics*," in Keyt and Miller, *Companion*, 57–74.
3 Balot, *GICA*, 44–55.
4 See, for example, A.R. Damasio, *Descartes' Error: Emotion, Reason, and the Human Brain* (New York, G.P. Putnam, 1994); M. Nussbaum, *Upheavals of Thought* (Cambridge, Mass., Harvard University Press, 2001); P. Goldie, *The Emotions: A Philosophical Exploration* (Oxford, Clarendon Press, 2000).
5 On a variety of issues related to distributive justice, see D. Keyt, "Aristotle's Theory of Distributive Justice," in Keyt and Miller, *Companion*, 238–78.
6 Cf. Salkever, *Finding the Mean*, 13–104.
7 I owe this formulation to David Depew. See also the very good pages of Kullman, "Man as a Political Animal," 108–14.
8 Depew, "Humans and Other Political Animals," has shown that variations in human practice are mediated by Aristotle's concept of the "way of life," or *bios*.
9 Cf. Nussbaum, "Non-Relative Virtues."
10 See D. Keyt, "Three Basic Theorems in Aristotle's Politics," in Keyt and Miller, *Companion*, 118–41; Miller, *Nature, Justice, and Rights*, 27–66; and, more concisely, Miller, *CHGRPT*, 321–43.
11 On the question of totalitarianism, see the pointed comments of C.C.W. Taylor, "Politics," in J. Barnes, ed., *The Cambridge Companion to Aristotle* (Cambridge, Cambridge University Press, 1995), 239–41.
12 On this and related issues, see Depew, "Humans and Other Political Animals."
13 See Nussbaum, "Non-Relative Virtues," "Aristotelian Social Democracy," and "Nature, Function, and Capability."
14 Keyt, "Aristotle's Theory," 256–9.
15 For an interesting modern development of such arguments, see J.D. Wallace, *Virtues and Vices* (Ithaca, Cornell University Press, 1978), 15–38.

16 For two different accounts of how freeing slaves fits into Aristotle's theory, see Frank, "Citizens, Slaves, and Foreigners"; Kraut, *Aristotle*, 295–301.

17 For brief discussion with references, see Kraut, *Aristotle*, 277.

18 For similar reflections in relation to arguing for freedom, see G. Kateb, *The Inner Ocean* (Ithaca, Cornell University Press, 1992).

19 Ober, *PDDA*, 344–51, offers an interesting discussion of such possibilities.

20 For an excellent exploration of such matters, see Mulgan, *Aristotle's Political Theory*, 53–77.

21 Depew, "Politics, Music, and Contemplation."

22 On Cleisthenes and "local knowledge," see J. Ober, "Classical Athenian Democracy and Democracy Today: Culture, Knowledge, Power," in J. Morrill, ed., *The Promotion of Knowledge: Essays to Mark the Centenary of the British Academy*, 1902–2002 = *Proceedings of the British Academy* 122 (2004), 145–61; on modern representation, see A. Rehfeld, *The Concept of Constituency* (Cambridge, 2005).

23 See Balot, Aristotle's Critique of Phaleas: Justice, Equality, and *Pleonexia*," *Hermes* 129.1 (2001) 32–44. On property in general in Aristotle's political thought, see Frank, *Democracy of Distinction*, 54–80.

24 Nussbaum, "Aristotelian Social Democracy" outlines this conception.

25 Kymlicka, *CPP*, 419–20, rightly makes of the "day care" of children an important political topic.

26 For discussion, see D. Keyt, "Injustice and Pleonexia in Aristotle: A Reply to Charles Young," *Southern Journal of Philosophy* 27 supplement (1988), 251–7.

27 As Salkever, "Deliberative Model of Democracy," shows, this legacy has been transmitted largely through the work of Rawls and Habermas.

Chapter 8 Hellenistic Political Thought

1 See Ober, *PDDA*, 342–51.

2 E.g., Long, *Hellenistic Philosophy*, 1–13; Shipley, *The Greek World After Alexander*, 176–91.

3 Tr. Goodenough, "Political Philosophy," 58.

4 On communication between the Hellenistic kings and Greek subject-cities, see, for example, J. Ma, *Antiochus III and the Cities of Western Asia Minor* (New York, Oxford University Press, 2000).

5 For an excellent discussion of this point and its ideological implications, see Raaflaub, "Father of All, Destroyer of All," 312–14. The traditional hierarchy that valued military glory over civic or intellectual accomplishments was also, later, a major source of tension for Cicero: cf., for example, *On Obligations* 1.61–92.

6   Tr. I. Scott-Kilvert, *Plutarch: The Age of Alexander* (New York, Penguin Books, 1973), 310. Compare the remarks of Hahm, *CHGRPT*, 459.

7   Cf. Hadas, *Aristeas to Philocrates*, 3–18.

8   Cf. Walbank, "Monarchies and Monarchic Ideas," 82–3 and Hahm, *CHGRPT*, 462–3, who helpfully connects this letter to the portrait of the early Egyptian kings found in Diodorus Siculus.

9   Cf. Walbank, "Monarchies and Monarchic Ideas," 78–9.

10   Tr. Goodenough, "Political Philosophy," 76–7.

11   Rowe, *CHGRPT*, 308.

12   As Sinclair (*History*, 251) argued many years ago.

13   Bracht Branham and Goulet-Cazé, "Introduction," in R. Bracht Branham and M.-O. Goulet-Cazé, *The Cynics* provide a properly skeptical account of the evidence concerning Diogenes and the tradition generally.

14   Long, "Socrates."

15   For a convincing and concise discussion, see Schofield, *Stoic Idea*, 133–4, 141–5. Compare also J. Mansfeld, "Diogenes Laertius on Stoic Philosophy," *Elenchos* 7 (1986) 296–382.

16   See Bracht Branham, "Defacing the Currency," 96–7 on the relationship between Cynic freedom and self-sufficiency.

17   Cf. Schofield, *Stoic Idea*, 141–5; Erskine, *Hellenistic Stoa*, 27–30. It is fair to add that though this view is widely shared it has recently and interestingly been attacked by J.L. Moles in "Cynic Cosmopolitanism" and in *CHGRPT*, 415–34.

18   Brown, "Socrates the Cosmopolitan."

19   R.P. Wolff, *In Defense of Anarchism* (New York, Harper and Row, 1970), 19.

20   As with the Cynics, I shall be dealing chiefly with the early adherents of Stoicism, to the extent that we can separate their views from those developed by later members of the school, especially those writing under the Roman Principate.

21   Long and Sedley, *Hellenistic Philosophers*, vol. 1, 436.

22   Schofield, *Stoic Idea*, 22–56; Erskine, *Hellenistic Stoa*, 18–27 takes a different view.

23   See the useful discussion of Erskine, *Hellenistic Stoa*, 64–70 on Chrysippus' views.

24   Tr. Bailey, *Epicurus*, 115.

25   This paragraph is indebted to Kymlicka, *CPP*, 168–75; the quotations are from 168 and 171, respectively.

Chapter 9 Epilogue: The Question of Politics

1   Nussbaum, "Non-Relative Virtues."

Index

LaVergne, TN USA
15 November 2010
204956LV00006B/8/P